TRUE TALES

FROM

ANOTHER MEXICO

TRUE TALES FROM ANOTHER MEXICO

The Lynch Mob,

the Popsicle Kings,

Chalino,

and the

Bronx

SAM QUINONES

UNIVERSITY OF NEW MEXICO PRESS

ALBUQUERQUE

Versions of some of these stories appeared in *L.A. Weekly,*
Mexico Business Magazine, Ms. Magazine, Paper Magazine,
San Diego Reader, and *United Airlines' Hemispheres Magazine.*

Library of Congress Cataloging-in-Publication Data

Quinones, Sam, 1958–
     True tales from another Mexico : the Lynch Mob, the Popsicle Kings, Chalino,
and the Bronx / Sam Quinones.—1st ed.
          p.   cm.
     ISBN 0-8263-2296-4 (alk. paper)
     1. Mexico—Politics and government—1988– 2. Mexico—Social conditions—
1970– 3. Mexico—Social life and customs. I. Title.
     F1236 .Q55 2001
     972.083'6—dc21

                                                                    00-010295

All photographs are the author's unless otherwise noted.

Book Design: *Mina Yamashita*

To my father and mother

—Ricardo and Laurel—

who gave me

everything I needed.

CONTENTS

INTRODUCTION

The best of this country has been built going against the current.
—*Gilberto Rincón Gallardo, presidential candidate for the Social Democracy Party, during the televised debate on April 25, 2000*

I came face to face with one side of Mexico not long after I moved to the country. It's an experience that I've thought about often since then, and it took me some time to realize that the side of Mexico I'd encountered was just the most notorious and most prominent. It wasn't the only side.

My run-in with it was due to the peso devaluation of December 1994. I had been living in Mexico as a reporter for seven months by that time. The country's dollar reserves dipped dangerously low. The new government of Ernesto Zedillo had nothing with which to support the peso and had to let it float. The peso plunged in value and took the country's economy with it. Another in a series of economic crises savaged Mexico.

This one bludgeoned the middle class. The middle class had gone on a buying binge and deeply into debt, believing Carlos Salinas's promises that with NAFTA, Mexico was entering a First World of stable interest and peso rates. By March 1995 interest rates were at 120 percent. Finally—after first cars, jobs, and businesses were lost—the middle class began removing their children from the private schools that they'd sacrificed so much to have them attend.

And so it was as part of a story on the middle class in crisis, in which I hoped to pay special attention to the question of private schools, that I walked headlong into the Mexican one-party state in the person of Severo Arellano.

Mr. Arellano was a licenciado—a term referring to anyone who has a bachelor's degree from a university. He was also director of the Asociación Nacional de Escuelas Particulares—the National Association of Private Schools. I had found the group's number in the telephone book. The address was Calle Lafragua #3. I called, and Mr. Arellano told me to come over.

Calle Lafragua #3 turned out to be an unremarkable thirteen-story downtown building of glass, metal, and a tower with a black-stone facade. The association was on the tenth floor of the building, at the end of a corridor. It was a small office, darkened by wood paneling, as I remember. The office had a large window, but it was smudged and grimy and didn't allow in much light.

Mr. Arellano appeared to be in his sixties. He was on the phone as I was ushered in. His secretary scurried to get him coffee. I sat down to wait. He was talking with someone, another *licenciado,* about getting his son into the army. This was difficult since the boy possessed the disadvantage, Mr. Arellano explained later, of being partially blind. As he talked, he swiveled in his chair, looking absentmindedly out the stained window. Below him, partially hidden by his desk, I noticed a shoe-shine man, hard at his craft. The secretary brought Mr. Arellano his coffee. He leaned back, oblivious to them both and, as he did, gave the impression of a Renaissance duke—down on his luck and holding to the remains of pomp and power. It struck me that in this small, neglected office, it still took two people to make sure one was happy.

On the wall paneling were pictures of Mr. Arellano with President Zedillo, which, after he hung up, he spent considerable time showing me.

Finally I edged the conversation toward the point of my visit: the predicament facing private schools. I figured he would make an impassioned plea for the nation's private schools during this most devastating crisis. I expected him to be the vigorous spokesman his position obviously implied. When I'd called, that's what I'd told him I was looking for.

Mr. Arellano did none of that. He did mumble something about private schools having a hard time these days. But his interest was other. It was in offering to sell me a copy of the association's database, containing every private school in the country, for the price of 500 pesos—roughly $100 at the time. I thought I'd misunderstood. All I needed was three or four good phone numbers of outraged private-school directors. I asked why I couldn't just have a few of the numbers for free. If he was their spokesman, this should be no problem. His answer had to do with the difficulty of calling up the list of member schools on the computer—that it reached a degree of difficulty worth 500 pesos. I told him I'd have to speak with an editor.

I left the Asociación Nacional de Escuelas Particulares angry and bewildered. It occurred to me on the way out that perhaps Mr. Arellano never actually did anything. That perhaps his job was not to defend private schools at all but instead to be attended to by shoe-shine men and secretaries and that he spent his day talking by phone with other *licenciados,* whom I now imagined spent their days in quite the same way. An amazing possibility.

My problem was that I didn't know where I'd been or none of that would have surprised me.

I had unwittingly wandered into the heart of the Mexican regime. Calle Lafragua #3, I later discovered, is the home of the Confederación Nacional de Organizaciones Populares—the CNOP. And its story, and how someone like Mr. Arellano came to be there, is really the story of the ruling Institutional Revolutionary Party (PRI).

What is now the PRI formed in 1929, the same era as the Nazi Party, the Italian Fascists, and the Bolsheviks. While those parties faded into history, the PRI has lasted to become the world's oldest one-party regime. Key to the PRI's longevity is its understanding of human nature. Its authoritarian brethren posited ideologies—a master race, a proletarian dictatorship—that needed an iron fist to keep people in line. The PRI's working concept was beautifully simple, more humane, and a lot easier. It bought people's loyalty. It became history's proof that every man has his price. As a powerful government in a poor country it found that men come pretty cheap. In return for loyalty, the PRI offered a candidacy, a professorship, money, land to squat, three years as a congressman, a construction contract, or a million other things a government can use to co-opt a poor people.

The PRI missed few details. I remember a criminologist telling me of a chess club he tried to start at his university when he was a student. The club held a few meetings. Then it received a visit from a PRI official, who informed the club that it had to belong to the PRI and use an official PRI union of janitors to clean up after it. And it wasn't until 1999 that a Mexican film was able for the first time to use the PRI's insignia. The party always made sure that where movies and television were concerned, it simply didn't exist. Both media always had a gaping hole where the treatment of the PRI and its vast influence on society should have been. These are examples of how deeply and

subtly the PRI controlled Mexico and insinuated itself into Mexican life.

Loyal *Priistas* were allowed to wallow at the public trough or break the law with impunity. Mexican corruption became not some unfortunate human failing but the machine's lifeblood, necessary for its survival and part of the political culture.

The PRI was inclusive, the big Mexican tent. For many years it had enough room underneath it for almost every person and way of thought. Despite its name, it was never a real political party. It was born to administer power, not to fight for it. Self-preservation and obedience to an imperial president became the guiding principles. The PRI apparatus, under the command of that imperial president, was a vehicle through which the struggle for power could take place peacefully. And in a country whose first hundred years of independent history roiled with *caudillos,* an imported emperor, ephemeral constitutions, and a revolution, it was at first a pretty good idea.

Three pillars of society came to make up the PRI/government apparatus: unions, campesinos, and what are known as popular organizations. The idea was to give these groups, which would normally be rousing rabble against the government, access to power. It was an appealing concept. The practical result, however, was to emasculate these organizations. Now part of power, each sector gave up the right to openly criticize it. Under the PRI regime, each organization became subservient to its leaders and its leaders to each successive president. Meanwhile the interests each group had formed to promote were quietly forgotten.

What I didn't know the day I walked into Calle Lafragua #3 is that the building is the depository for these withered popular organizations: National Confederation of Entrepreneurs, National Confederation of Nonsalaried Workers, Coalition of Taxi Unions, National Confederation of Small Businessmen, National Forum of Professionals and Technicians. Others were "revolutionary": League of Revolutionary Economists, Revolutionary Architects of Mexico, Revolutionary Popular Youth.

Calle Lafragua #3 is a pantheon to groups that I assume were once energized, rambunctious, and could have been competition for the ruling party. Some, I suppose, were out in the street—perhaps this was decades ago—demanding to be heard. Today these ostensibly revolutionary popular organizations never show up in the news. They gather dust at Calle Lafragua #3, neutered victims of that Faustian bargain they struck with the PRI and populated by somnolent *licenciados* on the party dole.

More than that, though, Calle Lafragua #3 is a metaphor for what seventy-one years of a paternalistic one-party state has done to Mexico's vigor. The building represents the great officialist tendency in Mexican culture—which, for lack of a better term, I'll call the culture of the *Priista/licenciado.* The day I walked into Mr. Arellano's office, I had unwittingly walked into that part of Mexico.

The *Priista/licenciado* is the modern version of the hacienda owner and the Spanish noble. He doesn't return phone calls to anyone less important than he is. He is accountable only to those above him. He keeps those seeking employment waiting in his lobby for hours because he can. His shoes are too well shined to belong to anyone who really works. His sinecure insulates him from the higher standards the world demands, and from this he derives his inertia.

The *Priista/licenciado* culture remains an anchor around the neck of Mexico's development. It assumes the superiority of those with power and thus is fundamentally unfair. Though clad in double-breasted suits, this part of Mexico remains emotionally stuck in the sixteenth century. It is the modern expression of the ossified top-down, hierarchical tradition left the country by the Aztecs, the Spanish, the Catholic Church, and the dictator Porfirio Díaz. This side of Mexico is hardly ready for the demands of democracy and the global economy. The very term *licenciado* is supposed to conjure up some kind of innate wisdom. The *licenciado* doesn't need to prove his worth; he is entitled to more than his labor produces. The *Priista* is a *Priista* precisely because adhering to the state endows him with special rights. Mexico's world-famous corruption has its roots here, and so therefore does Mexicans' belief that their society is unjust.

I mention all this because this part of Mexico is what the world seems to know best. Certainly the press, other governments, and tourists are most aware of the official, elite, corrupt Mexico; the Mexico that won't allow a poor man a chance; the Mexico behind the sunglasses. I've even been told by people, including Mexicans, that this *is* Mexican culture. But I know that's not true. There is another Mexico.

This other side is vital and dynamic and is often found on Mexico's margins. The other side of Mexico is not always pretty, but it is self-reliant and adventurous.

And this Mexico is what this book is about.

This Mexico gets very little press and is sometimes difficult to locate in the desert of *Priista/licenciado* culture. Yet it is the best of the country. On this side of Mexico are the Popsicle kings of Tocumbo, the Tepiteños, the folks from Chupícuaro—people who have the spunk to imagine something else and instinctively flee the enfeebling embrace of PRI paternalism. On this side of Mexico are untamed *valientes* like Aristeo Prado, the women who come to Ciudad Juárez to find a future, and the people who look for justice through the faith in the Narcosaint, Jesús Malverde. Here newly realistic telenovelas show the gray government censor that the country is too lively to abide his boss's dictates. Even the Bronxistas, the most perfect expression of *Priista/licenciado* culture, are attempting to retrieve some dignity through their minor rebellions.

On this side of Mexico are Chalino Sánchez, Zeus García, Luis Guerrero—all emigrants who dared to create something new. The emigrant stands for the country's vital side. He uses his wits and imagination. He strikes out on his own, looking for a future. One emigrant does not require two people attending to his needs. Some twelve million Mexicans reside year-round in the United States. Many millions more have lived and worked there or spend part of the year up north. The United States is now part of the Mexican reality and is where this other Mexico is often found, reinventing itself.

Official Mexico holds their absence against them. Emigrants are resented for their daring. In official Mexico's twisted point of view, emigrants must explain why they aren't traitors to their country.

A Mexican living in California told me once that he and a friend were driving to his home state of Michoacán for Christmas. They came to a roadblock near the sweltering city of Culiacán, Sinaloa. The roadblock is operated by federal judicial police ostensibly to check for drugs, but it's considered an infamous shakedown point by emigrants returning home from California between October and January, with the dollars their hard work has earned. A cop in sunglasses looked them over. He demanded their identification. They showed California driver's licenses. With a sneer, the cop insisted the cards were false. "Of course, I couldn't say anything," this fellow told me. "I just said, 'You're right. I'm nothing. What do I know?' You have to keep your eyes down and always agree. If you challenge them, they'll really hurt you." The cop slid the emigrant's license up his forearm, shook from it the sweat it accumulated, then returned it to my friend. The cop then took him to a room, forced him to undress, and body-searched him. My friend and his companion were allowed to leave the roadblock only after paying off the cop in dollars.

There has likely never been a clearer meeting between these two Mexicos.

The country's greatest modern catastrophe is that it has treated the emigrant this poorly and thus been deprived of his dynamism. His absence is of greater consequence to Mexico than the nineteenth-century territorial losses of California, Arizona, New Mexico, and Texas. Mexico survives today largely because the emigrant cannot bring himself to fail his country the way the *licenciado* so miserably fails him.

These two sides of Mexico are, in some sense, what the presidential election of 2000 is about as well. As I write this, the elections are a few months off. The time I've spent in Mexico has largely been a prelude to these elections. The PRI/government, after twenty-five years of economic crisis, no longer has the resources to buy the loyalty and control of enough of the country. Mexicans have actually been talking about politics—a pointless topic when the PRI was the political monopoly. The agency that oversees its electoral system is now independent. Opposition parties have gained strength and can now win elections. The congress has become plural, feistier, and more of a balance to presidential power. Mexican society has awakened from its catatonia. It has begun to flex its civic muscles. The media, business, churches, neighborhood, and nonprofit groups have all become more vibrant and alive.

All these changes have happened in spite of, not because of, the ruling party, which has had to be dragged kicking and screaming to the table of modernity and democratic reform.

The big question now facing Mexicans is, Are they willing to begin the arduous work of re-creating a nation, making it modern, the way the emigrant re-created his life? This can be done only when the PRI loses control of the government apparatus it uses to enforce loyalty and permit lawlessness. Can

Mexicans imagine something different after years of atrophy? They have the chance to punish a state party for its mountainous arrogance and biblical excesses. In so doing, they can also punish the hacienda owner, the imperious *licenciado,* the cop at the roadblock. They can require accountability from those with power. They can stage another revolution, quick and bloodless this time, and begin merging with the world.

Or they can shrink from the historical moment.

Still, no matter who wins the elections, this will be the country's great struggle for years to come: to shake from its back not just decades of *Priista* paternalism but centuries of suffocating hierarchical tradition. In practical terms, it will be to make *licenciados* and PRI bureaucrats produce something for a living, like the rest of the country.

When people speak of the country's emerging democracy, I think, in a larger sense, they are referring to the struggle between these two sides of Mexico. More than simply removing a state party from power, it is the battle against the inert, mediocre, and nonproductive tendency in Mexican society to allow the other, dynamic Mexico room to breathe.

* * *

As I was preparing this book, I showed the chapter outline to several professors. One professor wrote back that he felt the stories were too exotic, too much about the fringes of Mexican society. I thought about that. A good part of this book is about mainstream Mexico. But some of it, it's true, is about Mexico's outer reaches. That's partly just a reflection of my own journalistic taste.

But I also believe much is considered exotica only because it is ignored, and it is this Mexico that the book's title refers to as well. Drag queens, for example, are everywhere in Mexico. I saw a drag queen board a bus in the Hidalgo outback. I saw another in a small farming town in Baja California. A troop of them hail customers around the corner from my apartment on occasional Friday nights. I've seen drag queens everywhere in this country but seen nothing written about them, how they live or why they exist in such large numbers. So they end up being not so much exotic as simply erased from the official picture.

The same is true of lynchings—bizarre and seemingly so anachronistic. But I have newspaper clippings in a file that is now three inches thick, each telling of a lynching somewhere in Mexico since 1994. West Side Kansas Street might seem exotic until you travel across emigrant-sending states like Jalisco, Michoacán, and Guanajuato and see pueblos thick with U.S. gang graffiti. Nueva Jerusalén may seem just an exotic cult except that it has existed, generally immune from the law, with the help of the local PRI and one family in the kind of deal the ruling party has cut millions of times to consolidate its power. The conflicts surrounding the rise and fall of that family, the Villaseñores, though terribly violent are similar to confrontations that took place across Mexico from 1988 through the early 1990s.

Still, this book would fail were its tales bizarre for bizarre's sake. It seems to me that in a country with an arid officialist culture like Mexico, precisely on the edges is where some telling truths can be found. So while some of these snapshots—snapshots being what journalism is by definition—are from Mexico's fringes, I hope all the stories here can tell you something central about the country, about its complexity and how it is changing.

That is why I spent so much time in another Mexico.

—FEBRUARY, 2000

THE BALLAD OF CHALINO SÁNCHEZ

Saturday slides toward midnight at Rodeo de Medianoche, a cavernous club in Pico Rivera, as the duo Voces del Rancho begins the ballad of how Lamberto Quintero died.

Lamberto Quintero was a drug smuggler in the Pacific coast state of Sinaloa in the 1970s who was killed in a wild shootout. His ballad—or *corrido*—is now a classic. Voces del Rancho (Voices of the Village) have updated it with the sputter of machine-gun fire while maintaining the polka beat.

All the duo's songs are polkas or waltzes—*corridos* about events in isolated Mexican pueblos—backed by an accordion. Their crowd is a sea of bobbing cowboy hats. The duo's latest album shows them in boots and white cowboy hats, sitting on hay bales, with a barn in the background. Yet none of that—the hats, the song, the album cover, nor the music in general—has much to do with the singers' life experience or with that of their audience, for that matter. Nothing about the entire scene would indicate that Voces del Rancho are actually two L.A.-born young men who see a Mexican village about as often as they see a hay bale.

Mariano Fernández and Edgar Rodríguez, both twenty-one, grew up in the hard L.A. suburb of Bell, graduated from Bell High School, listened to rap, speak an up-to-the-minute urban slang, and, until recently, never dared sing Mexican country music. They and their audience are part of a profound cultural shift among Los Angeles Mexican-American working-class youth, who in recent years have rediscovered and remade their parents' folk music, including the traditional *corrido*.

The story of how all that happened is really the story of one man: a simple, rough-hewn, undocumented Mexican immigrant.

His name was Chalino Sánchez. His singing career lasted just four years and he was killed when he was only thirty-one, yet he's one of the most influential musical figures to emerge from Los Angeles or from Mexican music in

11

decades. "When we were small, we always wanted to fit in, so we'd listen to rap. The other kids were all listening to rap, so I guess we felt that if we listened to Spanish music, we'd be beaners or something," says Rodríguez. "But after Chalino died, everybody started listening to *corridos*. People want to feel more Mexican."

Six years after his death, Chalino Sánchez is a legend, an authentic folk hero. L.A.'s Mexican music scene and Mexican youth style were one way before Chalino Sánchez. They were another after him. After Chalino, guys whose second language was an English-accented Spanish could pump tuba- and accordion-based polkas out their car stereos at maximum volume and pretty girls would think they were cool.

Chalino renewed the Mexican *corrido*. In the Mexican badlands, where the barrel of a gun makes the law, for generations dating back to the mid-1800s the *corrido* recounted the worst, best, and bloodiest exploits of men. *Corridos* were the newspaper for an illiterate people in the days before telephones and television. *Corrido* heroes were revolutionaries and bandits—people who had done something worth singing about.

In Chalino's hands, the *corrido* came to reflect the modern world. The *corrido* became the *narcocorrido,* the Mexican equivalent of gangster rap, with themes of drugs, violence, and police perfidy and an abiding admiration for the exploits of drug smugglers. And because of Chalino, Los Angeles, an American city, is now a center of redefinition for the most Mexican of musical idioms. Chalino democratized the genre, made it modern and American, and opened it to the masses. In Los Angeles almost anyone can have a *corrido* about him written, recorded, and sold. "In L.A., without exaggeration, 50 percent of the [Mexican] music that's recorded here is based on the legacy he left," says Ángel Parra, the engineer who recorded most of his albums.

It boiled down to this, in the words of Abel Orozco, owner of El Parral nightclub in South Gate: "Chalino changed everything."

* * *

He was the youngest of seven brothers and one sister. His parents named him Rosalino, but no one ever called him that; he himself thought it sounded too much like a woman's name. He told people his baptized name was

Marcelino, but he always preferred Chalino. He was born in a small village in Sinaloa and had no more than three years of schooling.

He was not a tall man. He had a rail-thin body topped with a handsome, angular face that looked slightly bent. He possessed the hard, unwashable veneer of the Mexican rancho, or village; few photos show him smiling. He spoke the rolling, singsong, slurred Spanish of the Sinaloan coast. Those with money and position who would meet him later would say he was a shy man, not given to easy conversation. His friends say he merely had a rural Mexican's deference before power and education, since he had neither. He spoke no English. Onstage and around people he liked he was friendly, generous, and informal. They knew him as El Compa Chalino (Buddy Chalino). But the Mexican rancho never left him. He could be obstinate if he thought someone was trying to manage him and was more than ready to fight when challenged. "He had the reputation of being a *valiente* [tough guy]," says Nacho Hernández, his longtime accordion player and leader of the band Los Amables del Norte. "He was a very nice guy. You'd come up to him, greet him, 'Hey, how are you? Great.' But if you came up with the intention of fighting, he'd get into it. He was very delicate that way. He'd fight."

Like so many before him, he went north as a teenager. Of course, there was no work in his village. But the real reason he left had more to do with an event that had happened years before. When Chalino was about eleven, his only sister, Juana, was raped and sent home to her family naked by a couple of men. One was a *valiente*—or local tough—of the village known as El Chapo Pérez. The Pérezes weren't wealthy by any means, but they were better off than the Sánchezes. Chalino waited. He grew up. Finally, when he was about fifteen, he went to a party, honoring November 20, the day the Mexican Revolution began, at a local elementary school. There he saw El Chapo sitting with his two brothers. "Chalino told me he didn't say anything to him. He just went up to him and shot him to death," says Nacho Hernández. "He didn't give him a chance." Most people in the region went to parties armed, and El Chapo's brothers were no exception. So there, in the middle of the party, a shoot-out ensued between Chalino and Guadalupe and Florencio Pérez. None of the three men was wounded, and Chalino ran off. "He said he ran out of there and got home with his face ripped to pieces for having run

through all the brush and trees," says Nacho.

Chalino spent two weeks hiding out in the hills, then he left for the United States and never returned to Mexico to live. He came to Los Angeles, to the home of an aunt. For a while he worked on farms, following the harvests up through California to Oregon. But like many Mexican immigrants, he came to see the advantage in urban employment.

He settled in Inglewood as it and neighboring towns were forming into a belt of Mexican-immigrant suburbia around the city of Los Angeles. For a while he helped his older brother Armando, a *coyote* (smuggler of illegal aliens), who had an immigrant-smuggling business going in Tijuana. But he spent only a year or so at that and never liked it. The immigrants were always trying to skip out without paying. Finally the business ended in 1984, when Armando was shot and killed in his sleep in a Tijuana hotel.

Around this time, Chalino was thrown in the La Mesa jail in Tijuana for about eight months, charged with a variety of small crimes. Jail proved to be a crucible of sorts. In jail with him was his cousin Ismael Sánchez, who played the guitar. There were other musicians from Sinaloa. More important, there were other men from Sinaloa from the same kind of villages as Chalino, most of them doing time for drug smuggling. "In the jail there are a lot of guys with good stories to tell," says Lázaro Sánchez, Chalino's older brother. "They'd all get together, tell stories. Ismael played guitar." Tentatively Chalino began to put their stories to song. This stint in jail was Chalino's first stab at *corrido* writing.

When he got out, he returned to Los Angeles. There he washed cars for a time. He dabbled in drug dealing—small quantities of marijuana and co-caine, according to friends—but that stopped when his music career began. He did a stint as a driver for Rigo Campos—the owner of a restaurant in Bell Gardens, who was involved in the drug business, was killed by rivals, and about whom Chalino would later write a *corrido.*

In 1983 he met Marisela Vallejo, an immigrant from Mexicali, who worked at the same sewing factory as his aunt. They married the next year. That year Chalino wrote a *corrido* about his brother Armando. No one seems to remember for whom he wrote his second *corrido.* And no one remembers exactly how writing the ballads developed into a business. But slowly word spread that he would write the ballads on commission. Sometimes he'd set a fee. Early on, he'd also accept something of value—gold watches and a number of fancy pistols, as his fondness for guns and target shooting became well known.

He began singing almost by mistake. With his first batch of *corridos* composed, he asked a local *norteño* band to record them. But the singer dallied, and soon Chalino's *corrido* clients were asking for their cassettes. Finally Chalino decided to sing them himself. So in 1987 he and Los 4 de la Frontera, a local *norteño* band, went into Ángel Parra's studios on Olympic Avenue and in about four hours recorded fifteen *corridos,* including Armando's. Chalino knew nothing of recording. He didn't understand that inside the studio, you could stop the tape and talk. Nor did he care about the quality of the recording. "He didn't consider himself a singer. He just wanted to say, 'I composed a *corrido* about you. Here's your cassette,'" says Parra.

He made only fifteen copies of the first cassette, one for each corrido customer—just fifteen songs, no cover, no title. But six months later he was back, with another fifteen songs. On the third cassette the radar blipped. He made his usual fifteen copies. The next day he called Parra, asking for twenty-five more. His clients wanted copies for their friends. Parra suggested they go to a cassette factory. "We ordered up the grand quantity of three hundred cassettes, printed with side A and side B," says Parra.

Chalino had unintentionally hit a nerve. A lot of immigrants in L.A., it turned out, thirsted to hear their life stories in a *corrido.* "Often it really surprised me," Parra says. "He'd get his order, then he'd call again the next morning. His way of speaking was like, 'Jefe, grab a pencil. I need more cassettes.' 'But I just gave you some last night.' 'They're all sold.' That's how he began."

Taken together, his songs form a kind of oral history of the Mexican rancho. The ranchos were fertile ground for his songs. They were lawless places. In these poor, desolate villages, family feuds lasted for decades. Betrayal and ambush, paid killings, easy gunplay, and corrupted justice were common. Here parties could be expected to end with at least gunshots, if not a body or two. From the rancho emerged a legendary figure in Mexican popular culture: the *valiente*—tough, poor, barely civilized, and fiercely independent men—men who could be mean, decent, insane, generous; in the absence of a justice system, they made their own law, their own rules, occasionally challenging those with power. Everyone else trembled or went north.

In the ranchos of Sinaloa, the drug business flourished. Sinaloa, stretching down the Pacific coast across the gulf from Baja California, was where Mexican drug smuggling began; it is Mexico's Medellín. Chinese immigrants brought the opium poppy in the late 1800s, and marijuana grows nicely in the hills. Virtually all the Mexican cartel *capos* (bosses) of the last thirty years have been Sinaloan. Drugs and Sinaloa are now inseparable in the Mexican mind. So while Chalino rarely mentioned that some tough hombre in the hills of Sinaloa had a connection to the drug trade, he never had to. His listeners understood; they were rancheros as well, even if they now lived in South Gate and worked in Alhambra.

The stories of these drug-smuggling *valientes* became the stuff of Chalino's *corridos.* They were men who, now living in Los Angeles, spent a lot of time in cantinas and wanted to show off for their friends. Many of his *corridos* were about how their brothers or fathers had died back in Mexico. In the words of one man, they were "people who you never know who they are, what they do, or why they have so much money."

"He didn't write songs about people like you and me," says Nacho Hernández. "He wrote about people who were in the life."

Still, they were usually nobodies—hardly on a level with the famous revolutionaries and bandits who populated the *corridos* of old. Chalino wrote their stories anyway. As demand grew, he became more sophisticated, adding album titles, black-and-white photos, and finally color covers. Then he began selling at swap meets. "He began selling really well," Parra remembers. "We'd order five hundred of the latest cassette, then two hundred of the previous one, one hundred of the one before that. So they were orders of a thousand at a time." By 1989 he had given up his day jobs, had formed RR Records, and was hustling his cassettes full-time. He'd met Nacho Hernández in 1988. They turned out to be from neighboring villages in Sinaloa. By mid-1989 Hernández and Los Amables del Norte were his regular accompanists.

At about that time he met Pedro Rivera. Rivera had left Mexico as a young man in the early 1960s, picked melons near Fresno, then he, too, traded farmwork for the stability of urban life and moved to Culver City. In the mid-1980s Rivera started Cintas Acuario in Long Beach. In L.A. at the time, only the large labels served the Mexican community: CBS, EMI-Latin, Musart,

RCA. Musicians were at the mercy of these labels. Singers with finished re-cordings that they'd paid for themselves would go to these labels, where they'd be charged another ten thousand dollars to put their albums out under the label's name. Rivera figured he could offer these singers a better deal. He'd buy their recordings. Cintas Acuario was among the first of what is now a constel-lation of tiny and nimble independent labels on the outskirts of L.A.'s Mexi-can music industry. "What I did was to give opportunity to those who had no opportunity at all," says Rivera. "We began recording new artists. People loved it because there wasn't anything like it."

Cracking the established L.A. record-distribution system was nearly im-possible. So instead these labels made their primary outlets the racks (*raquitas*) at car washes, bakeries, butcher shops, and, above all, swap meets. For most Los Angelinos, the dozens of swap meets dotting southern California are places to unload unwanted junk on a weekend. But for many Mexican immigrants, who don't understand banks or can't hope for a business loan, L.A.-area swap meets are a shot at capital formation. For those entering the music industry, the swap meet became the distribution channel. The swap meets circumvented the Mexican music industry's normal promotion routes. They got product directly to the public without having to rely on advertising, big distributors, credit lines, or, especially, Mexican radio, which proved particularly unwilling to give these small labels a break.

"People who wanted to open a shop went first to the swap meet," says Abel Orozco, who also owns one of these small labels, Discos Linda. "Those of us who have record stores, dance halls, distributorships started in the swap meets."

"We didn't have money to give [the DJs] cars or cocaine. They never played us, and they still don't," says Rivera. "This is why artists record these *corridos prohibidos*—drug ballads—it's that the radio never plays our stuff. We had to promote ourselves by recording what was prohibited. To sell what's prohib-ited, you don't need promotion."

In early 1989 Rivera had learned this lesson after releasing, on a lark, a *corrido* about Panama general Manuel Noriega. The first two weeks it sold seven thousand cassettes. "I told myself that's the way to go," Rivera says. "Before that I had made a cassette for fourteen thousand dollars, with a musi-cal director, with a mariachi, very good songs that weren't *corridos*. It didn't even sell a hundred cassettes. People buy stories."

Soon after the release of the Noriega *corrido,* Chalino began coming to Rivera with his recordings of the stories of bad men. The fit was perfect. "Other people had recorded *corridos,* but no one was recording *corridos* that were so personal, about common people," says Rivera. "You'd be biting your nails waiting to hear what happened to the main character. People will always listen to stories that are true and original."

Acuario was a good fit for Chalino, too, because as time went on, it became clear that he horrified the established record industry. His voice, by industry standards, was famously bad. Starting out, he suffered frequent humiliations at the hands of bandleaders and club owners because of it. Critics might have called it "Mexican primitive" if they'd ever paid him any attention. "I don't sing," Chalino would say. "I bark."

Rough, moaning, and reedy thin, Chalino's voice was an echo of immigrants' rural roots. And that was about the last thing the Mexican music establishment was going to go for. Mexican pop by this time was far removed from Mexicans' daily reality—either at home or in the United States. And that was really the whole point. In a poor culture, the music industry put a premium on puff and polish. In Mexican pop the idea was to lose any vestige of the rancho, of poverty. Male singers looked like playboys and tried sounding like opera stars. In this world Chalino's raspy voice and menacing look of a *valiente* went down like battery acid.

"He had a voice you had to get used to," says Ángel Parra. "The bad sound at first, the rough production, the way he'd slur his words, all this made him difficult for many people to understand. Then he'd do strange things that people [in the industry] weren't used to. For example, instead of saying *'te fuiste'* ('you left'), he'd sing *'te fuites.'* That's how it's said in the hills. He knew how to say it correctly. But he'd say it that way so that people, campesinos, would hear it the way they were used to."

The Mexican music industry didn't take to it. "Producers never believed in the *corrido;* they never believed they could sell it," says Abel Orozco. "They didn't believe in poor people, in hearing real musical feeling."

The industry was too distant from its public—particularly its Mexican public that lived in the United States—to understand how they needed the memories Chalino's songs awoke. "Most of the people in L.A. are campesinos," says Fernando González, promotions director for Culver City–based Musart, one of the southland's large Mexican labels. "All these people come from villages, ranchos. We didn't realize it. They saw him as a singer from the pueblo. And the campesino buys records."

So Chalino had to promote himself. His friends remember him tooling around Los Angeles with first an old green Oldsmobile, then a Cougar, then a Chevy truck, laden with boxes of his own cassettes, taking them to distributors, car washes, swap meets.

Shut out of the established record industry, Chalino became the king of both the swap meet and the car stereo. Kids would play him as they cruised the boulevards. Soon their friends would be asking about him and heading to the swap meet for his cassettes. "That's what made Chalino," says Orozco. "In Tijuana, Guadalajara, Las Vegas—they'd all have Chalino going in their cars. That was his radio. It began here in Los Angeles. They'd leave here from El Parral with their stereos going at full volume."

Quietly, through 1989, 1990, and into 1991, Chalino's rough sound ignited immigrant Los Angeles. In 1990 he convinced Orozco to let him play at El Parral. So many people came that by 8 P.M. Orozco had to close the doors. From then on, Chalino had club owners avidly bidding for him.

He now began to clean up his *corridos*. "He didn't want problems with anyone," says Nacho Hernández. "Before, he'd record a *corrido* about someone who died and take the victim's side. In the song he'd insult the guy's rival or opponent. Sometimes the other guy would get mad. So he stopped singing that so-and-so, who killed this guy, was a coward."

As a performer, Chalino had a distinctly American ethic. He dressed not like an elegant star, but like his audience: a cocked cowboy hat, large belt buckle, cowboy boots, and usually gold chains and watches. He often tucked a gun in his belt. He broke, too, with the top-down entertainment style that is so traditionally Mexican, where the singer is the star, the audience the adoring public, and everyone knows his place. He would pose for photographs with fans who'd come onstage while he was singing, something every ranchero singer in L.A. does now. "Chalino liked people surrounding him when he sang. He started this tradition of people dancing while the singer sang," says Emilio

Franco, owner of El Farallón, the club in Lynwood where Chalino played most often. "If there were two hundred people in the hall, he'd mention them every one. 'Here's to my *compa* so-and-so, and my compa sitting over there.' He mentioned me one time."

In January 1992 a private *quinceñera* (fifteenth birthday party) in Compton where he was singing got out of hand when word leaked that he would be singing. Hundreds of people tried to crash the party. Windows were broken and the police came. He was becoming famous.

But his legend really began later that month. As a singer known as a *valiente,* Chalino would occasionally be challenged by men in the audience who wanted to test that reputation. On January 20 Chalino was booked into Los Arcos, a club in Coachella, twenty miles east of Palm Springs. His arrival was something special for the isolated, predominantly Latino desert town. Los Arcos was packed. He told police later that someone gave him a 10-mm pistol as he walked in, hoping he would wear it onstage, as was his custom. Actually the gun was his. "He always took a gun to a show. It was always loaded, with a round in the chamber," says Nacho Hernández.

Coachella police sergeant Vince Singleterry, who would meet Chalino later, remembers: "He explained to me about the facade, the showman, the *corridos,* the macho thing with the gun, the tough-guy attitude. That was expected, especially of somebody from Sinaloa. But he seemed like one who hadn't been bit by the fame and stardom. He still had the presence of mind to say that that was the showman part of him and he was really a normal person."

That night, shortly before midnight, Chalino was taking requests. Eduardo Gallegos, a thirty-three-year-old unemployed mechanic high on alcohol and heroin, jumped up on the short stage and, from a few feet away, fired a 25-mm pistol into Chalino's side.

Chalino pulled his gun, leaped from the stage, and ran through the packed dance floor, firing back at Gallegos, who was meanwhile cranking off more rounds. People rushed the doors and smashed windows, frantically trying to escape. A bystander wrestled the gun from Gallegos and shot him in the mouth; the crowd began kicking Gallegos. When it was over, seven people were wounded, including Chalino and accordionist Nacho Hernández, shot in the thigh. Rene Carranza, a twenty-year-old local, was hit in the leg and bled to death as friends lugged him to a car and drove wildly to a hospital. Police heard that other victims were taken by friends to Mexicali, ninety miles away. The floor was strewn with purses, shoes, beer bottles. Police arrived to find people energetically scaling the fences outside the club.

The shooting made *ABC World News Tonight* the next day and bolstered Chalino's standing as a *valiente*. As he convalesced, his cassettes sold better than ever. Finally his music was getting radio play, though DJs would air only one of his love songs—"Nieves de Enero" (Snows of January)—and didn't touch the *corridos* for which he was becoming notorious. Several weeks later, he played El Parral. The club had to shut its doors at 6 P.M., locking out hundreds of people.

But the Coachella shooting may have taken its toll on Chalino. In the months that followed, he did two strange things. To his friends, he gave away his prized gun collection. And to Musart, he sold the rights to his music. Chalino had always been wary of business dealings with people he didn't know. But after the Coachella shooting, something changed. He spoke of letting a company promote him and concentrating on his nightclub act, which was netting him ten thousand and fifteen thousand dollars a weekend. Every *corrido* he wrote now was getting him two thousand dollars on up.

His wariness in business did Chalino in. He demanded up-front money instead of royalties. Who could say whether there'd be any, and who could trust a record company to keep track? So he committed what his friend Ángel Parra calls "his greatest error." He sold Musart all rights to his songs—with no provision for royalties later—for a lump sum of 350,000 pesos, the equivalent of $115,000 at the time.

Chalino's royalties today are worth several million dollars. His widow, Marisela, and his son and daughter, though not penniless, must rely on relatives for financial help. "The quantity of money that this man lost was incredible," says Musart's Fernando González. "I think he was already thinking that he was going to die."

"The atmosphere in the bars and cantinas is dangerous, and he knew it," says Marisela. "He did what anyone does when you realize that you can die at any time. He put his life in order. He never thought his records would sell as well as they did or would have helped us out as much as they would have. He never felt

like an artist. He never knew the magnitude of what he would become."

Within a couple months of the Coachella shooting, Chalino was singing live again. With the Musart money, he bought a home for his family in Paramount—a once white L.A. suburb that Mexican immigration had turned into a kind of second Sinaloa.

Musart had plans for him. They wanted to dude him up, polish his rough edges, fit him with a mariachi suit and band. "More than anything, though, we'd have tried to teach him how to speak," says González. "He always spoke with his head down, didn't say much. He never engaged the conversation. We wanted to improve his conversation, make it more intellectual, more sociable."

And for only the second time, he accepted an engagement in Culiacán, Sinaloa's capital city. His friends and family told him not to go. He had been receiving threats after the Coachella shooting. Culiacán was a dangerous place. It was no longer his home, and he didn't like the region's oppressive heat; he knew L.A. better. But people in Sinaloa wanted him to come and were paying the equivalent of twenty thousand dollars. Plus Chalino had asked for and received half the money in advance. He had to go.

Culiacán is a city of six hundred thousand people, and that Friday night in May, two thousand of them packed into the Salon Buganvilias. The crowd exploded in cheers as Chalino took the stage, flanked by six scantily clad young women. After the show Chalino, his brothers Espiridión and Francisco, his cousin Carmelo Félix, and several young women, including Chalino's girlfriend in Culiacán, left the club. A short while later, at a traffic circle, they were stopped by armed men in Chevrolet Suburbans. "They were all real young guys," says Carmelo Félix. "Maybe one or two were police officers. The others might have been *madrinas* [thugs that Mexican police hire to do their dirty work]." First they took Espiridión from the car. There was some confusion as to who they wanted. Then one showed state police identification to Chalino and said, "My *comandante* needs you." Chalino and his brothers offered the gunmen money, believing them to be police officers. The gunmen didn't accept, but at Chalino's pleading they released Espiridión. "Chalino told them, 'Don't take him—he's not to blame for anything. I just met him at the show.' They didn't know he was his brother, so they let him go," says Nacho Hernández. Chalino talked with the gunmen for a while, then got in one of the Suburbans. It took off and the gunmen followed in the other Suburban.

A few hours later, as dawn broke on May 16, 1992, two campesinos found the body of Chalino Sánchez dumped by an irrigation canal near the highway north out of town. He was blindfolded, and his wrists had rope marks. He had been shot twice in the back of the head.

* * *

The reaction in Culiacán was immediate. "That night, all these guys, Chalino's fans, were driving around town with their speakers blaring, just waiting for someone to look at them funny," remembers Fernando Sauceda of the Sinaloan Human Rights Defense Commission.

Back in Los Angeles, news of Chalino's death clicked quickly along the informal network his music had created at high schools in Bell, Long Beach, Compton, Huntington Park. Girls cried at Paramount High. Spanish radio stations reported his death. El Parral got as full as it's ever been. People broke into tears. There was a minute of silence. Only his music was played that night.

Out in Coachella, Sergeant Vince Singleterry sent detectives to Culiacán to confirm Sánchez's death. The trial against Eduardo Gallegos proceeded without its key witness. (Gallegos was convicted and is serving fifteen years to life in prison. He never gave a reason for the Coachella shooting.)

Musart acted as you'd expect. "Immediately, obviously, we began to promote him," says González. "We advertised that he'd been killed, put out special posters. We said, 'Why should we keep all his tapes locked up?' But we didn't expect the gigantic reaction that followed."

Those who worked the swap meets could see it beginning. Lupe Rivera, Pedro's son, was selling cassettes that Sunday at the Paramount swap meet. "This lady walked up and said, 'Do you have any cassettes by Chalino? I want one of each. I just found out this morning that he was shot.' Her family had called her from Mexico. Then radio stations started announcing it. Pretty soon people just started buying his cassettes like crazy, you know: 'Let me have two of each.'"

If the Coachella shooting established Chalino's underworld credentials, his murder mythified him. Soon a Chalinomania gripped Los Angeles on down to Sinaloa. "It was an epidemic," says Marisela. "You could hear his music all

over the place. So many people would play him in their cars, their houses, their dances."

Arturo Santamaría, a sociologist at the University of Sinaloa in Mazatlán, remembers the next two months well. "I lived in an INFONAVIT [a government-built apartment complex]. From 6 A.M. until late at night, people would play Chalino. There'd be one neighbor playing him over here and another over there and another across the way. Then there'd be Chalino in the truck stereos. Chalino everywhere. My wife and I couldn't stand it after a while. We couldn't sleep."

Chalino had been known as a ladies' man. And several women came forward to claim that their children were his. None sued.

A cottage industry in cheesy Chalino reissues grew. Both Musart and Cintas Acuario quickly stripped the vocal tracks from his original recordings and wove them in with singers and bands Chalino had never met. Musart would put out ten, and Cintas Acuario twelve, of these lame ersatz recordings. All but one of his Musart albums still sell at least ten thousand copies annually.

Meanwhile a kind of "Sinaloaization" of L.A. Mexican culture was taking place. If tourists thought mariachi synonymous with Mexico, in L.A. the Mexican working classes were really listening to the music of Sinaloa: the *norteño conjunto* and the *banda,* a tuba-anchored marching band playing dance music. And if being Sinaloan—with its drug undertones—was suddenly cool, even more so was to be from the Sinaloan rancho.

Thus emerged the "Chalinazo," a new style of dress in which urban kids imitated Mexican hicks. At clubs they'd dress up in cowboy hats and boots, large belt buckles, and jackets with epaulets with the skin of some exotic animal; eventually gold chains and silk shirts were added. *Narcotraficante* chic. In Chalino's hands, Mexican folk music had become dangerous urban dance music. When he achieved that, he brought thousands of Mexican-American kids back to their parents' country music, of which they'd been thoroughly ashamed. A Mexican-roots renaissance took place, though this time undertaken not by a small group of Chicano college professors, intellectuals, and artists but by a large swath of working-class youth.

"I've listened to his songs a hundred times, and every time I listen to them, I hear and feel something different," says José Quintero, a twenty-two-year-old from Paramount, one night at El Parral. "Like the song about Tino Quintero. He was like a Billy the Kid. Everybody wanted to kill him, but because he was a man, they couldn't. They invited him to a party. At the party they began shooting at him. Surrounded by his enemies, he said, 'I'm going to take a few of them with me.' Then he ran out of bullets. He wasn't going to apologize to nobody. He died like a man. He inspired a lot of people. I want to die like that."

"There was a long time when, it seemed to me, young Latinos appropriated from black people an identity, a style of music, dress, a way of speaking," says Marco Galvez, a Mexican immigrant and employee at Cintas Acuario. "They didn't want to know anything about Mexico or Spanish. Now they've found their own identity. Chalino set the style."

In the years since his death, Mexican-American kids have transformed, probably forever, the music of their parents, giving it a nasty American edge. Dozens of young singers, who'd sung only in the shower or the car, figured that if Chalino could do it, why couldn't they? Following his death, one took the stage name Chalinillo—Little Chalino—another La Sombra de Chalino—Chalino's Shadow.

Among the new singers was Saúl Viera. "At first when Chalino came out, no one really liked him. Myself, I was like, 'Where the hell did you get that guy?' But then you pay attention to what he's saying and you start liking him," said Viera. "It's like gangster music about people getting shot, battles with police, growing marijuana."

Viera's own story was about as improbable as Chalino's. A graduate of Paramount High, in 1995 Viera was working for a courier company when one night he was getting drunk with some friends at El Parral. At their urging and because the club was almost empty, Viera got up to sing with the house band. As it turned out, Viera sounded like Chalino. Abel Orozco, looking for a new Chalino, figured Viera would do. Viera recorded his first album the next month.

Viera took the stage name El Gavilancillo (The Little Hawk). By age twenty-two he had recorded fifteen albums and become the biggest of the post-Chalino wave of L.A. *narcocorrido* singers. "A lot of people, when I came out, said, 'Man, you sound just like him. Why you trying to be like him?' I said, 'Man, I tried changing my voice. I can't sing no other way.' With time

people understood that," Viera said.

Viera became that wonderful urban immigrant anomaly: a young man who listened to rap and made a living singing polkas about Mexican drug smugglers—though like Chalino, Viera's biggest hit was a radio-safe love song.

"When I was in junior high and my dad would play the *banda* music, I'd be, like, 'Turn it down. My friends are going to hear.' Now it's the other way around," he said. "I'm turning it up and my parents are turning it down. When I was younger, I was ashamed of Mexican music. Now I know who I am. I'm not afraid of my race."

His goal, he said, was to "be as big as Vicente Fernández," the great *ranchera* singer.

He never got the chance. Four months after that interview, Saúl Viera and his fiancée were in the parking lot of a Denny's restaurant in Bellflower. A tall, thin young man approached them, pulled a pistol from his shirt, fired several times at Viera, and ran off. The singer died in the parking lot. His fiancée was unharmed. Viera was well known as a ladies' man—he even kept a scrapbook filled with photographs of himself with an array of stunningly beautiful young women, and he'd had children by three of them. Among his fans it's suspected that the shooter was a jealous boyfriend, friend, or brother of an ex-girlfriend of Viera's. Yet the case remains unsolved.

Soon hundreds of bands were following Chalino into the *narcocorrido*. From the small L.A. labels rushed a torrent of *corridos pesados* ("heavy *corridos*")—though radio stations still don't touch them. What was implicit in Chalino's music quickly became explicit and extreme. *Corridos* now frequently boast of the hero's drug involvement. Singers pose with massive weaponry. One singer, Jesús Palma, shoulders a bazooka on his album *Mi Oficio Es Matar* (*Killing Is My Business*). Singers who had never done many *narcocorridos* find they have to sing a few if they want to sell records. One company even released an Alvin-and-the-Chipmunks-style album of *corridos* for children.

At Cintas Acuario, Pedro Rivera's son Juan devised a series of compilation albums with photographs of staged drug deals and drug robberies: *Puros Corridos Perrones* (*Badass Corridos,* more or less). Volume 5, with no promotion whatsoever, sold sixty thousand copies in a week last year. Juan himself recorded an album called *Corridos de Poca Madre* (*Bad Motherfucking Corridos*, roughly).

Lupe Rivera, a *corrido* composer and singer like his father, released an album posing with an AK-47 (*Corridos de Fregadera y Media,* roughly *Bitch and a Half Corridos*), including an ode to drug lord Amado Carrillo—"The Lord of the Skies"—who died during a plastic surgery operation last summer. Lupe also recently recorded a *corrido* to Saúl Viera.

Since much of this music was recorded by—and sung by and to—Mexican-American kids who had grown up on gangster rap, the marketing debt was obvious. "When [rapper] Easy E was coming out, he'd have a gun. I'd say, 'Damn, I'm gonna buy it,'" says Lupe Rivera. "That's the stuff I liked. Plus when you see a cassette that says 'parental guidance,' you want to get it."

Beyond commercial production of *corridos,* the commissioned *corrido* that Chalino pioneered grew into a booming industry in Los Angeles. Today anybody, no matter how dull and insignificant, can have a *corrido* recorded about him in L.A. for between five hundred and two thousand dollars. Dozens of composers and most *narcocorrido* singers supplement their income by writing them. Unlike Chalino's songs, few of these commissioned *corridos* tell compelling stories. Usually they merely say that so-and-so has a nice truck, likes to go to bars and chase women, has a pearl-handled .45, and is real tough and respected by his friends, so don't mess with him.

The commissioned *corrido* barely exists in Mexico. It thrives in L.A. because, like *corridos* of old, it fills a need: this one of immigrants to show they have done well in *gringolandia*. The *corrido* has adapted to the new reality of Mexicans having to live and work away from Mexico. Immigrants use commissioned *corridos* as tangible proof—like a new car or Nike tennis shoes—that they've made it in the United States; the songs are especially effective if the immigrant also wants to leave the impression that he's connected to the dope business.

"If I write a *corrido* about someone who's made a lot of money here selling drugs, the first thing he does is grab my cassette and go back to Mexico to show all his friends," says Teodoro Peña, a landscaper and composer who followed Chalino into the commissioned-*corrido* business. "We can't write a *corrido* about Pancho Villa anymore."

"Before, they'd only do *corridos* about legendary figures," says Abel Orozco. "Now people want to hear about themselves while they're alive. Although they

may be nobodies, they want to make themselves known. *Corridos* have become, over the last several years, a little less news and a little more publicity for common people. They're fifteen minutes of fame that they pay for themselves."

Who killed Chalino Sánchez and why remains a mystery. Mexican justice being what it is and Chalino's circle of acquaintances being what they were, no one holds any hope that his murder will be solved. In the months following his death, close to 150 *corridos* were written and recorded about him. This makes Chalino Sánchez, according to ethnomusicologists, probably the most written about *corrido* subject in the century-old history of the genre, eclipsing even Pancho Villa.

Nacho Hernández believes it wasn't his death but the fact that someone was finally promoting Chalino that made him big. "He'd been a phenomenon without promotion, and with promotion, he grew even bigger," Hernández says. "His bad luck was that he became famous after he died."

A lingering rumor has it that he hasn't died, that he merely faked his own death to throw his enemies off his track, a rumor abetted by the phony recordings of him singing with living artists released by Musart and Cintas Aquario. Says Nacho Hernández: "I know he's dead. I saw his body."

Still, his musical legacy is as healthy as ever. El Farallón in Lynwood held a recent amateur talent show. "There were fifteen singers. They all sang like Chalino Sánchez," says Emilio Franco. "They all wanted to talk like him. They cocked their hats like Chalino, pronounced words like Chalino."

At home in Paramount, life goes on. Marisela Vallejo lives in the house Chalino paid for with the Musart money. (Actually Chalino had paid for only half of the house. After he died, the outstanding mortgage was forgiven and Marisela deeded the house by the owner, who was a big fan.) Her walls are hung with photos of her deceased husband and gold records of the legitimate Musart albums—records that went gold after he died. Marisela had to fight to get them. "I wanted him to have some kind of recognition," she says. Musart presented them to her at a ceremony a couple of years ago.

Chalino's son, Adan, is following in his father's footsteps. At thirteen he has a nascent singing career. Some people suggested he be called Chalino

Sánchez Jr. His mother nixed that idea. Instead his stage name is El Compita— The Little Buddy. Where her children are concerned, Marisela picks and chooses from her husband's legacy. She's proud her son sings Mexican folk music. But she won't let him record the *narcocorridos*—the "dirty *corridos*," she calls them— that his father's life and death have made fashionable. "They're harmful for young people," she says. She hasn't kept track of the people who were the subjects of Chalino's *corridos*. Many are long dead; others are on the run from the law or have faded into the cantina world that Marisela never liked.

Mexican essayist Carlos Monsiváis once said that during economic crises of the kind Mexico has suffered for twenty-five years, a hero is anyone who provides a job. Chalino's *corridos* are about the only two figures in Mexican popular culture during that time who can consistently claim economic success: the drug smuggler and the immigrant; usually, in his songs, the same person. His creation was literally Mexican and American. It showed the importance of the diaspora—primarily Los Angeles—in shaping contemporary Mexican culture. And though his creation was Mexican, his story is quintessentially American, one born of the opportunities, the reimagining of life's possibilities, that so many Mexican campesinos have come to the United States in search of. In Mexico, Chalino could never have been what he became; he'd never have had the chance. He was, after all, a barely lettered young man, once an anonymous campesino in the massive flow of immigrants north—a singer whose most important attribute turned out to be that he couldn't sing.

"We're not talking about Caruso or Placido Domingo," says Musart's Fernando González. "We're just talking about a poor boy who had a style people liked."

—1998

LYNCHING IN HUEJUTLA

No one much noticed the two men—one fat and one thin—who came lurching along the unpaved roads of the working-class López Mateos neighborhood in a gray 1980 Chevrolet pickup early on that afternoon.

Tuesday, March 24, was a hot one, as most days are in the town of Huejutla, Hidalgo, that time of year. The heat and humidity left a body with a well-lubricated feeling, as if it had been drenched with oil, then wrapped in a blanket. The sun bounced off the roads of creamy dust and made the most accustomed eyes squint. Without a breeze, even the fleshy fronds of tropical vegetation hung limp.

The López Mateos neighborhood is made up of humble concrete-block homes jammed crudely onto the hillside. The neighborhood is one where who owns the land is a question that can't always be easily answered. Residents make any improvements, chipping in to install things like electricity because the city hasn't stretched services to the area. There's no drainage or paved streets or public transport. When it rains, people walk to work in knee-deep water. A few mom-and-pop stores, usually operated out of a neighbor's home, are what most people rely on for food.

Stopping frequently at these stores, the men would stay a couple of minutes. Then they would slowly climb into the truck and roll off to the next one. No one was buying. The men were selling small packs of stamps, costing one peso apiece. In Mexico children buy the stamps and stick them to special cards that, once filled, they redeem for prizes. In the back of the two men's truck were toy guns, plastic swords, soccer balls, and dolls. The men traveled through east-central Mexico for a month or two at a time, hawking the stamps in neighborhoods like López Mateos.

The men were as poor as their customers. They hailed from Tihuatlán, a town of 25,000 people three hours away in the neighboring state of Veracruz. José Santes, thirty, a fat man with a bushy mustache, had been a taxi driver in

Tihuatlán, as had his father before him—his father, in fact, had been murdered years before in a taxi-union dispute. His uncles, a half brother, and a cousin were also taxi drivers. But taxi driving was unpredictable work. And Santes had a wife and four young children to support. So he had accepted the offer of a friend to work as a traveling salesman, which turned out to be more stable employment. While working as a cabbie, one of the people Santes met was Salvador Valdez, a thin, twenty-three-year-old orange picker from a small village near Tihuatlán. Santes needed an assistant on his sales trips. Valdez, recently married, left his seasonal job as an orange picker to accompany him.

Only later would store owners in López Mateos recall them, and then only to remember them as simple traveling salesmen like the dozens who pass through every month, and a little less pushy than most, the fat one doing most of the talking. About noon they stopped at a shop owned by Dominga Hernández. Her daughter, Esmeralda Maroquí, was watching the store. "I told them we didn't want any stamps because the children in our house get into them and we don't make any money off them," Esmeralda said later. In fact, of the eight or ten stores Santes and Valdez visited that day, only one took any stamps.

The day should have ended like that, with the two men drifting out of the neighborhood and out of mind. And it would have had the salesmen not found themselves in the López Mateos neighborhood just about the time the children were getting out of school.

Of all the things López Mateos doesn't have, one of them is a lot of crime. An occasional burglary is the worst the neighborhood is likely to see most of the time. So that Tuesday afternoon, neighbors were alarmed to hear the screams of a group of children coming home from school.

Valdez was standing by the truck while Santes was inside a store, trying to sell to a merchant. A group of children, seeing the toys, gathered around the truck. As a joke, Valdez said later, he ran after the kids. He grabbed Edith Hidalgo, eleven, on the arm and Dolores Hernández, nine, on a buttock. Valdez said later he was only trying to shoo the kids away from the toys in the truck. To Edith Hidalgo, he said something to the effect of, "What a pretty girl. When you're older, we'll come back and kidnap you." This terrified the children, who shrieked and ran for home, reporting to their parents that someone had tried to kidnap them.

A neighbor heard the children's screams, stopped a passing police truck, and reported what the girls had said. Officers stopped the men up a hill, where they had continued on, unaware anything was amiss. Arturo Moreno, the region's prosecutor, took the men's statement that night. Santes denied doing anything at all. Valdez admitted what he did, repeating that he'd meant it only as a joke. "See where jokes have gotten you," Moreno told him.

He could not have imagined. Valdez's joke, stupid but relatively minor and not an uncommon type of remark in the culture of working-class Mexico, was a spark that would smolder unnoticed over the next twenty-four hours, then suddenly ignite a towering firestorm of human rage. Yet even when it finally happened—that is, even when a mob of more than a thousand people finally lynched the two salesmen in the town's plaza the next night and left Valdez swinging from the bandstand—so much had contributed to creating a voracious mob out of a peaceful demand for justice that what was surprising was so many people could look back and say they didn't see it coming until it came.

For one thing, there was the sugar cane alcohol. The region is known to consume it in large quantities. "I don't know anyone who, with alcohol in his body, does anything great," said one man when it was all over. There was the thick heat and the crime the salesmen were said to have committed. Certain authority figures never intervened—notably the police, priests, and bishop, though the lynching took place in full view of city hall and the town cathedral. A local radio station assembled and riled the crowd by airing a spot every fifteen minutes urging people to the plaza to support a demand for justice. There was the area's profound poverty, lack of education, ignorance, and isolation. There were misunderstandings regarding the law. Added to that was a spectacular regional gift for exaggeration and willingness to believe the most preposterous ideas; so when it was all over, the men weren't salesmen at all but foot soldiers in a Texas-based ring of child kidnappers who not only trafficked in organs but had a liver or two in the cab of their truck, for which they were said to receive the awesome sum of $1,500 apiece.

Above all, there was the sense among people here, hardly unique to this part of Mexico, that their society is, at its core, unjust—that justice frequently is left undone—and that authorities, unless pressured, will let

nefarious criminals out of jail.

And who knows, a lot more than that probably went into the mix. It was a chaotic night. So many people gathered in Huejutla's plaza, each with his own reasons, his own story. And if most people in the plaza that night were there simply to see what happened and to support the demand for justice, they also didn't do anything to calm spirits. In the plaza that night, it all fermented, festered, and finally exploded in the tropical heat. Not even the governor, who hopped a mountain range in a helicopter late that night, could stop it. "This is a quiet town," says Cristóbal Cifuentes, a local dentist. "No one expected it to go as far as it did."

Huejutla is pronounced Hway-HOOT-la, and it is in fact a quiet town. Quiet and isolated and home to about 40,000 people. It lies sweltering in tropical lowlands on a northern edge of Hidalgo, one of Mexico's poorest states, just north of Mexico City. Huejutla is only 133 miles from Pachuca, Hidalgo's capital, but the distance is deceiving because between it and the capital is the massive Huasteca mountain range. Those 133 miles take about four hours to traverse in a car.

The city has three weekly newspapers of varying degrees of credibility and only two newsstands. Nightlife amounts to a movie theater and an estimated 200 cantinas. Unlike most of remote Mexico nowadays, Huejutla has no functioning pay phone downtown, though it's the seat of Hidalgo's third most populated *municipio,* or county.

Huejutla is the commercial hub for dozens of small Huasteca farming communities, where bony Indians live from harvest to harvest. Agriculture here is almost bankrupt. Despite its tropical climes, most of the year the region is dusty and humid. People grow crops when it rains and lose what they've planted when it doesn't, as it hasn't much of this year. So the town has become a magnet, as well, for poor campesinos, arriving as refugees from the battered fields and living in shantytowns of unpaved streets radiating out from the center.

Downtown, the Plaza de la Revolución sprawls pleasantly across three city blocks. To one side of it rises the town's dark, beautiful sixteenth-century cathedral. Across the plaza is a line of shops—stationery stores, shoe stores, restaurants, ice-cream vendors—that lead down to city hall, the jail, and, on a corner, the courthouse. Thick ficus trees line the square, home to thrushes whose constant chirping gives the plaza a light, cheerful feeling. Anchoring the plaza is the wrought-iron bandstand, painted forest green, that once stood in Mexico City's main plaza. According to one story, the bandstand was a gift to Huejutla after the revolution. Another has it that revolutionaries took it as bounty, and only later was it called a gift.

People speak of recent burglaries and car thefts in a serious tone of voice, but there's really not much crime in Huejutla. Last December reports circulated that some children had been stolen from the annual fair. That never happened, but the stories are believed. Still, Huejutla is the kind of town where you can understand people's awe at a sudden eruption of violence. This kind of thing had never happened before.

Nor was Prosecutor Arturo Moreno, a pudgy young man with a face indented with acne scars, expecting anything of the sort when the Santes and Valdez case landed on his desk in his office across town that Tuesday afternoon. After interviewing the two men and looking objectively at the case, Moreno concluded that the most the men could be accused of was attempted kidnapping. And under Mexican law, this meant bail.

In Mexico anyone accused of a crime not legally deemed "serious" is eligible for bail. Serious crimes, in Hidalgo, include murder, rape, robbery, rustling, and kidnapping, among others. But attempting to commit these crimes is, by law, not "serious." Moreno set bail at 5,600 pesos for the two men. But he didn't mention this to the girls' families when they arrived at his office on the outskirts of town the next morning. He merely told them everything would be taken care of. They thanked him and left.

The families assumed the two men would remain in custody, until they arrived at the jail and discovered they were eligible for bail. They were outraged. Why were criminals being given bail? The judge at the jail, Anastasio Hernández, studied the case and agreed with Moreno's decision. He told the families that the two men had the legal right to bail. The best he could do for the families was increase it. Edith Hidalgo's parents say they understood the bail concept well. "But you know these criminals pay bail and go out and do it

again and again," says Alfonso Hidalgo, Edith's father.

Any subtleties of bail got lost in translation as tempers flared outside the jail and a crowd slowly formed around the parents' outrage. It wasn't long before rumor had it that Santes and Valdez were caught with at least one girl in their truck. So onlookers were now being told a rough shorthand: that two child kidnappers were to be released after paying 5,000 pesos. Even those who did understand that bail was part of the picture couldn't understand how two child kidnappers would warrant it. To the people who began to gather at the jail that afternoon, it all began to reek of bought justice. And that sounded so familiar, a place they all knew far too well.

What they believed was happening and why they believed it have a lot to do with the rich history of corruption in modern Mexico, and politics in the state of Hidalgo in the last twenty years.

It starts with Mexico's ruling party, the Institutional Revolutionary Party (PRI), which has held power since 1929, the world's oldest one-party state. The PRI has achieved this simply by buying people off—a nationwide Tammany Hall and a remarkably successful one.

The price the ruling party has paid for loyalty usually isn't high. But it almost always involves some way of getting around the law. A great number of perverse results come from all this. But the greatest perversion of all, and the one important to the case at hand, is that of the justice system.

The PRI finally came to use the justice system as a lever to enforce support: those loyal to the machine could flout the law, while anyone who stepped out of line soon felt its full force. Accompanying this, naturally, was widespread corruption in law enforcement, where bribes can sway a verdict or get a person out of jail early.

Mexico's working classes know this. Without money or friends in high places, they possess a finely honed sense of just how solidly the system is stacked against them. They are the most affected by street crime and least able to do anything about it. And so a vast folklore has emerged pertaining to the treachery of the *autoridades*—much of it true, some of it fiction, and some of it based on popular misunderstandings of the law or the facts of certain cases— but all of it believed as gospel truth. Thus two men said to be child kidnappers and about to be released on bail would be taken for granted as another example of crafty authorities undermining the law for personal gain.

Moreover, the unpredictability of the justice system long ago forced large sectors of Mexico's working classes into *organizaciones populares* of neighborhoods, street vendors, garbagemen, teachers, farmers, and on and on. In these organizations they could protect themselves and force the system to let them break the law or at least leave them in peace. Across Mexico, for example, large groups of vendors sell in the public street without paying any rent or taxes or even having a permit. The PRI government allows them to break the law because they support the regime.

The party negotiates with an organization leader, who brokers his group's support in exchange for sweet political positions or kickbacks. The leaders are like ward bosses. They have access to the system that members lack, so they can get things done—say, obtain street space for a vendor. In Huejutla and in the Huasteca in general, these *organizaciones populares* became especially strong, dominating politics and the economic life of the region. Their leaders became "little gods," in the words of one politician. On their orders, members would close a highway or a community. They have been rumored to get people out of jail. They also enforced a mindless obedience and discipline. Only through the organization and the leader's blessing are members allowed to earn a living; dissidents are expelled to fend for themselves against the system. "Sometimes if you don't go to a meeting, they fine you," says María Maya, owner of a taco stand and member of the PRI's Union of Street Vendors in downtown Huejutla. "We go to support our leaders and for unity."

Coupled with that—indeed at the root of the Huasteca's history of strong *organizaciones populares*—is the Indian tradition of the community banding together to confront threats from the outside. "In 1986 a rumor spread that there were people running around cutting off people's heads," says Refugio Miranda, a teacher of the Aztec language. "Never was this seen. However, the rumor spread to all the villages and communities. People believed it. All through the region, communities got together to protect themselves. No one went around alone. Everyone went in groups. For any kind of thing—a cyclone, an epidemic—people come together to help. If there's a problem, people unify. Plus people automatically mistrust authorities. When there's no trust, people get together and protest in a very unified way."

And so the Huasteca was bequeathed the following peculiarities relevant to the lynching of Santes and Valdez: a history of a justice system prostituted to the will of a few; a belief that authorities will do nothing or, worse, will side with the rich and the criminal element over the hardworking poor unless pressured to action; a tradition of obeying leaders and quickly responding to community calls for action.

And all of that convened in the next ratcheting up in the day's events. Police say someone—perhaps Edith Hidalgo's father, Alfonso—paid the local private radio station, XECY, to put an announcement on the station. The station ran three different spots throughout the afternoon. The spots said nothing about mob justice but they did urge people to come to the plaza to support the parents' demands for punishment of the "kidnappers." They referred to child kidnappers caught trying to steal children. Some people said they heard the announcer say at one point that the two men had been caught with four girls in their truck, ages twelve, eleven, nine, and seven.

Huejutla, being poor, depends more than most towns on the radio. People listen to it at work and at home. Many Huejutlans don't have telephones. So radio is the town's most important medium both for communication and entertainment. XECY is one of only two local stations and has a reputation for yellow journalism. Starting at about 2 p.m. and lasting until about 6 p.m., XECY aired the spots at least sixteen times. Through the afternoon, the spots were an ominous drumbeat, sounding an awful lot like a call for organizational mobilization. So by nightfall that small collection of people in front of the jail became a massive crowd that filled Huejutla's plaza. "It was on the news," says María Maya. "Schoolteachers were telling children that they should go support the demand for justice. Plus they always steal children. There were a couple kidnapped at the annual fair in December. I think they stole like two or three."

Off in Pachuca that afternoon, Attorney General Omar Fayad was at work in his office when he received a call from Huejutla's mayor José Luis Fayad (no relation). People were angry that the two men would go free. So it was agreed: bail for the salesmen would be revoked. The people would be told the two men would remain jailed.

By midafternoon the crowd was upset, growing larger, though still manageable. Moreno was called to the jail at about 3:30 p.m. In front of the jail, he told the crowd that everything would be taken care of, though he didn't know what case the people were angry about. He was surprised to hear it was the case of the two salesmen. Moreno went inside, and immediately the crowd barred him and other courthouse employees from leaving. He called Attorney General Fayad. "Don't worry," Fayad told Moreno, "we're not going to let them go until there's a complete investigation."

To both Moreno in Huejutla and Attorney General Fayad in Pachuca, that seemed to resolve the issue. What else did people want? Moreno settled down to read some reports, figuring it would all blow over soon.

Judge Hernández went out again to tell the people that the attorney general had decided to revoke bail. Still, it's doubtful enough people heard him to make a difference. And even if they heard, it's unlikely many people would have believed him. For one thing, the radio kept its drumbeat going, never reporting that bail was now revoked and the kidnappers were not going free. And by now loudspeakers had been set up outside the jail, and a series of leaders of *organizaciones populares* took turns demanding that the authorities do their jobs. Plus one result of years of perverted justice is that Mexicans are simply unwilling to believe the justice system ever works.

In that regard, the citizens of Huejutla, as well as state police authorities, like to bring up the following case: Two years ago, Jaime Badillo Austria, a ten-year-old schoolboy and son of the owners of La Vega, the town's best restaurant, was kidnapped. His body was later found decomposing outside of town. This is the only authentic case of child kidnapping Huejutla has had in years. The kidnapper turned out to be not an out-of-towner but the boy's twenty-nine-year-old half brother. In something out of a Mexican soap opera, the half brother was born of a rape of a maid by the elder Badillo years before. He grew up rejected by his father and resenting his younger half brother. That, according to those who have spoken with him, was what brought on the kidnapping. He was arrested and is now serving thirty years in prison. Yet few people in town remember justice being done in the case. In fact, most Huejutlans are certain that no one was arrested and use the case to demonstrate to visitors their authorities' ineptitude and venality. Police investigators, meanwhile, use the case as proof that no matter how a case is truly resolved, people will always

believe the authorities have failed to do their jobs.

So just because Judge Hernández told the crowd that bail was revoked didn't mean anyone took him seriously.

Another factor complicated matters. Hidalgo state judges and prosecutors are never from the areas they serve, and they rotate frequently. The policy is intended to prevent corruption, but here the policy backfired. Neither Moreno nor Hernández had been born in the Huasteca—both hail from Pachuca, the far-off state capital. No one knew them. Witnesses say the judge and prosecutor's attitude early on was not one of conciliation, but of arrogance. Perhaps they were indignant at having a crowd attempt to dictate terms to them. "People are hardheaded," says Moreno. "They don't believe you no matter what you tell them."

Late in the afternoon Mayor José Luis Fayad met with a team of forty delegates—essentially PRI neighborhood representatives. The delegates told the mayor that people didn't believe the judge and that they were now hot, angry, and getting drunk.

Through the day Fayad had been at home and had not appeared in public. Fayad says the problem was not his jurisdiction but rather that of state judicial authorities, and that anyway he had spoken on the phone with the authorities in Pachuca. With no riot police in the region, the mayor says, he was left with his thirty-two-man municipal police force, armed with only .22-caliber pistols and unprepared to handle large crowds.

Fayad met with the girls' families, assuring them that the two men would remain in jail. As the day faded toward dusk, Fayad went to the balcony of city hall for his first public appearance of the day. While people insulted him from below, he told the crowd that he personally guaranteed that the two salesmen would remain in custody in Huejutla. Fayad went home and didn't appear in public again until the governor arrived at about 11 p.m. By then the court, jail, and city hall had been ransacked and the two salesmen were in the mob's hands.

It was one of the day's critical moments. Had Fayad, a man born in Huejutla and well known, been able to sway the crowd, the entire affair might have ended with his speech. But he could not. The reasons, according to many Huejutlans, had to do with his term in office so far.

José Luis Fayad, a tall, jowly, thick man with large spectacles, has for years been a beloved member of Huejutla society. His uncle was once a respected mayor. Fayad himself is a doctor, who often gave consultations for free to those who could not pay. He took office as mayor early last year.

But folks here say his administration has been marked by a distancing from the people that in turn affected his ability to convince the crowd that night. First, he got three thousand fewer votes than the previous mayor. In a region that has always voted PRI, this is a sign of weakness and thus cause for diminished respect. Plus many charge that nepotism has prevailed in the mayor's administration. A brother-in-law is chief of police. A cousin was appointed municipal judge. A sister-in-law is treasurer of the family-assistance program. Fayad's sister owns a building-materials firm that supplies the city's public works projects. Another brother makes all the ironworks for the city. Another brother builds schools. "People know all this," says Ánibal Torres, a teacher, who is the mayor's brother-in-law and a political opponent. "If he'd had the moral authority of being an honest man, people would have paid attention to him."

Two of Fayad's biggest public works projects have been highly questioned. He built a horse-racing track and he renovated the plaza, pulling out a couple dozen trees. People wondered why he would spend money on a track for horses when roads in so many neighborhoods are all but impassable. The plaza, though now very beautiful, was a luxury most people figured Huejutla also couldn't afford, given the numerous other basic needs of the city's population that go unmet. And in an area where summer temperatures stay well above 100 degrees, fewer shade trees is not necessarily considered an improvement.

Then came January 16. That day Fayad gave his first State of the City speech, as required by law. He invited people from Huejutla and the surrounding communities to attend. Close to four thousand people showed up, though the hall held only a thousand. Those allowed in were mostly wealthier folks and those holding posters applauding Fayad's administration. City officials erred in locking the doors to the hall. Had the doors been left open, people outside would have seen there were no seats available. But seeing the chains, they thought they were being prevented from coming in. Having lost a day of work—which in this region is tantamount to a day's food—to come

support their mayor, their mood turned nasty. Soon a torrent of tangerines, oranges, tomatoes, and jicamas was arcing through the hall's upper windows. So, too, were the traditional flower necklaces people had brought to honor the mayor. Fayad finally had to burst from the hall, protected by a phalanx of security guards. "Since then, people haven't respected the mayor," says Jorge Muhedano, who was Fayad's campaign photographer.

All of this tarnished Fayad's image leading up to March 25 and prevented him, the local voice of authority, from doing much to sway the crowd. Still, Fayad left the balcony believing he had resolved the situation. Some people in the plaza felt, too, that the crowd was beginning to disperse. Instead the night was about to get nasty and the possibility of a lynching was becoming real.

Lynching has a long, rich history in Mexico. For centuries communities occasionally rose up in spasms of mob violence against priests, tax collectors, and other authority figures. In modern Mexico, lynching has not abated. If anything, it has grown more common.

The *linchamiento* is part of the Mexico that tourists never see, lying beyond the shimmering hotels of Cancún and the sunny hillsides of Cuernavaca, in benighted towns and pueblos where any justice that does exist is hardly blind. Dozens of *linchamientos* have taken place in the last few years across Mexico. The state of Morelos, just south of Mexico City, in recent years has become known for them. Residents of one village once took some state police officers hostage, doused them with gasoline, and threatened to burn them. Finally the attorney general came and they took him hostage until the governor relented and came down to talk. In another Morelos town, in 1994, four men accused of robbing a bus were shot, stabbed, kicked, hacked, beaten, stoned, and finally burned. In another town one man was hung from the town basketball rim. In a village in Veracruz in 1996, a crowd grabbed a man suspected of raping and killing a woman, gave him a quick trial, judged him guilty, tied him to a tree, drenched him in gasoline, and burned him to death while someone videotaped it all.

The Mexican lynching is different from its southern-U.S. counterpart, which was a weapon the majority used to oppress a minority. Nor is it similar to the lynchings in the Old West, where there was no law. Rather it is a bellow of rage by the powerless majority against corrupt cops and politicians, protected criminals—against a justice system that people know to be unfair. Lynchings rarely change the cause of community grievances. They are, however, Mexicans' own clearest statement today on the quality of justice they expect—the horrifying, but not surprising, result of years of perverted justice.

And things began heading in that direction shortly after the mayor's speech. The crowd found the toys and stickers in the salesmen's truck. This kindled more rumor: the toys were used to lure children, people immediately concluded. Someone set fire to the salesmen's pickup. City police did nothing to stop it, and a line was now crossed. "I left about then," says Cristóbal Cifuentes, the dentist. "I could see people were ready to do things they don't ordinarily want to do."

Next the crowd broke down the door to the small courthouse where Judge Hernández, Prosecutor Moreno, and a half dozen other workers were hoping to ride out the storm. Again the police did nothing to stop it.

Here the night's leaders began to emerge. "You have these histrionic characters," says Ánibal Torres. "This was an open stage that called to people to act the role they always wanted to play. There was no control. They could act as they wished. The stage was ready. Write your own script. Put the ending on it that you wish."

Striding ahead of the crowd now was a man named Martín Hernández, an unlikely figure to lead a movement but an appropriate one for a lynching. Hernández, sixty-five, is poor, lumpy, and balding, with a healthy appetite for sugarcane rotgut. For many years he'd sold herbs and religious candles by the cathedral. Here Hernández rose from his anonymity for the one brief moment of notoriety in his life. He led the break-in at the courthouse.

"He had a large bucket filled with gasoline and he started splashing the floor with it, like it was water," says Moreno. "We were kind of huddled in the last little corner of the courthouse. He said, 'Now you're really going to get fucked.'"

Hernández splashed gasoline on Moreno's shirt and drenched Judge Hernández. With the courthouse about to burn, the courthouse employees made a run for it out a side door. Moreno said he raced through downtown and into neighborhoods he didn't know and didn't stop until he reached a government office on the opposite side of Huejutla. Moreno remembers

being stunned at the size of the crowd outside. He hadn't been outside since arriving at the courthouse in midafternoon. "There were just a few people then. When I ran out, there was this whole multitude," he says.

Judge Hernández wasn't so lucky. The crowd chased him, caught him, and beat him severely. They then took him to the jailhouse door, where they told him to order the release of Santes and Valdez. People had been banging on the jail for about an hour at this point. Hernández told them he couldn't do that and that they should speak with the jailer. The crowd's attention turned to the jail, and the judge was able to slip off. He ran a few streets away, where he took a bus away from the center, finally finding refuge in a private home.

The courthouse sacked and burned, the mob poured into city hall. The city's tax and payroll records went up in flames, and the births and deaths registry was destroyed. They hurled computers out the second-floor window to the ground, where they exploded like ripe melons. Police guns were stolen. People observing the action from rooftops a few streets away saw six or eight city cops escape by breaking a second-floor window in city hall and jumping to the roof of an adjacent building.

Sometime around 9 p.m. the mob set to work in earnest on breaking down the jailhouse door. Jailer Yasir Nochebuena remembers a continuous pounding on the door from early in the evening. Then Molotov cocktails began landing on the roof. The hammering and clamor outside got steadily more intense, with people yelling at the jailer and his employees to open up; otherwise things would go badly for them. The jail door is of imposing black steel, and witnesses say it took a couple of hours to finish the job. But shortly before 10 p.m. the crowd, led by Martín Hernández, smashed it open and rushed in for Santes and Valdez. A while later the crowd emerged leading the two men, who were now bathed in blood and gasoline. As people kicked and jabbed them with knives and machetes, the salesmen were dragged into the plaza.

Juan Ramírez, a sixty-seven-year-old campesino, was there. "The plaza was filled with people. They'd burned a car. There were fires and papers burning. The skinny guy [Valdez] was on the ground and people were kicking him and saying, 'Let's burn him.' Then they said, 'Let's tie him up.' They began dragging him by his feet across the plaza. So I picked up one arm and another man picked up another arm so he wouldn't hit his head. We took him up to the bandstand."

The bandstand soon was clogged with people. To one side was Santes, with his hands tied above his head. To another was Valdez, with both hands tied to the bandstand railing. Now at the crowd's mercy, the salesmen apparently came to their wits' end. Santes went onto his knees, begging for mercy. Both men began admitting to anything. María Maya, the taco vendor, went up on the platform and remembers people asking Santes what he'd done with the children. "He said he had two children in Tihuatlán and that he trafficked them to Texas. He gave the names of people who were his buyers," she says.

Martín Hernández, according to witnesses later questioned by police, was standing over Valdez with a machete blade under the man's right eye. "Isn't it true you trafficked in children and cut them open and cut their organs out?" Valdez said yes, and Hernández jammed the machete in Valdez's eye and flicked it out.

At about that time, across town, a friend showed a picture of Santes and Valdez, purchased from a photographer, to Esmeralda Maroquí and her mother, Dominga Hernández, who ran the store where the salesmen had stopped the day before. "I said, 'Mom, they're not kidnappers. They're salesmen,'" Maroquí says. Mother and daughter went to the square.

Meanwhile back in Pachuca, Attorney General Fayad had been receiving urgent phone calls from Huejutla. The promises of no bail and a complete investigation weren't working. The minor matter in Huejutla earlier in the day had mushroomed into something requiring immediate attention. Fayad called the office of Governor Jesús Murillo Karam. As people were sacking Huejutla City Hall, both men were on a helicopter heading over the Huasteca Mountains.

The trip was the culmination of a bewildering day in which the anger in Huejutla was a constant irritant in the distance but hardly anything that promised to incite open rebellion. "I was in Pachuca, and I didn't understand," Fayad says. "Finally when the governor decided to come here, I said, 'What could have happened during this time to allow things to get to this state?'"

As the helicopter hovered over Huejutla, the city was blanketed in low clouds. They were without radio support from below. "We circled, and then the pilot found a hole in the clouds. It was a terrifying moment. When you're

going down below the clouds, there's a moment when you can't see anything." Finally, though, the helicopter found a place to land.

The governor, flanked by the attorney general and the mayor, arrived at the plaza at about 11 p.m. Walking up the bandstand's circular steps, they found the salesmen tied and prone. The governor grabbed the rope that held Santes and threw it to the ground. Looking out onto the sea of angry faces, Fayad remembers thinking, "How did things get this bad? The crowd chanted, 'Justice! Justice!' The governor said, 'That's why I'm here.' He said, 'No one made me come. I'm here because I'm as upset as you are.' There were more chants for justice. 'That's why I'm here,' the governor said again, 'but we're going to do justice the way it should be done. There are laws, and we're going to respect them.'"

Here, though, people were too used to capricious justice for that argument to work. In Mexico people see their governor at election time and not much after that, unless it's to inaugurate some big public work and have people tell him how much they appreciate all he's done for them. Otherwise the governor is like a prince in a far-off castle, to whom the people must go to ask favors. Now, for a change, people saw a governor pleading with them. They could insult him. They began retrieving from their memory every sort of injustice, every affront they could remember. The noise could be heard ten blocks away.

"What about Colosio?" someone cried, referring to 1994 PRI presidential candidate Luis Donaldo Colosio, assassinated in Tijuana, whose killer is now serving fifty years in prison. Mexican popular opinion holds that other, more powerful people set the killer up for the job. In the crowd, Dorisela Austria, the mother of Jaime Badillo, broke into tears and yelled about injustice in her son's case; rumor has it that the decomposed body she was told was her son is in fact someone else and that her son is alive somewhere—though, according to Attorney General Fayad, DNA tests proved the identity of the remains. People yelled that they'd seen "little livers" (*"higaditos"*) in the cab of the salesmen's truck and clamored again for justice. They screamed about the children supposedly stolen from the annual fair the previous December—again, an event that never happened.

To the governor, the mayor, and others, the comments seemed absurd, the final proof that the crowd had lost all reason. But the Colosio case nationally, like the case of Jaime Badillo in Huejutla—as well as the fact that working-class people walk to work through rivers of knee-deep water when it rains while politicians build horse tracks—combine into the popular mix of fact and fiction that leads Mexicans to assume that there is no justice and any they do achieve certainly won't come from the authorities. And so on Huejutla's plaza that night all that pus, that resentment bloomed like a ripe pimple of popular rage and took as its focus Santes, Valdez, the mayor, the governor, the entire rancid system of justice and politics in Mexico.

The governor was finished. He had no microphone; the sound system had been stolen during the sacking of city hall. The crowd roared with boos, cat-calls, mimicry. Finally the governor left the bandstand and tried to negotiate with a group of thirty or forty people. "The authorities are used to people giving up," says Esmeralda Maroquí. "This time the people didn't give up."

Murillo Karam's aides would say later that the two salesmen were all but dead when the governor left the bandstand. With the governor gone, Santes, limp and unconscious if not already dead, was hoisted like a piñata, his hands tied above his head. His weight proved too much for the knot; he slipped through it and onto the bandstand. Undaunted, the mob tied the rope around his chest, lifted him above the bandstand's wrought-iron railing, and then swung him out over it. Again his heavy body slipped through the knot and he dropped like a rock fifteen feet to the plaza floor below. There he stayed and died.

Valdez's night continued a bit longer. Others on the stand lifted Valdez to the outside of the railing and tied him to it by his biceps. He hung there, splayed like Christ, before the crowd. "He was facing the crowd. Most of the time he was unconscious. Then he'd awaken and scream with pain. He was very beaten," says Simeon Bautista, Huejutla's chief agent for Mexico's Interior Ministry, who went to the plaza as the salesmen were being hauled from the jail. "He tried to lift up his legs, to support himself on the bandstand railing, but it was impossible."

Someone put a noose around his neck and then cut the cords around his arms that held him to the bandstand railing. "He was left hanging there," says Bautista. "They gave him a big pull to lift him above the railing, and he died. He didn't move. If he moved, it was from the yank they gave him."

Scattered applause emerged from the crowd as it watched what it had done. In the midst of it all, a few people could be heard yelling, "*Viva* Huejutla," and, in reference to Hidalgo's soccer team, "*Viva* Cruz Azul."

* * *

A few weeks later, Omar Fayad sits in his office discussing the events of March 25. "What we haven't been able to achieve is a clearer communication with the people," he says. The lynching in Huejutla, Fayad asserts, was stoked by the media's coverage of violence and crime. He has a point. Rarely do Mexican newspapers publish features about crime that help readers understand larger trends in criminality and the criminal justice system. Television never does. Mostly because it's easier and sells, papers publish whatever nefarious act happened the day before—accompanied often by pictures of some ne'er-do-well or a body crumpled in the street.

When Fayad took office two years ago, almost 5,000 robbery reports had been left unattended. Hidalgo, it seemed, was overwhelmed by robberies. Fayad commissioned a study of the reports and found that 30 percent were reports of stolen cellular phones, reported by people who had most likely lost them but whose company wouldn't reimburse them unless they were stolen. Another 30 percent were of stolen license plates. In Mexico police often remove license plates when giving a parking fine as the only guarantee the fine will be paid. Instead of paying the fine, people report the plates stolen. Of the 5,000 original robbery reports, only about 1,380 were of real robberies.

"That's an average of about four real robberies a day in the entire state," he says, picking up a newspaper that features mainly crime news. "But today they read about a robbery. Tomorrow a robbery, the next day, a robbery."

"Violence is the theme of the end of the twentieth century," Fayad says. "Imagine you're in Huejutla and you turn on the television, which comes from Mexico City, and there's a report of someone shot on the corner for his wristwatch. It didn't happen in Huejutla. However, the electronic media is constantly sending it out across the country. In this state we have one of the lowest crime rates in the country. Yet this inundation of news reports gives everyone the impression that all of Mexico is in the middle of a crime wave. It's not true.

"This creates a general consciousness that can expand into a kind of collective psychosis, which is what happened in Huejutla," he adds. "That night people were talking about an uncontrolled wave of kidnappings. What uncontrolled wave? In Hidalgo there were no kidnappings last year. This year we've had two, and they've both been solved."

In the days following the lynching, Huejutla remained keen to believe all kinds of bizarre rumors. One was that buses of folks from Tihuatlán, Veracruz, were coming to exact vengeance for the killing of their native sons. After a television interview with Martín Hernández in a hospital bed in Pachuca, another rumor quickly circulated he was dead. Not true, but not so far-fetched. Shortly after the lynching, riot police arrived in a bus from Pachuca and the governor called on them to clear the plaza. They likely also gave Hernández the beating that left him hospitalized with a broken left leg, a massive scalp wound, and deep purple bruises over other parts of his body. Hernández repeats again and again, for a stream of reporters, that he was drunk that night, doesn't remember much, but does remember that he wasn't in the plaza. "A lot of people look like me," he says. He blames the girls' families for putting the spot on the radio. As for his injuries, "Maybe it was the police who beat me, maybe somebody else," he says. "I don't remember."

Judge Anastasio Hernández spent the days after the lynching at first recuperating, then hiding from reporters. His assistant lied to reporters regarding his whereabouts before finally saying that all interviews had to be cleared in Pachuca. Prosecutor Arturo Moreno was rotated out of Huejutla a few weeks later and now works in the town of Actopan, near Pachuca. He'd been scheduled for a change anyway.

Huejutla's bishop, Salvador Martínez, issued a public letter decrying the lynching. He called it the "extreme manifestation of deeply held attitudes of consumerism, violence, aggression toward life that we have accepted and justified." He drew the parallel to the way Christ died and remembered Christ's defense of an adulteress about to be stoned to death by a mob ("He that is without sin among you . . ."). He didn't mention why neither he nor his priests attempted to intervene in the same way.

Prosecutors in Attorney General Omar Fayad's office have arrested six people and charged them with murder, assault, sedition, and some other crimes, for

which they are asking the maximum penalty of thirty years in prison. Among them are Martín Hernández; María Maya, the taco vendor; and Juan Ramírez, the farmer.

"I think what some people wanted [that night] was a kind of Roman circus, where the crowd gives thumbs-up or -down to feed the Christian to the lions," says Fayad. "They got one. As a civilization, it was truly retrograde to have this kind of spectacle in the plaza of a town."

Still, the case's resolution seems unlikely to forge a new popular appreciation of the justice system. All of those arrested are poor, working-class folks. "There were a lot of rich people there that night. Why aren't they here?" says Marco Antonio Hernández, a twenty-five-year-old encyclopedia salesman, who was seen in a picture on the bandstand that night and is now one of the six accused. "They've just picked up poor people. Why are we the only ones in here?" Indeed, Jorge Reyes, a businessman and owner of XECY, avoided all legal problems by firing his news anchorman and canceling the station's afternoon news show that broadcast the spots. He, too, avoided reporters for days afterward.

Huejutlans now have the tricky task of both condemning and justifying what happened that night. Generally this is achieved by insisting—falsely—that the six people arrested had lived in Huejutla for a very short time. "Huejutla was a stage. The actors were from someplace else," says Mayor Fayad.

On May 12 Omar Fayad went before the Hidalgo state legislature to say nothing showed Santes or Valdez trafficked in children's organs, were child kidnappers, or even had criminal records. He took time to note the impossibility of "little livers" surviving in the cab of a truck in the Huejutla heat.

In Tihuatlán the men's families blame authorities; discussions of the case set off lengthy descriptions of public officials' corruption and venality, up to and including the president. Governor Murillo Karam, especially, comes in for deep criticism. In Mexico a governor is imbued with such power that people have difficulty believing his presence alone couldn't have stopped such a thing from happening. "We're poor," says Filomena Santes, José's sister. "We don't have any money; that's why this happened." The assumption being that anyone rich would have been protected or wouldn't have been in jail in the first place.

Three days after the lynching, Tihuatlán staged a march behind the two caskets in the two men's memory. Santes, especially, was well known for his participation in the local cab-driver organization. Neighbors and friends insist that he was nothing more than a hardworking man trying to support a family. Santes's family is also trying to get over the economic catastrophe his death represents. Now they wait for some kind of financial settlement that Murillo Karam has promised.

Three weeks after the lynching, on April 15, Governor Murillo Karam came again to Huejutla, this time to give his regional State of the State address. He said he was approving funds for riot police for Huejutla. He also praised townspeople for having the most beautiful plaza in the state.

Meanwhile the families of the girls in the López Mateos neighborhood want very much to forget what happened. They say they never wanted a lynching and they were not present when it happened. "What we wanted was justice," says Eulalia Álvarez, Edith Hidalgo's mother. "We didn't want people to kill them."

"We put them in the hands of the authorities," says Antonio Hernández, father of nine-year-old Dolores, who is a janitor at the jail where Santes and Valdez were being held. "They were human beings. We just wanted them to be punished according to the law."

"Now we just want peace," he says. The families fear retribution from relatives of Santes and Valdez. "Look around," he says, sweeping his hand across the limp vegetation and the dusty, unpaved roads that will turn to muck when the rains come. "You can see from how we live that there's no one to protect us."

—1998

TELENOVELA

In 1992, as ex-Yugoslavia tore at itself in a frenzy of ethnic slaughter, a far sweeter note played on television. A Mexican telenovela—a soap opera—known as *Los Ricos También Lloran* aired in the warring republics. *The Rich Cry Too,* starring Verónica Castro, was the story of poor Mariana, an orphan and maid to a rich family, who falls in love with the family's son, has his child, goes crazy and gives up her child when her lover is unfaithful to her, then spends the rest of the show fighting to recover the baby. And every night while it played in Serbia and Croatia, where at the time happy endings were at a premium, life would stop for an hour.

Amid the chaos Kasia Wyberko worked as Balkan correspondent for Televisa, the Mexican network that produced *Los Ricos*. Wyberko traveled a lot between the two countries. Every night, she remembers, crowds would flock before department-store televisions and hang on the show's every subtitle. "The reaction was the same in Belgrade, Serbia, as it was in Zagreb, Croatia. The streets in both places were totally empty. For a moment this Mexican telenovela united two peoples who were at war." One squad of soldiers in the Croatian section of Herzegovina every night after returning from patrols would hook up a television to a generator and follow the trials of Mariana. "Every day on television you'd see reports from the front. Guns, guns, guns, and propaganda all the time," says Wyberko. "Then suddenly there's *Los Ricos También Lloran*: a beautiful woman falls in love with a rich man, with these beautiful homes. While here they're killing women and children, on the television there's a love story from Mexico, almost another planet for people here. It was so exotic, so refreshing."

And it was the highest-rated show on Croatian television that year.

Since then, Mexican telenovelas have swept the world up in their teary melodramas of romance, passion, good and evil, betrayal, lies, and happy endings. Televisa, Mexico's entertainment conglomerate and the world's largest

telenovela producer, has sold them to all of Latin America and to 125 other countries as well, among them Armenia and Azerbaijan, Belgium and Bophuthatswana, Iran and Iraq, Singapore and South Korea. China has aired twenty-two Mexican telenovelas. *Cuna de Lobos* (*Den of Wolves*) was a huge hit in Australia.

Telenovelas have taken over daytime television in the Balkans. Serbian television producers have even begun filming their own, with plot lines revolving around characters who inherit lots of money, then scheme to get more by cheating their relatives. Three Televisa novelas compete on prime time every night on Indonesia's three main stations. The network's newest sensation, Thalía, was mobbed when she visited the Philippines in 1995 and 1996. The press reported Philippine women naming their newborns Thalía or Marimar—one of the heroines the actress plays. In Romania a change in broadcasting law decreed less sex and violence on television. Mexican novelas perfectly filled the void left by more violent programming. One novela, *Esmeralda,* became so popular that women copied the hairstyle of star Leticia Calderón, and Bucharest ambulance crews were said to be getting to their calls late; finally televisions were removed from the station houses.

By 1996 Televisa could claim its novelas were Mexico's largest export product, ahead of car parts and Corona beer.

The telenovela is produced with international success—and, some say, with far more creativity—in Brazil, Colombia, and Venezuela as well. But Mexico—which is to say, Televisa—made it the enormous global business it is today. At its studios in southern Mexico City, the company has produced more than 600 telenovelas and maintains a pace of about twenty-five new series a year. Televisa invented the electronic prompter, a tiny speaker placed in each actor's ear allowing a prompter in another room to read them their dialogue—adding some stiffness to their performances but compensating by avoiding the time and expense of script memorization. Alone among world telenovela producers, Televisa can churn out half-hour segments in a day.

Other eras had Grimm's fairy tales or the feuilletons of Dickens and Balzac. The Mexican telenovela is the fable for the post–Cold War, high-tech global village. It offers a romance that in 160 to 240 half-hour episodes begins, falters, blooms, falters again, and finally succeeds—a simple formula that has captivated the world in the 1990s.

Ironically, as countries everywhere began shedding authoritarian pasts, they began consuming this genre that itself had emerged from an authoritarian state. Now forty years old, the Mexican telenovela grew to maturity with the PRI regime. The telenovela became Mexico's great cultural sponge, dominating entertainment in the same way the regime dominated political life. It supplanted cinema and theater and absorbed actors, writers, and directors, who found the pickings slim elsewhere. The genre ended up taking on characteristics of the country's centralized political system. "The telenovela has become the only show. Telenovelas have become so important that all the other forms of entertainment have become part of telenovelas," says Álvaro Cueva, a telenovela author and newspaper columnist. "If you want to promote a singer, put her in a telenovela. In Mexico everything converges in the telenovela. It has centralized show business in our country."

Apart from soccer, telenovelas are the most watched programming in Mexico. The novela belonged to Mexico's vast poor and working classes, watched mainly by maids and housewives. Hit novelas have created new hairstyles and social trends within those classes. In 1969 *Simplemente María*—the hugely popular novela of a poor seamstress who through hard work becomes a successful fashion designer—caused a run on sewing machines.

The ingenious PRI regime—never one to use the iron fist when other means were available—understood that in a country with enormous poor and working classes, the telenovela was a marvelous propaganda vehicle. The PRI government was rooted in revolution and leftist rhetoric. But when it came to television, the regime took seriously its duty as protector of the people's sensibilities and held to a distinctly prudish and paternalistic line. The government had, as one Interior Ministry agent put it, "the moral responsibility of looking after society." Televisa's founder, Emilio Azcárraga Vidaurreta, had a code of telenovela ethics that stated the programs should promote family unity, national pride, and personal advancement. Later the government and Azcárraga's son, Emilio Azcárraga Milmo—Televisa's late and legendary chief known as El Tigre—elaborated that into a series of strict rules regarding what a telenovela could contain. Novelas came to espouse the moral values the regime liked to believe it represented and wanted inculcated in its charges.

Certainly the lessons for women were clear: suffering was purifying and to be borne privately, life is nothing without a man, marriage was required for happiness, and certain subjects, especially sex, were not to be discussed openly. Large numbers of Mexican women learned how to conduct romantic relationships via the telenovela. Essayist Carlos Monsiváis once said that Azcárraga Milmo was the country's second secretary of education.

Above all, though, Televisa's television was to be fantasy. "The company has a theory that's worked, which is: people want to dream," says Raúl Araiza, a veteran producer and director of Televisa novelas. "They make novelas that are rosy, with princes and Cinderellas. It's a goddamn marijuana-smoker's dream because it's never existed. But people like to dream."

Azcárraga himself outlined his philosophy at a rare press conference in 1992 in what became a classic, if unexpected, piece of truth telling. Explaining the role of Televisa and the telenovela in the country's social life, he said: "Mexico is a country with a large class of people who are [economically] screwed. Television's responsibility is to bring these people entertainment and distract them from their sad reality and difficult future."

As it developed, the telenovela came to be a pillar for the Mexican regime. In a century that refined the use of propaganda, the Mexican telenovela stood out in its subtlety and effectiveness. For years at the filming or rehearsals of telenovelas, men in suits would sit inconspicuously at the back of each soundstage, watching it all. They were agents of the Interior Ministry, there to ensure that what was portrayed in telenovelas was a Mexico that did not exist. They were quiet men, usually, who tried their best to remain inconspicuous. Nor did they have much work to do, since producers and directors understood what was allowed and usually stuck to scripts the censors approved. These men made sure, for example, that no barefoot children showed up on film. No character could discuss money, his salary, how much something cost, or ever enter a bank. The gap between rich and poor was a delicate issue for the regime and not to be broached during a telenovela. Main characters, in fact, had to have social mobility, though that usually came through marriage and not through work or individual initiative. No politician could be mentioned, least of all the president. Terrorism, guerrillas, or coups d'état could not come up in the plot line. Nor could drugs or drug use. Water was served in coffee cups, not clear glasses, lest it be mistaken for alcohol. No cursing was permitted, much less any sex or naked bodies. Illegitimate children had finally to be recognized by their fathers and their parents properly married in a church.

Under these strictures, the classic telenovela plot quickly became the Cinderella story. The plot usually revolved around a woman named María, who was therefore poor and virtuous, often the maid in a rich man's house. María falls in love with him. Society condemns their love. Bad relatives scheme to separate them. She suffers unremittingly. She cries interminably. Finally a rich and childless old man proves to be María's long-lost uncle. The lovers can now marry and live happily ever after. These kinds of stories were refried dozens of times, in shows popularly known as "Las Marías."

The ending was crucial. For with it came a moral conclusion: love conquers all, the world's complexities are neatly resolved, and above all, the bad guys get what's coming. "Every telenovela is really a reflection on morality," says Miguel Sabido, a telenovela producer and Televisa's director of research. "It's trying to figure out who is good, who is bad, what is good, what is bad."

Understanding that the telenovela could impart a value-laden message, Televisa and the PRI/government began, in about the early 1960s, to intentionally exploit melodrama's power.

One important moment as far as that goes, according to Fausto Zerón-Medina, was 1965 and the production of a historical novela called *Páginas de la Vida de Maximiliano y Carlota* (*Pages from the Life of Maximilian and Carlota*). Zerón-Medina is a historian with a self-effacing manner and a thick black beard. He earned a master's degree in history from Cambridge University in England. His thesis was on the history of the Catholic Church in Mexico, specifically focusing on Bishop Clemente Munguía, a staunch conservative of the nineteenth century. Today, as a historian/entrepreneur, he is one of those rare people who makes a living from history. He worked for a long time for Clio, a publisher of popular books and videos on Mexican history and culture. He now publishes *Saber Ver,* an arts bimonthly magazine that he bought from Televisa. Years ago he was adviser to *Senda de Gloria* (*Path of Glory*), one of the most controversial historical novelas. One drizzly morning in a restaurant in Mexico City's Colonia Roma neighborhood, Zerón-Medina sat down to discuss how the regime has put the telenovela to use.

"The regime is paternalistic. The job of forming consciences, the national duty, was, for them, the state's job," he says. "They were very aware that Mexico was in fact many Mexicos. To fight against this they came up with the idea of the participation of the state in the formation of this [national] identity. They figure that since [the telenovela] has been used for other things, why not this job? Plus our history is rich, full of stories."

The story of Maximiliano and Carlota was one of the richest, and strangest, in Mexican history. In the 1860s the country, five decades after independence, was still at war with itself. Royalist conservatives and new-thinking liberals battled for Mexico's future. The national disintegration was such that some conservatives came to believe that Mexico needed a European emperor. About the best that can be said for the whole affair is that they drafted well, or at least that's how it appeared. Archduke Ferdinand Maximilian von Hapsburg was second in line to the throne of the Austro-Hungarian empire. But his brother Franz Joseph's longevity as emperor meant he spent his time looking for another sinecure. Mexican conservatives made him believe their country both needed and wanted him as its emperor. So in 1864 Maximilian and his wife, Carlota, arrived to rule Mexico. By most accounts they tried hard and had the country's progress at heart. Finally, though, after three years of intrigue and deceit and never quite understanding the country they ruled, Carlota fled for Europe and Maximilian was captured by liberal army forces under Benito Juárez. On June 19, 1867, he was executed by a firing squad. Mexico sheepishly went on, trying to forget that it once was so divided that it had actually imported foreign royalty.

The Maximilian and Carlota interlude became an important cornerstone of PRI legitimacy. "The myths that the regime used were the defeat of the conservatives, the defeat of the empire, the shooting of Maximilian, and the end of that era," says Zerón-Medina. "The revolution throws out [dictator Porfirio] Díaz and takes up the republic myth of Juárez. Everything that the revolutionary movement inherits, the entire twentieth century, is based on negating the past and the exaltation of nationalism. The confrontation of our party with the outsider, with the foreigner, with the United States, and foreign incursions into Mexico. The United States is the biggest example of that, but Maximilian and Carlota are as well. The regime substitutes a kind of secular religion for the old religion. The secular religion also has fiestas to observe, altars to venerate, saints to exalt."

In the regime's secular religion no one has a more exalted place than Benito Juárez, the stern Oaxacan Indian who became president and tried to install a liberal government in the mid-nineteenth century. In the way the Soviet Union revered a dead Lenin, Mexico came to officially adore Juárez. More than 800 streets and twenty-three neighborhoods are named for Juárez in the Mexico City metropolitan area alone. That doesn't count plazas, parks, or popular organizations. The Juárez Head, a bombastic piece of official art, sits at the center of a traffic circle on the outskirts of the city. Juárez's liberalism would have been at odds with the regime's strict paternalism. But his importance to the PRI regime lay in his opposition to Maximilian and Carlota, his attempts to forge nationhood from a disparate and dissolving Mexico, and his break with Porfirio Díaz, who would become the dictator the revolution was made to oust.

So sometime in the early 1960s, someone at Televisa had the idea of making a telenovela of the lives of Maximilian and Carlota, using it to instruct the Mexican people on the merits of Juárez, the revolution, and, not incidentally, the regime. Unfortunately, the story of Maximiliano and Carlota happened to be great telenovela material. Maximilian was at heart a decent man, a bit lost perhaps in his strange new country, but not devious. He and Carlota were in love. So their story had intrigue and romance, while his death provided the tears every novela needs.

Thus it was that every night on television in 1965, the novela wove their lives against the chaotic tapestry of mid-nineteenth-century Mexico and accomplished quite the opposite of its intent. "Mexicans identify with tragic figures in love. I remember people telling me later that as the figures of Maximiliano and Carlota grew in stature, Juárez became smaller," says Zerón-Medina. "They ended up looking like victims, deceived, with some ambition but not a lot. They began looking like people. People empathized with them." Juárez grew into a cold, impersonal figure—the villain of the tale—beside the warmth the telenovela cast on the unfortunate emperor and his wife.

The novela became a propaganda blunder, but it was important for two reasons. Not only did it foster a fascination within Televisa and the government with the telenovela as a vehicle for teaching history, particularly one view of

history, but after it aired, Televisa spent the next decade trying to repair the damage the series caused. The network produced four more historical telenovelas—*La Tormenta, Los Caudillos, La Constitución,* and *El Carruaje*—that took the country up to the end of the Mexican Revolution. All of them, this time, made the important points about Juárez and other of the regime's historical heroes.

Then in 1985, during the presidency of Miguel de la Madrid, the company decided to make *Senda de Gloria.* This was to be the historical telenovela to beat them all. Televisa and the government cooperated like never before. The series used seven hundred actors, five thousand extras, including members of Mexico City's police force, and cost 5 billion pesos. Costumes were imported from Europe, and the crew filmed for weeks at a time at the National Palace. Military historians were brought in to discuss uniforms, how soldiers saluted, and how trumpets sounded. The novela was coproduced by the Mexican Social Security Institute—the IMSS, which forgave Televisa a portion of its workers' social-security contributions in exchange for a producer credit.

The preceding fifteen years or so had seen an expansion in the history department at the National Autonomous University (UNAM) and the national archives. A boom in Mexican historical knowledge had taken place. *Senda de Gloria* employed a team of historians, led by Fausto Zerón-Medina, who combed the new sources, sometimes taking dialogue directly from the minutes of important meetings.

The novela was to cover the twenty-one years from 1917 up to 1938, when President Lázaro Cárdenas expropriated Mexico's oil fields from foreign companies. They were, moreover, years in which the PRI and the Mexican regime was forming and took control of the country that it has not relinquished yet. "They wanted to glorify Lázaro Cárdenas as one of the secular saints of the revolution, like Juárez," remembers Zerón-Medina. "In 1917 the Constitution is written. In 1938 there's the expropriation of the oil. There was an epic to tell. In the middle of it, there was a river of blood. But there was this idea finally that at the end of the story the institutions are safe, the country, the regime, everyone is united. There's problems with the church, but even the church finally says Cárdenas was right to expropriate the oil. The country goes into the era in bad shape and comes out looking good. Everything ends beautifully. They must have seen it as this unique story."

Senda de Gloria first showed in mid-1987 and achieved fabulous ratings, in part due to the blunt treatment of once untouchable historical figures and events. This was during De la Madrid's Moral Renovation, which ultimately failed to do much regarding corruption in politics but for a time allowed some measure of dissent and criticism. *Senda de Gloria* was the first uncensored historical telenovela. Zerón-Medina remembers people stopping him on the street to comment on the latest episode. His boss where he was then working frantically urged him to hide one day, certain that he would be imprisoned after an episode that showed one of the regime's leaders in the 1920s ordering a massacre. *Senda de Gloria* was a true media event in a day when the Mexican media were still controlled.

So pleased were the folks at Televisa that the next spring they repackaged the novela into two-hour segments and began running it every Saturday. Once again it gripped the country.

But a strange thing happened between the two showings. Mexico abruptly changed. That change would give an entirely different historical tint to *Senda de Gloria*. Art and current events began to intermingle, and apparently Televisa and the censors realized it only too late. What happened was that Lázaro Cárdenas's son, Cuauhtémoc, who had been governor of the state of Michoacán, broke with the PRI in December 1987, angry that he had not been selected as the party's presidential candidate. He and other prominent renegade *Priistas* formed the Democratic Front, which launched Cárdenas as its presidential candidate. The division in the once monolithic PRI electrified the nation. For the first time Mexico had competition in the race for president. Of course, the only coverage the Democratic Front was going to get from Televisa was witheringly negative. So Cárdenas took his campaign to the people. He led a wrenching, messianic tour through hundreds of small towns and large cities, concentrating especially on areas where his father had attained near sainthood for giving peasants land and nationalizing oil.

Then on July 6, 1988, Mexico went to the polls. That night, as Mexico City voting returns were the first to come cascading in, Cárdenas took an early lead, and somehow the impossible seemed to be happening. Then suddenly,

as if on cue, the government's election computer system crashed. When it was revived, the PRI's candidate, Carlos Salinas de Gortari, was leading in the polls and, finally, declared the victor. The month of July was spent in furious confrontation as the outraged Democratic Front brought hundreds of thousands of people to the streets. For a moment Mexico was at the brink of its worst civic unrest and the PRI regime faced its most severe crisis in twenty years.

Meanwhile *Senda de Gloria* had been plodding every Saturday through the early years of the construction of the modern Mexican state and by July, as the streets teemed with discontent, was moving into the apogee of Lázaro Cárdenas. Suddenly the political environment from a propaganda coup that legitimized the regime into something that did quite the opposite: it glorified the father of the regime's foremost apostate. It was almost like cheering Cuauhtémoc Cárdenas himself, who was now in the streets accusing the government of stealing the election.

Up to that point, Televisa had been running ads each week urging people to follow the show: "Don't miss the succession of Obregón," or, "Don't miss the betrayal of Zapata." Then in late July, as the streets roiled with people and the election was still in dispute, the ads urged viewers: "Don't miss the conclusion of *Senda de Gloria*." At home, Fausto Zerón-Medina remembers reading the ads and wondering, "How's that? Unless I'm wrong, there's a whole era missing."

Indeed, the conclusion of the novela that ran on Saturday, July 30, was a famously incomprehensible mishmash that bewildered the public. The final thirty half-hour episodes were cut and crammed together into two hours. Historical events were left out. Important characters just disappeared. One actress went from black hair to fully gray, almost from one scene to the next, for no reason the show made clear. Lázaro Cárdenas, and his presidency, barely figured in the ending.

No explanation was ever given, by Televisa or the government, for the mind-bending re-edit. But no one who was paying attention was really fooled. "Those episodes were [Lázaro] Cárdenas's great moment. He's supported by workers and popular organizations. Then it leads to the expropriation of oil," says Zerón-Medina, whose credit as the novela's historian was also cut. "I interpret [the cuts] to mean they were afraid of helping Cuauhtémoc Cárdenas."

To the newsweekly *Proceso,* Zerón-Medina noted at the time that between the ending of the telenovela's first run in November 1987 and the end of its second showing, "Cárdenas, the hero, became uncomfortable [for the regime], and the system that contributed to building his monument now hides it."

Since then, Televisa has attempted only two historical telenovelas— one dealing with the dictator Porfirio Díaz, a figure everyone can agree to dislike, and the other with the forty years leading up to Mexican independence in 1821.

Senda de Gloria ends with an image of the main character, a General Eduardo Álvarez, walking past the murals of Diego Rivera. As he walks by the murals, the general flashes back to moments in Mexican history. "We belong to a culture of images," says Zerón-Medina. "The Catholicism we received venerates the image, the icon, instead of the abstract word. This mixed well with the pre-Hispanic beliefs, which gave human bodies to gods. The evangelization of the country is done through images. Later, then, you politicize the country through images. Why, after all, have we had the murals of Rivera and [José Clemente] Orozco? Moreover, this is an illiterate people. People don't read; they listen. The telenovela creates the image that's so strong, it makes you feel as if you were a witness. They say much more than written words. [The telenovela] had an impact because it deals in images, in emotions, and because melodrama is the genre closest to simple people from the pueblos."

This goes a long way to explain why the telenovela has been such a potent cultural and entertainment element in Mexico. It also explains why, at the postliterate end of the twentieth century, Mexican telenovelas spread like wildfire around the world and found a reception in places as different as Indonesia and Romania.

The story of how that happened has to do with the demise of worldwide ideological conflicts in the twentieth century's last decade.

For many years Televisa had sold its telenovelas to Latin America with great success. When the 1990s brought an end to authoritarian and totalitarian governments around the world, company executives began toying with

the idea of selling their telenovelas elsewhere. Perhaps, the thinking went, telenovelas would provide a safe first step for formerly hard-line governments experimenting with relaxed censorship. Maybe telenovelas would find a market where people least imagined there was one. Out of New York, the company formed Protele, a subsidiary that now sells the company's product in the non-Latin world. At its head they put Pedro Font, a longtime company executive. "The telenovela is a family show. It's romantic, nonpornographic, with a lot of intrigue," says Font. "Plus the message of our shows is very different from those of American programs. In American programs, some guy takes a machine gun and kills 300 people."

So in May 1992 the network decided, on a whim, to send *Los Ricos También Lloran* to Russia. "It was a product we had around. The drama was nice. So we used it," Font says.

It paralyzed Russia. People there, with an economy in shambles and a political future to decide, stopped for an hour three days a week to follow Mariana's quest for her child. *Variety* estimated viewership at 100 million people, a record for Russia. In one town the director of a collective farm turned off the town's electricity after noticing workers were coming to work late when *Los Ricos* was on. *Pravda* reported that in the Caucasus, warring Georgian and Abkhazian soldiers arranged a tacit truce at the hours the show aired so they could all watch it, mesmerized by the woman with billowy brown hair.

Los Ricos made its heroine the first star of the global economy, just as the world was realizing that a global economy existed. It may be an exaggeration to say that Verónica Castro is as famous as Michael Jackson or Michael Jordan. But neither man has been invited to both Russia and China at the behest of the governments there.

No woman is more associated with the Mexican telenovela—at home or abroad—than Verónica Castro. She is the quintessential María, the good, sweet, hardworking heroine whose perseverance is eventually rewarded by marriage and love and living happily ever after. Her large eyes have shed countless tears, and her wide smile blessed many a baby and captured a good many husbands.

Now forty-six, she lives in an enormous mansion at the bottom of a canyon in the Bosques de las Lomas neighborhood of Mexico City—a house that was payment from Televisa in 1995 for hosting nine months of a nightly variety show. Her living room is jammed with chests from India, ceramics from Czechoslovakia, an enormous stuffed tiger, a stuffed leopard, a bearskin rug, sofas with towering backrests shaped like seashells, and bronze statues of Neptune and Arabs with sabers and upturned shoes, like something out of *Ali Baba and the Forty Thieves*. She lives here with her mother, sister, and youngest son, Michel.

Yet amid all this, Verónica is alone. This is not how a novela heroine is supposed to end up. Born in 1952, Castro grew up poor, the oldest of four children, in downtown Mexico City. Her mother worked as a secretary in government offices. Her father left the family when she was young. By age fifteen, Castro was working in theater and television. By age twenty she was making records. "My life is a kind of telenovela. I lived in a service room. I worked hard, studied hard. No one's given me anything. In the telenovela, the poor girl finds her Prince Charming and becomes rich by marrying him. My life was kind of like that; just I had to work hard to get ahead because my Prince Charming never arrived."

Her public image is perhaps that of a shallow, pampered woman—a diva used to the pretension of show business. And in fact, she resembles Joan Collins, from the *Dynasty* serial. Yet far from the superficiality of her public image, Verónica Castro has a seriousness and an awesome capacity for work that allowed her to succeed in a business and culture dominated by men. She was the first female producer of a Mexican telenovela, was once a member of a dissident actors union, holds a degree in political science, and was the first woman to breast-feed on television. She is the world's best-known Latin television actress.

Due to several all-night talk shows that ran from 11 p.m. to about 5 a.m. in the late 1980s and 1990s, Castro also holds a spot in *The Guinness Book of World Records* as the person who has been on television the most. During those years, she had to check herself into a hospital for a couple of days every six months to receive vitamin injections so she could continue.

"At times I'm not sure if it was worth it. Sometimes I think of all the times I was sick, the fatigue, or of having missed so many beautiful moments with my children or time for myself. I wasn't able to enjoy my childhood or adolescence. I spent it all on a television soundstage. People recognize me in the

street; they love me. But finally I'm alone, the same as any woman anywhere.

"It would have been nice to have some time to fall in love, to go out to eat once a week like normal people, or to leave town for a weekend every couple of months. Just disconnect yourself totally from your work. I never knew what that was like. I was only able to escape for a moment or two."

In 1974, while she was still a single college student and working in theater and Televisa part-time, Castro got pregnant. She was becoming well known by then. Her pregnancy scandalized Mexico. "I was one of the few women who were famous who said, 'I'm single, I'm not getting married and I'm going to have this child,'" she says. "This was really taboo." Soon photographers were hiding outside her house. Jacobo Zabludovsky, then host of Televisa's morning show, called several times, asking her to appear or to bring her child on when he was born. "Everyone wanted to know who the father was," she says. "Maybe [Zabludovsky] wanted to put on some kind of scandalous program: 'Verónica, the poor mother, suffering and rejected.' I said, 'I'm neither suffering nor rejected. I did this because I wanted to.'" That son is Cristian Castro, a Latin pop star.

She spent the next four years supporting her son, working in theater and in bit parts on Televisa novelas. Yet her star was clearly rising. In one supporting role, she became more popular than the heroine. Producers finally had to kill her off by having her character run down by a Volkswagen.

She had been out of work for several months when, in 1979, Valentín Pimstein, Televisa's most important telenovela producer, called her to his office. He was going to give her the starring role of Mariana in his next production, *Los Ricos También Lloran,* he told her. "He put a blank contract in front of me. It had nothing regarding the amount of money they were going to pay me. I said, 'How's this possible? I'm dying of hunger, but I can't work for nothing.' He said, 'Don't you trust me?' I said, 'I trust you, but the last time I worked, you all had me hit by a Volkswagen to kill me off.' Still, I signed it."

In the years since it was made, Televisa has made millions of dollars selling *Los Ricos* first in Mexico, then Latin America, Spain, Italy, and finally the ex-communist world. It is probably the most watched show Mexican television ever produced. Yet for the show's 240 episodes, Televisa paid Castro 500,000 pesos—roughly $20,000 at the time, or about $83 per episode—the minimum a supporting actor would make. Every time it runs somewhere in the world, Castro receives a royalty check for 17 pesos, the equivalent of about $2.

Nor did that blank contract include an assistant or a wardrobe. So for the year she filmed *Los Ricos,* Castro sang in theaters and cabarets on weekends. One weekend a month, she'd fly to Los Angeles and buy brand-name clothes with minor defects from the sewing factories, return to Mexico, and use them as costumes in filming.

Still, *Los Ricos* made Verónica Castro a star. It was a huge hit in Mexico. Mexicans still use the title occasionally in conversation to mean "Everybody has problems." Castro went on to make another twenty telenovelas in Mexico. She became the only Televisa actress who found much work outside her country. *Los Ricos* made her a star in Argentina, Brazil, and Italy as well. Televisa actually banned her from 1981 to 1986, when she left Mexico to make novelas in Argentina, then Italy. The company was known to go to some lengths to humiliate stars who left its stable. Verónica Castro was one of the very few stars Televisa had to entice back when it saw punishment wasn't working, finally offering her an exclusive contract to get her to stay home.

Over the next few years she grew into one of the two or three most recognizable faces on television. Then in September 1992, as she was filming a talk show in Spain, Televisa called. *Los Ricos* was doing very well in Russia, of all places. Castro hadn't even known it had been sold to Russia. But now Televisa was telling her the show was bringing the country to a halt. A visit had been hastily arranged. A few days later she was on a plane heading for Moscow. With that visit, the telenovela became international.

"I got there and they got me off the airplane and put me in a room at the airport. I thought there was some problem," Castro says. "They told me I couldn't leave because the airport was closed. Then they got me these huge guards. I walked in among them. Finally there was an opening, and I could see that the entire airport was filled with people. You couldn't see the end of them. I said, 'What's happening?' They said, 'Mariana is here.'"

Later she attended a showing of the Bolshoi Ballet's presentation of *Swan Lake.* Her presence caused a stampede of autograph hounds, and the ballet had to delay the starting of the next act; meanwhile the attendance of United

Nations General Secretary Boutros Boutros-Ghali caused barely a murmur.

"Flowers cost a lot in Russia, especially then," Castro says. "But there were times when you could not have put another flower in my hotel room, it was so full. It really bothered me, to be honest. I didn't like it that people might not be able to eat for two weeks in order to give me flowers."

She toured the Kremlin and met top Russian officials, including Boris Yeltsin. But the reaction of common Russians startled her most. "Wherever I'd go, they wouldn't clap or cheer. They'd cry," she says. "They'd cry and cry and cry. There were women and these enormous Cossacks crying. I said, 'Please don't cry. Let's be happy. I love you.' But they'd keep crying. I didn't understand it. But this was a country where women had it very rough and they knew what it was like to lose a child."

Russians are now fully addicted to telenovelas. In 1996 Boris Yeltsin arranged for a special showing of the Brazilian telenovela *Tropacaliente* on election day to keep people from leaving town. They stayed, watched the show, and voted. Press reports credit it as a key tactic in his victory.

In the lore surrounding the telenovela as an international phenomenon, *Los Ricos* has earned a hallowed spot. It is that rare thing, a durable product in a throwaway genre. *Los Ricos* has been shown in more than fifty countries, including Greece, Lebanon, Israel, and Zambia. It has done particularly well in countries at war. It was huge in Argentina during the Falkland Islands war with England in 1982. In Italy the telenovela has been shown twenty-seven times, and there are Italians who have memorized its dialogue and perform the action as it unfolds on the screen. Castro has been chosen best foreign actress in Italy. The telenovela was shown at 8:30 a.m. in Spain and disrupted work routines. Castro was invited to mainland China after the show became a major hit there as well.

Fernanda Villeli, a telenovela author, remembers her daughter, a Mexican diplomat, went to Vietnam at about this time. But instead of discussing trade between the two nations, Vietnamese government officials spoke of only one thing: How could they get photographs of Verónica Castro? Her daughter frantically called with the request. Villeli sent the photographs but thought this strange since *Los Ricos* had not yet aired in Vietnam. "Apparently what had happened is that they had obtained a pirate tape of the novela that was subtitled in Chinese," Villeli says. "They had a narrator, off camera, simply narrate the story in Vietnamese: 'Now this is what will happen. And she says this.' They didn't understand the language, but they knew what was going to happen."

Nineteen Mexican telenovelas have aired in Russia. But it was *Los Ricos* that showed Televisa that its most scorned product was a gold mine in disguise. Protele then got serious. It held focus groups of housewives in every country it sold to, and salesmen began trotting the globe. Televisa's telenovela sales outside Latin America have gone from 5,000 hours in 1994 to what they estimate will be 22,000 hours this year. "Now our goal is not just to sell a telenovela to a country but to move into more air hours in each country," says Font.

International sales meant Televisa very quickly began shooting chunks of its novelas on location. The public abroad wanted to see exotic Mexico. "Before, the entire telenovela took place in the living room, dining room, kitchen, maybe in the car," says Font. "Now we produce in parks, streets, office buildings. This has a lot of appeal. Besides following the drama, people like to see the beach, waterfalls, people walking in the street. There's a lot of interest in other countries about who we are in Mexico."

Ironically, it's at precisely this moment when who Mexicans are, as shown in their telenovelas, is itself changing.

* * *

"Before, you know, no one in a telenovela smoked," says Fernanda Villeli, sitting in her small office at Televisa's San Ángel studios, and as if on cue she fires up a Marlboro Light. "No one drank, either. We never had bedroom scenes. You never saw anyone actually sleep with anyone in a telenovela."

A short woman with short gray hair, Villeli has spent almost forty years putting safe but torrid words of passion and betrayal in the mouths of statuesque and sculpted actors. With sixty telenovelas to her credit, Villeli is at least as important a literary figure in world pop culture as Jackie Collins or Neil Simon. Still, she could easily walk down a Mexico City street unmolested. Call it a reflection of the low esteem in which telenovelas are held at home. Televisa stars, whose careers have taken flight on her words, can pass her by with barely a glimpse of recognition. Thalía has an office next to hers, "but I

know her only from television," Villeli says.

Villeli is a telenovela pioneer. In 1958 she wrote the first Mexican telenovela. *Senda Prohibida* (*Forbidden Path*) was the story of a scheming poor country girl who, to survive in the big city, uses her beauty to seduce a rich married lawyer. It was sponsored by Colgate-Palmolive. The production staff brought props from home and a number of actors declined the job, fearing overexposure. No tape of the program exists. "It was an experiment," says Villeli. "We didn't know what we were going to unleash."

Today, at seventy-six, Villeli is writing for the first time a script with language the way Mexicans speak it on the street. "Previous governments said, 'You can't use any word that begins with *Ch,* not even *Chihuahua.* Now we use the words we think are necessary," she says.

Curiously, the liberating changes around the world that meant so much to Televisa's international success came late to Mexico and the network. Through the early 1990s Mexico was selling telenovelas to newly open countries, while at home it remained governed by one of the world's now scarce one-party states that still thought it necessary to control what its people could see.

It wasn't so much that the country wasn't changing. On the contrary, the breech created by the Democratic Front in 1988 became a gaping divide, and by the mid-1990s Mexico was inching away from its one-party system. By 1996 opposition parties were making unprecedented electoral advances. The PRI was stunned with internal division and discredited after twenty years of economic crisis. Mexicans, housewives even, were talking politics as if it meant something. Still Televisa held stubbornly to its proven novela formula. There was no reason to change. "A person once said it seemed that televisions in Mexico came programmed with [Televisa's] Channel 2," says Bernardo Romero, a Colombian telenovela author, who has written for Mexican television as well. "Televisa spent many years getting audiences used to not changing the channel."

Yet flabby from years as a monopoly, Televisa had also been taking shortcuts. Its telenovela scripts were too often "refrieds" of previous successes. Inexperienced or unimaginative directors were using unknown actors. Characters, especially the women, seemed Victorian. Most important, a modern, more robust Mexico wasn't showing up in the network's novelas. Ratings began to slide. In desperation, and instead of taking novelas off the air, Televisa put more on and at all hours. It didn't work.

What did work, finally, was competition.

Toward the end of 1993 the government had sold two of its stations to a recently formed network known as Televisión Azteca. That ended Televisa's monopoly. In early 1995 newly elected president Ernesto Zedillo bowed to reality and announced that the government would no longer control the media.

It took a while for Azteca to get on its feet and longer still for the new network to actually challenge the Televisa behemoth. But in 1996, casting about for a way to break the Televisa headlock on the nation's viewers, Azteca took a risk and aired *Nada Personal* (*Nothing Personal*). Mexicans, by this time, had seen two top politicians assassinated in 1994 and were regularly hearing of foreign bank accounts worth many millions of dollars that Carlos Salinas's brother, Raúl, allegedly owned under aliases. *Nada Personal* reflected all that. It was the first telenovela dealing with political corruption and assassination—topics once very much banned from telenovelas by Azcárraga and the government. Plus it was more cinematic, using better lighting, longer scenes, and more complex characters. How well it rated is debatable. But the government let it run—it likely by now couldn't have done otherwise. And suddenly, to the fantasy factory known as the Mexican telenovela industry, reality began to matter.

Azteca, seeing Mexico changing before its eyes, began exploiting Televisa's dinosaur image. It took risks with telenovela subject matter. *Al Norte del Corazón* (*North of the Heart*) was a love story about undocumented immigrants and shows them beaten by the U.S. Border Patrol.

Last year Azteca aired *Demasiado Corazón* (*Too Much Heart*). The show was about drug trafficking, a once prohibited theme. It included occasional nudity and cursing and involved the Juárez Drug Cartel. The drug lord was named Armando Castillo, a thinly disguised Amado Carrillo, the cartel's leader, who had died in a plastic surgery operation a few months before the series aired. In the show Castillo faked his own death and lived on. *Demasiado Corazón* also included two nefarious gringos: one a Washington lobbyist fronting for money launderers, the other a corrupt DEA agent named Don Johnson. Alberto Barrera, the show's writer, explained the plot and characters this way: "We've

always gotten the theme of drug trafficking from the U.S. point of view. The dealers are always named Martínez or Pérez. Even though the United States is the country that consumes more drugs than any other . . . and no one's talking about the Smiths, the Robinsons, the Williamses. So this was a way of presenting a version different from that of *Miami Vice* or Hollywood films. I named the character Don Johnson after the actor in *Miami Vice*. I did it as a joke, to kind of say, 'Hey, that's your version. Here's ours.'"

The energy Azteca threw into its productions was a kick in the pants to ossified Televisa. The network began improving production, hiring known actors and movie directors and finally allowing writers like Villeli more liberty. When they did that, Televisa recovered a large part of its audience.

Televisa, too, began taking some thematic risks. *Los Hijos de Nadie* (*No One's Children*), for example, was a thin and maudlin series, even for a telenovela, but had the temerity to deal with the issue of homeless street kids, some of whom were, at long last, barefoot.

Verónica Castro saw the changes as a way to finally play a new kind of heroine. In *Pueblo Chico, Infierno Grande* (*Small Town, Big Hell*), she played Leonarda, a turn-of-the-century landowner in a small town who falls in love with a younger man, the first novela in which that happens. Powerful men in town hope to marry her and thereby ensure their fortune. They stand in the way of the couple's love. Castro did several steamy sex scenes, and the show had to be moved to a late-night time slot. Nor did *Pueblo Chico* have a happy ending. The men murder Leonarda's lover. She is left alone, pregnant with the young man's baby—the first time a Castro character doesn't end up with the man and rapturously happy.

Perhaps the most extreme examples of the new telenovela realism was to be *Tijuana*. *Tijuana* was to be a love story, around which swirled a cesspool of drugs, guns, and immigrant smuggling; discrimination against Indians; and life in *maquiladora* assembly plants and was even to include xenophobic U.S. politicians wanting to build walls between the two countries. The script outraged Tijuana officials, who, in what was likely a first, actually tried to prevent the novela from filming in their town, going so far as to try to copyright the city's name.

Raúl Araiza, the show's producer, said he didn't want to hurt Tijuana. "But they want a film about a city that doesn't exist. When I show Tijuana with no prostitutes, no crime . . . people will die of laughter. Mexico will have important television and cinema when we can make, as in the United States, films like *Hoffa* and *JFK*. What people in a democracy want is the truth. What's important is that people know what's going on."

In fact, the script eventually proved too much for folks at Televisa, and they never did make *Tijuana*. Nor has the network gone in as much for the "social telenovela" that Azteca is known for. Still, the new realism has surfaced in subtle ways at the network. Characters in almost every telenovela have become more believable. People are shown occasionally smoking, drinking; rich people are actually shown working. Above all, women's roles have changed substantially. No longer is the novela heroine always a poor, dim-witted maid who suffers until fate brings her Prince Charming. More heroines now are educated and middle-class. "The typical female lead in telenovelas is really fiction," says Paty Manterola, who starred as a chemist, the heroine of *Gente Bien* (*The Privileged*), a Televisa product that aired in 1996 and included a serious portrayal of a homosexual. "She's always good. She cries, she suffers. The man always mistreats her. My character breaks that mold. She's strong and in this case the man is weak. She makes decisions."

The role that likely changed for good how Mexican women are portrayed arrived on the screen in late 1997, played by an actress telenovela audiences knew, ironically, for playing the typically virginal, weepy heroines desperately seeking happiness through a husband.

Angélica Aragón had been in seventeen novelas by the time the role of María Inés Domínguez came her way in the novela *Mirada de Mujer* (*The Look of a Woman* or *A Woman's View,* depending on who you ask).

In her forties, Angélica Aragón is a strongly beautiful woman with high cheekbones. Like Verónica Castro, Aragón is a single mother. "Through books you become educated emotionally. You learn how people fall in love, why, what they do in certain situations," she says. "But people in this country don't read; even newspapers are read very little. So soaps, especially for women, have become that substitute, that sentimental education that is very necessary. Women have been taught that if they marry the right guy, they'll be happy and secure."

Mirada de Mujer had a different message. And it became Azteca's first real ratings coup in the telenovela wars. The series ended as one of the highest-rated shows on television and has gone into foreign syndication. In a sense the show took up the traditional Las Marías fable years later, with María now in middle age. María Inés Domínguez is a fifty-year-old woman whose perfect upper-class life is shattered when her attorney husband leaves her for his younger mistress. The story dealt with how a woman remade her life and found happiness away from her husband. The show touched on youth drug abuse, condoms, bulimia, and a variety of other formerly off-limits subjects.

But *Mirada de Mujer* stirred the most debate because María Inés, too, took a younger lover. Mexico takes on faith that men have a right to extramarital affairs and believes just as strongly that wives should suffer in silence and remain faithful. *Mirada de Mujer* posited that jilted wives can have lovers, too, and that went down hard. A Monterrey family-values group petitioned Azteca to cancel the show—though they'd never complained at the numerous portrayals of male infidelity. Mexico City archbishop Norberto Rivera suddenly preached a sermon deploring television artists who depict adultery and free-union relationships in their programs.

Meanwhile the set of *Mirada de Mujer* saw its own controversy. Only half jokingly, male stagehands formed FUSA—in English, the United Front of Offended Sanmillanistas—Ignacio San Millán being María Inés's cheating husband. They, too, were outraged that María Inés took a lover and invited him to the home she had shared with her now departed husband. They openly gloated over the prospect, once part of the script, that Ignacio take everything from María Inés in the divorce settlement. "Most of these guys will have a mistress," says Aragón. "They didn't want to be put on the spot by the story line. To accept that María Inés has the right to establish her own happiness, they're allowing for their own wives to do the same."

Azteca later aired a talk show in which guests and psychologists discuss the issues raised by *Mirada de Mujer*. Aragón, meanwhile, is planning a telenovela based on the life of Antonieta Rivas Mercado, a tragic figure from the revolutionary era. Rivas Mercado was a great patron of the arts as well as a strong-willed woman who, in 1919, divorced her husband, attempted an affair with a homosexual, was the longtime lover of 1924 presidential candidate José

Vasconcelos, and finally committed suicide. "It's a show that'll try to make parallels between the end of the last century and the end of this century; there's the same vacuum of leadership in the government," Aragón says.

* * *

As all this was going on, and as if it sensed what was happening in its country, monolithic Televisa was immersed in dramatic structural changes.

In April 1997 Emilio Azcárraga Milmo, El Tigre, the legendary "soldier of the PRI," died of cancer at the age of sixty-six. He was a man with little formal education but a steel-hard business sense, who loved tacos, tequila, and the Virgin of Guadalupe. He was a patron of the arts, had founded two museums, and possessed an art collection that reportedly contained works by Picasso. Physically notable with a pronounced dimple and a shock of white hair, he was one of the most influential men in Mexican life during the last quarter of the twentieth century.

At the time of his death, the Televisa empire included four national television stations, 280 Mexican affiliates, sixteen radio stations, forty magazines, as well as newspapers, record companies, movie production and distribution firms, and singing and acting schools—all of which allowed it to function as an entertainment factory that created and promoted television, film, and recording stars. The company also owned two soccer teams, Mexico's largest soccer stadium, nineteen bullfighting rings, and a cable television firm.

It was said that in his last years, particularly after the murder of PRI presidential candidate Luis Donaldo Colosio, Azcárraga came to regret his company's role as pillar of the ruling party; a newspaper quoted an associate who said Azcárraga had come to find politics a "dirty business."

"We can't even come to understand his importance today," Laura Castellot, an author of a book on Mexican television and a friend of Azcárraga's, said after his death. "He was transcendental."

Others cast his contribution differently. "Emilio Azcárraga repressed the creativity of many people, forcing them to work under ideological limitations and exclusive contracts," said Álvaro Cueva, the telenovela author and columnist. "His death can be compared to the end of a dictatorship."

Indeed, Azcárraga's departure was another chink in the armor of the once

invincible PRI. He left this $3-billion enterprise in the hands of his twenty-nine-year-old son, Emilio Azcárraga Jean, who quickly set about modernizing the company. Azcárraga Jean distanced himself from the PRI; Televisa news and talk shows soon featured guests from the opposition who were once banned. He cut five thousand jobs, eliminated exclusive contracts with many Televisa actors, and began contracting out services that the company once paid salaried staff to do.

The company's traditional personalities, too, were being cut loose. Jacobo Zabludovsky, Televisa's longtime news anchorman who many Mexicans viewed as the PRI's propagandist, retired at the end of 1997. Raúl Velasco, the host of the weekly variety show *Siempre en Domingo* and another symbol of old Televisa, stepped down a few months later.

It was probably only a matter of time before Verónica Castro felt the changes. Within eighteen months of the elder Azcárraga's death, Televisa told her bluntly that it had no work for her. Mexico's greatest telenovela diva and the world's most important Latina television actress was out in the cold.

Perhaps her image meshed too completely with the Televisa that was Mexico's television monopoly, a company that was politically compromised, the propaganda arm of the PRI. "I don't understand anything about it," she says, sitting in the darkened study of her mansion one afternoon. "You feel part of a company. I've been working for them for thirty years. I've always been careful to identify myself as part of the team so that people identified me with Televisa. Everywhere I'd go in the whole world, I'd always talk about Televisa. I felt like an important part of the company. Then I realized that I wasn't.

"They're trying to reinvent Televisa," she says. "I don't think it's going to be possible."

But it was happening, just as Mexico and the telenovela were changing. Both the company and the genre it invented were adapting to a domestic market where constant innovation and creativity were necessary to keep an audience that not long before had accepted anything it was shown. Increasingly novelas were striving for a middle-class public that advertisers were trying to reach. Productions were requiring a credibility they'd never needed before. A few novelas—*Mirada de Mujer* being one—opted not to use the electronic prompter to make the acting more at ease. "It's a little like Christianity," says Alfredo Troncoso, a communications professor at the Universidad del Nuevo Mundo. "It was a religion of the lower classes. It only became a powerful and lasting religion when it began appealing to, and adapting to, the middle and upper classes. If [the telenovela] is going to be destined for higher classes, then it has to get a little more refined."

So once again the telenovela was showing itself to be Mexico's most important cultural product, this time by reflecting Mexicans' recent civic effervescence and with it the slow crumbling of a tired regime. Neither the PRI nor Televisa controls Mexico as it once did. And so a genre that began as a foundation of authoritarian rule was subtly undermining the system that built it.

"Mexico is oxygenating," says Alberto Barrera, who wrote *Nada Personal* and *Demasiado Corazón*. "Five years ago we couldn't have done [these shows]. I think right now in Mexico there's a kind of anxiousness for democracy. Before, it was a society unaccustomed to competing, in politics, television, anything. Now it's beginning to get used to it."

—1998

THE JOTOS OF LA FOGATA

It was 11:00 a.m., and the sun was harsh in the sky on this day before the colony of *jotos* on the outskirts of Mazatlán showed signs of life. La Calabasa and Estrella awoke first and picked their way gingerly, barefoot and scowling, across the broken concrete and hot dirt of the colony's common area. Tonight was a rare moment to dream of glory for Mexico's sexual outcasts. So they immediately went to town for breast cups, panty hose, sponges, and glue.

The morning stretched into afternoon. Others emerged from their battered one-room dwellings. La Bella pranced out, her chest still tender and patched from injections of breast-enhancing baby oil three nights earlier. Abenamar, wearing the same top for two weeks now, took the quiet time to talk about his life. He is sixteen, of high cheekbones, a sexually precocious scamp. He has always known he's gay; so has his mother. But when he began sticking wads of paper in his shirt, pretending they were breasts, his junior high principal called home. At fourteen Abenamar was making money in drag-queen revues and working Mazatlán's streets. Now he's out here in the colony. "Most families of homosexuals fight with them. My mother accepts me. She just doesn't want me to be a drug addict," he says.

About twelve to fifteen *jotos*—depending on the week—live in this squat complex, where they share rooms and beds. Almost all of them work around the corner, in Mazatlán's Zona de Tolerancia, a red-light district of four clubs on Calle Pino Suárez, where prostitution is permitted.

Pino Suárez is an unpaved street southeast of town where steady traffic roils dust into a perpetual haze. One of the four clubs is La Fogata, which features a milky-green facade and an interior decked in shiny emerald palm fronds and chartreuse and gold pharaoh statues. At night all this shines in the club's colored spotlights. But during the day they reveal a layer of dust that is likely several years old, and the club's entrance smells of dog urine from the laconic pit bull that saunters about.

Once a year—tonight—La Fogata holds what is now Mexico's longest-running drag-queen beauty contest. The club is jammed to standing-room only as Mazatlán's gay community—poor drag queen, middle-class beautician, square professional—crams the small club, and for one night at least is unified and at home.

This year more than half the contestants live in the *joto* colony around the corner. La Mónica is a former farmworker from Nayarit in love with a hotel security guard; La Daniela, twenty-one, has been on his own and a *joto* since age eleven. La Cindi is fifteen, on the run after stealing a lot of money from dangerous people; La Calabasa—the Pumpkin—left home after fighting with his brother; Abenamar, flirting always, aware of his good looks; his half brother Martina, who is tall, leggy, and even better looking. And there are several more. Only one is over twenty-two.

Hidden across Mexico, colonies like this one are way stations for legions of wandering *jotos*—(pronounced HOH-tohs)—young, drag-queen prostitutes who have emerged from Mexico's working classes. The colony on Pino Suárez lives in close-clasped anonymity, fast friends for a while, known to each other only by their tinseled female pseudonyms—Selena, the late singer; Marimar, a soap-opera character; Estrella, the star. In a few months most of them will have faded away. But for now they are family. And today was going to be their big day.

* * *

"When I was a boy and began to realize I was gay, I began to say to myself, 'I don't want to dress like a woman.' But in my family there was no way of being gay other than dressing like a woman. I think this happens to a lot of gays in Mexico. There's no masculine model of gay life, one that doesn't involve cross-dressing. Mexicans don't tolerate, say, a masculine soccer player who also says, 'Yes, I like men.'"

—JUAN CARLOS HERNÁNDEZ, VERACRUZ ANTHROPOLOGIST

* * *

On the outskirts of Mexico the *joto* exists—machismo's queer and indispensable flip side.

Among urbane classes of gay men, two normally dressed men having sex is mildly acceptable. But amid the more than two-thirds of Mexico that is poor

and working-class, the deep dye of machismo still makes such a thing unthinkable. Mexico has almost no market for male prostitutes in normal male
garb. Instead it has the *joto*—a male prostitute dressed as a woman. *Jotos* are
found in conspicuous numbers in every city, every town, and in a good many
villages. They seem at times to be as predictable a part of the municipal scenery as the baker or ice-cream man.

Across Mexico *jotos* are a national caste of court jesters, or eunuchs, or
gypsies. They can be publicly goosed, whistled at, beaten, tortured, and laughed
at with impunity. In turn they are caretakers of the country's darkest secrets.
One secret is this: in manly Mexico, drag-queen prostitutes are so in demand,
they often charge more and usually do better business than female prostitutes.
Jotos can ignore the man insulting them on the corner because they know he'll
likely be coming around later to pay them to, say, anally penetrate him with a
soda bottle. They do consistent business in the cantinas where the toughest
hombres drink. Their clients are ostensibly heterosexual men looking for some
plausible deniability when they're alone with the police, or their wives, or
their own thoughts. After having a *joto,* a man can say, "I thought he was a
woman" and therefore, "I'm not gay."

Meanwhile, pretending to be a woman so his partner can pretend not to
be gay seems the only way an effeminate working-class homosexual can get a
boyfriend, or any sex at all for that matter. "I've had [drag-queen] friends here
who've gone to the United States to work and dressed up to look for a boyfriend while they were there. They're told, 'You're not going to have any luck
finding a boyfriend dressing as a woman,'" says Gil Castillo, a gay man who
owns a Mazatlán beauty salon. But among Mexico's lower classes, luck with
boyfriends comes clad in high heels, wigs, and fake moles, or at least a stained
halter top and plucked eyebrows.

One bizarre result is this: drag-queen prostitution has become part of sexual
maturation for a good many effeminate, working-class gay men—the equivalent of the high-school dating ritual for heterosexuals. It has become a fresh
breath of air after the claustrophobia of home, a first taste of sexual freedom.
Jotos can support themselves and live as they are, in apartments or colonies
like this one. They can have sex with a different partner every few nights and
get paid for it. Most of them will leave the life, and cross-dressing, by their

mid-twenties. But meanwhile they voraciously lap it up, amid a chaos of thievery, hormone injections, disease, and violence.

* * *

At rehearsals, in the days before the pageant, Marta Caramelo sits among the young queens and pronounces on the impermanence of beauty. True beauty comes from within, etc. The coquettish *jotos* pay her no mind and pass around a bottle of tummy-reducing cream. They hoist their nublike breasts and rumps, eye themselves obsessively in mirrors. Marta particularly lacerates Abenamar for earning her living selling her body. Marta has never done this and sees nothing but bad things ahead for those who do.

Marta is the owner, the transsexual diva, of La Fogata. At sixty-nine, her breasts sag and so do her eyes while her hair, dyed black, stands, like Don King's, at electric attention. She speaks in a haggard voice—twenty-nine years of dealing with screeching *jotos* will do that to a body.

Twenty-three years ago she was Martín Flores when she adopted a baby boy—the child of a friend who was mistreating the infant. Alejandro, her son, now helps her with the show. He's an affable guy unless he's coked up: cocaine transforms him into a twisted *cholo* gangster who occasionally nails the *jotos* and likes to demonstrate his partial command of L.A. Latino gang slang: "Whach you poblem?" "I watch a lot of movies," he says.

Three years later Martín Flores had himself operated on and became Marta Caramelo, the name, not coincidentally, of a famous 1920s Mexican singer. "I like to sing. Some people say I don't do it poorly," she says.

Almost single-handedly, Marta Caramelo built the Zona. She started with El Famoso, back when there was no Zona de Tolerancia. She sold that, then built Los Dos Gordos, which is currently considered the Zona's upper-crust entertainment venue. She sold that a few years ago and transformed a restaurant into what is now La Fogata. Every new place she's gone, she has brought the Miss Reina de Carnival Gay pageant.

A lot of people feel that Miss Reina de Carnival Gay has fallen on hard times. Unlike mainstream pageants, winning comes with no prize money and, probably worst of all, the winner doesn't keep her crown. Still, that doesn't change Marta's status as a pioneer in Mazatlán's gay community.

Mazatlán has what its residents admit is a frothing beauty-queen obsession. Firefighters, baseball leagues, soccer leagues, dance bands, taxi drivers, the chamber of commerce—all have their queens. Every private elementary, junior high, and high school has its own queen. Most schools within the major universities crown queens. There's Miss Mazatlán and Miss Sinaloa—major pageants that lead winners to Miss Mexico and, possibly, Miss Universe. But there's also a Miss Silhouette, a Miss Sexy Fat Girl, a Mother's Day queen, a Queen of Old Age.

Back in 1970, this craze was just developing, and the gay community, shut out of so much, ached to be a part of it. So Marta that year started his own drag-queen beauty contest as a way of promoting gay pride and unity in a community that had neither. "I saw that Mazatlán really liked beauty contests. I tried to do it, but well done, so it didn't look cheap," she says.

At the time, homosexuals were permitted to cross-dress only during carnival in mid-February. So Marta staged the pageant the Monday of carnival week. Her idea was to copy straight pageants: with cocktail parties weeks before to introduce the queens, bathing-suit competitions, evening gowns, and questions to decide the winner. "They don't win just because they're pretty," says Marta. "If among the last two the prettiest doesn't speak well, the other will win. They'll talk about Princess Diana or Mother Teresa of Calcutta: 'What would you like to do to help youth or the poor?' 'I'd like to be like Mother Teresa of Calcutta.'"

Marta's great bane is having to deal with a bunch of prancing, giggling *jotos* this time every year. Like court jesters, the *jotos* have fine-tuned their scandalous act. In public they shriek, lurch their hips, quiver their tongues, and spend their private time plucking chin hair. From the telenovelas—the soap operas—they have learned love's relationships, as have many Mexican women. Their hard-bitten cynicism dissolves into schoolgirl crushes on tattooed drug dealers, *cholos,* and bus drivers, and they are thrilled when these men hit them out of jealousy. Their photo collections have a ragged quality to them since after a fight they'll theatrically tear their boyfriends' pictures in half, then tape the snapshots together when they reconcile. Spurned, they turn smartly on a heel and shriek, "*Ooooi, no! Me has perdido.* You've lost me. I'm no longer speaking to you"—and await a plea for forgiveness.

Envious, backbiting, conniving, gold digging and shrill—they are parodies

of every rotten female stereotype. They generally embarrass the rest of the gay community, which feels they reflect a poor public image of the homosexual.

That's Marta's opinion as well, and she doesn't allow them in her club except during the beauty pageant and for rehearsals.

The designated *joto* bar, instead, is across the street from La Fogata, known as El Famoso. It's a cavern, painted black, with grimy floors, a small fading black-and-white television, and a shrine to the Virgin of Guadalupe overlooking an elevated dance floor.

Back in 1990, Francisco Labastida, then governor of the state of Sinaloa, where Mazatlán is located, banned transvestite revues statewide. The ban had minor effects in the rest of the state. But it electrified Mazatlán. A good many young gay men were making their living in shows impersonating female singers. At least three nightclubs, as well as several social clubs and cantinas, regularly presented drag-queen revues.

When the ban took effect, the now out-of-work queens immediately began hooking along Mazatlán's beachfront. Soon they were stealing clients from the female prostitutes. The public began to complain. The police began running them off. And that began a three-year battle, waged nightly, between *jotos* and Mazatlán police. "They'd chase us into the sea and they'd attack us in the water," says Rogelio Bonilla, who worked the streets around this time. "Once I almost drowned when a police officer had me in the water. If it weren't for a waitress at a seaside restaurant who helped me, he would have drowned me." Rogelio was arrested more than a hundred times in a period of four months. Another youth was arrested so often that, this being Mazatlán, he was crowned Queen of the Jail.

Finally the mayor ordered the Zona de Tolerancia open to *jotos*. They've been working at El Famoso ever since.

The afternoon of the pageant, Marta has scheduled a final, two-hour rehearsal. But concentration is contrary to *jotos'* chaotic lives. The dance routine planned for "La Bomba"—a brisk rhythm by pop star Ricky Martin—has always been especially muddled. The queens stampede around the club's runway, their chests out, shooting sexpot gazes at the few men in their seats. But at times they collide, and a few always end up out of place and scurry back into line after the music stops.

By 1:00 p.m. that afternoon, only a few contestants have arrived to re-hearse, all *jotos* from the colony. None seems to want to work at the routine or to help blow up balloons. So Marta dismisses them. "You're just in my way." And the *jotos* scurry out, relieved.

"The moral code that was imposed in Mexico suppressed all sexual diver-sity and only permitted homosexuality to be expressed through two extreme stereotypes: So if the woman cries, the transvestite shrieks. If the woman gets depressed, the transvestite dies of depression. Gay men who don't want to cross-dress go to the other extreme of machismo. The 'mayate' is very macho with transvestites. He's violent, jealous, possessive. So either you make yourself into more of a woman than women, or you're a man who is so much more of a man than other men that you wind up screwing men, thus killing off all the sexual diversity that existed between the two extremes. Everything becomes black or white, and the gray has to be very, very secretive."

—JUAN CARLOS HERNÁNDEZ

It is night in the *joto* colony, and Antonio has just punched Martina in the face. Martina is eighteen and was born Brian. After a good dousing of female hormones, she has the kind of beauty found in Italian fashion magazines: she's tall and hipless, with thick lips and tiny breasts. Despite the scabs and bruises on her legs and arms, the remnants of a working-class life, you can hardly imagine her growing old and wrinkled. She likely can't either.

Now she is outraged that Antonio has hit her face. "Goddamn *mayate*," she screams, and well-crafted invective arcs across the colony's courtyard. The next two days the colony will be mildly distracted by Martina's attempts to remove Antonio from their room.

Martina and Antonio have been "married"—which is to say living to-gether—for two months now. She washes and keeps the room tidy. He sup-ports her with his job at a metal workshop. He also sniffs a lot of glue, which is when he hits Martina. After all, she is, in his words, "my woman."

Along with the *joto,* Mexico's homosexual subterfuges have given birth to a

figure known as the *mayate*. Some are johns; others, like Antonio, are steady boyfriends. *Mayates* are supposedly heterosexual men who use a prison kind of calculus to maintain their psychosexual balance: he who goes with a *joto,* he who penetrates, can still tell everyone that he isn't homosexual. Often the word *homosexual* is synonymous with a man who dresses as a woman. The *mayate* gets off scot-free because he would never admit to having sex with a man who wasn't dressed as a woman nor let anyone penetrate him. After the exchange, only the *joto* is the homosexual.

"*Mayates* pay for men dressed as pretty women so that when they're discovered, they can say, 'She was so pretty, I thought she was a woman,' or, 'I was so drunk, I didn't know,'" says Vanni, a beautician, who spent several years of his youth as a *joto*. "And since they pay, everyone begins to dress as women. [*Jotos*] exist for a reason. There's a demand for them."

Many *mayates* aren't often seen with their *joto* girlfriends outside the Zona, certainly not anywhere hand in hand. A high rate of drug or alcohol consumption is another thing all *mayates* seem to share. "Whenever we're supposed to go to some event together, he arrives really late and he's always drunk," says La Mónica of her *mayate,* Jorge, the hotel security guard. The night of the pageant, with Mónica competing, Jorge won't even show. Police arrest him in another club for possession of cocaine.

* * *

On Saturday morning, two days before the pageant, the colony titters. Two *jotos* are in hiding. The night before, they drugged a client in his car and, as he slept, made off with $4,000 in jewelry and money. The man turned out to be a midlevel drug smuggler and is now vowing to kill them both. He has gone to the police, who have set up roadblocks around the neighborhood. The two *jotos* are La Fogata pageant contestants. But now they may have to forgo the event to run for their lives.

Jotos live in anonymity in part to avoid potentially murderous clients they've robbed. It's a poor idea to let a *joto* sit on your lap, hug you, or get anywhere near your drink. Most have learned the use of knockout drops. Many *jotos* are skilled practitioners of a deft pickpocket's movement involving the thumb and first two fingers, to slip money out of the billfold without removing the billfold from the pocket. This has apparently been passed down from one generation of *jotos* to the next across Mexico for some time now. The movement is effective anytime but is like taking candy from a baby when, in the dark, a drunk man's pants are down around his ankles. There being very few old *jotos*, "Get it while you can" seems the reigning ethic.

"One day there were six men sitting at a table and I stole money off each of them," says Cindi. "I'd sit on each one's lap, feel him up, lift his money, then say, 'Ooooh, you're too small.' And move to the next guy. I came away with 1,800 pesos."

Cindi is one of the most outrageous of the colony's *jotos*. Her real name is Orlando. She is young—sixteen—and pretty as a doll. She shrieks a high falsetto and collapses into men's arms, hand to her forehead, in a practiced Scarlett O'Hara. Cindi comes from a small mountain village of three hundred inhabitants that supports about a dozen *jotos*. "My parents always told me, 'Don't walk like that. You have to find a girlfriend.'" She once tried to join the priesthood.

Cindi treasures a furry white monkey doll that holds a pillow Valentine, embroidered with the words *I love you this much*. She got it from an accountant from Hermosillo, whom she met at a bachelor party in the Zona. "I was entering the Dragón Rojo [a straight club] and he said, '*Hija,* how much do you charge?' But he wasn't like a *mayate,* who'd say, you know, 'Get in the goddamn room!' He spent a long time talking with me, trying to please me, lighting my cigarette. He said, 'Where do you work?' I said, 'Over there in El Famoso.' 'Really, with all those fucking faggots in there,' he said. Finally I told him, 'I'm sorry, but I'm a man.'"

The accountant apparently got over the shock and returned a day later. "He likes seeing me dressed for the evening, like a fantasy, with my hair all done up, with my woman's body. He said, 'I don't want to see you dressed as a man. If I see you dressed as a man during the day, I won't even say hello to you.'"

By Monday morning, with the beauty pageant hours away, the two queens have given back the loot and are, in return, not murdered. The tension passes. The colony settles back into spats over rouge and panty hose and caustic judgments regarding the appearance of others. A *joto* walks across the broken

courtyard and Daniela screeches, "Five, five, five," imitating pageant judges giving low marks.

* * *

"The man who seeks out a *joto* is looking for some kind of different sexual experience, but something that has some relationship to what he's used to: a female appearance. That's why those who look more like women earn more."

So says Violeta, who is beefy and thirty-six, the oldest in the colony. With the pageant two hours away, Violeta sits on the only bed in her room, her heavy bosoms wrapped in a dirty hotel towel. Daniela, Mónica, and Martina look on as she glues sequins to a blue evening gown. The room's walls, long ago painted beige, are smudged and stained and occupied by posters of the Virgin of Guadalupe, the telenovela star Thalía, Mexican Madonna Gloria Trevi, and the indispensable mirror. The room has only one chair, a small tape deck, and a semiworking toilet. The smell of urine fills the room. Someone turns on a fan.

As a boy, Violeta was effeminate, tending to overweight, the kind most kids picked on. But he had a facility with words and for pleasing others. So the school would call on him whenever it needed a boy to speak from the microphone. Tonight Violeta will emcee the pageant.

At twenty-two he left home. "My mother is very religious. She has a phobia about homosexuals. Unfortunately, she gave birth to one," she says. Violeta lived in Tijuana in a houseful of transsexuals who worked as female impersonators. She began letting her hair grow, dressing as a woman. She left the transsexual house. Now living hand-to-mouth in a Tijuana hotel, she became a *joto,* earning twenty dollars on her first trick.

Later, to grow breasts, she injected hormones. Her breasts expanded, but so did the rest of her body, and she became so irritable that she finally had to masturbate to purge the hormones from her system. Her breasts and extra girth remained.

Mazatlán is her fourth red-light district. She has been here for three years. Mexican red-light districts serve many necessary social functions. One of them is as oases in the lives of *jotos.* Red-light districts offer *jotos* employment; they are places where they meet, share information and contacts, develop some kind of community, and live as they wish. The more isolated, the better. "Society is usually divided into upper and lower classes," Violeta says. "We're the third class. The rejected class. We're left only a few bearable alternatives as homosexuals. One is hairstylist. Another is *joto* in the Zona, tolerated because you live in the zone. We're an island. We're out here on the edge."

"If I have the gay man clearly identified in a beauty salon, I can control him. But if he's dressed as a man, teaches in a university, works in an office, or is an engineer or something, how do I control him? Almost anyone, then, could be gay. Making him very, very different helps in controlling him and allows people to say, 'No, I'm not like him.' Gays become visible and thus become a target. And making them so visible makes it hard for men with hidden gay feelings to act on them."

—JUAN CARLOS HERNÁNDEZ

Across town now, a Saturday night at Pepe Toro's, Mazatlán's only gay bar. The sons of the city's middle and upper classes are clasped arm in arm in their Gap casual finery and latest haircuts. Gay people can openly be what they are in only two public places in Mazatlán. One is out in the Zona. The other is here at Pepe Toro's. But unlike the Zona, in the crowd at Pepe Toro's there is no anomalous breast, no hot pants, no wigs, and only a few telltale plucked eyebrows. Men are dressed as men.

Onto the stage bounces an ample-breasted drag queen in a white Playboy-bunny-style suit, mouthing a Spanish version of Gloria Gaynor's disco hit "I Will Survive." The crowd explodes. Though the men watching her are atop the gay community hierarchy in Mazatlán, they live vicariously her freedom. They are young professionals—engineers, lawyers, or business executives—whose better education and family ties have allowed them greater economic opportunity while at the same time strait jacketing their personal lives. As one gay man said, "Acceptance of gay life drops the higher you get into society." Unlike this drag queen, *"los tapados"*—the capped—have more to lose and cannot be openly gay.

With most of the city's gay upper classes thus firmly closeted, Mazatlán society knows gays as beauticians, drag queens, or *jotos*. Few businesses will

hire a man who is too openly effeminate. Like *jotos* out in the Zona, the openly gay population is also segregated, into a few professions that confirm Mazatlán's belief in what a gay person has an aptitude for. In Mazatlán beauty-pageant organizing is one of these. So is cook and clothing designer.

Many gay men have earned money doing drag-queen revues ever since the 1990 ban was rescinded by a later governor. Mazatlán society, while it generally doesn't socialize with openly gay people unless it has to, isn't averse to having around a gay man who knows his place. So for a scream, drag queens are brought in to entertain at parties that celebrate life's important moments. At Mazatlán's bachelor and bachelorette parties, at birthday parties, as well as, of all curious things, at baby showers, it's customary to hire a drag queen revue to tell racy jokes and do a few numbers, mouthing along to the songs of famous female singers. The Lions Club is also known to be a big patron of drag-queen shows.

But the most important occupation available to working-class openly gay men is that of beautician. Beauty salons offer a variety of advantages to a working-class gay man. They require very little capital to establish; beauty school is cheap and quick; you earn well; you're your own boss; above all, any gay man who owns one is assumed to be doing his race's calling.

So Mazatlán has an enormous ghetto of gay beauty salon owners. Former *jotos* usually graduate to this social class. Others pass by the *joto* phase and head straight for beauty school. "Most people in Mexico prefer that a gay person cut their hair rather than a woman. They think he's got more talent for it," says Gil Castillo, who once was a drag queen and now owns Imagen Personal beauty salon. "More than half of the beauty salons here are owned by gays, and if they aren't the owners, they work in them. The owners look for gay hairdressers because that's what customers want." The idea that an openly gay man could be a mechanic, or plumber, or truck driver is inconceivable to most Mazatlecos, straight or gay.

Several of the contestants at La Fogata tonight are from this class of drag queen—hairstylists or clothing designers who occasionally dress in drag or work part-time in drag-queen revues. They bear a slight air of superiority toward the young, stained *jotos*. When competing at La Fogata—by virtue of their more stable lives and thus better preparation—they usually win.

And from early on in La Fogata's pageant this year, this is what appears will happen again.

Things begin late, around midnight. La Fogata, strung with balloons, filled with people, and glittering under colored spotlights, looks festive, no longer a red-light dive.

Marta comes out, dressed in a push-up bra, black headband, long white gown, and white face. Usually she sings, but tonight she is sick, her voice hoarse. She apologizes and hands the microphone to Violeta.

The contestants begin their show, and the lack of focused rehearsal is at once evident. The queens miss cues, take false steps. Two contestants drop out and slip out of the club. The "La Bomba" number is, as expected, a chaos of collisions and missed formations. Yet the crowd is forgiving, and the spectacle is dizzying nonetheless.

Still, the pageant proceeds like a mugging. Miss Durango is trouncing everyone, receiving straight 10s from the judges during the bathing-suit competition; her evening-gown victory is equally lopsided. Miss Durango is from Mazatlán's hairdresser class—never a prostitute. She has spectacular, sponge-enhanced hips packed into a golden gown, well-endowed breast cups, and a hair weave enhancing her already long, thick, curly hair. She has brought a throng of supporters, who chant "Durango! Durango!" every time she appears on the runway. She beams. It's clear who the crowd loves. Were it not for the flowers tattooed around her left bicep, she'd look like a regular Florida sunshine girl.

To one side of the stage and here to cheer Miss Durango on, dressed in a jeans jacket and baseball cap, is José García Medina. If Mazatlán's drag queen community has a legend, it is García Medina. He's known as La Prieto, for his dark face. He's a thin and muscular man, now thirty-five, with short-cropped hair, a soft, delicate manner, and large brown eyes. He now spends his life in his workshop, designing wedding and graduation dresses for Mazatlán society as well as an occasional dress for a La Fogata contestant.

In 1987, at the urging of friends, García decided to compete in Miss Sinaloa Gay, a short-lived contest held at a Mazatlán restaurant. His parents had no

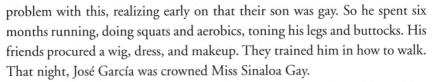

problem with this, realizing early on that their son was gay. So he spent six months running, doing squats and aerobics, toning his legs and buttocks. His friends procured a wig, dress, and makeup. They trained him in how to walk. That night, José García was crowned Miss Sinaloa Gay.

In 1993 he won La Fogata's Miss Reina Gay and Chica Piel Dorada (Golden Face Girl) in the neighboring state of Nayarit. The next year, in front of his parents and friends, he achieved his greatest triumph when he was crowned Queen of Queens at La Fogata.

Immediately he received proposals from men wanting to support him, to buy him an apartment. But this wasn't for José. "You wake up alone, with no one to say good morning to," he says. "Gay life is like that."

Today José has come to an accommodation that, if bizarre, seems to suit him as much as is possible under the limitations gay men face in Mexico. The September after he was crowned Queen of Queens, José wed María de Jesús Macías, a beautiful, tall, dark-skinned girl who was then sixteen. She had been a contestant for queen of her high school and needed training on how to carry herself. So her brother, a construction worker at José's home, put her in contact with José. José instructed her on how to walk like a queen, and she was crowned queen of Preparatoria Rosales. The two grew to be the closest of friends. "I told her, this is the way I am," he says. This seemed not to bother María de Jesús, who was aching to leave her family. The couple were wed in a civil ceremony. They now have a daughter who's three and a one-year-old son.

"Today I wake up and there's someone who calls me Daddy," José says. "You can never have children in a gay relationship. You're alone. You can't adopt because you can't marry. If before getting married I'd known I could adopt children in the United States as a gay man, I'd have gone there. But I didn't know."

María de Jesús's mother and brother were furious when they discovered the couple's plans to wed. The mother tried to prevent the marriage, attempted to place her daughter in a convent, spoke to the mayor to get him to stop the marriage since María de Jesús was still a minor, and later tried to steal the couple's daughter.

On the advice of a friend, the couple used a bit of witchcraft to put an end to their troubles. They wrote the names of the mother and brother on a piece of paper, wrapped it tightly in a piece of aluminum, placed the ball of aluminum and some water in a black film canister, and put the canister in the freezer. That was in 1995, and the canister remains in their freezer to this day. "Since then they've been frozen and we haven't had any problems," José says. "If we take it out, they'll become unfrozen and our problems will start again."

María de Jesús today is a housewife. Her husband is a dressmaker, a retired drag queen. And remains gay. It is the great secret of his life, but one that he cannot change. So while he carries on what he calls an active and enjoyable heterosexual relationship with María de Jesús, he also has as many homosexual relationships as he can without being infected with a disease and without María de Jesús finding out. Though they talk about a lot, they don't talk about that. Or at least José doesn't tell her, though it's common knowledge among his friends in Mazatlán's gay and drag-queen community.

"I've never spent a night away from the house. Never missed a meal," José says. "I don't think anyone accepts a person who has a double life. That's why I hide it. [But] you're never going to stop being who you are."

Back onstage, José's contestant, Miss Durango, is one of five finalists. Her only real competition, as it turns out, is Abenamar, the sixteen-year-old, who, with her gorgeous high cheekbones and elegant dark blue evening gown, is representing the border state of Tamaulipas.

Now it's time for contestant questions, time to prove that this isn't all about bimbo men in evening gowns and falsies. Marta has said that just having a good body doesn't guarantee victory. But everyone knows that a beauty contest is about one thing. And this one pits a hairdresser, most of whose tumbling hair is her own, against a *joto* from the Zona who enthusiastically sucks men's penises for a living and sometimes will do it for free. The crowd chants "Durango! Durango!" The result seems hardly in doubt.

The first question is for Abenamar: "If you could spend a day with the president, what would you tell him?" Abenamar grabs the microphone and from the speakers a defiant roar builds quickly to crescendo, as like a street-corner revolutionary she yells: "If it were me, I'd tell the president that he should give us gays the opportunity to be accepted the way everybody else is." Unlike a revolutionary, Abenamar knows when to shut up. Her answer screeches to a halt, as quick and jolting as an electric shock and it has that effect on the

crowd, which sits back stunned.

By luck of the draw, Miss Durango, Miss Sure Thing, is next. "What's more important, health, wealth, or love?" A limp question, and Miss Durango does nothing with it. Her answer meanders on about the importance of health in the time of AIDS and loses itself in the rasp of the speakers. Her momentum trips like a high heel on chipped linoleum.

Now, as the three remaining contestants answer, a chant can be heard at the back of the hall, slowly gaining strength and competing with the chants for Miss Durango. "Tamaulipas! Tamaulipas!" And as the contestants finish their responses, La Fogata begins to roar. "Tamaulipas! Tamaulipas! Tamaulipas!" What once was so sure is now in doubt. Miss Durango's smile etches across her face. As her victory begins to slip away, her eyes are wide and full of the agony her competitors felt fifteen minutes ago. Discreetly she chants out of the side of her mouth, "Durango! Durango!"

The contest is now officially over but has ended in a tie. The judges can't decide. The change has been so abrupt, when the winner appeared certain for so long. They will ask another question. The best answer wins. "What's more important, internal beauty or external beauty, and why?" Another stunningly dull question. Perhaps judges of straight beauty pageants have no monopoly on vapidity after all.

Miss Durango goes first. The "Tamaulipas" chanting quiets briefly. Of course, the answer is equally vapid, about how internal beauty is the real beauty, about external beauty not mattering. If anyone really believed that, no one would be here tonight. And coming from a drag queen, it's preposterous. Miss Durango's body, all cascading hair weaves and literally impossible curves, is itself an altar to external beauty.

The chanting picks up again. "Tamaulipas! Tamaulipas!" Abenamar's answer once again busts quick and torrid from the speakers and, though probably just as trite, is all but unintelligible as the crowd explodes. Men are dancing in the aisles. "Tamaulipas! Tamaulipas! Tamaulipas!" The Durango faction gives up.

And so, representing the beautiful state of Tamaulipas, which she has never visited, Queen Abenamar I takes her throne. Miss Reina de Carnival Gay 1999. Later one former winner says, "How strange that she won, because you know she is a, a . . . a prostitute." There's a well-supported belief among those who follow the pageant that *jotos* don't win because they simply don't have the command of language and the quick thinking to respond well to questions before a fevered public; maybe the hormones and the late nights make for a scattered mind.

But Queen Abenamar I is queen, too, of the *jotos,* of the outcasts; when she's not hooking, she sleeps on a tattered mattress with two other *jotos* and wears the same withered halter top and dusty jeans. Now she's mobbed. Everyone wants a picture with her, with the exception of Miss Durango. To lose so stunningly when she had it won, she, a hairdresser, to a *joto*. She slinks offstage and quickly out of the hall and probably won't be seen at a party for a while.

* * *

Later, outside La Fogata in a thickening fog, Violeta stands in a circle of friends in her wig and street clothes. In a few hours she will board a bus, return to Guadalajara, and leave the *joto* life forever. She has wearied of competing with new annual crops of round-cheeked sixteen-year-olds. She can sew. She can disc-jockey. She wants to start her own drag-queen revue. Tonight, though, there is news. "A friend of mine from Guadalajara just told me that my mother died a week ago," she announces. Violeta hadn't known. There's a pause in the conversation, perhaps as her friends inventory their parents' place in their own lives. Then quickly chatter resumes. Violeta hasn't seen or spoken to her mother in six years. She can't cry, and she wasn't going to be staying with her mother anyway.

After the pageant, life quickly returns to normal for the queens of the *joto* colony. Abenamar changes back into her dirty top and goes to show her family her crown. "They said, 'Congratulations, *hija,*'" she says. Violeta has left for Guadalajara. La Mónica is thinking of returning home. Martina and Antonio are again living in marital bliss. Meanwhile the endless spats and telenovelas dominate life in the colony. Talk turns again to which *mayate* really loves which *joto* and which *joto's mayate* is just using her.

Now it is night, a few days after the pageant, and Estrella, a nineteen-year-old runaway whose real name is Walter, stands out on the street near a few taco stands. Buses rumble by and stir up the dust. Estrella is a *joto* because he

likes the frequent sex. So far he has yet to inject himself with hormones. He's a sensitive, intelligent boy. If things were different, if effeminate working-class gay men didn't have to dress like women to get a guy, he'd probably be doing something else. Talking about his life, he once said: "I think after a while I'll stop this and study again. I want to do something with my life, not be just another homosexual," by which he meant "just another *joto*." "[*Jotos*] have no future. What future do we have? I want to be someone. I don't think I'll last long in this life . . . but I do want to keep doing it for now. I like walking the street, and a car passes and I get in and I don't know what's going to happen. I like the danger dressed as a woman. If I were dressed as a man, they'd never pick me up."

If he lives through it and reaches his mid-twenties without a disease, a criminal record, or debilitating emotional or physical scars, Estrella can look forward to a job as a beautician, a cook, or a clothing designer.

Now, through the din of the buses and wolf whistles from men in pickup trucks, Estrella comes to offer a hug and to say good-bye. Then, in his black evening gown and high heels, he daintily picks his way back across the rubble, and as stray dogs and barefoot children fill in behind him, he disappears into the neon and permanent haze of Calle Pino Suárez.

—1999

SAN QUINTÍN

October 1997

By the time Librada Ramírez arrived from her village in Oaxaca, the forest green tomato plants had climbed from the valley of San Quintín to the top of their poles and were pumping out enormous red fruit.

Librada is a stocky woman with a flat nose and wide smile that shows a couple of teeth bordered in silver. As she bent over these plants, she tried but could not remember the man back home saying anything about any airplanes. She didn't remember him mentioning that as she and her son labored twelve hours a day picking those tomatoes in the desert sun, crop dusters would occasionally fly over and spray them, along with the plants, with pesticides. Yes, he had left that out.

But they would come, buzzing low over the fields where she and others from her village of Cosolapa, Oaxaca, were working. This has happened repeatedly since their arrival in the Francisco Villa labor camp. The camp is owned by ABC Growers, one of the largest farms in this burgeoning Baja California valley.

Three months after their arrival in San Quintín, Librada, her son, and several relatives had no more illusions. They had been lured from Cosolapa by the promises of a man named Lorenzo, from a nearby town. This man Lorenzo had gone door-to-door, telling people of the marvelous work opportunities to be had far away in San Quintín. Cosolapa was as depressed as the rest of Oaxaca. So they had gone north.

Others in the labor camp had heard an ad on radio XEOA, out of Oaxaca City, making promises similar to those Librada heard from Lorenzo: three months of work at 70 pesos (about nine dollars) per eight-hour day, rooms with electricity and running water, work for children ten and up, and bus transportation to the valley and back to Oaxaca.

"They promised us three meals a day on the trip, but they gave us nothing,"

says Agustín Díaz, a thirty-year-old worker from Coatecas, Oaxaca, who took another recruiter's offer. Many people arrived malnourished after the five-day bus ride. The promised drinking water also didn't exist, though finally ABC put in a water tank. It occasionally stays empty for a day or two at a time.

"We're in the dark all night long," says María Jiménez Osorio, who heard the ad in her pueblo of San Andrés Niño, Oaxaca, and, with her husband and two daughters, signed up for the trip. The girls—ten and thirteen—work the fields like adults, for twelve hours a day, and get paid the adult wage.

The Francisco Villa labor camp has no electricity, and sundown begins the nightlong battle against boredom and the bitter desert cold. Without electricity, residents are saddled with another unexpected expense: candles, which run a peso apiece in the camp store; about twelve are needed to get through the week. Rooms here are four walls and roofs of corrugated tin. Beds are pieces of cardboard on black, hard-packed dirt. When it rains, at Francisco Villa people sleep in mud.

Saving money is virtually impossible. At the store, tortillas are 3.50 pesos a kilo, a peso more than at stores in town. Cooking oil goes for ten pesos a liter, when it costs seven in town. Sixty-seven pesos a day evaporates quickly at these prices. "We'd never left Oaxaca before this trip," says Librada. "Now we can't go back, given what we earn. They're eating us alive."

So by now Librada and her son show little indignation in adding that, oh, by the way, crop dusters also spray them with chemicals as they work the fields.

Spraying farmworkers with pesticides from crop dusters is a common practice in the valley of San Quintín. Workers from around the valley say it happens routinely on many farms and has for years. They describe how they break into a frantic dash, making for the sidelines before the plane buzzes the field—about fifteen feet above the valley floor—and dumps its load. "If you don't get out of the way, they bathe you in chemicals," says José de Jesús Toralba, a Oaxacan who works another farm farther north in the valley. Workers who can't get out of the way fall to the ground and huddle into a ball to cover any exposed skin.

Local doctors claim that being sprayed by a crop duster isn't that harmful and the residue can be easily showered off—though few farmworkers have access to showers. Rather, doctors here say, what leads to the high number of cases of intoxication they see is when water or food is contaminated and in-gested—as happens when the planes dust the trucks where drinking water and lunches are kept.

Besides the physical effects, though, the crop dusting makes it clear where farmworkers reside on the San Quintín hierarchy of economic importance—that is, somewhere below a tomato plant.

Thus it is remarkable that farmworkers, the valley's poorest residents, are its most powerful motor of community development and are making of San Quintín more than a simple story of victimization.

* * *

Straddling the black vein of highway running down the Baja peninsula four hours south of Tijuana, the valley of San Quintín looks like it just woke up. It begins in the north in Camalú, then on to Vicente Guerrero, San Quintín, and finally Lázaro Cárdenas. These are its centers of population. Which is not to say towns, for they have yet little of the community the word implies. Businesses spray-paint their signs on plywood boards, and fences lean crooked and gaping. Squatting hodgepodge along the highway are entire neighborhoods of gray concrete-block homes roofed in royal blue plastic tarp. Most valley streets are simply paths of rock and a fine milk-chocolate dust that clings to boots and trucks and is as hard as glitter to rub off. A clean and robust wind often blows in from the coast, and sunsets weave yellow and orange light into spectacular fabric across the sky each night, allowing even the smallest pebble to cast a grand shadow. But nothing man-made shines here for long.

The valley of San Quintín looks like a place people came to thinking they wouldn't stay long. Something besides civic beautification is on its mind. It is in the fields, loping off from the highway to the sea, and the foothills: perfect row upon row of tomato plants that carpet the valley floor, each plant tended by dozens of hands. It's as if people are so consumed with work that they don't have time to remember the normal comforts of life. Work. The valley is about work. There are only a few cantinas, a few mediocre restaurants, a movie theater—not much for 100,000 or so fully employed people.

Once an abandoned patch of coastal desert, this valley has become an important stop on the agricultural global economy—a primary supplier to San

Diego produce brokers who, in turn, supply U.S. consumers and food processors. Suddenly, too, it has become a major center of Mexican Indian life.

In the process, it has become known to Mexicans as the country's own stark "Grapes of Wrath"—an amalgam of fetid labor camps with high-priced stores, misused pesticides, high rates of disease and infant mortality, callous police, child labor, abusive foremen, and the sweat of desperate migrant workers—primarily Indians—from the country's south.

The non-Indian population has reacted to the arrival—and now numerical superiority—of the Indians much as Californians received Depression-era migrants. "They're human beings trying to get ahead," says Raúl Borbón, manager of Del Indio Market. "The problem is when they bring their customs with them that are so different from here."

One of these is courting. To Mexican authorities—in fact, to almost anyone outside the culture—Indian courting can look a lot like kidnapping and statutory rape. Sometimes men literally take wives. On occasion, San Quintín authorities throw in jail an Indian man who, say, has taken a fifteen-year-old bride, unaware he's broken any law. Some Indians aren't used to using a toilet and answer nature's call outdoors. And for many years children have been a common sight in valley fields, though growers are beginning to forbid them as the U.S. Department of Labor, and now Mexican authorities, have spotlighted the problem. "Poverty makes [farmworkers] see their children as another source of income," says Gabriel Neri, station manager of Radio XEQIN. "This creates a vicious cycle, in which a farmworker's son becomes a farmworker, too." The "Grapes of Wrath" parallels abound.

Yet John Steinbeck ended his novel too soon. In the postwar era, Okie families like the Joads became car salesmen and city councilmen in California's Central Valley and changed forever the towns that once scorned them. Likewise, San Quintín resists simplistic formulations. In a country known for backward agriculture, the valley is also a job creator and a gleaming example of productivity. No place in Mexico produces more tomatoes or strawberries per acre.

San Quintín is the story, too, of how an abandoned desert valley has suddenly become permanent home to more than fifty thousand Indians who are making it their own. They have brought Mexico to the border, with Day of the Dead and Las Posadas celebrations, in a region that once only feted Halloween and Santa Claus. Indian languages now echo through the valley, as well as on XEQIN, its only radio station. Moreover, Indians have transplanted their culture of organization and self-reliance to this atomized region, forcing services and civilized treatment on a place intent on denying them both.

For Indians, meanwhile, full-time work has been an invigorating elixir. Many have eagerly doffed traditional social and religious customs that kept them poor and benighted in their villages back home. They have joined Protestant denominations in huge numbers. Indian teachers complain that their children like to dress in tennis shoes and T-shirts and are enthralled by television and video games. "We've never thought of Indians as people whose identity is in the future, but rather in the past," says Federico Becerrer, a Mexico City anthropologist. "San Quintín is one of these places where you can see Indians looking to the future for an identity."

*　*　*

Perhaps that's because the valley has such sparse history. It was first settled only in the late 1800s. A government concession turned it into a colony for English farmers. After the Mexican Revolution, the new government canceled the concession. The English left, tearing up their train tracks and plugging wells as they went. All that remains of them is an ocean dock, a windmill, and a cemetery.

And with that, the valley again lay abandoned for almost twenty years. Dirt-poor migrants from the state of Michoacán were next to arrive in the 1930s. Over the next fifty years a small population of farmers somehow sucked a living from the desert.

By the early 1980s, however, San Quintín had found a way to make its desert bloom. Farmers in San Diego had been using drip irrigation—an Israeli invention allotting to each plant exactly the water needed through a system of tubes. Friendships and later partnerships were struck up with San Quintín's farmers, who began investing in the technology. "This valley never would have developed without drip irrigation," says Felipe Ruiz Esparza, a tomato grower.

Soon those dirt-poor migrants were coming up in the world. Others began arriving from Sinaloa, along Mexico's Pacific coast, and from Tijuana. Ruiz Esparza, an energetic man with a quick smile, arrived, college educated, from Ensenada in

1981 to manage the local bank. Drip irrigation was catching on. Within a couple of years Ruiz Esparza had left banking and was growing tomatoes, too. "My father wanted me to work in an office. I liked the farm better," he says.

Farmers had been customers of Mexico's national farm bank, Banrural, until the crises of the 1980s forced interest rates higher than any could afford. Increasingly they turned to the nearest source of available capital: San Diego brokers, U.S. growers and food processors, who urged their San Quintín counterparts to experiment with new crops, promising to buy whatever they produced. The valley went from a potato monoculture to tomatoes, then cucumbers, celery, radishes, and strawberries.

Mexicans generally view the border and those who live there as only semi-Mexican—too close to the gringo, where too many of his ways are imitated. In truth, that is what shaped the valley. With drip irrigation farmers saw the potential of growing for both the United States and Mexico and dropped subsistence farming for a very American capitalist ethic. Acres under cultivation went from two thousand in 1980 to almost twenty thousand in 1990. Nighttime electricity came to San Quintín. Then a few stores, a couple of motels, a movie theater, satellite television.

"I have uncles in the state of Zacatecas who grow chile," says Ruiz Esparza. "They harvest the crop, but only a part of the profits goes back into the fields. They're afraid of risking it all. Here, it seems they're a little crazy. They risk it all every year. People here aren't interested in having money in their wallet. Everything they have goes back into the fields.

"I look at the farmers of Oceanside, Bakersfield, Oxnard battling against the city, high water prices, taxes, and I see them keep going. They're very brave. I think having those people before us as examples inspires us to do the same. If they can do it, why can't we?"

From the north, San Quintín had its market, and from there it imported machinery, capital, and an entrepreneurial spirit. What the valley of San Quintín had never had was abundant labor. And that came from the south.

The Dust Bowl in all this became the states of Guerrero and, above all, Oaxaca, both states with enormous Indian populations who retain the customs and languages of their ancestors. Like the northerners with whom they now live, they are considered somewhat less than Mexican, disdained as "dirty

Indians." It was a strange yet perhaps appropriate pairing: two outcasts coming together to create something in the dust of the northern Mexico desert.

Agriculture in Oaxaca, like that in Oklahoma during the Depression, is a limp and stagnant thing. Inefficient farming and the division of land into ever smaller slivers have bequeathed the state a withering poverty, bloody feuds over land ownership, and generations of uneducated children. Hundreds of thousands of Oaxacan Indians—Mixtecos primarily, but also Triquis and Zapotecos—have been leaving home for four decades now. They are Mexico's migrants, the cheapest labor in a cheap-labor country. "They provided labor that was easily exploited," said Víctor Clark Alfaro, director of the Binational Human Rights Center in Tijuana. "They were docile, didn't speak Spanish, would accept almost any treatment and work hard."

First they cut sugar cane in the Gulf state of Veracruz. When Sinaloa received massive government investment in agricultural infrastructure, they went there. In the 1970s Tijuana became a stop on the Oaxacan Indian migration trail, especially for those heading to the United States. Thousands of them lived in the infamous shantytown known as "Cartolandia"—"Cardboardland"—in the concrete basin of the Tijuana River. Townspeople came to refer to them by the pejorative "Oaxacos" or "Oaxaquitos," and bus drivers often made them board buses after the "white people" had gotten on. Baja California police became notorious for their abuse of the newly arrived In-dians, using electric shocks, cigarette burns, and beatings to force confessions to crimes. From Tijuana many Indians moved on to California—to Vista and Oceanside, Los Angeles, Fresno, and Santa Rosa—always working at the lowest-paid jobs.

But in Tijuana, migrant Indians also discovered San Quintín's almost unquenchable thirst for cheap labor. Through the late 1970s and 1980s the valley evolved into a major stop on the Indians' migrant trail, part of what came to be known informally as "Oaxacalifornia"—the diaspora that starts in San Quintín and runs through North San Diego County and up the state. Entire families came to the valley to live in labor camps designed for transient men. The camps teemed, and the work was tough in the hot sun and choking dust. But it was work, which was something Indians had never had in Oaxaca.

April 1998

From the road, the valley fields seem barren of life now, covered instead with rows of black plastic sheets that hide tubes delivering water to incubating tomato seeds. The sheets run staccato into the distance before they gradually lose definition and become a dark and gleaming sea.

"People began coming faster than the area's capacity to receive them grew," says Felipe Ruiz Esparza. "In the early 1980s there was no radio, television, electricity—any of that. So you can understand how neither was there drinking water, infrastructure of any kind. There was nothing to receive those people because we never thought they were going to come here to stay. We thought they'd continue going to the United States. It had always been an escape valve."

But soon they were arriving. And largely because of one man, they stayed. That man is Benito García, a small, dark brown, forty-year-old Mixtec Indian who today is one of this valley's most controversial figures. For a while it looked like Benito García was San Quintín's César Chávez. "In 1984 he was the only leader who could make the bosses tremble," says Fermín Salazar, a teacher from San Juan Mixtepec, Oaxaca—García's hometown. "He had the support of thousands of workers. When he'd call a meeting in the park, they'd fill it."

García's life mirrors that of the Mixtec migration across Mexico. As a young boy, his family migrated to Veracruz. In the early 1970s his family was in the Mixtec migration to Sonora and Sinaloa. His life as an organizer began when an uncle was imprisoned in Sinaloa for inciting farmworkers. Benito, fifteen, would go to the jail every day to receive instructions from his uncle. Soon he was leading work actions himself. As a teenager organizing a strike, a soldier hit him with a rifle butt, permanently scarring his left cheek.

He was becoming a national leader of farmworkers when, a few years later, the government kidnapped him and took him to Oaxaca. There they tortured him and held him in a cell that approximated an iron maiden, so that he had to stand for several days. Three months later he was dumped, bruised and bleeding, by the side of a river. The Communist Party and students at Mexico City's National Autonomous University paid for his medical care. He convalesced for a year in hiding, then returned to lead the movement.

Over the next several years García would be abducted twice more and jailed frequently. By the mid-1980s he was well known as a fiery organizer of a frequently timid and submissive people. He was a leader of CIOAC, a nationwide independent farmworker union.

In 1984 García came to San Quintín and hasn't left. "People were working in subhuman conditions," he remembers. "The foremen would kick them. They wouldn't pay [legally required] Christmas bonuses. People would walk miles to work, or they'd transport them in tomato trucks. There were many accidents in which people died."

Farmworkers in the valley have always had a union representing them— the government-sponsored Congress of Mexican Workers (CTM). Yet in all the years of contributing to the CTM—a deduction that is now 2.44 pesos a week—valley farmworkers report never once seeing a union rep in the fields. Often workers are surprised to learn a union represents them. The need for a forceful farmworker voice has been clear for a long time.

When a tomato truck turned over and more than twenty workers were killed, García saw his chance and formed SINGOA, his farmworker union in San Quintín. The first battles were over working conditions. Under pressure to provide safer worker transportation, growers replaced tomato trucks with the buses that now line the highway at quitting time.

Still, too many workers would leave the valley every six months, weakening the movement. "We came up with the idea that for the movement to be permanent, the only way was to build permanent neighborhoods. So it became a fight for *colonias*, neighborhoods," says Celerino García, Benito's younger brother. "When we arrived, there weren't any *colonias*."

That decision would transform San Quintín. In 1985 SINGOA squatted land, then negotiated with the government and grower organizations. Finally the land was deeded to workers, and the first farmworker neighborhood, Colonia Flores Magón, was formed. Since then other groups have squatted and formed the neighborhoods that stretch across the flatlands and up hills. "People decided to stay in Baja California due to the climate," Benito García says. "They found work. It was close to the United States. Children could be in school."

They turned San Quintín into Oaxaca II; it became a place to work or to leave family while one emigrated to the United States. With housing permanence came the promise of economic advancement, of jobs away from the field.

Soon García's movement was leading San Quintín out of the Middle Ages. During high season, workers, once made to work seven days a week with no days off and no extra pay on Sundays, were now paid double time on Sundays, as the law requires. His movement, too, forced San Quintín growers to start giving time off for national holidays—like Mexican Independence Day. Labor camps slowly improved. If the barracks of today are revolting, they were in their day markedly better than how farmworkers had been living. For many years growers would simply provide some land and workers would construct their own shacks out of cardboard and pallets and plastic. García's movement forced growers to put up barracks and provide services like bathrooms and eventually amenities like basketball courts.

Yet the successes of the *colonia* movement brought with it the fall of Benito García. He had broken earlier with CIOAC over money. Now there were reports that García was selling land that the government had given to the squatters. There were even rumors that he'd become a *compadre* to a grower. García denies the charges, saying the government and growers spread lies to defame him and fracture farmworker unity. "I can't say he did it or he didn't," says Gregorio Santiago, a Mixteco DJ at Radio XEQIN. "But from 1987 to today, they haven't been able to prove anything against him."

Nonetheless, García's image was devastated and he lost followers. His fall also meant the end of the idea of a cohesive independent farmworker union in the valley. A confusing array of organizations took its place: UPT, MULT, MULI, MUJI, ALIAC, Organización Indigenista Bi-Nacional, as well as CIOAC and SINGOA—all products of the permanence that García's *colonia* movement allowed and the divisions his fall from grace created. Many of the groups are led by people who learned organizing at his side. Yet they don't seem able to pool forces or even spend much time in the same room. The feuding among villages that drove so many Indians from Oaxaca has its contemporary translation in the divisions in the valley's farmworker movement. Not surprisingly, none has won the right to represent workers at a single ranch in the valley.

Still, the wrangling among farmworker groups did not prevent the Indians from forging the valley into a home, and this they have set about doing with a unity and enterprise that astonishes their neighbors.

One place that's reflected is the emergence of Indian youth clubs.

In 1994 Radio XEQIN went on the air with music, news, political, and cultural affairs programs in the various Indian languages. XEQIN is one of sixteen Indian stations run by the federal National Indigenous Institute (INI). As the valley's only radio station, XEQIN has become a powerful catalyst in valley Indian culture. Five years ago Indians feared ridicule and were too shy to speak Mixteco or Triqui in public. Nor did Indian women wear traditional shawls or long dresses on the street. "With the radio this began to change," says Gregorio Santiago. "Now this is part of their way of life again."

A couple of years into its operation, station staff began getting letters from groups of Indian youths asking for song dedications, identifying themselves as neighborhood gangs: The "Flores Magón" gang, the "Lázaro Cárdenas" gang, and so on. "They were kind of imitating the gangs up there [in the United States]," says Santiago. "We began talking to them about what gangs were. Why not form clubs instead of gangs?"

Somehow a good talking-to was all that was needed. Almost overnight nascent gangs became clubs. This is how Indian kids are dealing with an adolescence spent stooping in the desert dust for up to seventy-two hours a week. Today in the valley of San Quintín, Indian farmworker youth culture is in the clubs. Indian teenagers have divided up into dozens of them, naming them after popular songs. The Yo Sin Tu Amor club, the Mi Luna Mi Estrella club, the Rosa Roja club, and a variety of "Corazón" clubs: Corazón Salvaje, Corazón Rebelde, Corazón Romántico.

XEQIN started a club show on Sundays—which budget cuts since forced off the air. Sometimes fifty different clubs would line up to get on the air.

Some clubs are simply a bunch of kids who like music and hearing their names on the radio. But others have taken an active role in community development. One of those is the Corazón Duro (Hard Heart) club, whose members live at a local labor camp. The club has held dances to benefit the camp school and the radio station and for victims of Hurricane Pauline, which hit Oaxaca in October 1997. Their dedications frequently admonish local youth to stay off drugs. "We try to help the community," says Alfonso González, a Triqui Indian and leader of Corazón Duro. "And we like listening to music."

San Quintín's clubs are what gangs must be like in heaven: no graffiti, no glue, no guns. Instead they are an example of a Mexican Indian identity that is forging in San Quintín—a defense mechanism for Indians who find themselves thrown together in a hostile environment. Corazón Duro is made up of four Mixtecos, a Triqui, a Zapoteco, and a mixed-blood Mexican. "It's like what happens in the United States: 'I'm a Latino even though I don't speak Spanish,'" says Gabriel Neri, the station manager of XEQIN. "Here it's, 'I'm an Indian even though I don't speak Mixteco.'"

Beyond that, though, clubs like Corazón Duro are part of Indians' most important contribution to their new land besides their labor: a community organization and self-reliance essential to their survival in this bleak frontier.

The tradition of the *tequio*—or community duty—lives strong in Oaxacan pueblos. Each member of a village is expected to contribute to its development. For those at home, this means turning out to, say, repair a bridge or help dig a well—similar to an Amish barn raising. Those who have emigrated from Oaxaca are still expected to send money home if they want to be respected and held in good stead in their village. This tradition has been transplanted to some extent to San Quintín. Part of neighborhood development has been Indians' willingness to help build local schools or to donate a day to clean a *colonia*.

Indians also brought with them their history of battle against a state government in Oaxaca that they have, charitably, viewed as deaf to their concerns. For some pueblos the fight against the Spanish Conquest hasn't ended. So when a Baja California government bureaucrat balked at, say, installing electricity in a neighborhood, Indians knew just what to do. Valley residents got used to them marching along the highway, shutting it down, holding sit-ins, and taking over government offices. "It's a way of pressuring the government that happens a lot in Oaxaca," says Eberardo Pacheco, a Oaxacan farmworker. "People from a village march to Oaxaca City [the state capital]. Sometimes they burn buses. It's all a way of pressuring the government to do what they want."

Thus episodes like the recent struggle with social security became commonplace. In Mexico social security provides medical coverage to a wide variety of workers. In September 1997 several hundred Indian farmworkers marched for six days to Ensenada, demanding a new clinic for the valley. Social security officials promised one would be built in a central location. Then last year officials decided suddenly to build the clinic in Camalú, at the northern end of the valley. Construction began. Outraged, Indian groups marched to Camalú, uprooted the construction sign, and closed the highway. Finally officials relented and stopped construction in Camalú. The clinic is now being built in a more central location.

Tenacity and tactics like these are why most Indian neighborhoods, looking to all the world like shantytowns, have what disorganized non-Indian neighborhoods in San Quintín lack: deeds of title, water and electricity, clean if still unpaved streets. Valley residents today count themselves lucky to live in a neighborhood that's predominantly Indian. "They are very organized, and they get whatever they want," says Miriam Verduzco, a local motel owner.

* * *

July 1998

Tomato plants are midway up their poles now, and their fruit are hard green boluses. Thick morning clouds blanket the valley until noon. And from the highway, one Sunday morning, as you pass the Apostolic Assembly of the Faith in Christ Jesus, you can hear a ringing, rocking beat.

The church itself is plain. Its floor is concrete, and its windows are of blue and yellow glass. But today is Sunday and the church is now packed, exploding with clenched, shaking bodies and the thunder of unison clapping and stomping feet. Drums and an electric guitar intensify the rhythm, busting out the raspy overhead speakers like a raunchy garage band. Young girls start their bodies to twisting and flap their hands. With faces cast down, young men shiver and hold their arms to the sky. Some dip and wiggle like James Brown. An old lady trembles. And soon almost everyone is crying. Only the front row of big-eared, gap-toothed little boys seems immune to the hullabaloo. They giggle and kick each other.

Most of this congregation—fully 80 percent—are Oaxacan Indians. Any Mexican will tell you that Oaxacan Indians are usually timid, taciturn people, not normally given to wild displays of feeling. But these Indians are here to praise the Lord and leave a life behind.

"We're of the Pentecostal tradition, which means we're more emotional," says Pastor César Meza.

Steinbeck's Joads and the Okies who came west in the 1930s brought with them their hollering religion. They stuck it into the state, and it made California different. Fifty years later those same denominations have been adopted by tens of thousands of Mexican Indians, who've made their own trek across land and time to their own part of California.

Indians transformed their new home when they came here to live. But just as profoundly, their new home changed them. And the clearest distillation of all those changes is the Protestant Church. "If you take a poll, you'll find that 80 or 85 percent of those who are established here now are Protestant," says Meza. That number might be high. But Protestant churches—especially of the more fundamentalist bent—proliferate in the valley. Indians here have become Baptists, Jehovah's Witnesses, Pentecostals, and scads of obscure denominations to which Luther's Reformation gave rise. The new churches are symbols of economic success, of modernity, of the monumental power and attraction of the United States. The adoption of a Protestant faith is almost standard issue in leaving Oaxaca for a future.

And that process is best told by one man who, now in his late forties, stands clapping in unison with the rest of the Apostolic Assembly of the Faith in Christ Jesus. Twenty years ago Luis Guerrero took his family and left his Oaxacan Indian pueblo and its traditions, moved to the valley of San Quintín, and hasn't yet looked back in fondness.

Guerrero, a Mixtec Indian who speaks halting Spanish in a thick Indian accent, faced a brutish dead-end life as a subsistence farmer, depending on unpredictable rains, in the village of Santa María Asunción, where landholdings were no longer measured in acres but in meters.

In 1972 Guerrero was among fifteen people who had to pay for the village's traditional party for its patron saint, the Virgin of Asunción. It was the custom: every year a few people had to become deeply impoverished to throw the three-day party for everyone else. His job was daunting: he had to give 2,000 pesos—the equivalent of two and a half years' local wages at the time—to buy food and alcohol for everyone, fireworks, candles, and more. The responsibility almost broke him. He borrowed the money at high interest rates, then left his young family and pueblo for that year to pick tomatoes in Sinaloa to pay it back.

In 1974 he began migrating to San Quintín with his family. Finally in 1978 they moved here to live, leaving Oaxaca forever.

Away from the cloistered atmosphere of his Oaxacan village, Luis Guerrero began a religious and secular awakening, one he likes to illustrate by talking about the books he bought.

In San Quintín he bought his first book ever—a Bible. In Oaxaca he had never read a Bible; though the whole village was Catholic, no one owned one. Like everyone else, he depended on a priest to know what it said. "I began reading it and I began to awaken my mind. That's where I understood that the priests hide part of the word of God. The word of God prohibits images, sculptures. I know how to read a little. I read the Ten Commandments, Exodus, chapter 20. Isaiah 44:9, which talks about idolatry. Psalms 115. I was working in the tomato fields. I met some people who spoke to me of the [Protestant] churches. I went. I like knowing myself. I went to the Catholic Church, the Apostolic Church, Prince of Peace, Los Olivares, Jehovah's Witnesses, the Open Door—to see how each denomination preached." He finally settled on the Apostolic Assembly.

Now thirsting for more, he bought his second book—a copy of the Mexican constitution. "In our pueblos in Oaxaca, we didn't know the earthly law, or how to defend ourselves [legally]. Also we didn't know spiritual law. So I searched on my own to discover what constitutional law said. I searched on my own to discover what the Bible said so that I myself could understand earthly law and spiritual law.

"Earthly law allows you to speak up for your rights with the police, the bosses. That's why I put forth an effort to learn it. [In the villages] people don't have education. The [local] authorities pressure them to fulfill tradition. They want them to put on traditional parties. [In Oaxaca] you can't give your children education because the little money you earn you have to spend on parties for the saints. Our children have no shoes because of tradition. We came here to leave all that behind."

Part of Luis Guerrero has not left the Oaxacan pueblo. He has eleven children—seven born in San Quintín—in the pueblo tradition of having enough

children to till the land without hiring outside help. When the community calls for help, he enthusiastically participates in marches and sit-ins demanding rights and services for farmworkers.

Moreover, there's a lot about the valley that Luis Guerrero doesn't like. Wages are too low, and thus he advocates child labor. Junior high is still the most school farmworkers can afford their children on local wages, and then only at great sacrifice. Bosses are callous. The fields are rife with mistreatment. And the government doesn't show it cares much about illiterate, brown-skinned farmworkers from 2,500 miles away. His first years here were spent in a shantytown shack. As he was working one day, a stone struck his right eye; without medical insurance or help from the grower, he lost the eye.

Still, the exodus from Oaxaca and steady employment has opened Luis Guerrero and Indian families like his to the world. And the proof stands before Luis Guerrero in his oldest son, Vicente.

Vicente Guerrero is a fast-talking, wide-smiling twenty-one-year-old. He speaks Mixteco at home, but that's about all of his Indian past he's willing to accommodate. "I've forgotten it all," Vicente says of the Indian traditions. "I want to begin anew. I don't want to go backward." He, like his father, has dropped the traditional Catholicism of the Oaxacan pueblo. He's now a pastor's helper at the Apostolic Assembly and occasionally preaches to the flock that includes his father, mother, and siblings.

Vicente and his family have worked hard so he can leave the fields in which his father still toils. He's now a clerk in a computer store and knows his way around Windows 95 and the innards of a computer. Vicente has caught the entrepreneurial bug and hopes to open his own shop in a few years.

None of this would have been imaginable in his father's village in Oaxaca. Children rarely went to more than a few years of elementary school. Moreover, language barriers and centuries of land swindles and other distasteful contact with the outside world bred both a deep suspicion among villagers toward outside influences and a rigid enforcement of traditional customs.

"Coming here is progress. People work and can buy food, even when it doesn't rain. They can buy land," Vicente says. "Before in Oaxaca, you couldn't spend time with mixed-blood people. Now you can. Before your parents would tell you to watch out because [non-Indians] were going to trick you. Now you have the confidence that won't happen.

"Most parents, what they leave to their children are their customs. My father had a different vision. I improved that vision. I said, 'No more fields.' I saw that my father was trying to get ahead. He did it a little. Not by much, but the mere fact that he left Oaxaca meant he could get ahead. I want to go further, to show that there's a bigger ladder to climb."

* * *

Day of the Dead, November 1998

The tomato plants are near exhaustion now. Many have given up, and their emerald green has faded to a dull brown. Workers are packing away the poles until next year. The breezes are sharper, the nights colder, the day's sun doesn't splash quite as warmly. The valley has shifted to broccoli, peas, squash, strawberries—all to supply the U.S. winter market.

"Ten years ago there were very few of these churches. Now there's two or three in each neighborhood, each of a different denomination," says Benancio López Chávez, who sits with several other men before an altar in a corner classroom at the Niño Artillero Bilingual Elementary School in the Maclovio Rojas neighborhood. The growth of Protestant churches like the Apostolic Assembly worries them.

López and his colleagues are bilingual teachers—schooled in Spanish and one of the four main Indian languages spoken in Oaxaca. The Mexican government has been training bilingual Indian teachers in Oaxaca since the 1960s, and today there are thousands of them. They often act as community spokesmen in Oaxaca when Indians deal with outside authorities. Teachers have also moved with their people along the migrant trail and into the United States. Like Talmudic scholars, they are charged with preserving Indian tradition in the diaspora. Among Benito García's victories years ago was to force the Baja California state government to reserve teaching slots in San Quintín for bilingual Indian teachers from Oaxaca. So two hundred of them now teach in the valley. They have also pushed the construction of some fifty bilingual elementary schools, built with government money and large amounts of community labor, that stretch down the valley—another example of Indian self-reliance and communal organizing in their new land.

Part of their responsibility is also quasi-religious: to construct each year an altar honoring the dead. The altar they have built is a gorgeous weave of orange and yellow flowers hooped over a table that holds bread, bananas, oranges, Coca-Cola, Fresca, cigarettes, tamales. A trail of flower petals leads from the school yard. Day of the Dead—actually November 1 and 2—the most traditional Mexican holiday, was itself a dead thing here in San Quintín. Instead every October 31 children would imitate Halloween as they saw it practiced across the border. Many children, including a large number of Indian kids, still celebrate Halloween here. They chant, *"Triki-traki,"* or, *"Queremos* Halloween, *queremos* Halloween" ("we want Halloween") as they go from door to door. It's the dominant holiday during these days. The United States is too close to ignore. And what kid doesn't want free candy?

But Indians have brought with them Day of the Dead, and the remarkable number of marigolds suddenly on sale along the highway attests to its growing popularity. The celebration is private. Each family sets out an altar at home to remember its dead and leaves something good for their spirits to consume when they return to visit.

Sitting now before the altar they have built, the teachers' conversation runs across Indian life in their new home and their future here. San Quintín is better than Oaxaca, they agree, because people can work; they can live closer to services like schools, health care, and markets. There's transportation. But children are losing respect for elders and knowledge of Oaxacan cuisine, and they're narcotized by video games. The communal bonds aren't as strong. Still, the teachers are proud of Indians' initiative in the new land, accomplishing in a few years what has taken longtime residents decades to achieve. "Colonia Santa Fe (a non-Indian neighborhood) has been around for forty years and just last year got electricity," says one teacher. And they point out that thanks to Radio XEQIN, Indian cultural practices are seeing a resurgence. The Triquis hold a traditional party every June. So do Mixtecos from the municipality of San Juan Mixtepec. Bowing to reality, no longer are a few souls required every year to go into debt to put on the party for everyone else, as Luis Guerrero had to. Rather, everyone pitches in.

Still, it's likely that in decades to come, Indian traditions will fade. Day of the Dead may lose the significance it holds in Oaxaca and become more a day of Indian pride, like St. Patrick's Day for New York's Irish. It's hard to imagine the grandchildren of these men speaking Mixteco if they remain in Baja California. The chances are slim, the teachers admit. The outside influences are great.

* * *

"Indians from the south have to abandon, I think, their customs and language because they're going to have to compete with us for jobs. Tradition is very nice— and lately there's been a lot of nice talk about conserving the language—but they have to compete for jobs with us. They have to leave it behind."

These are hard words, perhaps, but the man who says them is considered the most humane of San Quintín's growers. Liberato Romo runs Seminis—a world-class seed producer that he started in 1965, a few miles down the highway from where the teachers are sitting. Seminis is now part of a multinational agricultural company with headquarters in Monterrey, Mexico, and production sites in Europe, the United States, and Latin America. It's the high end of San Quintín agriculture since seed production is a high-tech thing these days. One pound of Seminis product can cost thousands of dollars.

Now nearing retirement, Romo sits at his desk and in a gravelly voice reviews what he thinks is San Quintín's future. It includes more reliance on technology and the use of greenhouses to increase productivity as labor costs rise. "We've found the way to overcome the obstacles that confronted us. We have poor land—highly alkaline—not much water, and we didn't have the technology. We've made the land productive. We have the technology, the ability. Now we're learning something new: how to treat people."

Seminis has doctors and nurses on staff, day care and a playground for children, lunchrooms, a human resources department, and a labor camp notably free of vermin and trash, and it trains employees for advancement beyond unskilled work to jobs that other companies hire agronomists and accountants to do. "People pay for quality," says Romo. "Treating people better, we're going to have employees who are more interested in working for us. The company depends on the work of its employees."

Despite the large *colonias* now lining the thin black highway, labor scarcity remains a problem in the valley. Retaining workers will be one of the great challenges for San Quintín. This raises the prospect that someday workers

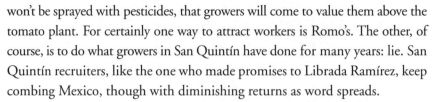

won't be sprayed with pesticides, that growers will come to value them above the tomato plant. For certainly one way to attract workers is Romo's. The other, of course, is to do what growers in San Quintín have done for many years: lie. San Quintín recruiters, like the one who made promises to Librada Ramírez, keep combing Mexico, though with diminishing returns as word spreads.

Still, San Quintín growers may take a while to follow Romo's lead. The tension between the old and the new way of doing things—between the traditional and the modern—will remain part of San Quintín life. This is especially true of its Indian residents. Coming here—like the Okies' arrival in California—has brought them into the world. They are finding a future in the global economy as they try to make sense of its disorienting cultural mishmash.

Recently bilingual teachers put on a community Day of the Dead celebration at a local dance hall. They erected Triqui, Mixteco, and Zapoteco altars. And with gushing parents ringing the hall, and teenagers in baggy pants, and Gap sweatshirts in the background, schoolchildren sang songs and performed traditional dances—some of them even dressed like Mexican Indians of centuries past.

Starting the evening, though, was a strange presentation. The announcer called it Baile Norteño (Northern Dance). Probably nothing the whole evening better reduced to its confused essentials the place in the world Oaxacan Indians in San Quintín now find themselves. Baile Norteño consisted of four Indian children—in cowboy hats, boots, and bandannas—doing a kind of square-dance hoedown to a Mexicanized version of a country-and-western polka beat that featured synthesizers sounding like fiddles, all performed in front of traditional Indian altars honoring the dead.

Slowly the economic forces that created San Quintín are also creating a new cultural mix that is a lot like Baile Norteño—part Indian, part Mexican, and part American. "The valley's advantage is that it's new," says Gregorio Santiago, the DJ at Radio XEQIN. "Everyone who lives here is a migrant. We're forming a new identity in the valley. In fifteen, twenty years, we'll all be the same, but with our own characteristics."

—1997–98

ZEUS AND THE OAXACA HOOPS

Zeus García, one of the greatest Indian basketball players to come out of the state of Oaxaca, got very little sleep in the weeks leading up to this year's Thanksgiving tournament in Santa Monica.

He took off work for three weeks. His days, which were often filled with basketball anyway, were now devoted entirely to the tournament's details and his team's practices. He was getting home regularly at one and two in the morning.

He contacted the Oaxacan Basketball Referee Federation. The Oaxacan government agreed to pay for four amateur-sanctioned referees—two of whom had reffed internationally—to work the event. Three months before the tournament, Zeus was already visiting the Oaxacan business community around Los Angeles, asking them to sponsor the tournament.

His nine-year-old son, Ervin, whom he'd named for Lakers star Earvin "Magic" Johnson, was reacting poorly to all this. "There have been times when I've abandoned him a lot," Zeus says. "I'll be out there organizing things, and I'll call my sister and ask her to pick up my son and fix him dinner. If there's something my son hates, it's my telephone. The phone will ring. I'll talk and talk and hang up, and it'll ring again. He'll be saying, 'Stop, I want to be with you. I want to talk to you. I need your help.'"

Still, the tournament consumed Zeus. He crisscrossed L.A., going to the homes of captains of more than twenty Oaxacan Indian basketball teams and inviting them to the tournament. With real referees, they would see how amateur basketball was called and not confuse it with what they saw in the NBA.

This was really the point of the tournament, the way Zeus saw it. He has played basketball for love all his life and thus has no interest in the pros. Despite naming his son for Magic Johnson, Zeus rarely watches the NBA and can't always recall Michael Jordan's name. He sounds often like an immigrant fearful his children will imitate the American's soulless ways when he talks about how the NBA is corrupting the way his people play hoops. "NBA players

don't play with anger and courage, to get to something," he says. "They can jump, land, then jump again with the ball. That's a violation. It's all for show. The NBA is a business. The sport's purity, that's what I want maintained. It's the same thing as preserving our language, the food, dance. There's no reason we should lose this part of our roots."

So the Thanksgiving tournament was to set a standard of tradition to be followed—a kind of sporting version of an Indian folk dance—in the Oaxacan diaspora.

Oaxacan mountain Indians have made basketball—that most hip-hop, twenty-first century of sports—as much a part of their ancient culture as their language, food, and handicrafts. They are among Mexico's shortest people, and the vast isolation of the state's rugged Sierra Juárez has kept them rooted to Indian custom. So they aren't obvious candidates for a serious basketball addiction. Yet their isolation is precisely why they have come to obsess over the sport.

Basketball proved a perfect match for the mountain range, which was too steep for soccer or baseball fields. The first courts in Oaxaca were built by villagers in the Oaxaca Valley in the early 1930s. From there, the sport ascended the Sierra Juárez, apparently first promoted by teachers sent up from Oaxaca City.

The first courts were made of dirt. Some villages had real hoops, but others simply nailed real baskets, enormous things in which two balls could fit, to a post. Men played barefoot or in sandals. Pueblos with money bought basketballs in Oaxaca City. Other villages made balls from deer skin that the women sewed with strands of fiber from the maguey cactus. These balls were filled with rags and didn't bounce. Often players were unclear about the rules and didn't know court measurements.

Still, basketball quickly replaced *pelota mixteca*—a sport similar to handball that is now dying out. However, *pelota mixteca* was seriously played only in some lower parts of the Sierra. Fernando Ramos thinks basketball caught on because it was similar to another sport called *pelota*. *Pelota* was an ancient game Oaxacan Indians played before the Spanish Conquest, in which players used hips and knees to put a round ball through a hoop. It, too, was played during religious festivals but died out centuries ago. No sport was played with such fervency, Ramos believes, until the arrival of basketball.

Ramos is one of a group of Zapoteco professionals and intellectuals educated in Mexico City who have returned to the Sierra. Ramos is from the village of Yavesia. He studied political science in the capital, then returned home fifteen years ago. He was among a group that started the magazine *Titza Keriu* (*Our Word,* in Zapoteco) and, in one issue, investigated how basketball came to the mountains.

"We think there must have been a sports vacuum that basketball filled," says Ramos. "[Basketball's appeal] may also have to do with the circular way of thinking in Indian culture. There is no beginning and no end. Ball games were based on the solar calendar, the sun and the moon. There's the cycle of day, night, life, and death. We think this might explain the fascination for games that involve agility, speed, physical training, and round balls."

By the 1950s highland villages had learned the rules and built courts, and the sport had become an important part of village life. Above all, basketball insinuated itself into the traditional fiesta each village holds to honor its patron saint. Today each village organizes a rodeo, folk dances, and a mass, but what everyone comes to see is the daylong basketball tournament. Hundreds of these fiesta tournaments take place every year across the mountains of Oaxaca.

In the 1970s Zeus García and his brothers and cousins had a team that dominated Oaxacan mountain Indian basketball—winning more than 250 of these village tournaments in its day, as well as dozens of trophies, nine bulls, two horses, a donkey, and legendary renown.

Now, twenty years later, Zeus works as a busboy in L.A. But he still lives for basketball. At forty-one, his playing days are over, yet Zeus cannot leave the sport. So he continues on, coaching a team of young Indian immigrants— all workers in West Side restaurants—which he has christened Raza Unida (United Race). Even in Oaxacan Indian basketball in L.A., defined by the pure devotion of its participants, Raza Unida is something special. It is the best team around, with the nicest uniforms, complete with warm-up jackets and pants. Its players pay coworkers to sub for them on tournament days, but sometimes they just miss work if they can't find a replacement. Three players have been fired for this. Raza Unida may have the only coach who shows up at neighborhood games with a clipboard and play diagrams, wearing a whistle like a cross. He has designed for his team an offense that involves ten different formations, with at least eight scoring possibilities off each formation.

To its coach, Raza Unida is more than a team. It is the continuation of a way of life, the American version of his former team—a monument in the new country to the best moments in the life of the immigrant Zeus García.

Zeus will talk about promoting basketball to keep kids off drugs and allow them time to be with other Oaxacan kids in Los Angeles so they can understand their shared roots. All that is true. But spend time with him, and it's clear the many Oaxacan Indian basketball tournaments in Los Angeles also give Zeus and Raza Unida a forum from which to say, with a certain healthy brashness uncommon among timid, self-effacing Mexican Indians, "We are the best."

* * *

Los Angeles is awash in Oaxacan Indian basketball tournaments. Between forty and sixty of them take place in the L.A. area every year: Santa Monica, South-Central L.A., Long Beach. Some are more than twenty years old. New ones start every year. From February to November there's at least one Oaxacan Indian basketball tournament every weekend—hosting between fifteen and fifty-five teams, including children's and women's teams.

These tournaments are some of the best indicators that the L.A. area, in becoming a major Mexican city, has also acquired one of the world's great populations of Oaxacan Indians. Today estimates of their L.A.-area population range between 60,000 and 200,000 people—mostly Zapotecos, the largest of Oaxaca's sixteen Indian groups. The Oaxacan Indian community reached a critical mass in the 1990s. Pockets of them live in Santa Monica, Venice, North Hollywood, Santa Ana, South-Central, and Koreatown. "It's no longer Koreatown; it's Oaxacatown," says Fernando López Matéos.

López Matéos is part of an emerging Oaxacan Indian business class in Los Angeles. He owns a money-wire service and the Guelaguetza restaurant near Koreatown. A decade ago a Oaxacan restaurant in L.A. would have died quickly. Now on Sundays lines are out the door. Other Oaxacan restaurants have since popped up. So López Mateos decided a newspaper could also work. In February he began publishing *El Oaxaqueño,* a free biweekly that exhausts the fifteen thousand copies it publishes.

El Oaxaqueño follows the great tradition of American ethnic newspapers. Yet it is not about people from one country—not the Armenian *Observer* or El Salvador *USA*—but from one state and thus is a measure of Oaxacans' separateness. To Americans, Oaxacan Indians may look Mexican. But their geographic isolation and firm hold on Indian customs and languages make them a group apart in their own country. They occasionally refer to Mexicans as "they." Other Mexicans often view Oaxacan Indians as ignorant and unassimilated. They call them "dirty Indians," "Oaxacos," or "Oaxaquitos." They insult them for speaking their languages in public and not learning Spanish properly.

"Mexicans always talk about discrimination, how they're being portrayed on TV," says Felipe López, a Zapoteco Indian, who arrived in the United States as a semiliterate restaurant worker and is now a graduate student in urban planning at UCLA and coauthor of the first Zapoteco-English dictionary. "The same thing that's being done to them, they're doing to indigenous people. A lot of people have told me, 'I don't want to live in a Mexican neighborhood. I want to live in a white neighborhood.' It's because of how they've been treated by other Mexicans."

Mexicans, the saying goes, prefer dead Indians to live ones. The country is full of monuments to ancient Indian kings, whose descendants can be found in the streets nearby begging or selling gum or playing the accordion. In the same way, many anthropologists have studied *pelota mixteca*—a sport that is all but dead—but no one, in Mexico or the United States, has studied basketball, though thousands of Oaxacan Indians play it avidly every day. "Basketball isn't exotic enough (to be studied)," says López. "But these are real people with real lives. That this is not an indigenous sport is beside the point. The question is . . . how have indigenous people made it part of their everyday life? It's become a ritual. Everyone plays basketball."

That Oaxacan mountain Indians have been playing basketball for more than half a century—not soccer or baseball—is a metaphor for their separation from Mexico. That separateness, in turn, is why Oaxacan Indians in America need basketball more than ever.

Basketball is the one familiar thing in the strange land. When Felipe López arrived from his village of San Lucas Quiavini in 1978, he made straight for the basketball courts on Venice Beach, where young men from San Lucas played. There, his Spanish being poor, he could speak Zapoteco in comfort. There, over time, he heard about work, saw old friends, and met new ones.

"Despite being so far from your community, you feel so close. You have that sense of being home," López says. "It's really reassuring that you've come to a place where you're accepted—the basketball court."

In the global era, basketball helps mountain villages maintain a kind of virtual community with their wandering children. Due to a lack of work and basic services, Oaxaca's mountains have been depopulating for years now. More than half the population of many pueblos in Sierra Juárez live in Oaxaca City, Mexico City, or the United States. Basketball keeps strong the ties to the village that would have withered years ago.

A sizable amount of public works in these villages now depends on the financial success of basketball tournaments in L.A. Many Oaxacan Indian immigrants send money back home to pay for community needs like plaza, church, and school renovations, ambulances, or street pavings. Zapotecos in L.A. often raise this money through basketball tournaments—where tacos and fruit drinks are sold. Immigrants from the village of Yavesia, in one tangled instance, won televisions and a cassette recorder at tournaments. They in turn used the appliances as prizes to attract teams to their own tournament. The money they raised there (four thousand dollars) was then sent home and used for prize money and referee salaries in Yavesia's fiesta tournament in Oaxaca.

Beyond that, though, much of a traditional Oaxacan fiesta—rodeos, fireworks, and the like—is illegal or difficult to stage in the United States. And though villages celebrate a mass here, American Catholic churches are famously unlike the churches in Indian villages. They are often cold and foreign, not places for refuge and succor. Nor does the fact that a priest is Latino mean he understands. "There was a mass for my town at St. Anne's in Santa Monica," says López. "The priest got really pissed off because we wouldn't answer back. But in my town, people don't recite back what the priest says. He was just screaming at us. It made us feel really bad. He was Latino. He thought all Mexicans were the same."

So the result is a strange one: basketball becomes church. The elaborate, centuries-old Oaxacan village fiesta honoring a patron saint distills down in Los Angeles to a basketball tournament and a dance a week later at which admission is charged and trophies are awarded. Thus in L.A., Zapoteco Indians can speak earnestly of preserving basketball tournaments in their New World—as if the sport were in danger of dying out in the country that invented it. "This is our religion," says a player. Perhaps that's a slight exaggeration. But basketball does amount to a secular faith through which Zapoteco villagers, flung across Los Angeles, find communion in a world where they are outsiders twice over.

***

And in L.A. Zapoteco basketball, Zeus García is the high priest. For it he has sacrificed everything, including two knees, two women, and one set of children. For it he has bridged divides within his own community.

"Basketball is my life. In my mind, basketball is never over," he says, sitting in the living room of the yellow stucco house on an alley in West L.A. that he shares with Ervin. The room is decorated with trophies, a stereo won as a tournament prize, banners, some team pictures, a ball over in the corner, tennis shoes, and a gym bag. Beyond that, the house has the look of someone easily distracted from happy homemaking.

Zeus is a busboy and a handsome man. He has a strong jaw, thick hands, a wide smile, and a deep voice. His dark eyes grow cast-iron black and fiery when the discussion turns to hoops. He's graying at the temples. He isn't tall—about five-foot nine. His given name is Rogelio, but at age eight, just beginning to play ball, he wore a jersey with the word *Zeus* on it and that became his name, though not until junior high did he discover the word's meaning. He works now at The Beach House, a trendy beachside restaurant. By candlelight, the restaurant serves high California cuisine to the coast cities' best-looking singles concerned with romance, savoring the fruits of a robust economy and oblivious, no doubt, to the fact that in their midst, imperceptibly retiring their plates of New Zealand lamb chops and ginger-crusted salmon filets, walks one of Oaxaca's greatest Indian basketball players. Zeus has worked at other restaurants. He works at The Beach House because its manager allows him extra time off to be with his team.

His basketball story begins years ago, 2,200 miles from Los Angeles, in the village of Santa Ana del Valle (population 1,000), in the Oaxaca Valley at the foot of the Sierra Juárez. Santa Ana has been a village of serape weavers since before the Spanish Conquest. But nowadays most of its young men want to play basketball. Every afternoon the court in the center of town is filled with

players. Years ago Zeus García and his brothers were there. They are scattered across Los Angeles now. But in their day the García brothers—Isaias, once a state MVP, Zeus, Arcadio, Gustavo—and their cousins, Alberto and Cirino Bautista, made up Equipo SAV.

For the last half of the 1970s Equipo SAV was the best team in the Zapoteco region of Oaxaca, though no player was over five-foot nine. Their practices consisted of running uphill for two hours every day with bike-tire tubes filled with sand tied around their ankles and thighs. Too poor for new tennis shoes, the players sifted garbage dumps for Canada-brand soles and Voltar canvas tops and sewed them together. Oaxaca was then largely cut off from the world. There wasn't much television, no NBA to watch. So Equipo SAV didn't know the finer points of basketball. Nor did it know the position names, which were irrelevant anyway since SAV was all the same size.

SAV's great advantage was its excellent condition and extreme dedication. While most teams played zone defense, SAV became famous for a fast-break, man-to-man full-court-press chaos all game long. "Back then, [Oaxacan] basketball was very stationary," says Zeus. "The older folks didn't really know how to dribble. We could, and we never got tired."

Most weekends, SAV headed for remote mountain village tournaments. Getting up at 3:00 a.m. to take a bus, the team would then walk for hours to arrive by the noon registration time, play all day, then sleep in a schoolroom that night. Once Equipo SAV walked ten hours to the mountain village of Yalina. SAV was the first valley team to play in Yalina. A village official interviewed the team as if they were visiting dignitaries and broadcast it over speakers around the town plaza. Equipo SAV won all six games that day. They also won a 1,300-pound tan bull named Trueno—Thunder. "We tied a rope around its neck and we walked down through the mountains for two days and nights," says Zeus. "There also happened to be a fiesta in Santa Ana the night we arrived. The entire pueblo, in the middle of the party, went to the entrance to town with a marching band. People followed us in, cheering and clapping, while the band played. It lasted all night." Livestock and poultry were soon common prizes in Oaxacan village tournaments.

By 1980, though, SAV's run was up. "Gustavo was the first to go. He didn't want to be poor anymore," says Zeus. "He went to Orange County.

Then Alberto went to San Diego." Isaias and Arcadio went to Mexico City.

But Zeus stayed in Santa Ana del Valle. "I couldn't give up basketball," he says. "I'd go to the fiestas in each pueblo. I'd play with the weakest team. To support myself, I'd weave serapes. I'd get up at about 4:00 or 5:00 a.m., and by ten I'd finish the serape. Then in the afternoon I'd work out. I ran up the mountain alone, just like we'd done as brothers. I spent about three years doing this, without my brothers. That's when the young guys got to know me."

Finally, though, Zeus too went north. He was living with a woman and couldn't support her.

He found work in the Chinese restaurants in Torrance, a suburb of Los Angeles, which employ many immigrants from Santa Ana del Valle. Torrance Chinese restaurants depend greatly on Oaxacan labor. They also often pay below the minimum wage and demand that employees work at least twelve hours a day, six days a week. Working for Chinese restaurants is usually the end of a player's basketball days. Zeus worked all of 1984 in a Chinese restaurant in Torrance. His apartment and the restaurant across the street were about all he knew of the United States. He went home after a year, hoping never to return.

"Back in Oaxaca, I devoted myself to basketball," he remembers. "I remember some girls would take pictures of my thighs. I had these huge thighs. Girls would warm up water for me to bathe. They'd pay for my tickets to the dance. During that whole year I played basketball, I got to know a lot of women. They came to my house, looking for me. But I'd be somewhere else, playing basketball. My woman got mad and took our children and left. I was such a coward that I couldn't handle it. I began drinking mescal and went off on a drunk for four or five months."

In 1986 Zeus left Oaxaca again for Torrance. This time, though, a chance meeting aboard a bus with another Oaxacan player changed his life. The player told him that far from Torrance, fifteen miles away in West Los Angeles, Zapotecos played regular pickup games at gyms and playgrounds. Zeus left Chinese restaurant work forever for basketball and West Side restaurants. Thus he settled into America and Zapoteco immigrant life and hasn't returned to Oaxaca since.

Here his story, involving restaurant work and basketball as the foundations of immigrant life, converged with that of the Zapoteco migration to L.A. Zeus was part of a larger Zapoteco migration to L.A. that began in the

1970s and accelerated mightily in the mid-1980s.

Highland Zapotecos were drawn to work in construction, painting, plumbing, and landscaping and to cheap housing in South-Central Los Angeles. The courts at Normandie Park, near Koreatown, became their gathering place, and the highlanders would become the L.A. area's great tournament organizers. Beginning in the early 1970s, the villages of San Pablo Macuiltianguis, Xochixtepec, Tlacochahuaya, and San Miguel Cajonos, among others, held the first tournaments at the park. The events soon became a measure of the growth of the Zapoteco community. At first men's teams from other mountain pueblos participated. Then in the mid-1980s organizers added women's teams. In the early 1990s children's teams were included.

Meanwhile Zapotecos from the Oaxaca Valley came to L.A.'s West Side restaurant work. Today they are prevalent as busboys, cooks, and dishwashers and have created a rich network of lowland Zapoteco pickup games. Basketball didn't attract the first valley Zapotecos to the West Side; restaurant work did that. But one reason young Zapotecos continue to come to the West Side is the many places to play combined with what is now a critical mass of good players.

Once discovered, Los Angeles revealed to Zeus a cornucopia of pickup games. For the next few years he consumed them, driving all over L.A., anywhere for a game. "That was the first time I played with black guys," he says. "They're arguing all the time. But I liked playing with them because they were tall and I liked trying to fight them for the ball. (White guys), you can't run into them even a little, because they'll turn and say, 'Are you all right?' They're very worried about you. Blacks don't care about that."

By the mid-1990s, after years of playground ball, Zeus could barely jump. His knees were giving out. He had operations on both, but he returned to the court too soon and this time ruined his knees forever. Suddenly Zeus García could no longer play basketball. It was nauseating to be reduced to watching others. "The first days I couldn't play, I left the gym in a really bad mood. [But] from that, I got the idea that I'd help another team—to coach," he says. "It's all you can do. You can't give up basketball."

He began haunting the Venice and Santa Monica courts, watching the games of Zapotecos half his age. They were now his lifeline to the game. He came to focus on one player in particular: his second cousin, Francisco Morales. Pancho, now twenty-five, is a cheerful guy with two children and a pompadour. Growing up in Santa Ana del Valle, Zeus and Equipo SAV were his heroes. Pancho grew to only five-foot six, but he developed a Zeus-like obsession for hoops. "After school every day I'd go to the court," Pancho says. "The older guys would play until dark. It's a poor pueblo and we didn't have lights. We'd play in the dark anyway. That was the only time they allowed us to play."

At age sixteen he left Oaxaca for California. He spent his first years in San Bernardino, about sixty miles from L.A., working in restaurants. Several years later he heard of pickup games in Venice with guys from the Oaxaca Valley. He began driving out to play on his days off because the games were good.

By now Zeus was hanging around these games as well. The younger players were timid in his presence. But slowly he pulled them toward him. He volunteered to referee a game. A week or so later he proposed a small tournament, with each player chipping in money for a trophy. Finally, after a few months of this, he suggested forming a team. This was all Pancho needed to hear. He quit his job and moved his wife and child from San Bernardino to Venice. Chiquis, Zeus's youngest brother, moved from a Chinese restaurant in Long Beach.

So Raza Unida formed—the first and only Zapoteco team in Los Angeles whose members are from different Oaxacan villages. From Union Zapata come the Aquino brothers—Julio, Miguel Ángel, and Nacho, who is six-one and probably the best Zapoteco player in L.A. Abel Jiménez, known as "Homes," is six-two and from Matatlán. Nacho and Homes form the tallest front line in southland Zapoteco hoops. The rest of the team—Piedra, Tomás, Eladio, Chiquis—are from Santa Ana del Valle. All work in West Side restaurants. At its heart is the scrappy general, Pancho Morales—sometimes point guard, sometimes center, and a busboy at Joe's Restaurant in Santa Monica.

Pancho has become a younger version of his boyhood hero. Like Zeus, he named his son Ervin—also for Magic Johnson. "The first thing in my life is my family. The second is basketball," he says. "I've been hurt—the ankles, the back. They tell me not to play anymore. But it's never been enough for me to say, 'That's it; it's over.'"

Zeus, in turn, calls Pancho "my son." "Francisco has basketball in his blood," says Zeus. "One time he dislocated his thumb. He was almost in tears, but he kept saying, 'I'm going in, Zeus.' I said, 'You can't play.' This was the first time he disobeyed me. I was doing something, and the next thing I know he's in the game. They threw him the ball, and it hit his hand and went out of bounds. Somehow, though, he forgot about his hand. He began to shoot and the ball began going in. Pancho won the game for us.

"When I see a basketball player like that I want to cry."

* * *

In the gymnasium at the El Sereno Recreation Center one fall Sunday, Zeus and Raza Unida saunter around the court in their effusive red, white, and blue uniforms. Some of the players keep their heads down, affecting a calm detachment. But this is hard to maintain in the bedlam enveloping the gym. Here in this corner of Los Angeles, clarinets are screeching and cymbals are crashing madly over a humphing tuba as a brass band brays the "Zacatecas March" and leads fifty-five teams of Zapoteco Indians into the packed gymnasium and in a short parade around the court. Both the public and the players spend lives blending into L.A.'s background—painting homes in Malibu, cleaning them in Pacific Palisades, or waiting for day work at corners of Santa Monica. But here they aren't so quiet.

This is the opening ceremony to a tournament sponsored by the immigrants from the Sierra Juárez village of Atepec, in honor of their patron saint, San Juan. It's only Atepec's third tournament in L.A., yet it has become a central event in the immigrants' lives. They are spending five thousand dollars to put on the tournament and dance. Their reputation back home is at stake.

In 1991 the village of Atepec built a gymnasium with money earned from its sawmill. Its immigrants in L.A. decided to contribute a new electronic scoreboard to christen the building. They ordered it from a company in Chicago. The scoreboard cost $3,500, was as big as a bed, and weighed seven hundred pounds. Three men put it atop a van and drove it to Oaxaca. They left on December 22, hoping to arrive Christmas Day. But Mexican customs stalled them at the border, forcing them to arrive in Oaxaca the day after Christmas. Worse, the duties, food, gasoline, and road tolls cost more than the scoreboard itself. The immigrants didn't have the money, so the village had to pay the transportation. Village elders pointedly did not put a plaque by the scoreboard honoring those in L.A.

Now Atepec's immigrants are hoping for some redemption. Their tournament will raise money for a community park the village has planned in Oaxaca. "We don't want what happened to the scoreboard to happen [to the park]," says Isauro Contreras, president of the Atepec tournament committee. "It should have our name. It should say something about Los Angeles. The village wants to build a garden with plants, but nothing for the children. We want a playground, with swings—in the style of playgrounds we see here."

So, like most tournaments in the Oaxacan diaspora, this one is about bigger things than basketball. For Atepec's immigrants, it's about the park back home. For Zeus, it's about discipline and class. As it gets underway, Zeus assembles his proteges outside the gym. There's been some on-court arguing lately, and Zeus finds this entirely undignified. "We have to show how good we are. We can't be yelling at each other. We look ridiculous.. . . Through making baskets we're going to show who we are. We each know what we have to do. We need to go out and do it and show people we know how to play basketball."

It is a theme he brings up often—demonstrating you are the best. It was his consuming passion in his playing days. Remarkably, the young men sit still for this—an amateur coach, who can't get them scholarships, talking to them so firmly. But this is Oaxacan hoops—another kind, from another part of the world. It's not about scholarships and shoe deals. It's about being the best because it feels good and you can say later that you were and everyone will know you're telling the truth, even though by day you were a busboy.

The fact that Raza Unida is here at all makes Atepec's tournament an important moment in L.A. Zapoteco Indian life.

Atepec is a highland village, and Raza Unida comes from lowland villages. In Oaxaca the two regions are suspicious of each other. Zapotecos from the Oaxaca Valley are nearer the state government, with access to better facilities, and thus are better basketball players. However, those from the Sierra Juárez, while poorer, are more self-reliant due to their isolation from the government's paternalism.

In Los Angeles the two groups have historically had little to do with each other. This division, not surprisingly, was for a long time expressed most clearly in basketball tournaments. Highland Zapotecos organize all the best L.A. tournaments, and for many years lowland teams never participated. "People from the valley are always wanting the government to do things for them, to orga-

nize a tournament, say, so they can just show up and play," says Zeus, himself from a valley town. "The highland folks don't want anything to do with the government."

So Zeus and Raza Unida were viewed warily when, in 1997, they showed up at a highland tournament asking to play. Zeus had played in the highlands, and he was well known. Yet when he asked if Raza Unida could play, the organizers said no. Zeus said, "We're all Oaxacans, suffering discrimination, working the hardest, lowest-paid jobs—and then among each other we discriminate."

The captains argued. Some felt Raza Unida would crush the mountain teams. After lengthy discussion, though, they voted to allow Raza Unida. This wasn't exactly breaking the color barrier. Still, basketball has since then brought together highland and lowland Zapoteco communities that in L.A. once kept their distance.

It was after playing in several of these highland tournaments that Zeus concluded Oaxacan basketball was at risk here. He saw the influence of the NBA was deep and nefarious and resolved to combat it in a struggle he now calls "my fight." With captains and referees, he has argued with a believer's conviction over when to call traveling, palming the ball, and charging. He has had many discussions over when players can enter the key after a free-throw attempt. All these violations are called one way in the NBA and another in international amateur competition.

"In Oaxaca the players adapt themselves to what the referees allow," he says. "Here they make their money, they buy the best shoes and the shorts endorsed by Michael Jordan and shirts that cost a hundred dollars, and they go to the court and try to play like Michael Jordan. They don't know what they're doing. They'll ask, 'Give me a chance to play for your team, Zeus.' I have to say no. 'How do you play defense?' They don't know. Basketball is played with fundamentals. But all they see are the dramatic plays of the NBA."

Yet despite Zeus's warnings regarding the NBA, Raza Unida is the most American of Oaxacan teams. It defies tradition by using the best players from different villages. It is taller and faster than the highland teams. Like Equipo SAV before it, Raza Unida has laid waste to the competition in Zapoteco L.A. At the El Sereno gym, as expected, Raza Unida wins Atepec's event for a second straight year with very little trouble, beating many of its opponents by twenty points or more.

As the Atepec tournament makes clear, there is little competition left for Raza Unida in the Zapoteco tournaments in L.A. Unless one of its stars is hurt, it always wins. Flyers circulate through the rec center announcing two upcoming tournaments. But neither promises to test Raza Unida. So this and Zeus's Thanksgiving Day tournament might be their last for a while. "Maybe we should look for some black teams to play," says Chiquis, with a wince—a daring thought—as the players file out of the center into the darkness and Atepec's volunteers hurriedly sweep the bleachers.

* * *

The fifteenth annual Thanksgiving Oaxacan basketball tournament actually begins the Sunday before the holiday. Thirty-six teams line up on the court at Marine Park in Santa Monica. An honor guard of uniformed players carries the Mexican and U.S. flags onto the court. The national anthems of both countries are played.

Zeus and his brother Isaias began organizing this tournament at Marine Park after they arrived in the United States. Only seven teams from Santa Ana del Valle participated that first year. But as the West Side Oaxacan community grew, so did the tournament, until it is now a fixture in Zapoteco L.A. life.

Still, it has never been this organized. Zeus wanted it to set a new standard this year. This is the first Oaxacan tournament in L.A. to have sponsors, who have donated uniforms for prizes.

Standing before the teams lined up across the court, Zeus welcomes the players. One of the referees then makes the players swear an oath to play hard and fair. Marcial Santiago, a local union activist, officially inaugurates the tournament. A guitar duo plays "Hymn to Sport," a song written by Isaias, who shoots the ceremonial first free throw. Only after all this pomp—lasting half an hour—do the games begin.

Raza Unida has taken every precaution. The team has been running on the beach instead of the local high school tracks; practices are extended to three times a week. The first day's events are therefore predictable. Raza Unida beats two teams by a combined margin of fifty-five points. No one roots for Raza

Unida, not even at its own tournament. As the night falls, a cold, brisk wind approaches gale force and blows Coke cups and pine needles across the court. The nets are at forty-five-degree angles, and every free throw becomes an adventure. The action ends around 9:00 p.m.

For the Thanksgiving Day finals the weather is mercifully mild. The refs enforce all traveling and charging violations and call technical fouls on those who protest. Zeus couldn't be happier.

To one side stand the Luna brothers. None of the Luna brothers are over five-nine, but they are the only team to have beaten Raza Unida lately—defeating it twice in a tournament in July. Anticipating a rematch, the brothers have added Mario García, who measures about six-three.

The Lunas form one of the oldest Zapoteco teams in the L.A. area. Their coach and father, Fidencio Luna, is from Luvina, a woodcutting village in the Sierra Juárez of Oaxaca, where when he was young, people played on dirt courts with balls made of leather sewed around a ball of rags. Fidencio Luna is a small man, with dark skin, a graying mustache, and a nervous and shy way about him that fades as soon as he begins talking about anything dealing with basketball, and especially when talking about the team he coaches. He left Luvina as a young man and spent a few years in Mexico City working as a welder. In 1972, at the age of twenty-three, he made his way to Orange County, where a relative lived. He found work as a gardener. Two years later he brought his family. Through it all he has played basketball. Fidencio Luna formed a team with a brother and some cousins. It played its first tournament in 1978. He began to bring his children to the Zapoteco tournaments that were becoming more common around L.A. Fidencio and the rest of the first generation of Lunas are now retired. But like Zeus, Fidencio cannot leave basketball. These days he coaches his sons and nephews. The team is one of the best around, characterized by frequent fast breaks and the slashing, stutter-stepping drives of Fidencio's twenty-three-year-old son, Benito.

At 2:00 p.m. the Luna boys face Raza Unida. This is the game of the day: lowland versus highland, L.A.'s best team versus the team best able to beat them. But before it begins, Zeus questions whether Mario García, the Luna boys' new center, is from Oaxaca or of Oaxacan parentage. If not, according to tournament rules, he can't play. Zeus is unpopular among Zapoteco crowds in part because he's a stickler on fine points like these. "He's always complaining. He doesn't like it when another team is equal to his," says one man in the crowd, which is now three deep around the court and chanting for a ball game. Finally Mario García is allowed to play, though his provenance is never made clear. An announcer is brought in to call the action.

Both teams start nervously, bricking shots. But soon they loosen up. Low-post play gets brutal, with Homes and Nacho slamming against the Luna brothers. The crowd hangs on every basket. Benito and Israel Luna carve through the Raza Unida defense, dishing to García, who gives the Lunas what other teams lack, an imposing and agile center to match Raza Unida's. Still, Chiquis is having the tournament of his life, cutting and passing off to his big men. He and Julio Aquino foul out with seconds left in the game and Raza Unida ends up with four players on the court but victorious: 30–24.

This is a double-elimination tournament: each team must lose twice to depart. So the rest of the day is spent waiting for the rematch. Raza Unida gets a scare but emerges victorious against Colosos, a team of West Side restaurant workers from the mescal-making village of Matatlán. Meanwhile the Luna boys reach the finals through superhuman effort, playing five games nonstop beginning at about 5:00 p.m.—and winning them all. At 7:45 p.m. they must again face Raza Unida, which has played only twice today.

The championship game takes place in bitter cold, yet with hundreds of spectators still on hand. For a while the Lunas keep things close. At halftime they trail by only five points. Zeus takes his team aside. The Lunas all have three fouls; four is the limit. "You have to finish them off," he tells them. But Raza Unida cannot. The Lunas don't foul, and though this is their sixth game without a rest, they start desperately pressing the length of the court. The cold is forgotten. Each basket brings an explosion of cheers from one side of the court or the other. Passions run high. "Learn to lose," comes a call from the Raza Unida cheering section. "It'll be the first time," the Luna side responds. In the last minutes of the game the cold, the grinding games it took to get here, and Raza Unida's speed and height wear down the Luna boys. Homes's warlike approach to rebounding is too much. Nacho Aquino is unstoppable. Raza Unida wins the game, 32–23, and the tournament, which ends under the lights at 8:20 p.m., three hours past sundown and more than twelve hours after it began.

The awards ceremony follows. Again Zeus has seen to every detail. The hosts of a sports show on Radio KWKW (1330 AM) have been invited to preside. Zeus has printed certificates of recognition for the referees, the sponsors, and others who helped out. Each is called upon to say a few words. Edgar Ruiz, of the New Oaxacan Alliance, says: "I'd hope tournaments like this would establish once and for all that we're not 'Oaxaquitos.' We're Oaxacans. Long live Oaxaca!" Then Zeus speaks. He's happy that the standard of Oaxacan basketball has been reinforced in this land of hoop infidels. This tournament is done, but for Zeus it is also prelude. Basketball is never over. Every detail he cared for is intended to make this year's tournament a success but also to facilitate next year's. He thanks the crowd and the players. Next year, he announces, he'll be organizing a series of southland tournaments, with the winners appearing on Thanksgiving in a tournament of champions.

Thanksgiving is evolving into the biggest Oaxacan-immigrant basketball day of the year in L.A. Though Zeus speaks of preserving Oaxacan tradition in the United States, his tournament is the most American of them all. It has sponsors; it is a secular event, not tied to any traditional village fiesta. America has given Zeus García something more than a livelihood; it is a place where Oaxacans need basketball as much as he does. With the L.A. Zapoteco community so large, the possibility of a second basketball life is only now becoming apparent to him. Several teams have asked him to coach. Others need help with their own tournaments. Some lowland villages have even begun organizing tournaments. At some point Zeus wants Raza Unida to tour Oaxaca for a few months, challenging teams around the state. Eventually, though, Zeus sees his current players leaving to form their own squads. He will continue to coach Raza Unida. He hopes it will become akin to a pro team—where players file through, then leave, but the institution remains to maintain the purity of Oaxacan hoops in the diaspora.

Late that night Chiquis and other teammates sit at a restaurant on Santa Monica Boulevard. "Are you going to write that we achieved something great?" he asks. Sure. Raza Unida achieved something great on that cold court on Thanksgiving Day after the sun went down. So did the Luna boys. Zeus and Isaias, too. You should have been there. Next year's should be even better.

Chiquis spoke once about winning tournaments. "It's like winning a piece of Oaxaca," he said. "To play here with my friends in a tournament is as if I were there in Oaxaca. When I retire, I want them to say, 'That guy, he played.' There's no money, but there is satisfaction from the competition, the game, the desire you put into it. That's what stays with you. Later they'll say, 'Those guys were good.'"

—1999

THE DEAD WOMEN OF JUÁREZ

Seven men were already in jail in Ciudad Juárez, charged in the serial murder of seventeen young women—the case apparently solved—when Sandra Juárez's body turned up on the banks of the Rio Grande.

One Saturday in July 1996 Sandra, seventeen, walked into Ciudad Juárez from Lagunillas, a village of forty adobe houses, thirty miles from the nearest telephone, in a parched region of the state of Zacatecas. She was no match for the city. On Monday she went looking for work in the *maquiladoras*—the assembly plants—that dominate the Juárez economy. A few days later they found her blouse on the Mexican side of the river. She lay strangled to death on the U.S. side. Her case has not been solved. No one knows where she went, or with whom, that Monday.

For the people of Ciudad Juárez, Sandra's case, and others that turned up that summer, played havoc with some accepted beliefs. Until then, for example, they had believed that the city's first serial-murder case, which had attracted news media from across Mexico and the United States, had been put behind them. They believed that a foreigner and a group of U.S.-style gang bangers were responsible. Given the town's border location, Juarenses are used to blaming things on people from somewhere else; 80 percent of the town's prison population is from somewhere else, is an oft-quoted statistic.

But about the time Sandra Juárez died, people in town finally had to start listening to Esther Chávez. Chávez is a thin, almost frail retired accountant who lives in a middle-class neighborhood of Juárez and wouldn't seem the type to get involved in a serial murder case. Nor did Chávez have much history of feminist involvement when she organized a women's group known as Grupo 8 de Marzo. But from newspaper clippings, Chávez had been keeping an informal list of cases involving dead young women ever since she noted the rape and murder of thirteen-year-old Esperanza Leyva on November 15, 1993. By that time the list was already thirteen cases long. "We

had gone to talk to the mayor," Chávez says. "He promised to get higher authorities involved. He was my very good friend, but he never did anything for us. What we were trying to get people to see was a general climate of violence against women."

The cases were notable in that the identifiable victims were usually young and working-class. A good number had worked in the *maquiladoras*. These were not murders of passion, taking place in a bar or bedroom. Some of the women had been raped, many had been mutilated, and a good many more had been dumped like the worn-out parts to some machine in isolated spots in the deserts surrounding the city. Their killer or killers didn't even take the trouble to cover them with dirt, believing, with good reason, that the sun and the desert's scavengers would quickly wipe their corpses from the face of the earth. By the summer of 1996 Chávez had counted eighty-six of these cases, dating back to Esperanza Leyva in 1993. Actually, that turned out not to be a whole lot in the larger scheme of things; Juárez tallies more than 250 homicides a year, of which a good number are drug-related executions and well more than eighty-six are gang killings. But Juárez is also a place where, according to the assistant attorney general based in the city, those who aren't gang members or drug smugglers can live free of the fear of murder. So the women's deaths, finally, were notable in their number as well. By the time Sandra Juárez's body appeared on the banks of the Rio Grande, people in town had to listen to Esther Chávez and consider the possibility that behind the dying women of Juárez was something even more disturbing than a lone serial murderer, something that had to do with what the town had become.

* * *

Ciudad Juárez spreads low, bleak, and treeless across the valley floor south of El Paso and the Rio Grande. The smell of fetid sewers is a constant companion through town, a nagging reminder that the desert is no place for a major industrial center.

Years ago Juárez thrived because it understood that beneath America's puritan rhetoric, a buck was always waiting to be made. During Prohibition, Juárez produced whiskey and beer and ran it across the border. Bars emerged along Avenida Juárez, the main drag leading to the bridge into El Paso, and have never left. "Divorce planes" brought American couples in to quickly end their marriages. To women looking for work, Juárez offered prostitution. Until the mid-1960s Juárez was a bustling city of sin.

Then the *maquiladoras* arrived. Over the next three decades the assembly plants turned dusty border outposts into major stops in the global economy, assembling televisions, telephones, appliances, clothes, calculators, car parts— all for export to the world's wealthiest market across the border. In Juárez several *maquiladoras* even count America's coupons.

Mexico began allowing *maquiladoras* on the border in 1964. The idea was to sop up migrant workers returning after the United States ended the so-called *bracero* treaty, a twenty-two-year-old agreement that allowed Mexicans to work seasonally and legally in America's fields. The *maquilas* began as an after-thought. But beginning in the late 1970s, the country lurched through recession after recession, and the peso steadily lost value. Many U.S. and foreign firms saw a payroll paid in a currency that always lost value as a nifty proposition. As Mexico staggered, the *maquiladora* sector along the border became an increasingly important job provider. Today some 970,000 people—mostly unskilled and low paid—work in more than 3,800 *maquiladoras,* completing in twenty-five years one of the most remarkable industrial transformations anywhere in the latter half of the twentieth century. Virtually all the plants are owned by foreign companies: General Motors, Ford, Hughes, Phillips, RCA, Sony, Toshiba, Daewoo, and on down to minor candy and clothing manufacturers.

Juárez saw the twenty-first century in the *maquiladora*. The city always had more *maquila* jobs than any other city—178,000 today. As the *maquila* grew, so grew Juárez. The city went from 407,000 inhabitants in 1970 to what townspeople can only estimate is about 1.5 million people today, with several thousand more wandering through in any given month.

But since in Mexico, border towns barely qualify as Mexican, Juárez was always last on the list when the central government in far-off Mexico City doled out the resources. The city couldn't provide basic municipal services for everyone the *maquiladoras* pulled from the interior. Urban planning was an impossibility. And on a *maquiladora* salary, no worker could afford much rent. So shantytowns leaped into the desert. They were without drinking water, sewers, parks, lighting, or paved streets. An apocalyptic folk craft—

shack building—developed, using plastic tarp and barrels, wood pallets, cardboard, wire cord—anything that was *maquiladora* detritus. Bottle caps were used for bolts. Nor was moneyed development controlled. A lot of people got rich selling the desert to foreign *maquilas*. Meanwhile a collection of cheesy strip malls hunkered down around town as developers mimicked what they saw across the border.

Juárez grew rootless and cold under the desert sun, a place to make money but not a place to love or know or drink from a faucet. Here five hundred street gangs fought a war of attrition among themselves; walking among the cars at intersections were Indians in plastic sandals hawking gum and Mennonites in overalls selling cheese; narcos in gold chains and snakeskin boots, driving Chevy Suburbans and carrying assault rifles, winked again at El Norte's puritan rhetoric and used Juárez as the mainline into the American vein. Coming off the border is a gaudy collection of neon nightclubs, advertising the profiles of buxom, naked women, and cheesy curio shops that sell tequila and serapes to day visitors from El Paso.

As Juárez grew, an anonymity that characterizes many large U.S. cities settled on it. Police make a lot of the fact that so many of the dead women—more than half on Chávez's list—are unidentified. Nor do they have missing-person reports matching their descriptions. No one claims these bodies. Their families in some isolated part of Mexico may believe they live somewhere in the United States or simply don't care where they are. This, police say, is what they're up against. One Mexican politician has suggested lowering *maquiladora* salaries and building a wall fifty kilometers out of town to staunch the flow of Mexico into Juárez. Meanwhile one citizens' group now gives seminars in high schools to educate newcomers on the city's history on the theory that people won't love what they don't know. It's hard to imagine a city with more bars over its windows and doors than Ciudad Juárez. Even in the shantytowns, where people have little to steal, some shacks of cardboard and plywood have barred windows. Everywhere, too, is the incessant babble of gang graffiti marking Juárez as a border town—too close to the gringo is what the rest of Mexico would say.

But Juárez offered jobs, and that makes it like America in the most important way. Like the United States, Juárez attracted Mexicans from the interior who were restless and willing to risk a lot to change their lives. People from rural states of Durango, Zacatecas, and Coahuila continue to trudge into Juárez in huge numbers, figuring anything is better than the brutish life of the bankrupt Mexican *campo*. But unlike the United States, which attracts mainly men, Juárez became a magnet for women, especially young women. The *maquila* did not, as Mexican planners hoped, employ many men returning from the United States. Instead the plants pulled young women to the border from deep in Mexico's countryside. In Juárez for many years, more than 80 percent of all *maquila* workers were women. Even today, with *maquila* work heavier, two-thirds of the *maquila* workforce is female. These were women with few of the skills that the industrial economy would reward. They were interchangeable and they moved frequently between jobs, which were generally similar in their monotony. Juárez thirsted for them, and the *maquilas* put up help-wanted banners that fly almost all year round.

* * *

One of the women that Juárez attracted was Elizabeth Castro, a seventeen-year-old who had come from the state of Zacatecas. On August 10, 1995, Castro's decomposing body appeared along a highway. At the time no one thought much of it. For a few days she even remained unidentified. Then, through August and September, the bodies of more young women began showing up, several of them in Lote Bravo, a magnificent sprawl of caramel-colored desert south of the airport. The doctors autopsying the bodies said some showed signs of being raped. Several of them were too decomposed to identify. Pressure mounted and headlines grew shrill. Juárez had seen a lot, but never this.

Juarenses were comforted, however temporarily, by the arrest in early October of Abdel Latif Sharif, an Egyptian chemist. Police accused him of killing the women, including Castro. (Witnesses were later found who said they'd seen Sharif and Elizabeth Castro in a club together.) The case finally had something Juárez was used to—a foreigner with a history. Sharif had lived in Florida for a number of years and there had been convicted of a variety of sex crimes against girls and spent time in prison. When the United States deported him, he didn't return to Egypt. He came to Juárez.

Police claimed the forty-nine-year-old Sharif had been prowling the downtown clubs that *maquiladora* workers frequented, seducing young women, then

killing them. But Sharif said he was innocent, a scapegoat for police under public pressure. He predicted the bodies would continue to appear. He was right.

Lomas de Poleo is a stretch of desert west of town littered with the wind-blown trash of clandestine garbage dumpings. Within a few months of Sharif's arrest, the decomposing bodies of young women began appearing amid the debris. A goat herder found three of them.

It takes a lot to shock Juárez, but the continuing discovery of bodies did the trick. Civil patrols were now organized to protect children getting out of school and young women as they returned home from their *maquila* jobs. The shantytowns of Anapra and Lomas de Poleo formed squads to comb the desert areas for more corpses. The newspapers were filled with the latest news, clues, and conjecture about the case. Police competence was routinely questioned.

Then one night in April 1996 the police raided clubs along Avenida Juárez, the bar-studded drag leading from El Paso, where officers had been working undercover. They arrested a gang called Los Rebeldes (The Rebels). The police theorized that Sharif paid Los Rebeldes to kill women while he was in jail to make it seem that the real killer was still at large. And there stood the police case.

But then came the summer of 1996. More dumped bodies showed up. They continue to be found. So while evidence points to a serial murderer in some of the cases, what now seemed clear was that Juárez had something much larger on its hands.

Indeed, since the arrests of Los Rebeldes in early 1996, the bodies of almost fifty women have turned up. Rocío Miranda, a bar owner, was raped by seventeen young men, then dumped in a vat of acid. The only parts of Miranda that remained when she was found were her hands, feet, and the silicon implants that police used to identify her. Silvia Rivera, twenty-one, was stabbed to death by her husband and buried out near the prison; she was first identified and buried as one Elizabeth Ontiveros, who'd been reported missing, until Ontiveros showed up, having run off with her boyfriend. Soledad Beltrán, a stripper known as Yesenia, turned up in a drainage ditch, stabbed to death, her killers unknown. Sonia Yvette Ramírez, thirteen, was raped and killed and left a block from police headquarters. Her father spent two months tracking down her boyfriend, who had fled south to Chihuahua City. There he cornered him in an auto-repair shop, thrashed him, and turned him over to police, who charged him with Sonia's murder. Brenda Nájera, fifteen, and Susana Flores, thirteen, were both raped, tortured, and shot in the head. An autopsy showed Susana had had four heart attacks before dying. And there were more women who turned up whose identity still is unknown, leaving behind only the grimy detritus of a dime-store novel: a tattoo on the wrist, black jeans, fingernails painted dark red, green socks, white panties, a black bra, and often the signs of rape. One woman was found with two brassieres lying by her side. Two others were found on a motorcycle racetrack in the desert, wearing slippers and bathrobes.

There was no one thing—or one person or group—to pin the bodies on anymore. If a serial murderer was at large, there was a lot of horrible other stuff going on as well. It came to seem as if Juárez was awash in dead women merely because it was Juárez.

✳ ✳ ✳

Among the corpses that summer was Sandra Juárez's. A lot about Sandra was typical of the young country women whose labor forms the backbone of Ciudad Juárez. Like many of these women, Sandra's last little piece of the world was a concrete-block house on the outskirts of town in a neighborhood with neither pavement nor a sewer system. Her street—Capulin Street—got electricity only five years ago. This is where her aunts and cousins live.

You get there by heading out Avenida Tecnológico east from downtown. Amid a battalion of billboards you spot Space Burger and the last gasp of Thunderbird Motors. A little ahead is Peter Piper Pizza, where "Lunch Paquets" can be had for 9.90 pesos. Over Wrinkled Bridge (Puente Arrugado) is the Mini-Super and a Del Río Superette, then the Autotel, with curtains over its parking spaces for maximum privacy, next door to the Silver Fox Piano Bar. Along the way is Autos Hawaii with its *"facilidades de pago"* ("easy payments"). As you head farther east you begin to see the squat *maquiladoras* where Sandra thought she glimpsed a future: Cadimex, FCM, the Los Fuentes Industrial Park now under construction ("Come Grow with Us").

In coming here, Sandra followed a new tradition for women in her family, indeed in most of her village. "There's no work there," says her cousin Joel Juárez, who left Lagunillas twelve years ago. "The men work part of the year

in the fields. For women there's nothing. Life's hard. About twenty years ago the first family left [for Ciudad Juárez]. They came back and told us about it, and we came running."

Behind her relatives' concrete-block house are signs of the limbo world between rural and postmodernity that Sandra's family occupies: a traditional adobe bread oven, a chicken coop, and a one-room shack made of pallets, cardboard, and plastic tarp discarded by *maquiladoras* where family members have worked. Their house stands as a symbol of the wrenching social changes that Ciudad Juárez is as unprepared to address as its residents' demand for paved streets.

People here surmise that these changes are one reason why women are murdered and tossed away. On display in Juárez is the quick and brutal mashing of a rural people into an industrial workforce. Thousands of women like Sandra come here, hoping to be part of it. The *maquiladora* yanked these women from the farm with the offer of their first paycheck; they became Mexico's "Rosie the Riveter." In a matter of a few years the *maquiladora* turned time-honored sex roles upside down: women became the family providers. *Maquiladoras,* for all the nastiness associated with them, created a new Mexican woman. *Maquila* workers often came to see the world, and their place in it, differently. But this same process did not create a new man.

The case of Marcela Macías, a thirty-five-year-old mother of four, is instructive in that regard. On June 19 Macías's decomposing body was found buried under some tires near a highway leading out of town. Two days later police arrested her husband, Ramón Ochoa, forty-nine. Ochoa told police that his wife had become more independent since taking a job at a *maquiladora* and had been talking back to him. He believed she had a lover. He said he would spy on her at work and see her eating lunch with other men. She told him she was going to sit with whomever she pleased. "My sister was very independent," says Macías's half sister, Silvia. "He was afraid of that and felt she was unfaithful." In the year since she took the job, the couple fought constantly. Ochoa said he strangled her during one such fight, buried her, and reported her missing.

"This is so symptomatic of the way men respond when women begin to leave home and to their not being dependent on them," says María Antonietta

Esparza. Community pressure surrounding the deaths of the women prompted officials to set up an office to handle reports of sex crimes and domestic violence, staffed entirely by women. Esparza, an attorney, is its director. She says men from rural areas are used to controlling women down to how they dress and speak. Women, once they get to the *maquila,* often aren't as disposed to take it as when they were down on the farm. No one knows how many of the cases of murdered women have to do with domestic violence or a general male resentment toward uppity women. But the reports Esparza's office handles have risen steadily every month in the year since it opened and show no sign of tapering off. Says Esparza: "We don't stop being part of a culture. In some sense, men may feel unprotected in not having a woman to cook and clean for them, like a mother. This vision of women's work is what makes them feel, when the woman does work, like they're losing control."

Esparza believes the crude and quick modernization of country women going on now in Juárez has another role to play in the killings. Nothing about Mexican country life prepares a young woman for Juárez. In their villages they're prohibited from even being out after dark; the first boy they sleep with they marry. But in Juárez all the chains come off. "They come from an atmosphere where they couldn't do anything to one where everything is within their reach. They're easy prey," Esparza says. "They come looking for work. They don't know the city. Don't know the conditions. Perhaps all they know is what they've heard in songs: 'Ciudad Juárez is *número uno.*' They go to these clubs, which are fertile fields for the commission of these kinds of crimes."

* * *

As the killings of young women progressed, police looked for reasons and thought they found one in the glut of clubs that thrived with the arrival of 178,000 *maquiladora* jobs. Following Sharif's arrest, detectives claimed the victims led double lives, unbeknownst to their families. After their *maquila* jobs, according to investigators, these women doubled as party girls in the dance halls of downtown Juárez. These claims earned the police no love among the victims' families, who vigorously denied them.

But whatever the truth of the matter and investigators' lack of tact notwithstanding, police were right about one thing: the bars and dance halls now

play an essential function in *maquiladora* life and for that reason probably have something to do with the killings. "*Maquila* work is long and monotonous. [The women] work eight hours, plus the time they spend in buses getting to work," says Esther Chávez. "So on Fridays and Saturdays they go dancing. They're looking for affection. Men there take advantage of them. [Women] have been taught to work. But they haven't been taught to live in a violent city with problems like this one. They come here very trusting, because in rural areas customs are much different."

The clubs are likely where some women met their killers. It's not a coincidence that these clubs are also the best public display of women's new economic place in this town. Juárez is full of young women with money and the freedom to enjoy it for the first time, thirsting for an escape from tedium and willing to throw caution to the wind.

Go to Juárez's central plaza before dawn on Friday and you'll see them. At 4:30 a.m. in Plaza de Armas the hulls of buses stand vacant and a light breeze blows the sounds of a taxi driver's radio across the square. By 5:00 a.m. more buses are arriving, here to take workers to the *maquiladoras* by starting time. And then suddenly the square teems with silent, scurrying people, an open-air Grand Central Station muted except for the sound of wrenching gears of dozens of *maquiladora* buses. The buses lurch to a stop, quickly take on passengers, then move out to deliver the assembly plants their workers by 7:00 a.m. This is simply part of many workers' withering daily routine; to get here on time, they must arise from their shanty at 4:00 a.m.

What makes Friday different is that on that day many women arrive at the square as if bound for some fashionable dinner party instead of eight hours of tedious assembly work. They're decked out in sheer black dresses, tight mini-skirts; an occasional ankle-length gown shuffles by on high heels over the cracked, gum-smeared sidewalk; hair is piled high, lips sparkling red, and fingernails glittering with polish. Since many workers live in shantytowns on the edge of town, going home after work is incompatible with having fun on Friday night. So every Friday before dawn, Plaza de Armas looks vaguely like a cocktail party.

Through the day they work. Then in the afternoon, they hit the clubs. By 4:30 p.m. on Fridays—an hour after work and well before the sun goes down—young women have packed the city's bars and dance halls, where they stay until early Saturday morning. It brings to mind a 1960s Friday night in Pittsburgh or Detroit, except the workers are usually teenage girls, not burly men in their thirties. To watch them arrive at the clubs is a remarkable and rare sight for Mexico: groups of three, four, and five women at a time file in, pay their own way, order their own drinks, light their own cigarettes. "They're all looking for a man," says a bouncer at El Patio, one of the most popular dance halls with *maquiladora* line workers. That's true. But the other truth is that the bars that once offered women for sale to gringos now must cater to Mexican women's new economic power. At some clubs women don't wait for men to ask and fill the floor dancing with each other. Moreover, a routine offering these days is "sexy boys" shows—male strippers. Nothing measures the cultural distance between Juárez and the isolated villages that provide it with workers like a woman who pays her own money at a club and gives a thumbs-up-thumbs-down to a man feverishly undressing on stage for her pleasure. Mexican village life leaves no room to conceive of such a thing.

One favorite place is Casino Deportivo on Avenida Juárez. Police say that Sharif was seen in this club with Elizabeth Castro. *Maquiladoras* do hire people in their late twenties and thirties, but they also wink at hiring kids under the legal age of eighteen. From Deportivo's clientele, *maquila* employees all, it seems that Mexico is industrializing on the backs of high school students. Under black lights kids dance to the polkas of a *norteño* band and then to the thunking bass of disco. They paste their home-state identity on their clothes in letters of white gothic script: ZAC—Zacatecas; COAH—Coahuila; DGO—Durango.

"We work all week, and on the weekend we've got to get out," says Anahy Rentería, a twenty-two year old.

She and her cousin, Marisela Martínez, seventeen, have come from the village of Canatlán in the state of Durango in the last six months. Now they're living with relatives and making television components at the Haromex plant. They are dressed identically in silver lamé blouses and black jeans, with DGO in enormous letters spelled out down their right pants legs, each of which cost them a week's salary. At home in Canatlán, there's nothing to

do and little work for women. Juárez is a fun park in comparison. "Things were so boring at home," says Martínez, "so I bugged and bugged my parents and they finally let me come here."

* * *

"Have you ever seen the film *Citizen X?*" asks Ignacio Alvarado, a reporter who has covered the murder cases for the *Diario de Juárez* newspaper, sitting in a cafeteria one morning. *Citizen X* was an HBO production starring Donald Sutherland and is based on the investigation into the first serial murder/rape case in the Soviet Union. Officials at the attorney general's office in Juárez played the film for their detectives investigating Sharif and Los Rebeldes. How much it influenced their investigative strategies depends on who you ask. Using the film was a bold move by a department looking for any edge it could find in its first serial-murder case. But it also highlighted what Juarenses say is another factor in the continuing murder of young women: a criminal-justice system utterly unprepared for today's Juárez.

Alongside the virtually absent public-work and social-work infrastructure, the city never developed a criminal-justice infrastructure worth the name. Detectives send bodies to the local university laboratory since they don't have a morgue lab of their own. They don't have gloves with which to handle evidence or bags to put that evidence in. Police officers number only about 1,200— 300 per shift—for a wild city of 1.5 million. The local jail was built for eight hundred prisoners yet now holds sixteen hundred. And in a city that has depended on female labor for three decades, Esparza's sex-crimes and family violence office has only been open since August 1996.

All this has become an issue because besides the continuing appearance of dead women—many of whose murders are unsolved—police have had no success in their case against the one man they have caught. The Egyptian has been in jail for almost two years, but he has yet to be convicted of anything. Judges have been reluctant to find him guilty on the available evidence and just as reluctant to face public wrath by letting him go. So he exists in legal limbo as investigators try to find enough dirt on him to convince a judge.

Police are undaunted. "Look how long it took to catch the killer in *Citizen X,*" says Jorge López, assistant attorney general. But the lack of results has simply confirmed Juarenses' fears regarding police competence. Victims' families generally feel that if they had been wealthy, police response to their daughters' deaths would have been overwhelming and more sensitive.

Astrid González sees more systemic problems, related to the city's inability to keep up with its population. Homicide detectives still receive only six months of training before they're put on the street, and then they're allowed only five gallons of gasoline per day, says González, who has organized a group known as the Citizen Committee in the Fight Against Violence. She remembers a case in which a man wanted for a long series of rapes was arrested robbing a woman. The judge, about to get off work, quickly set bail for the robbery but ignored the other cases that, though requiring lengthy paperwork, would have kept the suspect in jail without bail. The man hasn't been seen since. "Judges are poorly paid, too," says González. "Impunity promotes crime. People believe they can commit crime without punishment. They don't just believe it, either. They prove it."

The lack of confidence in the police has confused the case of the growing numbers of dead young women. Juárez wonders whether it's in the midst of an enormous serial murder, a variety of unrelated crimes with serial murder included, or whether there's been serial murder at all and the whole thing's just been bungled by the cops.

"I'll tell you about a case that says a lot about Juárez," says Jorge Ostos, a psychologist who runs the state police academy south of town. Ostos is a young, thin, articulate man given to diagramming his ideas on paper as he speaks. At one point he took a lot of derision for suggesting that the reason for Juárez's violence was that people had stopped believing in the Virgin of Guadalupe. As a metaphor, though, the idea isn't that far-fetched. The normal ties that bind Mexicans in community don't exist much in Juárez, which is a point Ostos likes to make. "When I was a kid, the parents in the neighborhood took part in raising you," he says. "If they saw you smoking or drinking, they'd say something. But today society is separated from itself."

The story he tells is of a ten-year-old girl, Ana-María García, who left home alone to visit her father, who lived a couple of miles away. Toward dusk she began the walk home, again unaccompanied. Near a liquor store her path crossed that of four teenage boys who had spent the afternoon inhaling a

variety of industrial solvents and were by this time quite out of their minds. They grabbed her as she walked by, put her in a car, taped her mouth, and took her to a nearby hill, where they raped her and stabbed her seventeen times. Her body was found a few days later.

To Ostos, the case illustrates two other problems that have accompanied Juárez on its march to modernity. One is the breakdown of the family—both the girl's family, who let her walk home alone, and the youths' families, who raised thugs. Accompanying that is the rise of drug abuse and gang activity. "I tell you this because a lot of people talk about a serial killer in Juárez. I don't discard the possibility," Ostos says. "What I'm sure of is that there are as many potential killers as there are drug addicts in this town. You've got the possibility of psychopaths on every corner. What happened [to Ana-María García] could have happened in all these cases involving murdered women in the last three years. The question is, do we have a serial killer or simply a whole bunch of psychopaths roaming the streets?"

Sitting in her office at FEMAP, Graciela de la Rosa tries to answer this question. FEMAP is a nonprofit organization that educates *maquila* workers on workplace rights and health issues. De la Rosa, a Juárez native, is a thick woman, a well-known firebrand around town. She has watched waves of *maquiladora* workers arrive in town while her city has moved out farther into the desert.

"It's obvious that many of these girls went willingly with their murderers," she says. "Why do they go? Because they're young. Sex plays a role. But most important is that they don't have the psychosocial resources to understand what's happening, to ask themselves if they should go, and to say no to a man.

"This is part of the collision of the migrant who's just arrived and has no resources to confront the dangers and complexities of this forced 'modernization' we have going on here.

"Children are blind before the *maquila*. Choosing between the village and the *maquila*, the *maquila* is better because although you're not paid well, at least you have food. But what happens to the migrant when she arrives? She immediately enters into this process of modernization that U.S. culture and Juárez offer her, which is without any substance.

"People never thought that the city needed housing, education, artistic activities. They only saw the money to be made selling land to the *maquiladoras*. So they created an industrial sector in a city without water. The city center is the mirror of Juárez's crisis. It's the proof that this is a sacked city. The only thing that remains intact is the cathedral. The church is the only value remaining in downtown. The rest is nausea. What do the businessmen do? They open their 'Juárez Moderno,' where there's cineplexes and malls.

"Meanwhile the *maquiladora* is now part of the family duty. The same in France during the 1800s, when the whole family had to work in the mines because one salary wasn't enough. Here the mother, the children, the whole family enters the *maquiladora* to survive. Here they're modernized through production.

"If you add to this education in crisis, institutions in crisis, government in crisis, what are you going to have? Crime, murder. The only way we're modern is in the producing.

"Crime has always existed," she says finally. "There are many mysteries in the human heart that contribute to that. So you can understand two, three, four of these killings from that point of view. But eighty-six murders is really the product of the circumstances; it's a product of the social decomposition of a place. The collective madness is making itself felt."

* * *

Juárez today is part Dodge City, part Dickens's London, nestled at the dawn of the twenty-first century.

The growing stack of unsolved cases of murdered women is in some twisted sense a measure of the city's growth, of the distance it's putting between itself and the Third World. "Perhaps the life that people led in Zacatecas or Durango, or in Juárez twenty years ago, was saner," says Jorge Ostos.

Perhaps that is part of what's behind these killings: that growth does not necessarily equal development or sanity, and Juárez's expansion was too quick, tore too many bonds that gave life balance. Juárez has married itself to the *maquiladora* for thirty years and, without an accompanying social development, those eighty-six women are the downside. Perhaps, too, it's that Mexico's rural young women have changed Juárez, responded to what it asked of them, and now are resented for it.

What can be said with more certainty, however, is that these cases reflect Juárez's anonymity. No one knows, or seems to care, what happened to most of the dead women of Ciudad Juárez. The cases have a public half-life of about three days anymore. They pile up, people shake their heads, and the women are left to be remembered only by their families. *Anónima* is the word that appears frequently on Esther Chávez's list. This is what Juárez has come to accept about itself today. The murder in 1979 of one *maquiladora* worker generated more outrage than most of the current cases combined. Life, after all, is not a Hollywood mystery. There is no resolution, no evil madman to conveniently pin it all on. The perfect murder is, it turns out, unusually easy to commit, especially when the victim is no one important, an anonymous figure, and Juárez has enough of those. All of which leaves Sandra's people up on Capulin Street with a lifetime of wondering ahead of them. "What we'd like is to know something," says her aunt, María de Jesús Vásquez, pleading, holding out her hands. "We don't know anything."

—1997

WEST SIDE KANSAS STREET

The Cervantes boys were wearing their long coats and their best Dickies on the eve of the celebration of the Virgin of Guadalupe as they waited for things to get as serious as they ever do.

Memo Cervantes had a bat tucked away. His cousin Juan de Jesús "Chin" Cervantes had a television antenna. José Cervantes, not related to either of them, was walking about with a lead pipe. The plastic jug of mescal was going from hand to hand as about fifteen Kansas Street guys huddled near Chin's family's house of stacked brick and corrugated tin.

"The Virgin doesn't like to see you like this," said his mother, María Aguilar, to the crowd of *cholos*.

In front of the house stood the moss-covered altar to the Virgin, backed by green, white, and red sheets of plastic. The altar was lit with candles and a string of blinking Christmas lights. María Aguilar watched it all and shook her head. "The Virgin is the mother of all Mexicans," she told me, watching Chin as he crouched near his friends. "With her, we leave our worries and our pains. With Chin, I've left it all in her hands. I just don't know if she's listening."

Florencio Cervantes rode up on a three-wheeled low-rider bike of his own design, blasting the *narcocorridos* of Chalino Sánchez from the speaker box between the two back tires. It was then that two unlucky fellows from a barrio down the street happened by. The Cervanteses got in a couple of solid kicks and a punch or two in the few furious seconds before mothers and fathers stepped in. Only Memo's father, Guillermo Cervantes, also known as John Lennon because he has long hair, stumbling drunk, wanted to pursue the issue. His son held him back. It was over. And it wasn't much. But they had proven to themselves that they were *cholos* worthy of the name and that this strip of Avenida Juárez, on the outskirts of Zamora, Michoacán, deep in the heart of Mexico, especially on the Virgin's night, belonged to a gang whose identity was borrowed from the streets of Los Angeles.

The Virgin of Guadalupe is the patron saint of Mexico's Indians and her poor. When Juan Diego saw "the dark virgin" in 1531, near the sanctuary of the Aztec goddess Tonantzin, his vision allowed millions of Indians to make their own peace with the culture of the conquering Spaniards. On her night, on Avenida Juárez, about every third house has an altar before it in her honor. Together they add some sparkle to what is normally a bleak two-lane thoroughfare. Looking down it that night, you couldn't even see the graffiti insisting that this ninety yards of Zamora is in the hands of a street gang called, in English, West Side Kansas Street.

I had first come to Avenida Juárez six months before, looking for a Mexican translation of the American dream. I found one version of it there amid West Side Kansas Street. The gang alighted on Avenida Juárez in 1991 after two young men returned from Los Angeles with tales of thrillingly bad things. The real Kansas Street is tiny and in the L.A. suburb of South Gate. The original West Side Kansas Street gang now claims large chunks of Maywood and Bell, other suburbs of L.A. But Los Angeles, as well as being the world's second- or third-largest Mexican metropolitan area, is Mexico's culture factory, an unswerving force that defines modern life with its image and its product. Mexican Indians centuries ago adopted and transformed part of an incoming foreign culture as a matter of coexistence when they transformed Tonantzin into the Virgin of Guadalupe. In the same way, in Zamora and other towns and villages, Mexican youths are performing their own syncretism with L.A.'s gang culture. Over the years a kind of gangland minor leagues has emerged across Mexico, a pre-NAFTA export mimicking L.A.'s big show. In Zamora gangs claim barrios from Venice and San Gabriel. One bunch of youths in Tangancicuaro, five miles from here, claims East Side Wilmas from Wilmington, where many townspeople have emigrated. The largest gang in Uruapan, seventy miles south, is from Long Beach. Its main competition is a gang from Pacoima. One short-lived gang there claimed East L.A.'s 18th Street. They also took English nicknames: Enrique became El Henry; Jaime, El Jimmy; Jorge, El George.

The trappings here are the same: baggy pants, tattoos, hand signs, graffiti. Here *homeboy, cruising,* and the classic L.A. *cholo* challenge to rivals, "Where you from?" have joined *diet* and *lite* as English additions to the Spanish vocabulary. What *cholos* here can't match, they work around: low-rider bicycles of spit-polished chrome instead of low-rider cars.

"If you think that there are two thousand miles between Zamora and Los Angeles, all this is strange to see," says Gustavo López Castro. "But when you think of the fact that there's no cultural distance, then it's not strange at all. The United States, speaking of its culture in the broadest terms, is here in Zamora."

López Castro is a spectacled, soft-spoken professor who specializes in immigration studies at the Colegio de Michoacán in Zamora. As a student in Baja California in the early 1980s, López Castro set out to write a doctoral thesis on *cholos* along the border. "I found that it was impossible to understand *cholismo* without understanding immigration," he says. The result was *La Casa Divida—The Divided House*—a book about immigrants from Gómez Farías, a nearby village, in Watsonville, California, that included a chapter on *cholos*.

"The border with the United States is here, not up there," he says. "The United States for these kids represents maybe not El Dorado but something very close to it, and not just for money or the access to work but also because of what they've lived through culturally here. The families speak of the United States almost every day—they're talking about relatives, their lives, their experience, their family history. They talk about the United States in the schools.

"If the kids can't go, they go to supermarkets and buy cereals—Cheerios. So the contact with the United States isn't imaginary anymore, but you can eat it. With *cholos* the United States is consumed not just by buying Cheerios but also through an attitude."

This describes many of the families of Kansas Street members. Few have many connections with the United States. But their children have walked out of Mexico into a corner of Los Angeles like it was home.

This is particularly true of one extended family, who over the generations has steadfastly ignored America's beckoning call. Julio Cervantes and his wife, María del Refugio, a half century ago cast their lot with Mexico, figuring that the United States was just too far from family.

Instead America came to them.

Today many of their grandchildren are the L.A.-style gang bangers of Avenida Juárez. Of the forty or so guys in the gang, about half are Cervanteses:

a bewildering web of cousins, second cousins, uncles, brothers, nephews, and brothers-in-law, all under twenty-five. The family's story is of what happens to Mexico's poorest who don't go to the United States, who have no access to dollars and must depend on what their country's economy can provide.

* * *

Field work and love brought Julio and María to Zamora in 1942.

Julio Cervantes met his wife while he was working on the railroad that passed through her hometown of Zacapu, Michoacán. Her brothers never liked him, but he was a tall, tough man and he stole her away to his home in Silao in the neighboring state of Guanajuato. "Now let's see what your brothers do," he said.

Railroad work couldn't support a family, so Julio hired himself out as a farmworker. Soon his children did too. But the fields of Silao were never as rich as those of Zamora, where wages were twice what Julio was making. And besides, María had some sisters there.

The couple came to Zamora at the beginning of a massive agricultural migration to the city lasting three decades. For a while the jobs in agriculture would come, pulling country folk from their unproductive land. Zamora was from time to time known as *El Norte Chico*—the Little North—because people knew only one place where jobs were more plentiful. But then the industry would bust, stranding new migrants. People like the Cervanteses found relatively steady work but at wages so low that economic progress was unthinkable.

Julio Cervantes remained a farmworker. But only with the added labor of his wife and children could the family support itself. They worked in the fields or in packinghouses. Combining their wages, they could afford nothing better than a rented barn for their first twenty years in town. Still, the Cervanteses stayed at it as Zamora lurched into becoming the second-largest city in Michoacán (population 225,000).

The change that created modern Zamora arrived, as many changes do in Mexico, from the United States. Until the 1940s Zamora was a small town, with an economy largely based on subsistence agriculture. The Green Revolution changed that. Imported fertilizers and pesticides brought new possibilities to the area. Zamora turned away from subsistence agriculture—away from beans and corn—and toward supplying the U.S. market with tomatoes, onions, and potatoes. When in the 1960s California investors found that strawberries could be grown in Zamora during the U.S. off-season, a boom brought thousands more people to town.

The agricultural revolution offered promise to a hungry and growing Mexico. But in Zamora it also posed the problem of how to provide jobs to a swelling population at higher wages. It was a dilemma Zamora never solved. The city's agricultural interests knew they had a good thing. They barred the door to industry, not wanting competition for their workers. Even in agriculture the town only hobbled along. Land remained in the hands of the wealthy while a poorly paid underclass went to the ever-extending edge of town. No one bothered to imagine anything different; in one of the most fertile regions of Mexico there is still no agency or university promoting agricultural research.

The year the Cervanteses moved to Zamora, 1942, was also the first year of the *bracero* treaty between the United States and Mexico. America, with its men at war, needed workers for its fields. Human labor being Mexico's main natural resource, the treaty worked well for both countries. Millions of Mexicans went north with seasonal contracts to pick fruit, cotton, and vegetables. Along with legally contracted workers, an even larger number of illegal workers made the trip as well. When the treaty ended in 1964, many areas in states like Michoacán and Jalisco had developed deep traditions of emigrating, legally or not, to *El Norte*.

Beginning with the *bracero* program, hundreds of thousands of people— sometimes whole communities—left northern Michoacán for the United States. The state is second to Jalisco in the number of emigrants it has sent north. Zamora and the surrounding towns contributed heavily to this exodus. Many nearby villages are virtual ghost towns, home now only to children, old people, and abandoned women.

For many young Mexican men, the United States became a short-term adventure, a rite of passage, a Mexican version of the American college graduate's trip to Europe. They would leave to find out if everything they'd heard was true, then return a few years later to say that sure enough, it was, adding some of their own tales to the body of lore.

But there was another large group of Mexicans who weren't looking for

adventure, for a rough two-thousand-mile journey to a hostile land away from family and friends. "Emigrants to the United States, independent of the social class, are more daring, more ready to change, than those who don't emigrate," said López Castro. "Zamora attracted people who wanted to change, but only within certain limits. They were not so ready to change everything they know."

That pretty much described Julio Cervantes. He worked for years picking crops for large landowners at a small fraction of the wages he could have earned on the other side. But the United States never appealed to him. "He always said, 'How can I leave my wife and family?'" his son, Florencio, now fifty-four, told me.

Julio's reluctance to change has been passed down. Only one of Julio Cervantes's nine children and only about a half dozen of his estimated forty grandchildren have ever been north—a minuscule number for this part of Michoacán. "I always wanted to go," said Roberto Cervantes, his oldest son. "But my father always said that I'd forget I had a family and get involved in bad things up there."

Still, the Cervantes family and thousands like them couldn't escape the heavy influence of the United States. Local agricultural barons were content simply to own the land, which always seemed to be worth more. Instead foreign capital, primarily from the United States, built and now owns Zamora's packing, processing, and refrigeration plants for the produce that, in one form or another, supplies the U.S. market. Even the new strawberry plants are grown in the United States, then transplanted in Zamora.

Today Zamora is an agricultural city—a paradox that is the essence of the street where Julio and María del Refugio eventually wound up.

* * *

Avenida Juárez runs through Zamora as straight and foul as a stiff middle finger. About two hundred yards past the center is the Zamora Refrigeration Plant, which was once on the city's outskirts. After that two thin lines of houses follow Juárez west out of town. Behind these houses stretch potato fields and untilled lots. The multinational Bimbo Corporation's food-processing plant stands in the distance. Here Juárez is inhabited by the poorest of the migrants of the last fifty years, whose lives and customs remain a rough mix of rural and urban, featuring little of the best of either. Here Avenida Juárez is an urban calamity. Traffic—screeching, dusty, unrelenting traffic—dominates life. The houses are sunken and set back only a couple of yards, swallowing all the exhaust and filth the road can cough up. "The traffic's so loud, it makes you stupid," said one woman.

In the mid-1960s, when Avenida Juárez was still a dirt road, Julio and María bought a couple of lots and stayed there as it grew out in unplanned, illegal developments that still don't officially exist. The Cervanteses are now starting their fourth generation of tomato sorters. Sorting tomatoes is a job that pays by the box—2 pesos per 25 kilos. It requires only rapid movement and the ability to get up at 5:00 a.m. and determine by quick feel whether a tomato is of good quality. "We're *cholos,* but we're hardworking," says Memo Cervantes. "We've all learned real young how to select tomatoes. When I was ten, I was working in that. Fast. My father, my uncles, they've all worked all their lives in that."

Amid the chaos on Avenida Juárez are modest but well-tended two-story houses of emigrants, freshly painted and with tiled floors. They are tangible evidence of what emigration to the United States can do for a family willing to risk a little. Yet none of the Cervantes clan seems too anxious to head north anytime soon. They and their Zamora-bound neighbors remain an insulated bunch. No one votes. No child has gone beyond elementary school. There's not a newspaper on sale for blocks. Not many people even leave Avenida Juárez for any length of time except to sort tomatoes downtown or pick them in the fields. "All the time I've been alive, I've been on La Juárez," Antonio Contreras, a seventeen-year-old Kansas Street member, told me in a statement that may be almost literally true.

As the gang was hanging out one day, I pulled out a tiny plastic box that carried a microcassette tape. I was besieged by kids and teenagers who examined it like a scientist would a moon rock. So, too, did photographs and my camera's zoom lens go over big.

Most houses have television, which brings some outside influences, usually the most cynical entertainment Hollywood has to offer. About the only other major agents of change are the young men who have briefly left Avenida Juárez to test their mettle and earn some money in the great Norte and return to tell about it. One of those young men was Manuel Ramírez, who, in 1991, reappeared along Juárez after two years of running and ducking on the streets of Los Angeles.

* * *

Manuel—also known as Simio or Monkey for a nose twitch he sometimes affects—is a gaunt, handsome young man with brushed-back hair and a mirthless laugh. Now twenty-seven, with one son and another child on the way, he's married into the Cervantes family and his gang-banging days are drawing to a close. But his attitude toward life remains grounded in a few street principles: an unbending disdain for police, an unwillingness to question the morality of almost any act he can get away with, and thus utter scorn for anyone—cop or rival gangster—who didn't do him in when given the chance.

Simio doesn't hang out much on Juárez anymore. The police have been looking for him since he stole a couple of cars. He spends a lot of time raising his fighting cocks and with his "business," which he's not too anxious to discuss. But he strives hard to maintain his place in history as the one who brought West Side Kansas Street to the Avenida and taught everyone how things are done in Los Angeles.

In 1989 Simio left Zamora running. He and a friend, Alejandro Camarena, had been planning an L.A. trip for a while. The morning of the day they left, they went to an acquaintance's house, intending to simply take a boom box from him. In the struggle Simio stabbed the owner in the stomach. The tape player fell to the ground and shattered. That night they took the bus to Tijuana.

Simio's years in Los Angeles weren't an example of the admirable contribution immigrants make to America. Compared to Zamora, L.A. was for Simio a fun park of bedazzling criminal possibilities, allowing his highly developed street instincts their fullest expression. When Simio says he liked the United States because "it's not like here. You could go around the corner and make five dollars," he doesn't mean the boundless job opportunities America offers an immigrant; rather, the houses and cars were busting with stuff to steal. He spent two years there in a prolonged spasm of burglaries and drug use, of running out of a.m.-p.m.s with hot dogs, or liquor stores with beer, of cutting car-lot fences and rolling out new Buicks, and chases with cops and rival gangs—stories that invariably end with Manuel Ramírez outwitting everybody.

The first thing he did on arriving in Bell, where his sister and her children lived, was to ditch the coyote, whom he owed four hundred dollars for the ride from Tijuana. Bell is just south of Los Angeles, a working-class suburb of small single-family homes that years ago was all white and now is virtually all Latino. On first glance, Bell was disappointing. It wasn't the opulent Los Angeles he'd been promised. "I thought it would be cooler. I thought it'd be more like what people had told me. But it wasn't," Simio says. "All the houses were the same. It was kind of dead, though I saw there were all kinds of chances to steal."

Simio met up with West Side Kansas Street that first week in Bell. They were hanging out near his sister's house. He traded them a gold chain for some weed. People along Avenida Juárez in Zamora have been paying for that chance meeting for several years now. The way Simio tells it, after a while he was being recruited by both 18th Street and Kansas Street, but the latter seemed a better fit. "I was going around with them every day anyway," he said.

The gang hangout was the railroad tracks or the home of Bobby Cerna, "Zapata," who was that rare thing, an old junkie. The gang would help Zapata fix, and take him to the hospital when he got sick. For Simio, joining Kansas Street was a natural extension of his Zamora life. He and Camarena had tried to set up "Barrio Juárez" on the Avenida. It hadn't amounted to much. Now, with Kansas Street, he was clearly in the big time. And as he tells it, he stood out. "I woke those guys up," he told me. "They were all asleep. They didn't have the urge to rob. They were afraid. They weren't stealing anything."

He also discovered crack. He smoked it for the first time with some Kansas Street guys about three months after arriving in Bell. "I had only been smoking weed and I was looking for something stronger, pills or something." Crack was a revelation for Simio. He had picked up a strong taste for marijuana and glue as a youngster in Zamora. But there was nothing like the fantastic, short-lived high of the hard-boiled cocaine. It came to embody everything electric and powerful about the United States and remains the aspect of American life of which he speaks most fondly. The car exhaust on Avenida Juárez reminds him constantly of the drug.

Within a few months he had quit his minimum-wage job at an Alhambra ceramics factory, after stealing several boxes of plates. He left his sister's house, and the street became his home, crack his constant companion. "When I went

[north], I told myself I'd go to earn money, but that was just talk," he says. "It all went for drugs. I'd even go out in the rain, go buy a little piece, go back, smoke it. It'd still be raining and I'd go back, buy another piece. It was great.

"I'd rob two houses during the day, then one more at night. Jewelry, money, the VCR. I'd sell it all on the street. I'd spend a thousand dollars in a night. More and more. The crack worm was always wanting more. By the morning I'd have nothing."

He remembers breaking into a house and finding handcuffs, leather wear, and a vibrator. He remembers going to the beach and stealing a cooler filled with beer and yogurt from a car: "Those American girls really love their yogurt." And he remembers a few close calls: surprising a woman who was in bed watching television; breaking into a home he thought was unoccupied to find the owner in underwear listening to music on headphones.

The beginning of the end of his U.S. tour came as he, Camarena, and a Kansas Street friend were breaking into an apartment. Simio was lookout. He saw a patrol car swing onto the street and gave three sharp whistles. Their friend heard the warning and took off. Simio began walking and dropped his .22 pistol into an open car window. Camarena was too busy inside to hear anything. He served fourteen months in state prison for burglary and was deported.

Simio told the police he was seventeen and spent three months in juvenile hall on a weapons charge. Eight months later he returned to Mexico to visit his mother. Zapata told him not to go. "You'll just starve to death in Mexico," he told Simio. It was supposed to be a two-month visit, but Simio wound up getting married and not going back.

Zapata wasn't that far wrong. Simio returned with almost nothing. The thousands of dollars he'd made working and thieving had fed the crack worm. He spoke only a few words of English and he'd seen almost nothing of the United States but the streets of L.A. The most important things he brought back from his adventure were West Side Kansas Street, his tattoos, his stories—usually beginning with words like, "I stole this car one time"—and a baggy pair of brown Dickies. And his first day back he took it all out onto Avenida Juárez.

The Cervantes family *cholos* and others in the gang today speak ardently of their devotion *"para siempre"* to Kansas Street—which their mouths sculpt into something that sounds like "Kansas City." Many have tattooed KST on their backs and hands, homage to a street they've never seen and can barely pronounce. When I asked them why, they'd look at me quizzically and tell me that Simio brought the barrio back with him. That's reason enough.

"I talked to them about the barrio there," Simio told me. "I taught them the hand signs. I told them how it was almost like the mafia was there. I came back dressed real down and I told them how all the guys there went around dressed down in their Dickies. I told them about how we attacked other gangs, how we hung out. I told them that when somebody came into the barrio, we ran them out. When I got here, they weren't doing that."

And as he taught them, he changed the face of Juárez. Along side the BJZ—for Barrio Juárez—he sprayed KST and 13, the symbol of La Eme, or Mexican Mafia, California's first prison gang, which has been appropriated by virtually all southern California Latino gangs and now gangs in many emigrant towns in Mexico. Soon the Kansas Street graffiti dominated the road between the Zamora Refrigeration Plant and the adjacent barrio, Generalíssimo Morelos. "He wanted to unite us and he did it," says Antonio Contreras.

Simio became a major source of information on L.A. life for the Cervantes youth and their friends. His stories still mesmerize the guys who've never been north, their general impression being that Los Angeles, and by extension California and the entire United States, is no place for the timid. "From what I hear, I don't think I'd like it," says Pepe Cervantes, Simio's twenty-one-year-old brother-in-law. "All I hear is bad news. You know, here you can hang out anywhere without being bothered. But a Mexican who goes over there, he can't leave his apartment like he can here because of all the gangs, the drugs, violence. Plus he'll get hassled by the *migra*."

For the younger Cervantes crowd, a safer alternative to heading north was joining West Side Kansas Street, the Zamora chapter. It was convenient, obviously less dangerous, and all that grabbing a piece of L.A. involved was a thirteen-second beating and a trip downtown to the market for a pair of Dickies. Most of the guys in Kansas Street made sure I knew that before Simio returned, everyone was wearing tight pants, like some farmhand from the *campo*. But seeing Simio in his Dickies, straight out of L.A., was enough to

spark a sea change in Avenida Juárez fashion.

Dickies are sturdy, cheap pants—coming in routine colors of black, brown, gray, blue—made for those who work as janitors, as landscapers, in construction, or in the fields. They're also worn by the preppie sailboat crowd. The ingenuity of the L.A. *cholo* has turned his father's work pants into high ghetto style. Dickies are all over Zamora. In the market it's hard to find them with less than thirty-eight-inch waists, though the inseams are twenty-eight inches or shorter.

The transition was lightning quick. They say Juan Briseño was the first along Juárez to jump in. "Simio came back all dressed down, with his Dickies. I just liked how it looked," Juan says. Memo Cervantes, tall, husky, and good-hearted, felt the same way and jumped in next: "Miguel Núñez and I had a little fight. But I told Manuel, I'm not going to hit him because he's my friend. So we just kind of lightly hit each other. We weren't really hitting. It went on for thirteen seconds." Pretty soon guys along Juárez were jumping into Kansas Street every day. Camarena remembers that when he came back three months later, "there was Kansas Street graffiti all over the place."

All this was duly noted by the children on the block, for whom Simio and Camarena and the newly christened Kansas Street crowd became the guys they looked up to. One of them was José Cervantes—despite his last name, not a member of the Cervantes clan—who was eleven when Simio returned home. He remembers watching Simio and the older guys play video games. "I liked how they hung out. They were into marijuana, thinner, glue," he said. "I said when I'm older, I'll jump in."

Now fifteen, José's thin body curves and hunches into a perpetual question mark. It matches his face, which is screwed into a look of constant perplexity. His words come as if squeezed from his body, every sentence requiring immense energy to finish before the thought collapses in exhaustion. He rarely sits but rather crouches on his haunches, a position for which the kids in Kansas Street have developed a Zen-like tolerance. José smoked marijuana for the first time when he was thirteen, alone in a field off the street, made from the remains of smoked joints and rolled in an old bus ticket. A week later he jumped into Kansas Street. "I just wanted to hang out," he says. "To hang out you have to jump in." So three of his friends beat him up for thirteen seconds.

Suddenly José was a *cholo*.

The first thing José did was buy a pair of Dickies—the first pants he ever bought, using money he made picking potatoes for 25 pesos a day. "They're size forty-four waist," he remembers. "They fit my old man and he's a fat guy." Not long thereafter, he began having Camarena tattoo his body. José's hands and back are engraved with his gang's initials. His torso bears the name of his mother and her last name, Cervantes, which he prefers to his father's name of Macías.

Mercedes Cervantes is an elderly lady whose life has ill prepared her to understand what her son has become. She grew up near Guadalajara and followed her husband around Mexico for a few years before they finally settled on Avenida Juárez in the 1960s to work in the strawberry fields. There she's remained, caring for the family home, though almost everyone in her life— her husband and eight of her children—has left it. Only José remains. "He turned out bad," she says, standing in the doorway as the deafening trucks roll by. "He goes around with these baggy pants, hanging out with his friends. He never wants to work. I tell him he shames me. He embarrasses me going around like that. People reproach me. I tell him I'm going to have your brother in the United States take you and get you lost up there."

As we talked on her doorstep, Mercedes Cervantes remembered better days. She pulled out a photo album, filled with pictures of weddings, babies, and baptisms. The best shot is of a younger José, smiling widely and dancing arm in arm with his mother. On the album's inside cover is the evidence of what José has become: KST, SUR, X3 in gothic script, the hieroglyphics of L.A. streets.

José's Kansas Street membership has split the family. He once stole 1,500 pesos from a brother and with two Kansas Street friends took a bus to Tijuana, planning to visit L.A. and the gang he claims but has never seen. "They've been telling me that everything's great there, that there's money and you never lack for food," he told me. "I just wanted to go so that no one can tell me about it, so that I know.

"Manuel told us that all we had to do was get to Maywood and look for Kansas Street—West Side Kansas Street, not South Side Kansas Street—and tell them that we knew Simio, but that we'd probably have to be jumped in

again. He told us we'd get there all poor looking and that they'd give us some money for clothes. He told us we'd be able to check out houses, break in and just steal money, jewels.

"On the bus a guy saw my tattoos and my Dickies and he told me to watch out when I got to L.A. and that I should pray to God to bless me."

They got as far as the Pacific coast state of Sinaloa before police stopped them for traveling underage. An understanding bus terminal manager allowed them aboard a bus back to Zamora. When José returned, his mother threw him out. Most of his siblings wanted his mother to leave him on the street. But Mercedes Cervantes couldn't reject her youngest for long. Two months later she took him back in, and several of her children haven't spoken to her since. José reciprocates by not smoking cigarettes around the house. "It's just the respect I have for her," he says.

* * *

Like Mercedes Cervantes, none of the Kansas Street parents profess any understanding of what has happened to their children. "It's a disaster," says María Aguilar. "They're lost. They don't have any self-worth and they don't know how to say no to people who lead them along. Plus they don't do anything."

That's true. Despite their exotic look, West Side Kansas Street spends each day in a pitched battle with persistent boredom, unleavened even by violence. They work sporadically, don't read, and along Avenida Juárez, or anywhere in Zamora for that matter, there's not much to do. Most girls in the neighborhood are under strict orders to avoid Kansas Street unless they have the misfortune to be married to one of the gang members. Then the guys usually do their best to avoid them.

One day melts unspectacularly into the next, taken up *cotorreando*—hanging out—which is to say consuming withering quantities of pills, marijuana, glue, cheap mescal, and nonfilter cigarettes. The Kansas Street *cotorreo* doesn't involve a lot of philosophical discussion on its place in the world, perhaps because it's too painfully obvious what that place is. Rather the talk gets disjointed and bizarre. Homosexuals, it was decided one night, had a surplus of female blood. But no one ever determined once and for all whether an albino could actually be Mexican.

Having spent several days mired in this boredom with them, I was eager and surprised when they told me that the following Monday would be a soccer day. It was something different, a break from the tedium, so I showed up early. As it turned out, soccer day was the *cotorreo* taken about as far as it could go.

The terrain was a weed patch leading to the potato fields behind the home of Filiberto Hernández, a former member of the federal judicial police, Mexico's version of the FBI. The judicial police are charged with combating the drug trade. Beto, while still a police officer, one night a couple of years ago ate some hallucinogenic mushrooms, began playing with his favorite pistol, the one he calls *La Morena*, and shot out his right eye.

We cleared the field of broken bottles, jagged rocks, and dirty disposable diapers. Near the houses children scampered about shoeless and shirtless, riding crooked tricycles or bouncing on rusty mattress springs. The game began. I lost my team two games as goalie, sprained my thumb, and decided to retire to the full enjoyment of cheap cigarettes. I sat down next to Huacho—Juan Sánchez. Huacho can be a pleasant sort. But now he was hard at work burning his mind with the fumes of shoe glue, the start of what would become a four-day binge.

No one in Kansas Street really trusts Huacho. He's had children with a Cervantes woman, but he also beats her. Plus he has the poor manners to hang out with Barrio Pobre Generalíssimo when the odds seem to warrant it. Barrio Pobre is what passes for Kansas Street's mortal enemies ever since Barrio Pobre attacked some Kansas Street guys for no reason. Since then the gangs have developed a tepid rivalry—trading rocks and fists—which Kansas Street does its level best to take seriously. So Kansas Street looks askance at people like Huacho who straddle the line.

At the soccer field, as I sat down next to him, his eyes were wide and raving. Glue was stuck to his lips, and he wanted money for more. When I told him to forget it, he growled and gave me a couple of seething looks. I moved away.

Soccer day continued on through the afternoon, ending hours later in a marijuana-and-mescal haze, consumed around a table where some older

Cervanteses were playing dominos. Inside the shack in front of us, women with kids on their hips cooked supper over a fire on the hard-packed dirt floor.

The houses are pretty much as they were when Julio and María moved here thirty years ago. Corrugated tin and two-by-fours. The houses sometimes flood when it rains. One Cervantes shack is long and narrow, with wires running the length of it, providing electricity for bare lightbulbs. The shack actually has two floors, the second of which is a bedroom for a few children. Between fifteen and twenty people, all Cervanteses by birth or marriage, live in an area of twenty by fifty feet. A massive homemade television antenna rises above it. "It gets three channels at the most," says Memo Cervantes, passing me the jug of mescal.

Meanwhile Juan Briseño rolled joint after joint. Marijuana grows rather nicely in the hills of Michoacán, and it's pretty cheap (ninety dollars a pound). So Juan has developed a powerful taste for the herb. He spends large parts of his day rolling joints and has thus become a true craftsman. Marijuana may be cheap, but rolling papers aren't. So he and the Kansas crowd use almost any paper available. Not restricted by the limitations of regular rolling papers, Juan's joints become long, thick creations.

Juan spent a few years in Watsonville, California. That's where he bought the parts for what is regarded as the toughest low-rider bike in the whole set. Juan's *bica* has a purple frame and a black banana seat, riding a little more than a foot off the ground. The whitewall tires are encased in chrome rims, with seventy-two chrome spokes each. The bike has chrome fenders, mirrors, and handlebars and an ornamental chrome welded-chain steering wheel. In Watsonville, Juan has a crown that fits in the center of the steering wheel and emits perfume. The parts to all this cost him one thousand dollars. It's the only thing besides clothes he brought back from three years in California.

Still, it's a lot. Not many kids in Kansas Street can afford even a stripped down *bica,* which generally run about 300 pesos. For them and other *cholos* in Zamora low-rider *bicas* remain the status symbol, a car being beyond the realm of possibility. Since the bikes are so close to the ground, only the shortest kids can really pedal them without knocking their knees against their arms. Everyone else, like Juan, spends a lot of time walking them down the street.

To Florencio Cervantes, all these *bicas* means business. The low-rider bikes

that mesmerize his cousins and uncles and many other Zamora *cholos,* Florencio
has transformed into a cottage industry. Florencio is a friendly twenty-four-
year-old with no schooling. In Cervantes tradition, he began working at seven,
sorting tomatoes in packing plants. Two years ago he got a welding job that
pays 400 pesos (sixty dollars) for a sixty-hour week, no eye protection. He
began indulging his tinker's instinct. His first *cholo* bike didn't go well. But
since then, Florencio has created some low-slung masterpieces.

His imagination may be a reason why he's one of the few Cervantes grandchildren who have ventured off Avenida Juárez and north to the United States.
"You know, I saw guys who came back and they were saying that everything's
cheaper and what I'd earn in a month here I'd earn in a week there," he says.
Florencio was thirteen when he asked his father if he could go. Absolutely not,
he was told. He knew no one there and nothing about the country. So one day
after the tomato work was done, Florencio packed two shirts, two pairs of
pants, and 180 pesos and without telling anyone hitched a ride on a coal train
north to the California border. He arrived blackened from head to toe.

He crossed the border with a boy he met in Tijuana. They ended up in San
Bernardino, where they slept in a garbage dumpster for a week before Florencio
decided he'd had enough. "It was my little adventure," he says. "I came back
humiliated. People would ask me about it and I'd say, 'I don't even want to tell
you.' I was down to eating moldy bread covered with ants that I found near
the freeway."

Since then, Florencio has settled down. He's married with two children,
whom he supports with money from his welding job and the sale of his odd-
fangled *bicas*. His newest creation sits in his front room. It's built around a
purple Schwinn frame, with the front forks stretched forward. It has ten speeds,
a black banana seat, three twenty-inch whitewall tires, a headlight, foldable
mirrors, a digital clock-radio and tape deck, an equalizer, four six-inch speakers in a wood compartment that also has room for a six-pack of beer, a fifty-
watt amp powered by a rechargeable car battery, and shock absorbers that
support the whole thing and allow the rider's butt to glide about eighteen
inches off the ground. A *cholo* in a neighboring barrio has offered him 1,500
pesos for it, but Florencio wants 2,000. "These little *cholos* really love to go
around on these things," he says. "I figure that they just want to be like the

low riders up there. They can't afford cars, so they just get these bikes."

* * *

After people noticed me hanging around Kansas Street, several adults began to strike up conversations, wondering what a gringo was doing on Avenida Juárez. "I hope you tell them not to cause any more trouble," one Avenida Juárez shop owner told me one day.

For their neighbors, Kansas Street is another cross to bear for a barrio already burdened by so many. There's the traffic, the poor wages, the lack of trustworthy drinking water, and now the children are strange-looking hoodlums. After a while many of the residents and businesspeople began offering their analyses regarding the kids of KST. Some told me they're not surprised the gang exists: that's what happens to Mexicans who venture north into America's decadent gut. "Here we have the bad habit of imitating the bad habits of the United States," said David Silva, director of the city police department. "They're not a mafia or even well organized. These kids are just trying to imitate people who come back from up there."

I spoke to Javier Partida, who manages a fertilizer warehouse the gang had also broken into. Partida has been threatened by Kansas Street but didn't look too spooked. "I think they're just misdirected kids," he told me. "I think it's just their way of feeling important, of not being ignored. Mexico's problems of unemployment, the economic crisis, the lack of education, all come together in these kids—though that doesn't justify what they're doing."

A few blocks off Juárez, José Luis Manzo, director of the CRREAD drug rehabilitation clinic, was mildly amused at the thought of *cholos* in Mexico. Manzo has fit a lifetime of madness and grief into his twenty-three years. He spent time as a teenage heroin dealer in Los Angeles and Washington state where, while he had the smack, money was as easy as sex with fourteen-year-olds. He wound up a few years later an addict, sleeping near garbage dumpsters. "In Los Angeles all the *cholos* go around with big fancy cars, nice shoes and pants, big muscles. In Mexico they're walking around in sandals.

"The United States is number one in movies, number one in clothes, number one in drugs, number one in gangs, in guns, in money, in everything," Manzo says. "People see this on television, in the movies. I used to go watch

Bruce Lee and Jackie Chan movies. *Aiiiiiyah,* knocking people all over the place. I wanted to do that.

"Everything that's from the United States is number one. People want to be the same. People come from down below, and what do they want? U.S. clothes. They want American tennis shoes. They don't know it's made in China. It's that they bought it in the United States. Reebok. Nike. All that. It's American."

When sociologists talk about *cholismo* in the United States, there's usually a lot of discussion of the ghetto Chicano's nihilistic rejection of U.S. dominant culture. The kids of West Side Kansas Street stand that interpretation on its head. They fully embrace the part of American culture they know. They proudly told me they are "100 percent Mexican," but Mexico has given them little to hold on to. They are poor and barely literate, Mexico's glue-fried, undernourished, barely employable future—empty vessels into which can be dumped almost anything that glitters.

If Avenida Juárez is any indication, the beacon of the United States shines a different image to the world's poor than most Americans like to think. Here America is not about grassroots democracy, individual initiative, every man a king. It is not the country of Thomas Jefferson, Duke Ellington, and Mark Twain. Instead America is the land of Madonna, of diet Coke, the Dallas Cowboys, and a pair of pants known as Dickies.

Wandering down Avenida Juárez once more before I left, I passed a video store that rented nothing but Hollywood high-tech shoot-'em-ups and their Mexican low-budget imitations. This is America to the kids of West Side Kansas Street: a rootless, Walt Disney urban nightmare of tantalizing glitz and violence, where a boy becomes a man and women, guns, and money are easy. Standing in front of that shop, it occurred to me that U.S. marketing has won the battle for Avenida Juárez; America is now a product for mass consumption, and the kids of West Side Kansas Street bought in long ago.

Yet this is also why there's something about West Side Kansas Street that doesn't ring true. Like a Japanese blues band—Kansas Street is playing all the right notes, but something's missing. This comes out in their attitude toward guns. Though *cruising* and *homeboy* are now part of the Mexican gang lexicon, *drive-by shooting* isn't yet. To some extent, Mexican law has restricted firearms.

And West Side Kansas Street is still only a ragtag group of desperately poor drug users, not dealers. For the time being Mexican street gangs are without the income that would catapult their minor neighborhood beefs into major wars.

Nor does that seem to bother anyone. Kansas Street picks and chooses when consuming L.A.'s gang culture, happy to overlook the high-powered artillery. Most still prefer rocks or knives. The boys from Kansas Street say they could come up with a gun if the need arose. But Julio Quiroz told me: "We just stick to what people are throwing at us. If they're using rocks or knives or something, that's what we'll use."

Quiroz is chubby cheeked and eighteen and, like a lot of the guys in Kansas Street, he's quiet and generally polite around strangers. He referred to me always in the formal *Usted,* even after I asked him to use *tú.* Having a gun might appeal to him at times. But he seemed content to avoid them to also avoid proving he was willing to use one. *Cholos* here can sneer with the best of them. But despite their wholesale appropriation of a corner of Angelino culture, they're looking for a lot less trouble than they'd find on L.A. streets. Donning *cholo* garb is a way of getting through adolescence as much as anything else. As tough as their lives have been, they're still the product of a Mexican province, where innocence still lives. Here the streets aren't as mean. Teenagers don't spray neighborhoods with bullets. And they don't smoke around their parents. Not yet.

—1995

1. Chalino Sánchez. *(Courtesy of Pedro Rivera, Cintas Acuario.)*

2. José Santes and Salvador Valdes on the afternoon of their lynching.
    (Courtesy of Jorge Muhedano.)

3. *Luis Guerrero, formerly of Oaxaca, now of San Quintín, Baja California.*

4. *The Apostolic Assembly of the Faith in Christ Jesus in San Quintín.*

5. Zeus García
and Raza Unida.

6. The monument
to the paleta at the
entrance to Tocumbo,
Michoacán.

7. *St. Isaac and St. Martín de Porres*
   in Nueva Jerusalen on All Saints' Day.

8. *Saints lining up to vote.*

9. *St. Zachariah at the guard shack at Nueva Jerusalén on All Saints' Day.*

10. *Verónica Castro. (Courtesy of Enrique Caballero.)*

11. Miss Durango.

*12. Left to right,
La Calabasa, La Karen,
La Daniela,*

13. *Queen Abenamar I.*

14. *The cholos of West Side Kansas Street, with author.*
   Simio is at far right.

15. *The grave of Aristeo Prado in Jaripo, Michoacán.*

16. *The Narcosaint, Jesús Malverde, with his apostle, Eligio González.*

THE BRONX

It was getting toward 3:00 p.m. one spring day in Mexico's Congress, and the Bronx wanted to get to lunch. Standing before it at the podium was Gabriel Llamas, of the opposition National Action Party (PAN). Llamas was commenting on some social security reforms that were up for a vote and looked to be finishing his speech, which was what the Bronx, muttering under its collective breath, was fervently hoping he'd do. Then he asked to be allowed a few more minutes before the recess.

I was standing amid the Bronx, and I could see this was going to be unacceptable. A groan went up. The Bronx was hungry. Their stomachs were growling. They had little patience for guys like Llamas who could waltz up to the podium to speak anytime they pleased. I don't remember if anyone in the Bronx stood up and grabbed his crotch in response to Llamas's request, though it wouldn't have surprised me. The Bronx did do what it does best: it let Llamas have it. "Put a lid on it!" "Pinocchio!" "Sit down!" "Hypocrite!" "Go get paid!" The catcalls pelted down from their far corner of the Chamber of Deputies.

"When dogs bark, you have to feed them," said Llamas from the podium. "Woof, woof."

This was my *bienvenida* to the Bronx—the bad boys of the Chamber of Deputies, Mexico's lower house of Congress.

The Bronx is the name given to, and proudly worn by, those PRI congressmen who sit in seclusion in the chamber's right field and spend their time heckling and insulting speakers from other parties. Their party doesn't let them publicly participate in chamber debates. Nor does it often ask them how they'd like to vote, or what changes they'd like to see to proposed legislation, or their opinion on budget priorities. There isn't much that the Bronx gets to do at all except do what it did to Llamas.

Thus relegated, *Bronxistas* have developed their own style of being deputies that is based on vulgarity, mimicry, and loud wisecracking on chamber

events from which they are otherwise barred. Imagine a Greek tragedy with a chorus of pro wrestlers and frat boys, and you have a good idea of Mexico's Chamber of Deputies with the Bronx in the house. When a speaker discusses a gripping issue facing the nation, the Bronx can be counted on to point out that he is a . . . "Clown!" or a . . . "Fatso!," a "Baldy!," or an . . . "Ox!" To the overweight opposition congresswoman who threatens a hunger strike, "Don't let us stop you."

I was able to spend an intimate few weeks with the Bronx during the chamber's spring session of 1997. I could do this because journalists still had the run of the chamber at that time. It was a symbol of how little had ever happened here, of how meaningless the Congress had been in Mexican life for so many years, that a reporter—and an American at that—could freely walk its aisles during legislative sessions. The chamber was at this point taking on new strength and importance and debating the major questions facing the country. Nevertheless, it retained the customs of the past. Therefore, I, or any reporter, could still sit down in an empty, high-backed seat, strike up conversations with deputies even as debates were going on, take pictures, and be offered soft drinks by the hostesses in their almost miniskirts and ogle their legs along with the rest of the congressmen. At times I could have raised my hand and voted if I'd wanted. Within two years, that would change. The chamber modernized. Reporters were penned into a small corral at the back of the room. But before that, dozens of reporters and photographers meandered through the hall all day. Frequently like a cloud of locusts they'd swarm down the aisles to get to some congressional leader or commission president, then a few minutes later swing over to another side of the chamber to talk to his rival. But one place they almost never went was the Bronx. The Bronx is the Bronx because it has no decision-making power. No one pays it any mind. No one knows the names of *Bronxista* deputies. The only time anyone looked their way was when the Bronx was shouting at the podium. So I had the Bronx pretty much to myself.

The first *Bronxista* I met was Aurelio Marín, from the state of Hidalgo. Marín is a funny and generous man. He's an attorney who grew up through the National Confederation of Popular Organizations, one pillar of the PRI, to become mayor of Tulancingo, Hidalgo, then a state legislator. He's short, with a wonderfully ample and quivering double chin and the kind of body you'd politely call "portly," though to *Bronxistas* he was simply known as "fat." He had once visited Pleasanton, California, as part of a city exchange program with Tulancingo, he told me. Marín stood out because he possessed the quality *Bronxistas* prize most—a ringing loud voice, a baritone, in his case. It would boom across the chamber as Marín excoriated some opposition-party speaker. For that reason, Marín became one *Bronxista* whose name people knew. "There are a lot of ways of being in disagreement. When we disagree, we're loud. We participate in the chamber. We participate by supporting the decisions that are made in that part," he said the first day we met, pointing toward the chamber's center field.

With that began my lesson in chamber geography. The PRI wing of the Chamber of Deputies, it turns out, faithfully reflects Mexican society: a mass at the bottom dominated by a select few at the top. The PRI leadership, sitting in center field, is known as La Burbuja—the Bubble. There decisions are made, orders are given, and reporters hover. Bubble deputies have the pretty personal secretaries, chauffeurs, computers, travel budgets, meetings with the president and cabinet members. The other deputies follow voting orders, rarely speak at the podium, and live in anonymity, content with pool secretaries and money to get home on weekends. Deputies will tell you that technically speaking, anyone not in the Bubble is by definition in the Bronx. But true connoisseurs know that most of the PRI wing is made up of "Bronx Lite"—deputies less committed to the ribald retort—or "Bronx Argentina"—the brownnosers who fawn over the Bubble. The true Bronx—the real meat eaters—are out here in the chamber's deep right field. This is the section for deputies from hot states like Veracruz, Tabasco, Oaxaca, and Sinaloa, where people have a well-earned reputation for particularly loud, profane Spanish.

I also learned that opposition parties, not surprisingly, view the Bronx as a bunch of dinosaurs exiting history's stage in a chorus of "fatsos!" and fart noises. This is the opinion of Alejandro Rojas Díaz-Durán, a Mexico City deputy and one of the few *Priistas* to ever go against his party on a major vote. Rojas told me of a debate over a proposed political reform that he believed was unconstitutional. He went to the podium and asked: "Do you know that this is an antidemocratic reform?" The Bronx replied: "Yeeeessss!" "Are you aware

that this is an unconstitutional reform?" Rojas asked. "Yeeeessss!" "Then why are you going to approve this reform?" "Becaaaaause!" "After that I began calling them 'the Children's Chorus of San Lázaro,'" Rojas said, referring to the district of Mexico City where the chamber is.

During the 1995 recession, President Ernesto Zedillo insisted on raising the sales tax from 10 percent to 15 percent. It was an unpopular idea. But *Priistas* did the president's bidding and pushed it through the chamber anyway. Rojas cast the lone dissenting vote among them. The Bronx exploded in fury. "Out of the PRI! Traitor! Throw him out!" Rojas smiled amid the bedlam and waved a Mexican flag. In thanks, his neighbors the next day brought a mariachi band to his home to serenade him. Months later Rojas went to the podium and resigned from the party, to a thunderous hail of "Good riddance!" from the chamber's right field.

"They're an instrument of the PRI leader in the chamber—his firm hand, used against dissidents, opponents, and critics," Rojas said.

But the Bronx also seemed to me to be a symbol of Mexico midway in the throes of democracy—an indicator species of how far the country has gone toward democratic modernity and how far it still has to go. The Bronx was, in some small way, a rebellion of the rabble against its betters, and any public rebellion in PRI ranks was rare. It was also the bellow of an authoritarian political system under attack.

No Bronx was needed during the decades of PRI hegemony, when virtually all congressmen were *Priistas*. An occasional opposition critic at the podium was even a welcome sight, adding a democratic veneer to an authoritarian exercise.

Congressmen then were known as *levantadedos*—finger raisers. Cartoonists portrayed them asleep in their chairs with their hands in the air. They took orders from the president and approved whatever he proposed. Some deputies couldn't read or write. It didn't matter. They had been powerless since 1933. That year, in a move aimed at strengthening the president, congressmen were prohibited from reelection. Since then a new crop of rookies entered the chamber every three years. The constantly vacant seats gave the president plums with which to reward sectors loyal to the PRI/government. The chamber became about filling quotas in the ruling party. Each legislature had deputies who were actors, teachers, oil workers, campesinos, and so on. Each sector of the Mexican state was represented, though only a few congressmen had any power. The rest spent three years yawning.

But in 1988 the *levantadedos* had to wake up. The 54th Legislature (1988–91) was the first with more than token opposition representation. Many opposition deputies, particularly those from the center-left Party of the Democratic Revolution (PRD), had been members of the 1968 student movement and had been fighting the government since then. They came to the chamber enraged at the presidential election they were certain Carlos Salinas de Gortari had just stolen. Confrontation, not lawmaking, dominated those years. The opposition invented Super Barrio, a caped superhero with a pro wrestler's mask, a fighter for social justice who began showing up at chamber debates. The chamber's rigid group discipline and somnolence dissolved. Heckling became a tradition. "It became a different legislature in the sense that it wasn't so oppressive. People expressed their thinking. You didn't always repeat this dogma," Jaime Castrejón Díez, a PRI legislator in the chamber at this time, told me one morning in his office in Mexico City.

I had searched out Castrejón because I wanted to know the history of the Bronx. Several *Bronxistas* had told me that its beginnings lay with Castrejón and the 54th Legislature. The new circumstances of that legislature created new conventions. One was that the chamber had its first popular chronicler in a hundred years: Castrejón. A professor of biology, Castrejón had joined the PRI in the mid-1960s while Carlos Madrazo was party president and trying to reform it. He served as mayor of Taxco, Guerrero, but distanced himself from the PRI after Madrazo was removed as party president, then died suspiciously in an airplane crash in 1969. For the next two decades Castrejón wrote extensively on education in Mexico. He eventually became rector of the Universidad Autónoma de Guerrero. In 1988 the PRI invited him to become a congressman and, along with poet Jaime Sabines and poet/journalist Andrés Henestrosa, he made up the PRI's intellectual wing amid the battle royal that was the 54th Legislature. "We were decoration," Castrejón said. "But in a way [PRI leaders] were mistaken in thinking we intellectuals were amenable to what had gone on before."

One day Henestrosa gave Castrejón a book called *Los Ceros de Cero—Zero's Zeros*. "You like writing stories," Henestrosa said. "Why don't you try

writing something like this?" Published in 1882 by an author named Vicente Rivapalacio, the book was a collection of anecdotes making fun of the political figures and legislators of the time. Rivapalacio began publishing his anecdotes in newspapers in 1879 under the pen name Cero. His columns became popular. His identity was discovered and his columns published in a book that became a best-seller.

Nothing like *Los Ceros de Cero* had been possible in the intervening century, during which Mexico saw a dictatorship, a revolution, and the consolidation of the PRI regime under an imperial president with Congress as his rubber stamp. But the 54th Legislature was different. And Castrejón was both an honored intellectual and a member of the PRI's chamber leadership, then popularly known as *La Pavada*—the Group of Peacocks. So he was less bound by the limitations of party discipline than a rank-and-file deputy. He began to write. What he came up with were less anecdotes than farcical flights of a well-educated imagination: Dante visits the chamber to judge how far civilization has advanced and discovers, among other things, that "Mexicans are really adding new things to the art of torment"; the PRI leadership asks Freud for a psychological analysis of the chamber; Zeus, bored with politics on Mount Olympus, comes to earth incarnated as José Luis Lamadrid, the second in command of the PRI wing of deputies, because in the PRI people respect hierarchy and authority. The 54th Legislature could only be recounted with "literature of the absurd," Castrejón wrote. Even so, "with the presence of Super Barrio in the parliament's lobby, any imagined story has to take second place."

Castrejón photocopied his stories. They circulated through the chamber as a kind of clandestine press. Snippets of his writings began showing up in newspaper columns. Castrejón's noodlings were eventually packaged into a 120-page paperback: *Fantasía Política: La "Histórica" Legislatura*. The book was intended for sale within the chamber so only one thousand copies were printed. But then a publisher bought it and marketed it to the public and it sold twenty thousand copies—a best-seller. "People like to laugh at politicians," Castrejón said. "If the book had one quality, it was its irreverence. It didn't pardon anybody." It was also daring for its moment. Mexicans had for years been enormously creative in the jokes they told about their ex-presidents, but few people had printed anything that so mocked PRI leaders.

Something had changed in the culture of the chamber. Deputies' new rambunctiousness. Castrejón's stories. It left an opening that PRI leaders couldn't quite close. There was now room for parody aimed at taking power down a notch.

Castrejón's torch passed to the 55th Legislature (1991–94). Taking it up was the unlikely figure of Dr. Arturo Nájera, a surgeon and an anonymous deputy from Veracruz. A dark-skinned, dapper man, Nájera would become part of the first Bronx and its unofficial theorist. He had been a student doctor in 1967, when he and his colleagues struck, demanding better scholarships and studying conditions. The doctors' strike was a precursor to the army's 1968 massacre of student protesters. The regime crushed it. Some doctors had their scholarships rescinded. Some went to jail. Nájera was able to finish his studies but then moved to Xalapa, Veracruz, and into private practice. The doctors' strike made clear that only within the party could change be achieved. Outside the party, dissenters were easy prey. This lesson Arturo Nájera learned well. He distanced himself from the party for a few years. But by the early 1970s he had returned. "I'd always been a *Priista,* but always with the idea of never submitting to authority," he says. In 1987 he was made a state legislator, and in 1991 he was elected to the 55th Legislature of the Chamber of Deputies.

A fire in the chamber that year forced the 55th to spend many months in an auditorium at Centro Médico—the medical center several miles away. The auditorium had no offices, no secretaries, no telephones. Simple things like writing a letter were major undertakings. Most PRI deputies were already shut out of the decision making, which was the exclusive domain of an elite crew of twenty or so *Priistas.* Now they didn't even have secretaries. They felt like schoolchildren. Ghettoized, they commiserated, and soon a collective bond emerged among sixty or so deputies. As the months wore on, they hit on the idea of publishing a newspaper as an outlet for their festering frustration. The precedent of Castrejón's tales was before them. Their newspaper, too, was to be a clandestine organ of dissent and barbed humor, written anonymously. Nájera was put in charge of collecting articles.

The paper was first published in December 1991 and was known as *La Daga—The Dagger. La Daga* looked like a junior high school newspaper. Only eleven editions were ever published. If Castrejón's farces were an intellectual's

take on chamber life, *La Daga* was by and for the rabble. It had no budget. It was written on a typewriter—full of spelling mistakes—then xeroxed and stapled together. *La Daga* was a collection of gossip, anecdotes, sexual innuendo, and cartoons making fun of important chamber members—and in that lay whatever transcendence it achieved. Soon dozens of deputies were contributing. "You know, there were 250 or so underemployed congressmen," said Nájera. "If you're sitting there with nothing to do, in two hours you can write a poem or an article." There was often too much to publish.

Yet if this group of deputies showed signs of rebellion, its main function was to ridicule opposition deputies at the podium. "Lumpendeputies," one opposition-party colleague called them. Wisecracking sustained them in their discredit. Relegated, disrespected, crude—the group developed an esprit de corps around its name. How it got that name is in dispute. Nájera says it was given them by Esteban Zamora, a PAN deputy. One day, the story goes, they were attacking Zamora as he spoke from the podium. "You over there in the Bronx, leave me alone," Zamora supposedly boomed in response. Zamora denies coming up with the name, though he admits calling them *"la broza del PRI"* ("the PRI's rubbish"). "They'd already named themselves the Bronx. I didn't invent that," Zamora told me. "Please don't attribute it to me. It would be an insult to the district in New York."

Whatever the case, Mexicans had long associated the term with aggressive behavior. The group donned the name—*La Daga* became its voice. *La Daga* eventually published a map of the chamber. The PAN section was labeled Queens; the PRD, Harlem. The PRI leadership section was commonly known as the Bubble by this time, but it was labeled the Holy Sanctuary, while the group of powerful *Priistas* directly behind it was christened Manhattan. Left field, made up of *Priistas* who didn't yell or participate but more or less bided their time, was dubbed New Jersey. In right field was the Bronx. "I think among many of us who formed the Bronx, there was this spirit of independence, of not enslaving ourselves to an orthodox, closed regime," Nájera said. "We formed a wing that superficially could be seen as '*rudos*'—with the yelling and all that. But that wasn't the intention. Rather it was a way of permeating this impenetrable bubble of power."

La Daga and the Bronx were unprecedented outbreaks of PRI rank-and-file independence. Party leaders were worried. Congressional leader Fernando Ortiz Arana called a luncheon with the Veracruz congressmen. They arrived to find Veracruz Governor Dante Delgado and the state's congressional leader, Gustavo Carbajal, at the head table as well. Soon they realized the meeting was to put a halt to *La Daga*. They pretended not to know who published it. The lunch had the feeling of naughty students meeting with their principal and parents. It ended with Carbajal assuring Ortiz Arana that the newspaper would not reappear. However, the next day *La Daga* circulated again through the chamber. Carbajal later told his charges, "Just let me know next time, so I don't make a fool of myself."

Unable to suppress *La Daga,* party leaders offered to subsidize it. This was a crucial moment. *Bronxistas* knew all too well the party's history of co-opting dissident groups. Their independence was now at stake. They refused the offer. It was a risky move. Few in the Bronx had the renown, and thus the protection, that Castrejón had enjoyed. As a precaution, they kept the newspaper anonymous—articles would just show up on Nájera's desk and he could claim ignorance of authorship. The Bronx, meanwhile, remained leaderless. "Without a leader, no one could be bought off. They'd see us all in a group, but they couldn't cut off the head," said Nájera. "So they might have been able to co-opt a few, but the rest would have continued on. And it would have cost too much to buy us all off." The Bronx, the base of a party that made corruption an art, knew how to remain incorruptible.

But the leadership's tolerance went only so far, and then it was time to fall in line. This was the heyday of Carlos Salinas and his free-market reforms. The president's worldwide popularity was cresting on his attempts to modernize the Mexican economy. To the 55th Legislature, and the Bronx, fell the duty of passing major Salinas reforms: the privatization of Telmex, the state telephone company, and a liberalizing of agricultural laws, among others. The Bronx may have believed themselves critics of leadership, but they couldn't be reelected. They owed their jobs and their future to the party hierarchy, not to constituents back home. So they obeyed when ordered. Deputies who supported a state-run economy, as most *Bronxistas* did, passed reforms that they believed betrayed Mexico. "When agricultural reform was an issue, many of us were opposed and we expressed ourselves strongly in the commissions,"

said Nájera. "We weren't simple *levantadedos*. We'd go complain to the leadership. We'd tell them privatization hurts Mexico. [But] often congressmen were incapable of rebellion because they wanted to preserve their positions. So we weren't in favor of [these reforms], but we voted for them. A few times we'd ask the leader for permission to be absent, so as not to feel the shame of voting in favor of something we so opposed."

Yet none of this dissent made it into *La Daga*. With their stand on the important issues decided for them, the newspaper and the *Bronxistas* became about petty rebellions. They complained about the awful cafeteria food. They fought a move to rescind one of the few privileges rank-and-file congressmen enjoyed: a card that allowed them to pass through highway toll booths without paying. *La Daga* came out strongly in favor of changing the uniforms of the chamber hostesses. It decried the fact that congressmen had to share telephones. *La Daga* published doggerel and nicknames about each other. There was Deputy Hot Blood, who spent more time watching the hostesses' miniskirts than the debates, and Deputy Doublewide, who destroyed the "butt meter." It ran cartoons of leaders with inflated noses and drooping bellies. All this was taken as daring attempts to speak truth to power. And for the PRI, it was.

The Bronx grew to relish the act of voting itself. The chamber didn't yet have electronic voting. So on important issues, there was a roll call. Each member would take the microphone as it was passed along the aisles and announce his vote. These developed into moments when the Bronx attempted redemption. For each *Bronxista,* sweet seconds of individuality lay in how he voted in favor of whatever the regime told him to. With what flourish or smirk would he take the microphone and say, *"Sí."*

In 1994 the 55th Legislature ended, and with it *La Daga* died raw, as free as it could be, and everything its originators had intended for it. It left behind some meek precedent of *Priista* dissent and the term for the attack bloc of deputies that remains part of Mexico's congressional geography. In its last issue *La Daga* defined the Bronx as "a state of mind, an outburst, the chamber's gaiety.

"We're proud to belong to the Bronx," it went on. "We're autonomous. It's not the power of one person. It's a collective action."

This was clearly an insider's version. "There's a phrase in Spanish, *'echar relajo,'*" said Esteban Zamora. "To take everything as a joke, take the seriousness from everything. They made a joke of what should have been serious. Moreover, they were the shock troops, the PRI's triggermen. Their bosses never reined them in. [The Bronx] may have emerged spontaneously, but they were permitted to act that way." Four *Bronxistas* from the 55th would become governors before the decade was out—Antonio González Curi of Campeche, Tomás Yarrington of Tamaulipas, Joaquín Hendricks of Quintana Roo, and Ángel Aguirre of Guerrero—proving again that in the PRI loyalty to power, however expressed, is always the smartest move.

* * *

By the time the 56th Legislature was sworn in, in the fall of 1994, the Bronx was assumed to have taken the place of the *levantadedo*. It was an advance, however small. At least chamber debates were now loud and important enough to keep deputies awake. With the opposition invigorated, the PRI could no longer afford *levantadedos*.

Early in the legislature, a banner over the chamber's right field was unfurled, announcing the Bronx was present once again. The Bronx was now part of political discourse. Newspapers referred to it with no explanation, as if none were needed. *Bronxistas* arrived knowing they were expected to be bawdy and coarse. This Bronx elected its own president, Rafael Ruvalcaba, a deputy from Sinaloa. One of his functions became to preside over the occasional lunches the Bronx now organized.

Aurelio Marín invited me to one of these. As I sat in the corner with some deputies I didn't know, fine Herradura tequila flowed freely. *Bronxistas,* their jackets open, ties loosened, leaned back in their chairs and traded jibes across the dining hall. They broke into chants at the slightest provocation—*"Cu-le-ro! Cu-le-ro!"* ("Butt fuck-er! Butt fuck-er!"). I was sitting at the core of *priismo*. Before us tables were laid with a main course of barbecued goat, with peanuts and dried apricots, Coca-Cola, tequila, and ashtrays that waiters emptied often. Mexico's tax dollars at work. Ruvalcaba rose to thank "especially Humberto Roque Villanueva, who as our chamber leader . . ." "Time's up!" *"Cu-le-ro!"* "Homo!" "Time's up!" Marín got up to speak. He, too, was drowned out. Marco Rascón, a PRD deputy, had recently suggested from the podium that Marín—who had made a career out of attacking him—was homosexual. So as

Marín spoke, the Bronx broke into, "Rascón *tenía razón!* Rascón *tenía razón!*" ("Rascón was right!")

Marco Rascón had become by this time both the Bronx's foil and, in a weird way, friend, or at least respected foe. A chubby fellow with graying long hair, a beard, large nose, and infectious smile and laugh, Rascón is Mexico's Abbie Hoffman. He's less interested in politics than in political theater. Rascón grew to prominence as an organizer of the Asamblea de Barrios—a group of neighborhood organizations that formed in Mexico City after the 1985 earthquake. He invented and copyrighted Super Barrio and has been a constant critic of Mexico's free-market reforms. As deputy, he would occasionally wear masks to legislative sessions; he brought in a puppet once and another time wore sunglasses shaped like the crown of the Statue of Liberty. Rascón's defining moment came on September 1, 1996. As President Ernesto Zedillo stood at the podium giving his annual *Informe,* Rascón put on a pig mask, stood below, and unveiled a series of placards printed with sayings like, "We bankers want more government support," "July 4th: Our Independence Day," and "Thanks for continuing my policies and following my instructions: Carlos Salinas." With that he incurred the undying wrath of the Bronx, who now save their most luxurious insults for Rascón, questioning the fidelity of his wife—singer Eugenia León—and referring to him on occasion as "Babe," after the movie about the pig of the same name.

Not long after the pig incident, and interested in Rascón's new prominence among *Bronxistas,* I spoke with him as he sat in the chamber during a debate. The Bronx was trash talking him incessantly. He relished it. "I do it to make them mad," Rascón said of his political theater. "I do it so they'll defend a ritual in which they don't believe either. I simply decided to play the game according to their rules—to see who could be the heaviest. I think I'm winning. I do what they'd like to do but can't. I get up at the podium every time I want. They can't. They're deputies from the provinces, from the worker sectors, who don't have connections among the leadership. Being here means they've fulfilled requirements of their party, such as not protesting at acts of corruption, taking part in those acts. This is a reward. They're here for three years of vacation. The most they've done, in the way of rebellion, is to go urinate when it's time to vote. This is the most dignity they can muster.

Abstaining is a kind of rebellion here."

Just because a new party emerges, talking democracy, doesn't mean the old patterns disappear. Rascón sees himself fighting a top-down structure in the PRD that is similar to what exists in the PRI. He has adopted the Harlem label—the PRD's Bronx, in other words. "Those of us from the Bronx and Harlem have our own way of understanding each other in the face of the establishment. Look around you," he said, waving at the chamber fanned out around him. "This is just a product of your imagination. Here we're not five hundred deputies. We're really four party leaders, and those four decide the course of the legislative agenda for the rest of us. This is a virtual assembly. What [the leaders] are interested in is the form, the protocol. Decisions aren't made here but rather someplace else. Before they were made in Los Pinos. Now I think they're made in Washington."

Back at the Bronx luncheon, Francisco Peralta sat in one corner. A deputy from Tabasco, Peralta is light skinned, soft-spoken, and spectacled. Amid his colleagues' riotous behavior, Peralta can be counted on for sober and honest analysis, however poorly it might reflect on his own status in the chamber. This I found to be a common trait among *Bronxistas*. Though they behave like brutes in public, most of them want to be taken seriously and play a role in chamber business. They bray from their seats at a deputy at the podium, then privately offer stinging critiques of Mexico's authoritarian political traditions. Even Aurelio Marín seemed embarrassed that his real usefulness to his party lay in his booming baritone. He shuffled quickly by me one day, shaking my hand. I asked him where he was going. With a gleam in his eye, he said, "To participate." The golden words. Later that session he proudly went to the podium to support the proposed privatization of part of the nation's petrochemical industry.

Peralta, like the rest of his Bronx colleagues, has been cut out of decisions on legislation. He's an ex-judge, former mayor, former state secretary of education, and author of seven books. As a thoughtful man, his second-class status in the chamber disturbs him. "I got here with a lot of enthusiasm to do legislative work," he told me. "I'm a lawyer, plus I love political and judicial analysis. However, I got here and they wouldn't let me do anything.

"[The elite deputies] are the ones who have the privileges. They go to the

podium during the most important debates. They're presidents of commissions, the ones who travel abroad. It's a social class within the chamber. You just don't come here and be part of it. They've worked together for a long time. I've been involved in politics only at the state level, not at the federal level.

"I've been to the podium twice, but not on issues I wanted to speak on. I went to defend the governor of Tabasco. That's why a lot of deputies from the provinces are allowed to the podium—to defend their governors who are under attack. But on the great national issues—in my case, say, during the debate over judicial reforms—we don't go up. Many people have never gone up, not because they don't want to, but because they aren't allowed."

So Peralta has found himself with a lot of time on his hands to pursue what he now loves best: recording the anecdotes and behavior of his 499 colleagues, mostly those from the Bronx. He publishes them in a newsletter. This can safely now be called an obsession with Peralta. He is the Bronx's Boswell. Other deputies watch their mouths around him lest they wind up as fodder for his newsletter. Chamber sessions are, to Peralta, not moments to attend to the nation's business but rather anecdote-collection opportunities. In the two years of his term he has found the time to publish three books and more than fifty editions of his glossy newsletter—a better-looking descendant of *La Daga,* yet without the erudition of Castrejón's *Fantasía Política.* The newsletter, *Crónicas, Anécdotas y Otras Cosas,* is crammed with quips, comments, and the color of life in Mexico's 56th Legislature.

In one section, recorded as Peralta answered nature's call, congressmen discuss how often they leave the session to urinate: "I've never gone so much in my life"; "I come here to kill time"; "It depends on the level of liquids and your biological functions"; "Ten or twelve times a day"; "Depends on how often you want to say hello to a friend." As Christmas approached, one congressman waxed poetic with a ditty that roughly translated into: "They pay us tomorrow. We'll get our check very early. A large Christmas bonus. For raising our hands."

The newsletter's popularity has created for Peralta what his judicial experience in Tabasco never could: room to participate in chamber decision making. After more than two years as a deputy, he's been invited into the Bubble, if only part-time. But Peralta isn't interested; it would take time away from his newsletter. "I don't want to stop doing what I've been doing for two years to become part of something that's only got a few more months to go," he said.

The 56th Legislature dissolved in September 1997 and with it another Bronx. Rafael Ruvalcaba spent the last months of the legislature trying to interest *Bronxistas* in forming an *"asociación civil"*—a nonprofit organization, El Bronx AC—that will make the Bronx an institutional part of future legislatures. "Perhaps as time goes on," said Ruvalcaba, "the Bronx will be defined as the expression of people who've been pushed to the side. If we didn't have the Bronx, we'd spend the whole time as spectators."

Some form of the Bronx will likely survive as long as congressmen can't be reelected. When deputies must justify their votes to constituents back home, bloc voting, especially on unpopular issues, will fade quickly. So will the Bubble's control. But until that happens, *"rudos"* will continue toeing the line while demonstrating their independence in meaningless minor rebellions.

Less clear than the Bronx's future is its legacy.

I sat with Arturo Nájera in a coffee shop as he discussed that question one evening. He went on for a while in a rambling discourse. He touched on Galileo and Copernicus and Freud and Christ. But mostly he dwelled on the quality of Mexican rebellion that is possible after seven decades of rule by one of the twentieth century's most paternalistic and debilitating one-party states. Though he didn't say it in so many words, the Bronx is a metaphor for the Mexican people at the end of that century. Torn between rebellion and submission, it wants desperately to be part of the world after years of isolation. Yet only slowly can it bring itself to break with habit and tradition and move toward something new.

"The human being emerges in the moment he's able to disobey," Nájera began. "To disobey is to contribute, to rebel against what's established and create new ways of doing things. This, at some point, became the idea behind the Bronx. [But] a total break with the past wasn't possible, a cutting of the umbilical cord to the system. [The leadership] would have replaced us.

"To go against that, we would have needed to cultivate each individual . . . a new Prometheus, a new human being free of his chains, who could cast a

free vote. There was always, 'My union will take my job away if I vote like that. I'll lose my office.' People mortgage their convictions out of hunger.

"In the Mexican there is a germ of democracy, of internal liberty. What happens is that there's this fear of standing out, this fear of breaking with the preestablished, with the government, the system, the party. This part of the human being that continues depending on what's come before is what the system manipulates to make individuals dependent on this All, this Party.

"Each Bronx has had one thing in common. None could throw from its back the control of an all-powerful leadership. We tried to break and do something important. But the fear is terrible. The Bronx were a handful of Mexicans who became deputies, with the anxieties and aspirations of any Mexican, and who wanted to rebel against established practices they didn't like. They didn't like uniform votes, this monolithic control, that only ten or so deputies could participate.

"I can't pretend we obtained freedom. I can't claim that we were autonomous or that we did great things. What I can say is that internally, we were consistent with ourselves. When we said the food is bad, we said it frankly."

—1997

LEAVING NUEVA JERUSALÉN

When in June 1998 seventy-five families were expelled from Nueva Jerusalén, they told the world a strange story about why they'd been forced to leave the strict theocratic community of four thousand people.

Their story involved the attempted murder of the secretary of Padre Nabor, the renegade priest who founded Nueva Jerusalén, and within that the story of how a street gang of drug users emerged in this isolated village that was intended to replicate heaven on earth.

The families began their story by returning to the origins of the community, to 1979. Nueva Jerusalén was just forming in the western part of the state of Michoacán. Believers from across Mexico were flocking to the place where a peasant woman had reportedly seen a vision of the Virgin. Papá Nabor had been excommunicated and was setting up his own version of the church. Borderline hysteria gripped the region. Legions of buses backed up along the rugged road leading up to the village. Men were selling land and animals in other states to bring their wives and children out of the sinful world to where they could live praising the Virgin and praying for mankind's salvation. And here their children grew up.

Years later, in the mid-1990s, as these young people were in the full romping bloom of young adulthood, leaders at Nueva Jerusalén imposed a new strictness. Daily attendance at mass and rosary, starting at 4 a.m., was now required. They forbade contact with the opposite sex. They prohibited "fashionable" clothing and hairstyles. These rules were enforced by the secretary to Padre Nabor, a man in his thirties named Padre Matías. Padre Matías apparently felt that the generation of kids between the ages of, say, fifteen to twenty-four had grown up soft, were thus not to be trusted, and needed a bit of the lash to stay in line. One afternoon, as young people were going to rosary, Padre Matías jailed all the young men—about 150 of them. They were stripped of their clothing and their hair was cut.

Not surprisingly, this went down poorly among Nueva Jerusalén's youth. They remembered a time when the Virgin didn't require daily attendance at 4 a.m. mass and when a casual conversation with a girl wasn't call for damnation. So gradually there emerged in Nueva Jerusalén a rebel generation—fifty to seventy youths who had grown up in the community. And within this group was a subset of young men who used drugs. These young men especially resented Padre Matías's new regime.

They formed around Juan Ulloa, a young man who had recently moved with his family to the community from Guadalajara. Being from the big city and unwilling to go along with the daily regimen Padre Matías had in mind, Ulloa became leader of a gang of eight or ten of the most resentful young men. These kids would buy marijuana or glue in nearby towns and get together at night to get high. "It was well known among young people that these guys used drugs, but their parents weren't aware, being simple people," says Jorge Hernández, a young man who came to Nueva Jerusalén in 1985.

On the night of March 7, 1998, several of them went to the home of Padre Matías with the intention of murdering him. Padre Matías suspected something was up and sent his younger brother out to meet the gang. They fell upon the brother, stabbing him three times in the stomach. They later shot another man who had once reported them to the local police. Both men were sent to a hospital in the state capital of Morelia, survived the attacks, and are living again in Nueva Jerusalén. No one outside the community was told what happened.

The gang fled. Ulloa headed for Guadalajara. "So Matías, what he does is look for people to blame," says Jorge Hernández. "He looks over the lists of those who don't go to mass or rosary. Those are the ones to blame. All of us."

And that, they say, is one reason why three months later, on June 7, seventy-five families were expelled from Nueva Jerusalén in a Salem-style ostracizing, a purging of bad blood. The families were given twenty minutes to leave the community or face a beating with wooden clubs. They left behind their animals, homes, and land—everything they had in the world—as state police officers looked on to make sure they left in peace.

The expelled families went to authorities in the *municipio* of Turicato, to which Nueva Jerusalén belongs. They also spoke with reporters. And that was how, for the first time in many years, the world heard news of Nueva Jerusalén. Not since the great schism of 1982, when a sensational rupture within the community forced four thousand residents to leave, had there been anything like it.

The families described life inside the village. They told of the current seer and apparent successor to Padre Nabor, an old man who has raped young girls and who for four years had a warrant out for his arrest that police never got around to executing. They said the village had a private jail, underground, with no windows or bathroom and a private police force, which allegedly made arrests and possessed high-caliber rifles that Mexican law says only the military may own. And they said marriage was now prohibited in Nueva Jerusalén.

These were violations of Mexican law. But Nueva Jerusalén got away with it. The stories of how the community did that became these families' great contribution to Mexican political science.

The Nueva Jerusalén they described was more than just a screwy theocratic village with its own street gang; it wasn't only a community governed by a priest who believes that Pope Paul VI is held hostage in the basement of the Vatican. Nueva Jerusalén, they said, was also a theocratic community that always votes for the ruling Institutional Revolutionary Party (PRI). Its leaders continually receive precise voting instructions from the Virgin of Guadalupe and from Mexico's most beloved president, General Lázaro Cárdenas, who governed from 1934 to 1940 and died in 1970. According to these families, both the Virgin and the general insist that the PRI is holy, that it's the party of the Virgin, that it's a sin to vote for any other. So in return, PRI/government authorities allow Nueva Jerusalén to be an island where the Mexican constitution doesn't apply. As political competition has become fierce in Michoacán, the village has actually become a swing bloc of votes in its region, tipping local races to the PRI.

In a century known for great experiments in authoritarian political control, Nueva Jerusalén stands out as a masterful achievement. It is a testament to the PRI's remarkable ingenuity in using the government and the justice system to enforce loyalty and conserve its own power. If the PRI is, in the words of historian Lorenzo Meyer, "the world's most successful authoritarian regime," it's because the party could see the potential for its own political self-preservation in places like Nueva Jerusalén, while a less subtle state might have seen it as

competition and jackbooted it right into oblivion. Cracks now furrow the regime's artifice. PRI discipline has weakened, and opposition parties are stronger than ever. Yet the PRI still relies on its myriad arrangements and deals to keep functioning, especially in rural Mexico, where it remains strong. One of these is the special relationship the party developed with the cult run by the priest named Papá Nabor in this poor, isolated, and hot part of Michoacán.

* * *

From its entrance, Nueva Jerusalén looks a lot like any other Mexican village, nestled in the hills above a valley green with sugarcane. Rocky, unpaved roads stretch up a hill, and farm animals wander about. A group of men in sweat-stained shirts and rumpled straw hats lounge at a shack guarding the entrance to the village.

Nueva Jerusalén grew out of a reaction to the Catholic Church's 1965 liberalizing reforms known as Vatican II. Nabor Cárdenas Mejorada was a priest assigned to the town of Puruarán, in the *municipio* of Turicato, at the time. Vatican II was designed to modernize the church, to adjust it to a world where religion was no longer life's center point. Masses were now to be done in native languages instead of Latin. Catholics were urged to cooperate more with other religions. Laypeople were given enhanced roles in the church. But to Nabor Cárdenas, a priest for thirty years by then, this was heresy.

In 1973 there came to him a peasant woman named Gabina Romero, who claimed to have seen a vision of the Virgin. The Virgin, Gabina Romero said, had selected Nabor Cárdenas as the man to build a community where pilgrims could praise Her and pray for the salvation of mankind. The Virgin went on to condemn the teachings of Vatican II. She said the priest was now to be called Papá Nabor, and Gabina was to be known as Mamá Salomé.

By the mid-1970s Papá Nabor was building Nueva Jerusalén on communal farmland that he squatted. People learned of Mamá Salomé's vision. Pilgrims began to visit. A community began taking shape. Later a millenarian component was added. Communism in Nicaragua and the Socialist Party victory in post-Franco Spain—it all spelled the end of the world, which at first was scheduled for 1980, then for 1983, then was predicted for 1988, and is now almost certain to happen in 1999.

Nueva Jerusalén was approximate heaven. So saints, too, were necessary. Papá Nabor anointed hundreds of people with the identities of saints from Catholic history.

Nueva Jerusalén never quite got to heaven, though. Early on, many pilgrims came seeking cures for illnesses. The community suffered outbreaks of disease, including leprosy. The community had no sewage system and only one source of water. People lived in shacks. Through the mid-1980s health workers in nearby towns began seeing young girls hemorrhaging from botched abortions; these girls, according to health workers, had been "quarantined" with saints, who impregnated them, then midwife abortions were performed to hide the rape.

Pope Paul VI died in 1978. That year the Catholic Church excommunicated Papá Nabor and called Mamá Salomé's vision false. Papá Nabor came to believe that Pope Paul VI hadn't died but is being held hostage by communists, Masons, and Jews in the Vatican and will emerge at the apocalypse to save mankind, with special consideration for those who live in Nueva Jerusalén. The community maintains a house especially for his return.

Papá Nabor organized a squad of preachers to travel Mexico, telling of the Virgin's appearance. In 1979 Nueva Jerusalén accepted more than 8,000 pilgrims, most of whom had sold their land and possessions to come live, and buy property, in the theocratic village.

Then in 1981, Mamá Salomé died. This left the renegade priest with the problem of succession. The Virgin appeared to him and proposed two women as possible successors: Mamá María Margarita and Mamá María de Jesús, a bespectacled young woman who was born Arcadia Bautista. She was said to be a former prostitute and had come from Monterrey with a remarkable sexual appetite and possibly a mental illness to look for her boyfriend. She had stayed to move into the community hierarchy. Nueva Jerusalén divided over who would succeed Mamá Salomé. One group followed Mamá María Margarita. The other believed Mamá María de Jesús to be the chosen one. She became pregnant with, it was said, a "child of God." For a while it looked as if she might truly be in the Almighty's favor. But when the child reportedly was born dark skinned, her opponents attacked. How could God be the child's father, they reasoned, if both God and Mamá María de Jesús were white?

Papá Nabor finally anointed Mamá María de Jesús as seer. She was the

designated communicator with the Virgin and General Lázaro Cárdenas. In November 1982 the followers of Mamá María Margarita—some four thousand people—left the community en masse, making national news as the press converged to write salacious stories about the community.

For several years Nueva Jerusalén lived in relative tranquillity. But in 1989 Papá Nabor announced that a revolution would take place in the community. He scuttled the now out-of-favor María de Jesús to a convent and named a new seer. His name was Agapito Gómez.

Agapito, now in his late sixties, has a tumor the size of a baseball on the right side of his neck and ropes of greasy hair slicked across his balding pate. He was a pilgrim in 1979, when he arrived from the state of Guerrero. But ten years later he had worked his way into Papá Nabor's graces. Soon after he was anointed seer, he declared that he was holding regular conversations with the Virgin and Lázaro Cárdenas. Upon announcing this, Gómez played a tape for the community in which he supposedly talked with the dead. The voices of the dead, according to those who've heard the tape, were high-pitched, sounding something like a Spanish version of Alvin and the Chipmunks. Since then these conversations have governed life in Nueva Jerusalén. They have determined whether people can stay. After one such conversation Gómez decided one man was a witch. He was expelled June 7 and lost all his property.

Agapito lives up on a hill in one of the largest homes in Nueva Jerusalén. He is the owner of the community's sole television—a twenty-inch color television, according to those who've seen it. He also has a videocassette recorder. The expelled families say Gómez uses them to attract young girls to his home and seduce them. Young girls no longer go there without an escort. Shortly after his anointing as seer, Gómez began inviting girls to his home to watch movies. He'd give them money. And there, too, according to ex-cult members, he would rape them.

One such girl was María Remedios Cruz Vigueres, who is now fifteen. María Remedios was often invited to Gómez's home to watch movies. One day—María Remedios was then twelve—Gómez sent for her. Afraid to go alone, she took her little brother. Gómez gave her brother a bag of bread and told him to go give it to his siblings. Once alone, Gómez put María Remedios in a room and threatened her with a pistol, put a bandanna over her mouth, and raped her. For six months María Remedios told no one. Then her father came home from working in the United States and noticed his daughter had grown fat. She asked to go to the doctor, saying she thought she had worms in her stomach. The doctor discovered her pregnancy.

María Remedios now has a two-year-old daughter, Neri, whom the family claims is Gómez's. She also has a horror of men and can't be around them alone. Her mother and father filed a complaint with authorities. Gómez now has an arrest warrant out for him. Expelled family members say state police have visited Nueva Jerusalén many times. Each time they receive money and leave without the seer in custody.

Agapito's continued freedom was one of many signs that Nueva Jerusalén had become a state within a state. Its residents also paid no taxes, and the village barred entry to anyone it pleased. It had no public school, though it is required by law to have one. Initially Nueva Jerusalén was an illegal settlement, and nearby communities tried hard to evict them. The village also needed basic municipal services that its neighbors wanted to deny it. Later Nueva Jerusalén needed protection from the scrutiny of outside authorities so that the community could, say, jail young men for having long hair. Neighbors came to believe that part of the community's floating population were wanted criminals who knew Nueva Jerusalén was off-limits to police. In the mid-1980s there was a shootout between state police and marijuana smugglers, who had supposedly used Nueva Jerusalén as a transfer area for their dope.

For all this, Papá Nabor needed the system's protection. And despite constant reports of violations of Mexican law, the local and state PRI government left Nueva Jerusalén alone. What the system got in return, it soon became clear, was its most valued commodity: loyalty. Every election Nueva Jerusalén voted 1,100 or 1,200 to zero for the ruling party.

"If you didn't vote for the PRI, you weren't with God or the Virgin," says Santiago Aparicio, who sold his property in Guerrero in 1979 to come to Nueva Jerusalén. "The seer Mamá María de Jesús received messages. She said the Virgin told her that we had to vote for the PRI."

The meetings at Nueva Jerusalén got increasingly insistent about how citizens should vote as competition from opposition parties increased in the late 1980s. Before elections there'd be sermons at which believers were told that

the Virgin wanted them to vote PRI. Followers had to attend classes on how to vote. They were shown where to mark their ballots. The holy trinity in Nueva Jerusalén became Virgin, Flag, Party. The colors of all three are the same: green, white, and red. "They told us that the flag comes from the Holy Virgin," says Andréa Hernández. "They said that the PRI is the party of the Holy Virgin." But finally it got very simple. "They'd tell us all, 'You vote for this party,' and so we'd vote. Otherwise they'd run us off," says Lucio Pérez, another of the expelled members.

So the PRI/government allowed Nueva Jerusalén to stay where it was—on land it didn't own—and to grow into a village that isn't legal, that pays no taxes, and that doesn't show up on maps.

In this, though, Nueva Jerusalén was not unusual. This kind of wink-and-a-nod arrangement is how huge swaths of Mexico have developed. Deals like it have led to the invasion of national parks, ecological reserves, ravines, hilltops, and private farmland and are why urban planning is virtually impossible in Mexico. Nezahualcóyotl, a city of three million people adjacent to Mexico City, was once nothing but illegal squatter settlements. They were allowed to stay in exchange for voting PRI. The large quasi-Protestant sect Luz del Mundo (Light of the World) has an enormous neighborhood in Guadalajara; it grew from nothing with the protection of the PRI/government. Its members, too, vote PRI in every election. The shantytowns that ring most large Mexican cities exist in a twisted way precisely because they are illegal. Their illegality allows the PRI/government to control their residents. The deal is once again simple. The government doesn't enforce the law and throw them off the land so long as residents promise to support the system, usually represented by a powerful politician or family who can protect them.

This is what happened in Nueva Jerusalén. The community received the protection of the ruling party. It became especially tied to one family within the local PRI. And here the community's story cannot be told without also telling the story of its patrons, the Villasenores.

* * *

The Villaseñores were the peasant kings of Turicato. Their saga is a sweeping real-life version of a Mexican telenovela. The Villaseñores were once peons on a sugar cane hacienda. Using iron will, impetuous violence, the political system, and Papá Nabor and the pilgrims of Nueva Jerusalén, they rose from the dirt to own that hacienda and attempted to extend their dominion to the region. Their arrogance and ruthlessness that brought them power also tempted fate and finally broke them. Their empire collapsed in a hail of political gunfire that echoed across the Turicato region and left a legacy that years later was still being felt. Local folks simply observe that the Villaseñores "got involved in politics"—as if nothing more is needed to explain their rise, their inevitable corruption, and their fall. Today in the *municipio* of Turicato, the Villaseñores are a cautionary tale, the moral of which is, not surprisingly, "never get involved in politics." Through it all, though, Papá Nabor and the pilgrims at Nueva Jerusalén were the family's close allies.

Turicato is where Michoacán's Tierra Caliente—the Hot Land—begins. The thermometer rises quickly during the drop of fifteen miles from the mountain city of Tacámbaro into the sugar cane valley and the towns of Puruarán, then Turicato. On the road between the two is the turnoff to Nueva Jerusalén. In all, 283 hamlets and villages—over 453 square miles—make up the *municipio* of Turicato. Most of these communities are collections of a few homes, ranchos baking in the sun and gasping in the isolation. Very few are accessible by more than the most rudimentary roads. Rickety, coughing buses make the trip once a day. Temperatures and humidity reach unbearable levels the farther into the Tierra Caliente you travel.

Accompanying the rise in temperatures is a kind of descent into barbarism. So while the people in Tacámbaro have always held their lowland cousins from Turicato and Puruarán in fear and disdain, in the same way those from the towns have always been wary of the poor peasants—*"la gente brava,"* "the wild people"—from the hamlets and outposts farther into the Tierra Caliente. "From childhood, they'd believe that death didn't matter. It was very important to them to die fighting," says Sergio Trigo, who runs the biweekly newspaper *Tacamba* in Tacámbaro. "At a party, let's say, someone would yell something. Someone else would answer from another side of the party. They'd keep it up until they were going at it with machetes in the middle of the party." For years young men spent afternoons jousting with these machetes, training like sword fighters by whacking at sticks hung from trees. Even today the casual

observer quickly notes a belligerence, as well as a disturbingly high rate of mental retardation, physical deformity, and lost eyes and limbs, among the people of the *municipio*—living testaments to the poverty, alcoholism, lack of medical attention, probably no little inbreeding, and the prevalence of the machete.

The *municipio* of Turicato has always divided along these town-rural lines. The hill folks resented the power, money, and education, relatively speaking, of the people in town. The city folk feared the hillbillies but saw no reason to extend power, or municipal services, to people they considered ignorant and barbaric. In these years the Barajas family—a family of local merchants—dominated Turicato politics. Up until the 1980s the Barajases controlled the office of mayor. "I remember on several occasions they wouldn't even put on a campaign," says Adolfo Villaseñor. "They'd circulate a petition, 'Are you agreed that this guy be made mayor? Sign here.' We'd sign it."

In this atmosphere "Los Villa," as the Villaseñor family was known, emerged first as rebels. They took up the cause of the hillbillies and peasants—the *"huarachudos,"* the "sandal wearers"—whom they rallied to their cause against the city folk.

People remember them distinctly. Andrés Villaseñor was light skinned and walked with a limp from a shooting accident as a boy. He was always armed, was always looking for trouble, and was often surrounded by a ring of *pistoleros,* usually men from the nearby village of Cuámacuaro. José Villaseñor, the oldest brother, was darker and more reserved. He tended to business but was the family's true *valiente.* He had lived for many years in the United States; he had money and was the brains behind the family's economic advance. A hard worker, he also knew how to manage a farm-and-livestock operation. "He didn't go looking for trouble, but if you wanted some, he'd give it to you," remembers one man. Adolfo Villaseñor, short and thick, seemed to live in the light his brothers cast.

At the head of the family was their sister, María Villaseñor, a woman of white skin, dark eyes that grow quickly fierce, a round face set off by high cheekbones, and a Tierra Caliente temperament that she admits is *"muy duro"*—"very hard." She was at one time a powerful politician in the state and once a student activist whom the Mexican political system co-opted in classic PRI style.

Now fifty-four, María Villaseñor's star has faded from Michoacán's political cosmos—"a relic" is how one man described her. Once a congresswoman, once a state legislator, once a favorite of Mexico's first lady, she is now unemployed, divorced, and caring for both a son crippled in a car crash and her youngest brother rendered simple by what her family has been through. She lives in a poor neighborhood near the soccer stadium in Morelia, Michoacán's state capital, and has trouble paying her phone bill. She hasn't returned to Turicato in years.

"The poor still come to me for help. They're the ones I still care about," she says. "The government functionaries don't want me near them. They don't give me anything. The party doesn't give me any work. When people say, 'Thank you, Marí, because thanks to you we have electricity,' I say, 'No, we all fought for it together.' Power never comes from one person."

The Villaseñores were *huarachudos* themselves. They were sixteen children whose father, Tomás, had been born a peon on the hacienda San Rafael. In the 1930s President Lázaro Cárdenas ordered a section of the hacienda transformed into a communal farm—an *ejido*—owned by those who had worked it as peons.

The change of ownership did not change the Villaseñores' lot in life; they lived in a one-room hut with a grass roof and worked the remaining hacienda for 50 cents a day. María remembers, as a girl, washing her face in the dew of the grass and carrying hay on her back into town to sell to passing horsemen. She remembers, too, girls from Turicato throwing rocks at her and her sisters because they didn't want to go to school with hillbillies.

Years later ex-president Lázaro Cárdenas came to town. María and a sister asked him for help in attending school. Cárdenas arranged for them to attend junior high school in Morelia. This changed their lives. They left Turicato's limited horizons. They studied hard and in the early 1960s were enrolled at the Universidad de Michoacán San Nicolás. In college María's firebrand nature overcame her shame at having no money for nice dresses or a social life. She fought for a house where rural girls could live and study. That struggle developed into a student movement that demanded freedom of speech and better education.

When in 1966 students went on strike, the state government closed the rural-student houses and the army arrived with parachutists and tear gas and kicked down dormitory doors, looking for the leaders. María spent the next two years on the run and penniless in Mexico City. At the National Autonomous University (UNAM)—which was becoming a hotbed of student radicalism—she asked one director who knew her plight for permission to continue her studies. She was denied. After that, she says, "I didn't believe any of that talk about socialism, class warfare, the proletariat. Everyone protects his own interests, his group's interests, the interest of his generation." This would become core Villaseñor political philosophy.

Finally María found work with the PRI's Confederación Nacional Campesina (CNC), though still a wanted woman in Michoacán. In 1968 the political climate in Michoacán softened, and María returned home. She campaigned for a spot on the CNC state board and won. One of the PRI's great talents is its ability to assuage the fervor of dissidents and radicals by bringing them into the system. This was now happening to María Villaseñor. In 1973 Esther Zuno, wife of President Luis Echeverría, proposed María Villaseñor as candidate for Congress from Turicato, to the thrill of the region's poor campesinos. María was "the candidate of the poor," fighting against injustice. And since the PRI had no real opposition, she won handily. Turicato's *huarachudos* were now in Congress.

Meanwhile the Villaseñores were slowly buying up Hacienda San Rafael. The family had been partners with twenty other *ejido* families in buying the rest of the hacienda in the mid-1960s, when the owners lost it to the bank. Soon the Villaseñores were pressuring their *ejido* partners to sell to them. "They were dangerous people. So rather than being in bad stead with them, it was better to sell them your share of the land," says Francisco Sánchez, a local tailor. By the early 1970s the Villaseñor children owned outright the hacienda where their father had once been a peon.

And suddenly the unwashed Villaseñores were prosperous. They had 650 acres dedicated to sugarcane alone. José's business ability soon increased the family's livestock operation to about 400 head. They bought new trucks, and in the hacienda's big house and in the fields they had dozens of employees.

The Villaseñor *piloncillo* operation also grew. *Piloncillo* is a small cone of brown sugar about an inch in diameter, processed by a simple mill. It is used to sweeten coffee, in household cooking, or by the soft-drink industry. In the

1990s *piloncillo* has all but vanished as a product from the Turicato region. But in the 1970s and 1980s many sugar cane growers were producing *piloncillo*. It was generally a cash business, and for many years it was very big. In the Turicato region in the 1970s and 1980s, owning a *piloncillo* mill was the difference between a life of comfort and one of hopeless poverty. "Those who owned a mill were doing well," says Sergio Trigo, the newspaperman.

With María Villaseñor a rising PRI star, by Turicato standards the family was doing very well. Now with money, land, and political connections, the Villaseñor brothers turned their attention to local politics and Turicato city hall. "I have the impression that her brothers abused her power," says Domingo Rodríguez, a public-works engineer who worked in Turicato for a long time. "The brothers feel powerful because their sister is a congresswoman. So, 'Since my sister is a congresswoman, I'm going to decide who is the next mayor.'"

The emergence of a hillbilly family brought with it the kind of abuses that town residents had feared all along. "What happens is they form into groups," says Trigo. "There's one who's a leader, and around him form people who like to fight and look for trouble. They like to walk into a cantina and throw everybody out. They figure that's a real achievement. This grows; the group gets larger. Then it becomes, 'Let's take over this land.'"

Their allies became other *huarachudos*—the Cervantes and Piña families from the village of Cuámacuaro. The Villaseñores had helped these families gain legal title to land they had been farming. The Cervantes and Piña families were made policemen under the Villaseñores. For several years they were the only band of heavily armed men in the area. In 1986 María Villaseñor was elected to Michoacán's state legislature. The Villaseñores became a de facto government in Turicato, and soon they were doing as they pleased. They were said to provide protection for drug smugglers. There were many killings; bodies turned up in the river. The Cuámacuaro police thugs killed Jesús García, from the village of Piedra del Agua, for his gun as he walked along a country road. Talk was that they'd murdered a government engineer who had come with money for a mill project. And there were reports, unproven but part of the reputation anyway, that members of the Villaseñor family had raped wives of its peons.

The family warred repeatedly with rival factions in town. In 1984, when the Villaseñor candidate and a rival candidate were in essence tied after a mayoral

election, then Governor Cuauhtémoc Cárdenas placed a local rancher, Octavio Sierra, in the post as a neutral candidate. Villaseñor followers from Cuámacuaro showed up at Sierra's ranch, demanding that he resign and promising to take over city hall. Sierra says: "I came out of my house and said, 'If you want to take city hall, come by tomorrow; just come armed because we're going to get into it.'" Sierra remembers that seemed to calm things.

Today people remember that María Villaseñor didn't do a bad job as state legislator. But her brothers seemed intent on using her political prominence to dominate the *municipio*. "They were blinded by power," says one man.

Yet the Villaseñor family never did fully dominate local politics. They proved in the end to be poor politicians. Their frequent warring—"their bellicose nature" as one man put it—earned them many enemies. By 1989 a significant part of the *municipio* nurtured in dark silence a pure and vital hatred of the Villaseñores, and among them were many of the same poor peasants—the *huarachudos*—that the family once rallied to its side.

Amid all this, a few miles from Turicato, Nueva Jerusalén was taking shape. As congresswoman in the 1970s, María Villaseñor remembers writing a report to the Interior Ministry warning that the sect's illegal settlement "would lead to conflict if it wasn't channeled properly." She took it upon herself to properly channel Nueva Jerusalén. "For a while 300 buses of pilgrims a day would come," she says. "It began to grow into a village, like one of those squatter shantytowns around Mexico City. We had to give them services. Puruarán refused to give them water or land for a cemetery. I was invited to speak to them, and I promised to negotiate for services."

That was the initial contact in what would develop into a mutually beneficial alliance between the Villaseñor family and Papá Nabor. They quickly came to need each other. To the priest, the family's power meant that his village could receive services that nearby communities were intent on denying it. With Villaseñor protection he could keep squatting the land and run his village as he saw fit. The Villseñores saw Nueva Jerusalén as a source of cheap, hardworking, noncomplaining labor. This was crucial. The Turicato region had been consistently losing people to the United States. Returning emigrants were unwilling to tolerate brutal sugarcane work. Nueva Jerusalén took up the slack. The thousands of poor and devout pilgrims became an enormous labor pool for the region's sugarcane industry and even today are famous for their willingness to endure work that others will not, at the minimum wage, and for singing while they do it.

Soon Los Villa were being treated like dignitaries at Nueva Jerusalén. Their arrival was cause for a community feast, with believers turning out with their best food and their finest dress; the pilgrims would put on special dances that the Villaseñores would watch from the table of honor. "When it wasn't work season, we'd only see them occasionally," says Lucio Pérez, who came to Nueva Jerusalén in the mid-1970s as a teenager. "But when there was work, they'd come by every week or month. Sometimes they wouldn't be able to find any-one to work, and they'd come and say, 'Give me a hand.'" So that week Papá Nabor would end mass saying there was a religious duty to perform: everyone was to go work the Villaseñor sugarcane fields. Those who didn't were barred from mass and from receiving communion. The pilgrims expelled from Nueva Jerusalén tell of spending at least a couple of years working in the Villaseñor *piloncillo* operation. "Sometimes they'd just give the workers food and they'd pay Papá Nabor the money," says Martín Yáñez, who worked on the Villaseñor farm for two years.

It's not clear when the village cast its lot with the PRI. Many people as-sume that the PRI cut a deal with the priest early on, threatening to evict him from the property if he didn't support the party. Luis Martínez Villicaña, run-ning for governor in 1986, rode by the village's entrance and saw hundreds of the pilgrims welcoming him. "At that moment, I think the PRI got it that here was a large group of willing voters," says Domingo Rodríguez, the public-works engineer.

But whenever the arrangement with the party was made, Nueva Jerusalén's ties to the Villaseñor family were there from the beginning. The family's economic connection with the sect naturally became a political one as the family ventured into local politics. Besides providing cheap labor, Nueva Jerusalén was also a solid source of votes for the family. Before each election, the Villaseñores would send over a cow to be butchered and eaten. This treat was usually enjoyed by the nuns, priests, and Papá Nabor rather than the village commoners.

The political connection grew especially strong in 1988 and would ignite years of turmoil. That year saw the great national schism in the PRI.

Cuauhtémoc Cárdenas and others in the party broke to form the Democratic Front. Cárdenas ran for president and lost amid harassment and suspect circumstances that included the last-minute crash of the electoral computer system. In 1989 the Front became a political party, the Party of the Democratic Revolution (PRD).

For the first time Mexico had real political competition, and it tore many parts of the country to shreds. The PRI-PRD conflict was often window dressing, a disguise for deeper conflicts rooted less in ideology than in old land disputes, family feuds, or battles for regional economic and political power. While one party ruled Mexico, these battles were fought under the PRI umbrella and ignored outside their regions. But after 1989 these feuds took on a political tint that got noticed because supposedly they were part of the country's fitful transition to democracy. Yet if after 1989 one family donned the PRD banner, leaving the PRI to their rivals, it didn't mean that either side had any deep appreciation for the political ideologies involved. Nor was one side necessarily more versed in the tenets of participatory democracy. It was simply an institutional way of continuing the feud that had begun years before.

Some of these feuds did evolve into fragile exercises in democracy—though only after climaxes of awesome bloodletting. It was as if certain people just had to die, and the old rancor buried with them, before the place could advance. This is more or less what happened in the *municipio* of Turicato.

Cuauhtémoc Cárdenas had inherited, in Turicato, a deep wellspring of love created by his father, who as governor and president had redistributed land to peons. So when Cárdenas, the son, broke with the PRI, large numbers of people in Turicato followed him, as they did across Michoacán. However, the Villasenores remained Priistas, and locally the party more than ever became associated with the family. This meant that the PRD in Turicato attracted people whose priority in life, as much as supporting Cárdenas, was revenge against the Villaseñor family and their henchmen from Cuámacuaro.

None of this, however, was understood by a young man, a twenty-four-year-old graduate from the Universidad de Michoacán with a degree in pharmacology. Efraín Barrera returned to Tacámbaro in 1989. He was the third child of Salvador Barrera, a respected campesino from the village of

Santa Cruz de Morelos in the Tierra Caliente. Salvador Barrera had once fervently supported the Villaseñor family but now had followed Cuauhtémoc Cárdenas into the PRD. Everywhere people were talking about the upcoming state elections. The Barrera family had moved from Turicato to Tacámbaro years ago. But Mexican law allows anyone to run for office in the place of his birth. So people from the PRD in Turicato began recruiting Barrera as a candidate to run against Adolfo Villaseñor. Efraín did notice that no one was too anxious to run for mayor, but he was flattered and young and filled with the idealism of the moment. "They painted me this rosy picture. 'You'll win.' People I'd talk to would say, 'We'll support you.' People wanted me to do it. I said, 'If there's unity, let's do it.' But really I didn't know anything about the *municipio* of Turicato," he says. "If I'd known the political conditions there, I never would have run for mayor."

The campaign featured only a couple of armed standoffs with Villaseñor *pistoleros* and some death threats. Barrera's campaign was supported throughout the *municipio*. Adolfo Villaseñor had no campaign team to speak of. He toured the *municipio* with his bodyguards/policemen from Cuámacuaro.

At Nueva Jerusalén, there was no question who the village would support. Papá Nabor believed Cuauhtémoc Cárdenas to be a communist. From the afterlife, Lázaro Cárdenas was telling the village seers that he was ashamed of his son. The general wanted the community to vote PRI.

The residents of Nueva Jerusalén had always voted in Puruarán. Now the PRI insisted that a voting booth be put in the community itself. Barrera and the PRD opposed the idea. The local elections committee finally decided to put a voting booth in the village, then annul the votes later.

Election day came. Barrera won twenty of twenty-two voting places and was ahead by 800 votes. Then arrived the votes from Nueva Jerusalén. The community voted 1,295–0 for Adolfo Villaseñor and the PRI. As surprising as the sect's final count was the quantity of votes cast in the ten-hour electoral day. Even today, voting simulations by Mexican officials show that at peak efficiency, one voting booth processes about a ballot a minute, or about six hundred votes in a day. Nueva Jerusalén had more than doubled that.

Barrera and the PRD claimed victory. Yet at the last minute the state electoral committee reversed itself and decided to allow the Nueva Jerusalén ballots. Adolfo

Villaseñor now claimed victory. That set off what essentially became a civil war that lasted five years, in which a worm of violence dug its way into Turicato, began to twist, and didn't stop.

On January 1, 1990, as Turicato prepared to swear in Adolfo Villaseñor as municipal president, Barrera and about five hundred others marched into city hall. They occupied the building and swore Barrera in as mayor. He in turn appointed a cabinet and police force. Meanwhile Adolfo Villaseñor set up his government in a building across town. For two months Turicato had two municipal governments. Two police forces would pass each other on patrol, guns cocked and pointed.

In late January, Villaseñor gunmen ambushed a squad of soldiers, mistaking them for PRD supporters. Two soldiers died in the shootout. Barrera's followers now decided to keep a pile of weapons under a canvas tarp in city hall. They hid gunmen in a nearby house and deployed many others in the hills.

In mid-February, Villaseñor *pistoleros* and police officers descended on the town plaza. A shootout erupted. Barrera and the PRD hunkered down in city hall, firing out its windows. The Villaseñor *pistoleros,* meanwhile, took cover behind benches and the graceful tamarind trees that give the plaza shade. Two people were wounded, yet nothing was resolved. At the end of the day Turicato still had two governments.

A few days later Andrés Villaseñor came to visit Efraín Barrera. "I invited him in," Barrera says. "He had a pistol in his shirt, but when he comes into the house he takes it out and he puts it in his waistband. He says, 'I've come to tell you that if you don't leave city hall in twenty-four hours, I'm going to kill you.' I said, 'I don't think that's the best way to resolve the problem.' He left angry."

The next day Andrés Villaseñor was gunned down near Puruarán by two men who were following him. Barrera says he had nothing to do with the murder. And in fact most people in Turicato today believe Andrés's killing was paid for by a drug smuggler that the Villaseñores had unsuccessfully tried to ambush. Later people said that the two men who killed Andrés were his friends and were seen drinking in a cantina, singing "*Maldito dinero*—'cursed money'— for you I betrayed a friend."

Meanwhile in Nueva Jerusalén, Papá Nabor was commenting frequently on the warfare beyond the village walls. The Villaseñor family, he told his flock, was fighting for the party and for the Virgin. He asked them to pray for a Villaseñor victory.

It wasn't to be. In March, Michoacán's state legislature voided the Turicato municipal election and appointed a teacher from Tacámbaro, Ramiro Chávez, as mayor.

Efraín Barrera retired to Tacámbaro, where he tried to wind down from the tension of the previous months. María Villaseñor took her brother's murder as a sign to stay away from Turicato. José Villaseñor, however, who was less involved in politics, saw no reason to leave. It was a poor calculation for a man whose good sense had impressed even his enemies.

Stalwart supporters of Barrera's campaign happened to be members of the García clan from Piedra del Agua, whose father, Jesús García, had been killed for his gun by the Cuámacuaro police/thugs years earlier. For some reason, perhaps because he was oblivious to this key connection, Ramiro Chávez appointed men from Piedra del Agua's García clan as police officers.

On July 15 a city truck full of these policemen shot and killed José Villaseñor and his foreman as they sat in a pickup in Turicato's plaza. Figuring to settle accounts once and for all, the officers proceeded up the rugged road winding above Turicato to the village of Cuámacuaro, home of the Villaseñor *pistoleros* who'd killed Jesús García. There they opened fire on a group of men standing around the basketball court. Seven men died that day in Cuámacuaro, along with an unknown number of pigs and chickens. The García clan from Piedra del Agua returned to their village and dug in, their police career at an end.

The Villaseñor family was now damaged. But the war against it wasn't finished. Their sugar cane fields were burned and their livestock wells poisoned. The family fled to Morelia. Suddenly the Villaseñor empire was wiped from Turicato.

Yet the violence did not go with them. If the Villaseñores weren't around, their enemies would now collect vengeance from the folks from Cuámacuaro, who themselves were deeply aggrieved and vowing revenge for the basketball court massacre. Ramiro Chávez resigned as mayor, citing severe health problems. A former army general was brought in as interim municipal president. Some kind of relative calm settled over the *municipio* for the next two years.

But 1992 was again an election year, and the *municipio* hunkered down as

the parties set about choosing candidates.

Versions of the Villaseñor political model were now repeated. In the region's harrowing political atmosphere, each candidate needed the support of *pistoleros* for protection. But it was a deal with the devil. Victory meant three years of doing the bidding of thugs who, when the candidate won, would want to be paid off in police badges.

The PRD nominated Everardo Duarte, a man of limited education but intense energy, who had risen from poverty to become a mildly prosperous cattleman. Duarte won the election and this time the results were not disputed. Anger at the Villaseñor family and the PRI and the excitement of the times overwhelmed the Nueva Jerusalén vote.

But as Duarte's swearing in approached, rumors flew that the *Priistas* from Cuámacuaro, the ex-*pistoleros* of the Villaseñores, would descend upon the town to shoot anyone attending the ceremony.

Indeed, that day the *Priistas* from Cuámacuaro crept down the mountain into Turicato. The PRD was holed up in a restaurant a block from the plaza. Occasionally one of them would go outside to urinate, then knock on the door to be let back in. About 10 a.m. there was such a knock at the door. Baldemar Ambriz, a campesino, opened the door, then reached for his gun in his waistband. But it was too late. Shots rang out. Ambriz fell dead, and for the next hour the two sides shot it out across town. There were gunmen on the roofs and others taking cover at each street corner. Duarte ducked into the Livestock Association building. Finally the Cuámacuaro gunmen retreated up the hill. Three days later Duarte was sworn in as municipal president.

A month after the swearing-in shootout, Cristóbal Medrano, a *Priista* from the village of Zárate, was murdered in Puruarán. By coincidence, Everardo Duarte had to visit the village of Zárate a few days later to swear in municipal officials. He was met by armed Medrano family members who demanded that Duarte turn over the killers. There in Zárate the two sides—the Medrano family and supporters, and Duarte and his contingent of cabinet members and police officers—faced off, tense and silent until, in something out of a Western, Ramiro Medrano's son, Armando, let slip the finger that held the trigger to his gun. A round accidentally fired. The ensuing shootout lasted most of the day.

Seven people died. Duarte and his cabinet holed up in a farmer's house. They would have died, too, had not the farmer been a man the gunmen respected, the son of a general, who forbade anyone to take a life in his home. For two days the mayor and cabinet of Turicato remained hostage in the farmer's house, with the gunmen from Zárate circled outside. Finally the army and the state police arrived and rescued the constitutional government of Turicato from the farmhouse.

By now it seemed the violence would never leave the *municipio*. Every killing was a bellow on the righteous fire of revenge. Each shootout, every ambush added another fiber to the complex web of hatreds that canopied across the *municipio,* linking families who had never met but had heard that the other had something to do with the death of a brother, a father, a cousin, a friend. The Villaseñores had been arbiters of feuds like these. But Villaseñor power was no more. Now each region of Turicato had its own dominant family, armed and with something to fight about.

Beneath it all lay the absence of authority, the isolation, the ignorance, the limbs lost to machetes, the alcoholism; it was another Wild West at the end of another century. "Where there's no control, where there's a lot of weapons, a lot of unemployment, and no way to lead a life of dignity, this is what happens," says Efraín Barrera. "It's the law of the jungle."

Over the next three years of Everardo Duarte's term there were many more deaths. Thugs from Puruarán had supported his campaign, so Duarte had to make them police officers. They came to control the government. They threatened the municipal secretary. They believed the *síndico*—or city attorney— had been ratting them out to the state police. So one day they put him in a pickup truck, put a gun to his head, and drove him a few times around the plaza. He resigned soon thereafter.

Duarte had a spooked look about him and often considered resigning. Yet he served his term, spending it largely in the safety of city hall, then took his mistress and moved to the United States.

During these years economic life stopped in the region. No one could put down his weapon long enough to work the fields or tend livestock. Every rocky country road was an invitation to an ambush. Corn didn't get planted, and sugar cane went uncut. The thriving *piloncillo* industry died as growers

abandoned their mills and moved away.

Entire families, sometimes entire villages, were dug in and alert, waiting for their enemies or the military. With no way to make a living, they turned to banditry. And so the political violence evolved into pure criminality. The gangs hijacked trucks, robbed marijuana growers, rustled livestock. In Piedra del Agua the García clan—whose hatred of the Villaseñores for the killing of Jesús García had brought them to Efraín Barrera's campaign—evolved into the region's most famous gang. El Grupo de Los Treinta—the Group of the Thirty—they were called. For two years, from about 1992 to 1994, the name of Los Treinta rang across the *municipio*. They seemed to be everywhere—rustling livestock and robbing travelers here, shooting it out with state police over there.

In 1994 the military put a roadblock between Turicato and Puruarán and set about arresting or killing off the bandit gangs. Others saw that the military meant business and laid down their guns. So five years after the Nueva Jerusalén vote threw Turicato into civil war, a version of peace came to the *municipio*.

* * *

It is another hot day in Turicato, this one in October. The road to Hacienda San Rafael turns sharply up a hill above town. It's rugged, steep. "These are the much commented on roads of the Villaseñores," says Humberto Hernández. Humberto is twenty-two. He has swept-back hair and a thin mustache. When he laughs, his eyes and his mouth break in straight lines across his face. Humberto was among those expelled from Nueva Jerusalén in June. At the time he had been working as a mechanic in Puruarán and had purchased a car—a Nissan with suspect suspension and a wobbly left front tire. The car is now his saving grace. On being expelled, he painted it white, emblazoned on it the red lettering of the local taxi crew, and almost overnight became a cabdriver. He now navigates carefully around crags and crevices on the way to what was the center of the Villaseñor empire.

"I remember they would ride these roads in these really new trucks," he continues. "They had a Ford and a Cheyenne. I remember working in their fields when I was about nine or so. Papá Nabor would send us with a foreman." He pauses, swerves around some rocks, then, as he approaches the top of the hill, he says, "Who knew how they'd turn out?"

The hacienda the Villaseñores once worked, then owned, then lost was a marvel in its day—three large houses, a mill, and about a thousand acres of land falling away into a valley. Enormous shade trees protect the patio from the harsh sun. Visitors remember seeing Nueva Jerusalén pilgrims at work in the kitchen and as farmhands. But neither the family nor the pilgrims have been back in years. Plows and tillers rust slowly, and the brick walkways are overgrown with brush. A stone aqueduct that served the family's *piloncillo* mill is only damp now. The family rents the land to the local sugar mill. But no one tends the houses, and no one has dared squat. After years of neglect, the buildings' roofs have caved in and shards of tile are everywhere. A mattress has rotted away to the springs.

In the patio, under mounds of dirt and broken tile, buried like some archaeological artifact, lies the final remnant of the Villaseñor empire. All but covered beneath the patio's debris, it is a large oil painting, about three feet by five feet. The canvas is rotting in the damp dirt and is falling from its frame like overcooked meat from a bone. But wipe the dirt and tile away, shoo off the spiders, and a face appears. It is the face of a woman, round, with white skin, high cheekbones, and big, dark, fierce eyes. María Villaseñor.

About three thousand miles away, Adolfo Villaseñor lives now in a dingy house in a working-class neighborhood of Pittsburg, California. After his brother José's murder, Adolfo left the region—not waiting to attend the funeral—and emigrated to the United States. He hasn't returned. His two brothers are dead. So is a son, murdered in Morelia. Adolfo has nothing. "I've had a very tough time since I left," he says as he remembers his son and sobs slightly.

He wandered from job to job in Napa Valley, Las Vegas, and Washington State before finally settling in Pittsburg. Now in his fifties, he's a dishwasher and suffers from pains in his hands. He asks for help in finding a new job.

Adolfo Villaseñor now sees Turicato's civil war and his family's fall as something planned from above, by state politicians. "They said, 'Kill yourselves, and we'll see who's left standing,'" he says. These politicians, Adolfo Villaseñor believes, viewed the people of Turicato the same way Turicato's town folk viewed the *huarachudos* from the Tierra Caliente—as ignorant barbarians who needed to let blood every so often. So they let the violence happen.

"Our biggest error was getting involved in politics," he says. "We were very hard workers. We worked the sugar cane. We'd go to the United States—José and me—and use the money to pay off the [hacienda] land. Then we'd come back to work the sugar cane. Finally we owned the land. But we got into politics, and it did us a lot of harm."

* * *

But the area had advanced. In 1995 election day came to Turicato and calmly went. Pedro Reyes was elected municipal president. Reyes had once been a *Priista* but had switched to the PRD. The party chose another man, Leonel Galván, as its candidate. With the campaign about to start, Galván was murdered by nephews as part of a long-standing family feud, and Reyes became the PRD's emergency candidate.

Reyes won the election only because Nueva Jerusalén ballot boxes were delivered several hours late to voting authorities. Reyes sued and had all the votes—roughly 1,200—annulled. "If that hadn't happened, I'd have lost," he says. But no one was killed after Reyes and the PRD were sworn in.

At Nueva Jerusalén the enforcement of the stricter rules regarding mass, rosary, and the opposite sex coincided with the arrival of the PRD in power in Turicato. The PRI government has moved in to fill whatever void the Villaseñores' departure may have left. Governor Víctor Tinoco Rubí campaigned in the village when running for office in 1995. In late 1997 Nueva Jerusalén received 60 percent of the federal money sent to Turicato to reduce dropout rates among schoolchildren—though the community has only 12 percent of the *municipio*'s population, has no recognized public school, and pays no taxes.

Meanwhile the expelled families say they continue to believe in the Virgin. Many want to return to their homes despite the expulsion. They don't believe Papá Nabor knows of their plight or of his leaders' abuses.

Barring that, however, they want indemnification. They are poor and mostly illiterate and have spent a lifetime dedicated not to accumulating wealth but to praising the Virgin. Most of the families have nothing but the clothes they wear. A state official has offered them 10,000 pesos apiece to forget their complaint. Who would pay this money—Michoacán taxpayers or the people who remain in Nueva Jerusalén—wasn't made clear in the offer. The families refused, saying their property is worth more. Santiago Aparicio figures his home, possessions, and animals are worth about 150,000 pesos: "When are we going to earn it all back, earning twenty-five pesos a day?"

* * *

I visited Nueva Jerusalén twice in the summer and fall of 1998, but the entrance was the most I ever saw. The guards said journalists have been prohibited since 1982, when the exodus of Mamá Margarita's followers attracted reporters from all over the country and their stories angered Papá Nabor.

However, Nueva Jerusalén has been forced to allow observers on election day. On that day anyone can drive into the village without questioning from the guards, as long as he pretends to belong there. So I returned for a third time on November 8, election day in the state of Michoacán. And thus I finally entered Nueva Jerusalén.

As it turned out, Nueva Jerusalén is better appointed than many Mexican villages. It has come up in the world since the early days of leprosy and open sewers. The houses on the interior of the village are mostly of concrete block; most of the streets are paved. The market buzzes with a few flies, but it, too, is cleaner than markets elsewhere. Nueva Jerusalén is uncommonly quiet, due to the absence of cars and stereos. Its streets are for walkers. Here and there are ads for Fresca and Pepsi. Small shops sell food, fruit, and soda. One store sells cassettes of hymns to the Virgin and Kodak film. Street dogs wander aimlessly.

In fact, it would have been hard that day to tell this from any other Mexican village were it not that November 8 is also All Saints' Day in Nueva Jerusalén.

On All Saints' Day those ordained residents of Nueva Jerusalén dress up as the saints they were ordained to represent. And since the Catholic Church recognizes saints from across history—from the deserts of Palestine to the royal courts of Europe—November 8 in Nueva Jerusalén ends up looking a lot like backstage at some elementary school Christmas pageant. Just all the actors are adults.

Hundreds of people calmly stood in line to vote while strapped to their heads were halos, apparently made from clothes hangers wrapped in aluminum foil.

I got up on a wall to look down the lines of people. The halos grew tangled in the distance, like bunches of television antennae, and from that angle looked like a convention of 1950s-style spacemen.

The women were dressed as if for a Renaissance convent. Most had colored robes of linen. Others had billowy dresses of green taffeta or velvet of black or bright red. Some wore crowns and looked like queens, their flowing gowns reaching the ground; others dressed like brides, like princesses, like fairy godmothers. They had wands, some of them. A good many women in black habits could pass for nuns were it not for the ever present wire halos affixed to their heads.

The men of Nueva Jerusalén, too, were dressed like kings and knights and Moses, with tunics and staffs made of broom handles and wooden swords that looked like wood shop projects. They walked about calmly, their quiet normalcy contrasting starkly with the craziness that clearly gripped the town. A lot of men wore fake beards. These were ratty mats of polyester fur hanging from their faces by wires or rubber bands that stretched around the back of their heads.

Beside one road, two men sat talking. One had a staff, a fake beard, a wire halo, and an Arabic headdress of black and white stripes. The other was dressed in a kind of Roman centurion garb. His linen tunic was red and blue and yellow. Perched on his head was a centurion's helmet. This, on closer inspection, proved to be a construction worker's hard hat, painted silver and worn backward. Atop it was fixed a column of red nylon bristles, taken from an industrial broom, that formed the helmet's comb. In one hand he held a wooden sword, also painted silver. Neither man was too anxious to talk. But they told me they, too, had taken saints' names. Saint Martín de Porres was the man with the jerry-rigged centurion helmet. The man with the beard and staff was Saint Isaac.

At the entrance to Nueva Jerusalén, as I was about to leave, several more men were sitting and talking. One of them wore another of these fake beards, with the ubiquitous wire halo attached to his head. He wasn't happy to talk about his getup, either. His friends laughed and made fun of his beard. His saint name was Zachariah. "In life, Zachariah had a beard," he said.

I wandered about the village that day half the time in awe and half the time busting out laughing at the full-bloomed insanity around me. Yet there was something deeply disturbing about it as well. This was an entire village of grown-ups going about their daily business in painted swords fit for third graders, golden crowns, wedding gowns, and those preposterous halos and fake beards. Entering Nueva Jerusalén on All Saints' Day is awesome testimony to the combined power of religion and isolation. It was like being dropped into some lost world, a bad science-fiction movie Shangri-la, where everyone takes for granted that dressing as if for an elementary school pageant is what the Virgin wants.

Yet later it occurred to me that this unhinged pageantry—this seeming non sequitur—wasn't so out of keeping with the region's unstable history. Perhaps the violent lunacy that gripped Turicato mutated into something less barbaric to find its last expression in the weird mental meanderings of a lost priest.

On this election day, Nueva Jerusalén cast 1,012 for the PRI and none for any other party. The PRI won. In part this was due to the Nueva Jerusalén vote. But mostly the PRI victory was due to the PRD, which proved no more democratic than its adversary. The local PRD chapter had elected one of its founders, the tailor Francisco Sánchez, as its candidate for mayor. However, departing mayor Pedro Reyes and his allies in Morelia decided that the candidate would, in fact, be Fidel González—the treasurer under Reyes—and suppressed Sánchez's nomination.

Fidel González proved a tepid candidate. He stumbled over speeches he read from papers that he held close to his face. Meanwhile Sánchez the tailor joined the small Labor Party (PT). Based on Sánchez's popularity, the PT, which had never before proposed a candidate in Turicato, took second place. González and the crippled PRD finished third—an astounding self-inflicted defeat for a party whose victories had come at such a high and recent cost in human life. With the opposition vote thus divided, the PRI won.

And so it was that years after the Villaseñor family had tried the strong-arm route to power, the PRI earned via the ballot box and Nueva Jerusalén what it had lost through the barrel of a gun and returned to govern Turicato.

—1998

JESÚS MALVERDE

Every third night Florentino Ventura can be found sleeping outdoors, guarding the large blue shrine that honors the belief in a lawless man.

His faith keeps him there.

The summer when Florentino was twenty-three, he was working as an oyster diver in Mazatlán. One day he became tangled in his rope underwater. He wrestled with the cord and began to drown. Then suddenly the face of the bandit Jesús Malverde appeared to him. Florentino finally freed himself. He rose to the surface and came immediately to Malverde's shrine to give thanks. From the way Florentino describes it, the experience led to the kind of spiritual catharsis that makes people change their lives. Florentino changed his. He'd been on track for what would have been at least a minor political career. He'd been a PRI youth leader and won a scholarship to study political science in Mexico City. He was taking a break from studying law when the diving accident happened. But he gave it all up, and, now thirty-six, he's been here ever since. "The Mexican political system is useless. It was false, pure lies," he says. Florentino found more truth in Malverde.

Florentino Ventura is one of thousands of people who believe the bandit Jesús Malverde—"the Angel of the Poor," "The Generous Bandit"—works miracles in their lives. And all year long they come to his shrine here in Culiacán, capital of the Pacific coast state of Sinaloa, to ask Malverde for favors and thank him for those he's granted. They leave behind photos and plaques with grateful inscriptions: "Thank you, Malverde for saving me from drugs," writes Isaias Valencia Miranda, from Agua Zarca, Sinaloa; "Thank you, Malverde, for not having to lose my arm and leg," reads the dedication on a photo of a man in sunglasses identifying himself as Lorenzo Salazar, from Guadalajara. There are plaques from the Guicho Ríos family from Mexicali, the León family from Stockton, the Chaidez family from North Hollywood, and many more from the great Mexican diaspora in Los Angeles.

"Dear holy and miraculous Malverde," reads one letter to the bandit left at the shrine. "I'm writing this letter so that you'll help me with a problem I have with some friends I had, so that they won't look for me anymore. Make them forget the problems we had. Make them please leave my parents and my sister and me in peace. This is what I ask of you, Malverde, that you do this favor. I promise that when I go to Sinaloa, I'll go visit you and I'll bring you what I can because I live in Los Angeles, California. Malverde. Your son, Ángel Cortéz. Sept 15, 1992."

Sinaloa is one of those places in Mexico where justice isn't blind and the lawless aren't always the bad guys. Having the government as an enemy can improve a reputation. So maybe, then, it's not such a stretch to understand how thousands of people could come to believe that Jesús Malverde, a renegade supposedly long dead, performs miracles in their lives.

Nor is it hard to understand how over the past two decades Jesús Malverde has also become what he's now known best as: "the Narcosaint," the patron saint for the region's many drug smugglers. Mexican drug smuggling began in Sinaloa. Here smugglers are folk heroes, and a "narcoculture" has existed for some time. Faith in Malverde was always strongest among Sinaloa's poor and highland residents, the classes from which Mexico's drug traffickers emerged. As the narcos went from the hills to the front pages, they took Malverde with them. He's now the religious side to that narcoculture. Smugglers come to ask Malverde for protection before sending a load north. If the trip goes well, they return to pay the shrine's house band to serenade the bandit or place a plaque thanking Malverde for "lighting the way"; increasingly plaques include the code words "From Sinaloa to California."

* * *

The story of Jesús Malverde takes place during the reign of dictator Porfirio Díaz (1877–1911). The Porfiriato, as the era is known, was a time when big business, especially foreign-owned big business, was encouraged above all else. Díaz saw himself as the rest of the world saw him: as Mexico's modernizer. Yet progress passed by millions of Mexicans, who remained as impoverished as ever. As the century turned, the country fermented with the social anarchy that would explode in the Mexican Revolution. The hills and back roads of

Mexico were alive with bandits, some of whom would become folk heroes to the country's poor.

The legend is that Jesús Malverde was one of these, a bandit who rode the hills near Culiacán. They say Malverde robbed from the rich and gave to the poor, a Mexican Robin Hood. It must have been true, for they say the government hung him and left him to rot in a tree. That was on May 3, 1909. Every year on that day there's a great party at Malverde's shrine.

There are two movies and one play dealing with Malverde's life. But historians have found no evidence he ever existed; a likelier prospect is that Malverde is an amalgam of two bandits—Heraclio Bernal from southern Sinaloa and Felipe Bachomo, from the north part of the state. "If he lived, faith in him is a remarkable thing," says Sergio López, a dramatist from Culiacán, who has also researched and written about Malverde. "If he never lived, it's even more remarkable because people have created this thing to achieve the justice that is denied them."

What does exist is a rich and fluid body of lore about Malverde's life. Supposedly his Christian name was Jesús Juárez Mazo, and he was born sometime in 1870 near the town of Mocorito. In some versions he was a tailor. Others have him as a construction worker or a railroad hand, who built the tracks that were just then extending through northern Mexico and that brought with them the opportunities that made some men wealthy and other men bandits.

Some say Malverde began a life of crime after his parents died of hunger. Some versions say he was finally betrayed by a friend, who cut off his feet and dragged him through the hills to the police to collect a 10,000-peso reward. Others have him betrayed and shot to death. His betrayer dies three days later, and the governor who wanted him put to death, Francisco Cañedo, dies thirty-three days later, from a cold contracted after going out at night without slippers.

López believes Cañedo may have invented the Malverde legend himself to keep the state's hacienda owners thinking twice before indulging in the more extreme abuses of their peons. But there's also a story that the governor challenged Malverde to rob him. Malverde, as a construction worker, slipped into the mansion, stole the governor's sword, and wrote on a wall, *Jesus M. was here.*

Malverde's first miracle, according to one version, was returning a woman's lost cow. Eligio González, whose work to keep faith in the bandit alive has

earned him the nickname "The Apostle of Malverde," tells still another story. "The rural police shot him in the leg with a bow and arrow," González says. "He was dying of gangrene. He told his friend, 'Before I die, *compadre,* take me in to get the reward.' His friend brought him in dead and got the reward. They hung Malverde from a mesquite tree as a warning to the people.

"His first miracle was for a friend who lost some mules loaded with gold and silver," is the way González tells it. "He asked the bones of Malverde, which were still hanging from the tree, to find his mules again. He found them. So he put Malverde's bones in the box and went to the cemetery where the governor is buried. He bribed the guard to let him bury Malverde there. He buried him like contraband. No one knows where."

Malverde's shrine stands near the railroad tracks on the west side of Culiacán, well known to just about everybody in town. Nearby are Malverde Clutch & Brakes, Malverde Lumber, and two Denny's-like cafeterias: Coco's Malverde and Chic's Malverde. Outside the shrine people sell trinkets, candles, and pictures. Inside the shrine are two concrete busts of the man. Malverde, supposedly a poor man from the hills, turns out to look a lot like a matinee idol— dark eyes, sleek mustache, jet black hair, resolute jaw. Near the main busts are stands of pendants, baseball hats, tapes with *corridos* to the bandit, countless picture cases with photographs of the bandit and a prayer to him in thanks, and rows of plaster busts wrapped in plastic.

To one side sits Doña Tere, rocking the day away. She is a cheerful, plump woman, made up with bright red lipstick. She, too, has her tale of faith. Eight years ago, doctors diagnosed Doña Tere with cancer. She decided not to take medicine. "I said, 'Malverde, they say you do miracles. I'm going to ask you for a miracle. I don't believe in you. I know I'm going to die.'" Doña Tere's still around. "I have four Malverdes in my house," she says. "One in the kitchen. One in the dining room. One going up the stairs and one in the bedroom. I bless myself every time I'm at the foot of the stairs." Last time they operated on her, Doña Tere paid for two hours of music to be played to Malverde. "Rich, poor, sick, not sick—everyone comes here," she says. "When they come here and pay for music to be played, people here say it must have gone well for them on their trip [sending drugs to the United States]. I don't know. It's their own private business. I don't ask. But I'll tell you. More people come here than go to church. If you go to church asking for food, the priest will give you advice, but if you come here asking for food, you'll get food."

There was a time not so long ago when the Malverde shrine was a funky thing, awash in the artifacts of Mexican working-class life. You'd see piles of baby pictures and faded, out-of-focus Polaroids of men in cowboy hats and poorly spelled thank-you notes in twisted handwriting. There'd be slats of cardboard warping under the weight of pasted plastic flowers and photo collages of extended families. One man had left a Baggie of hair, thanking Malverde for allowing him to survive a term in San Quentin. There were artificial limbs and corncobs and a lot of photocopies of recently obtained passports. Fishermen would leave large jars containing enormous shrimp in formaldehyde— thanks for a successful catch. González remembers two different men—one left a pistol, the other an AK-47 rifle.

But that's been changing lately. Families have built glass enclosures—in essence, shrines within a shrine. Malverde has gone a little more high-class. There isn't as much room anymore for all those piles of homemade thank-yous and photo collages.

Still, faith in Malverde remains above all a private affair. There is no ceremony here. A constant stream of people arrive, place a candle near one of the busts, sit for a while, bless themselves, touch Malverde's head, and leave. Some are poor. Others arrive in shiny trucks and cars, looking very middle-class.

Jesús Gastelo, a rugged, aging farmer, enters in sandals and a shirt buttoned halfway up his plump torso. In his arms is his newborn son, Sergio, now thirteen days old. Gastelo lights a candle. "I'm really old," he says. "How old do you think I am?" Gastelo is sixty-four, once widowed, and he's just fathered his eighth child, this with his new wife, a woman of thirty-one. A lot to thank Malverde for. "I've believed in Malverde since I was a little boy," he says, dropping his index finger to his knees as an indication of how tall he was at the time that faith began.

Back then, faith in Malverde didn't get the press it gets today. It centered around a pile of stones and pebbles, which is now about fifty yards away and across two streets. "It was just a pile of rocks and stones, like a grave," says Gastelo. "It was where they say he was hung."

Believers will tell you the reason there are so many of them is that Malverde

answers faith like Jesús Gastelo's. But there are other reasons. One of them is Eligio González, a fifty-year-old jack-of-all-trades who wears his "Apostle of Malverde" tag with pride. The other is a bright idea the state had in the late 1970s. Government officials decided to build new state offices on the land where people congregated to pay tribute to Malverde. Opposition to the idea was fierce. Newspaper columnists opined over the idea. "The protest lasted two years," says Gastelo. Finally, state officials were forced to provide land where the shrine now stands, and another plot for the stones and pebbles that mark his grave.

They say all of Culiacán turned out for the demolition of the pile of stones and pebbles. They say, too, that stones began to jump like popcorn and that the bulldozer operator had to get drunk to have the guts to roll over it; they say the machine broke down when it touched the grave. Finally, though, the job got done. The massive state government building now sits over Malverde's original tomb. The tomb itself was moved across the street from the shrine, at the corner of Insurgentes and 16 de Septiembre streets.

Researchers say it was during these years that the media christened Malverde as the Narcosaint. In the late 1970s Sinaloa was embroiled in the great military strike against the region's drug smugglers that was known as Operation Condor, during which the army went through the hills attacking traffickers and innocent ranchers with equal vigor; the state lost an estimated two thousand hamlets and villages during those years as people abandoned homes, land, and livestock and streamed from the hills to the cities. "The press, sharing the same view as the authorities, or perhaps so as not to be left behind when the graft was being handed out, added their two cents," says Luis Astorga, a researcher of the narcoculture who lived in Culiacán during this time. "They labeled Malverde as the 'Narcosaint.' The drug smugglers, due to their social origin, had inherited the belief in Malverde. But the media gave it a kind of yellow slant. They were really the ones who made Malverde into the drug smuggler's saint, forgetting how old the belief in him really was."

Today the pile of pebbles signifying Malverde's tomb now shares a vacant lot with Tianguis Malverde—Malverde Market –a consignment car lot where Víctor Manuel Parra and Marco Antonio Osuna will try to sell your used vehicle in exchange for a commission for themselves. The pebbles sit in the middle of the lot, surrounded by weeds and Suburbans, Nissan pickups, Monte Carlos, and dented Volkswagens. Atop the pile is an iron cross and a weather-beaten bust of Malverde, now for some reason encased in a rusty birdcage. Like many parts of Sinaloan life, the car mart depends largely on drug money. In the fall, marijuana growers are tending their crop and about to harvest. So sales at the lot are slow, this being October. The men say they are biding their time until December and January, when the growers will have sent their loads north and have money to burn. So they have more than enough time to talk about Malverde and the tomb of stones they work around every day. "He'd rob from the rich and give to the poor. This is where they say he was hung," says Parra. "[The owner] wanted to build on this site, but he couldn't get rid of it. The soul of Malverde wouldn't permit it. They brought in machinery, but the machines broke down."

The truth, it turns out, is more mundane. José Carlos Aguilar, the lot's owner, says he wants to build a high-rise hotel or office building on the site but hasn't been able to find funding or a suitable partner. Still, if he did build on the site, Aguilar says he'd leave aside a corner of the building, or maybe a section of the hotel lobby, for the bandit's tomb. "You can't be inflaming people's sensibilities," he says.

The building dispute with the state government may have distressed many of Malverde's believers. But the faith emerged from it energized and publicized. Eligio González has built and added to the new shrine. Now it has what it lacked before: a true focal point.

González is protective of the faith's image. "All this stuff about the Narcosaint, they say it, but he's for people from all walks of life," he says. González is a small man with leathery skin and sandals. He says the outlaw Malverde cured him of gunshot wounds in 1973. But he punctuates his speech with the words "God first," so no one gets the wrong idea. "If it weren't for God, Malverde couldn't do anything," he says.

He spends his days driving through outlying villages selling newspapers and Pepsi-Cola. Pepsi-Cola, it turns out, is a stalwart Malverde sponsor. Local distributors often give González discounts so he can sell the soda at concerts and dances and keep the profits for Malverde. Once during a large encampment of campesinos outside the state building that lasted two months, he sold

four thousand cases of Pepsi. Not surprisingly, Coke products are scarce at the shrine. With the money González feeds his family, and the leftovers go to Malverde. Money taken in donations and sales at the shrine goes to help with burials—more than 9,500 so far—and to buy wheelchairs for the crippled and cots for the poor. Nor was faith in Malverde hurt when González won a raffle recently—a Volkswagen Golf car was the prize—which he promptly sold. Proceeds, he says, went to buy more cots, coffins, and blankets for poor families. (He's said to have won the national lottery twelve times.)

González is a controversial figure in Culiacán. Local reporters wonder slyly what else he might be doing with the money. There have been reports that González hasn't shared royalties from cassettes sold at the shrine with a crippled man who wrote ballads to Malverde. But if this is the case, González doesn't seem to be getting rich. He has no phone, and his clothes are humble.

"Thanks to God and Malverde, there's something for everyone," he says. "Not much, but something. Little by little we've built this. Before it was just tiny. People have put in a lot of faith. If there's no faith, there's no miracles."

—1997

TEPITO

Entering from Eje 1 Norte in the center of Mexico City, Tepito yanks you headlong into its bewildering maze of tunnels with a rude assault of noise, color, and the chaos of commerce. The first timer loses all bearings in the steep cliffs of stereos and Rubbermaid containers and striped tennis shoes and ringing alarm clocks. People who live here will tell you not to look lost. Tepito's thieves and pickpockets watch for the look of shell shock. But it's hard. Within a few yards the thump-thump-thump of disco blends with the *cumbia's* bounce and together they almost overwhelm the constant, wailing pleas of the vendors as you pass: *"Escójale, joven. Qué quería?"* (Take your pick, kid. What do you want?) An awesome army of consumer goods stands at attention. Many years ago vehicles moved down these streets. But now these streets are jam-packed with metal-frame stalls hung with merchandise each morning and denuded each night. Reebok knockoffs—Reetok, Retbok, Redbook, Reeboh, Reecher, Reewer, Reedlaak, Ruddock, and so on—far outnumber trees.

Several blocks later, the barkers' tune hasn't changed but the metal frames have given way to sheets spread on the ground. Here cars can at least pass. This is where Tepito remains basically as it has for decades, lined with Mexico City's *cháchara* (junk)—the frazzled televisions, old encyclopedias, warping Santos and Johnny records, letter openers, wrenches, lensless sunglasses, crooked silverware, and pile upon pile of used clothes. The junk evokes the barrio's grit and gives an idea of what Tepito must have looked like before contraband changed everything in the mid-1970s.

Sooner or later you make your way to the center of all this, to *saldero* (remainder seller) corner at Toltecas and Matamoros streets—a maelstrom of discount merchandise that best typifies what this historic neighborhood has become. Under a low-hanging plastic awning, vendors shriek the benefits of Flintstone toys from an expired McDonald's giveaway, of Hard Rock Café boxer shorts, of Planet Hollywood T-shirts and Playboy underwear—all *saldos,*

remaindered.

In the middle of all this stands Francisco Moreno. A silk shirt is buttoned about halfway up his ample stomach. Gray chest hairs peek out above the shirt. Moreno and his guys are selling reject shoes from a Guadalajara factory. He did have them at 20 pesos a pair, but since he lowered their price to 10 pesos, customers are three deep and picking like pigeons at a park.

Tepito's evolution over the last fifty years is reflected in the Moreno family story. His grandmother resoled old shoes and sold them. His father sold *cháchara*—junk—and his mother darned panty hose for resale. When Moreno was in his thirties, he turned from *cháchara* to selling contraband merchandise and made a ton of money. Now he's a *saldero,* selling remaindered goods. As the new century approaches, Moreno's only son uses cocaine heavily. "You know, there were guys whose trade it was to turn old coats inside out and make you a really great-looking new coat," Moreno says, his voice rising above the clamor around him. "They did the same with shirts. I knew a guy who carved the head-board to the bed for [movie actress] María Félix. It was beautiful. There's none of that anymore. Now we're all *salderos* or coke dealers. The rest is all gone."

* * *

In the republic of Mexico, no barrio is older, more famous, or more infamous than Tepito. Tepito was here when the Spanish arrived, and many an urban-renewal attempt since has died on its hardened streets. Just east of Mexico City's downtown, Tepito is a fifty-seven-block Mexican Hell's Kitchen: insulated, suspicious of outsiders, with its own speech, humor, and such a wide range of social problems—alcoholism, sexual promiscuity, child abuse, mental illness—that health authorities call it "multipathological." Yet people here remain fiercely proud, and the neighborhood owes its continued existence to their intense resistance to any change the outside world might propose for them. The motto "Proud to be Mexican, but it's a gift from God to be from Tepito" puts things in what people here would call the proper perspective.

Tepito has also been a barrio with an inordinate importance to Mexico's economy. Tepito has been: Mexico's central black market, Mexico City's thrift store, a key component in the government's fight against inflation, and the city's recycling center. It is still such a major marketplace that it sets the prices nationally on a number of consumer goods. Out of Tepito came a string of great boxers. Modern anthropological studies of the urban poor were born here after Oscar Lewis used people from the barrio for his landmark examinations of what he called the "culture of poverty": *Five Families* (1959) and *The Children of Sánchez* (1961).

As much as anything, though, Tepito has been Mexico's crucible for the formation of a pure capitalist ethic. When Mexico's economy was run by the state, Tepiteños were guerrilla free traders, scavenging value from society's detritus. Tepiteños entered the global economy well ahead of the rest of Mexico and got rich selling the illegal merchandise their countrymen craved. The mercantile spirit, for better or worse, still burns bright in Tepito. The saying here is, "Everything's for sale, except dignity", and these days that includes cocaine and some sixty-five million pirate cassette tapes a year.

"The attitude is, 'If you'll buy this from me, I'll sell it to you. I don't care what you do with it,'" says Alfonso Hernández, a Tepito native, a citizen representative in the city government, and director of the Center for Tepiteño Studies. "It's a kind of urban neoliberal survival in which only exchange is of value. You give me the money; I'll give you this. I don't care if it kills you, poisons you. That's your thing. And since you like it, I'll also sell you the pirated version."

The capitalist ethic—selling whatever someone will buy—was the secret to Tepito's resilience and essential to its survival. But that which made it strong now corrupts it. Today a once poor but productive barrio is one where residents' only skill is for bringing in the mounds of Flintstone giveaways and Retbok tennis shoes that choke its streets. In that sense, Tepito's transformation over the last three decades is one metaphor for Mexico's entry into the global economy, raising the question of whether what the country, like the barrio, might get in the bargain is nothing more than streets awash in *cháchara*. And even that it can no longer afford.

* * *

"My grandmother was a remontera [resoler]. She'd put on a heel, a shoe sole. She'd find a pair of shoes at the dump and if the top looked good, she'd throw them in this bag she carried. She'd take off the sole. She'd have a bunch of tacks in her mouth, even

though she was toothless. She'd put on a new sole and put the shoe together.

"My parents were merchants. My mother darned panty hose. She also resewed old shirts and blouses, sold used dresses. My father was the classic chacharero. *They had no education. They sold used stuff. For us, selling was like an inheritance. We sold anything, not just one line of items. All of us who worked as* chachareros, *we'd go to the* colonias *far from here and the people would sell us whatever they were throwing out.*

"Now I'm a saldero. *Stores or factories will give me a call, tell me they've got something to sell, remaindered or discontinued. It doesn't matter. I'll go get it. Shoes, dresses, jackets, blouses."*

—FRANCISCO MORENO

Tepito's die was cast years before the Spaniards ever arrived. Tepito was, even then, the humblest neighborhood in the Aztec capital of Tenochtitlán. And even then its residents were making something out of nothing. Tepito was the place where beans and corn that were unacceptable for Aztec nobility were brushed up and resold to the rest of the city. "If it had been a submissive place, they would have eaten it," says Ivette Cardenia, who is writing her doctoral psychology thesis on Tepito. "But they generated an economic subsistence system out of waste. It was their own system of commerce."

Modern Tepito has its roots in the reign of the dictator Porfirio Díaz (1877–1911), when Mexico City began to grow. Tepito was the first stop for thousands of migrants, all finding temporary lodging in its *vecindades*—the complexes of small apartments surrounding a common patio. The city grew quickly, though, and for the poor Tepito's *vecindades* became permanent housing. "The *vecindad* was the very spinal cord of Tepito," says Hernández. "It kind of forced living together. Because there wasn't room in the house, life spilled out onto the common patio, and from there it spilled out onto the street."

Through most of this century, Tepito was that urban anomaly—an independent barrio where life could go on with little contact with the outside world. As the postwar "Mexican Miracle" unfolded, poor people from other neighborhoods joined the industrialized rank and file. Tepiteños kept working for themselves. "Everything you needed was made here in the barrio," says Luis Arévalo, one of the last surviving shoemakers. Tepito became one of

Mexico's shoe-making centers, with hundreds of families living from the trade. There was a time when it even competed with León, Guanajuato. The *vecindad*—from the family apartment to the patio—was the workshop.

Tepiteños were urban artisans who ingeniously invented new trades as necessity demanded. Besides the *remonteros* and *chachareros, pantaloneros* turned used adult pants inside out, cut them up, and made a pair of children's pants. As the century progressed, and technology with it, Tepiteños focused their ingenuity on cast-off blenders, irons, telephones, and other appliances. They learned to repair them using scavenged parts, producing a functional appliance for a fifth the price of a new one.

The ability to extract value from almost anything, letting nothing go to waste, applied to food as well. You could buy live chickens in Tepito or, for a whole lot less, the dead ones that had suffocated in the truck on the way to Mexico City. Tepiteños invented *las migas,* a soup made from spices and stale bread, with cow bones for taste. A few neighborhood cafeterias still serve it. No one serves *escamocha* anymore, probably because it was, literally, garbage. A few Tepito vendors toured downtown restaurants every night, gathering in large barrels whatever customers didn't, or couldn't, eat. They'd sell the concoction by the kilo back in Tepito. Mothers would pick out the cigar butts and other inedibles and stew up the rest. "If you were lucky, you'd get a piece of fish, or chicken, or something," says Moreno. "They used to say, 'Only lazy people die of hunger in Tepito.'"

Mexico knows Tepito from its role models. Thieves were one. When Oscar Lewis was in Tepito, the barrio was known for its thieves market, in which all manner of stolen goods were for sale. One of the more famous criminals in Tepito's pantheon was La Jitomata (The Tomato). La Jitomata—Leonor Aguilar was her name—followed at least two grand Tepito traditions. She salvaged value from waste, restitching torn panty hose and selling them. Then she discovered her second talent lay in that other hallowed Tepito tradition: holdups. Something of a female Fagan, La Jitomata ran a gang of young boys whom she trained as robbers. They were known as "The Diaper Gang." Instead of using guns or knives, they'd keep the victim's attention with ferocious pit bulls and Doberman pinschers. La Jitomata once hired some mariachis for a party. Later she refused to pay, killed three of them instead, and buried

them in her *vecindad*. The police found out and dug up the bodies. La Jitomata became a convict and a legend.

But no one better embodied the nature of the barrio than the topflight boxers Tepito produced from the 1950s through the mid-1970s. The list was long: Raúl "Ratón" Macías, Luis "Kid Azteca" Villanueva, Salvador "El Negro" Torres, Octavio Gómez, Chucho Hernández, José "Huitlacoche" Medel, Rodolfo Martínez, and more. They were small, scrappy men—flyweights and bantamweights—who fought as if their lives depended on it and made Tepito proud. "My mother would lock me in the house to run out and touch 'Ratón' Macías," says Rodolfo Martínez, who in 1973 would become the only world champion Tepito produced.

The pugnacious boxer was an appropriate symbol for the neighborhood. Beginning in the late 1950s and continuing through the 1970s, city planners devised ways of razing the barrio. Tepito hung on and withstood them all. "Many parts of the historic center of Mexico City have been eliminated," says Ivette Cardenia. "Whole residential zones of the 1950s don't exist anymore. Tepito is still there because they've developed this spirit of resistance."

It took the earthquake of 1985 to transform physical Tepito. Nearly half of the neighborhood's housing stock—*vecindades* all—was destroyed and much more was seriously damaged. The government in its haste to rebuild put up duplexes and three- and four-story apartment complexes. The new apartment buildings isolated families and snapped Tepito's communal lifestyle that the *vecindades* had fostered. Apartment walls were thin, unlike those of the *vecindades*, so fights between neighbors became more common. "You can design a maze that will drive a rat crazy. This is what happened," says Alfonso Hernández.

The earthquake dug deep into Tepito's heart. But its effect on the barrio's way of life was nothing compared to the wrenching changes that had begun a decade earlier. Fittingly, this transformation wasn't imposed on the barrio. Rather Tepiteños themselves, the arch-free traders, invited them in.

"We were making huge amounts of money. Rivers of money. We were eating chicken every day. We weren't prepared for it. In this barrio, the standard of living

has always been low, underdeveloped. I'm from here and I'll tell you we weren't prepared for it.

"It was like a movie. You'd close your eyes, open them, and you thought you were in a wonderland. When I was growing up, there were a lot of thieves on this street here, Tenochtitlán. People from here knew not to go there for fear of getting robbed. Tenochtitlán was the street where the fayuca *really took hold. After that there were many times when you couldn't walk on Tenochtitlán because it was so packed with people and stands.*

"Most of us thought it would never end. People were coming from all over the country. Tepito was the distribution center. There were people who didn't know how to read or write but who'd go every night to these nightclubs in the Zona Rosa.. . . You'd see some guy and he'd have a car. 'Look at that guy. He's got a car. What's he up to?' 'He's bringing stuff back from Laredo, the –.'"

—FRANCISCO MORENO

* * *

Fayuca. The word meant contraband, illegally imported merchandise: stereos, televisions, calculators, cameras, silk shirts, tennis shoes, blue jeans, blenders, and blouses. The government slapped this stuff with steep tariffs when imported legally as a way of protecting Mexican industry. Tepito brought it in illegally. To Tepito, *fayuca* meant easy money and lots of it. Despite the official prohibitions, Mexicans gorged themselves on the outside world's baubles. Tepito was their dinner table. It was a time tailor-made for the Tepito mind-set. In the go-go era of *fayuca,* what mattered was not what you sold or how you brought it in but how fast it would move. The trickle of suitcases containing small items like perfume, watches, and jewelry in the mid-1970s became, by the 1980s, torrential truckloads of twenty-one-inch televisions and full home stereo systems.

To a government running a desiccated economy, it quickly became clear that the contraband did two things. First, it appeased the middle classes, who didn't really care where they bought this stuff so long as they could buy it. Second, *fayuca* also helped dampen inflation. The prices in Tepito were usually well below what the same goods sold for in the stores that had legally imported them. "The authorities wanted to lower prices without really entering the global economy," says Gustavo Esteva, a sociologist who lived in Tepito for several

years during the *fayuca* boom. "So the government used Tepito and the *fayuca* to fight inflation." Though *fayuca* was illegal, it was bought and sold openly in Tepito. The regime couldn't appear to allow it in and yet didn't dare keep it out. Eventually the industry was carved up among Tepito's *fayuqueros,* commandants of customs, the judicial police, the highway police, and other government officials. After a while the highway police in San Luis Potosí, midway between Laredo and Mexico City, decided they wanted their cut too. The wife of President José López Portillo, Carmen Romano, was said to be one of the greatest *fayuca* importers.

The arrival of *fayuca* was a key moment in Mexico's economic history. *Fayuca* was in its own way as important in rocking the regime's credibility as the 1968 Tlatelolco massacre, the periodic peso devaluations, and the fraud-riven elections of 1988. Its presence showed that the protected, state-run economy no longer had a prayer of providing what Mexicans now expected out of life. Though Mexicans talked economic nationalism, they voted with their feet and mobbed Tepito, looking for the smuggled imports.

And for the first time Tepito got rich. In Tepito the *fayuquero* took the place of the boxer as the model for economic advancement, though in this case the road to riches was accessible to thousands of people and few of them missed the turnoff. Since the *fayuca,* Tepito has produced no great boxers. Instead Tepito's *fayuqueros* took on the status of legendary renegades; at least two B movies were made about them.

But to Luis Arévalo, *fayuca* hit Tepito like crack in an urban U.S. neighborhood. Arévalo, a portly, spectacled, fast-talking man, speaks like the purist he is when the subject of Tepito and *fayuca* arises. He's been a shoemaker for most of his fifty-five years. In the mid-1970s he formed the Free Workshop of the Art of Shoemaking specifically to counter the effects of *fayuca* on Tepito's traditional trades. "This barrio was 100 percent artisan," he says. "Everything that was sold here was made by people in the barrio. *Fayuca* came along. Cheap products flowed in. People, seeing they could make money overnight, dropped their trade. Overnight it changed people's economic station. It was like a drug. It began generating huge amounts of income. The barrio has always had a lot of sin and vice. But it was limited because people didn't have the money to indulge their every desire. Along comes the *fayuca* and now the women want to dye their hair blond, the men don't want to leave the bars."

Though the 1985 earthquake was the coup de grace to Tepito's shoe-making industry when it knocked down the *vecindades* that had been makeshift workshops, the trade's decline was apparent as early as 1980—the height of the *fayuca* years—when Tepito was no longer the second-largest shoe producer in Mexico after León.

Enrique Gallardo was one of those who left the trade. Gallardo is a small man, given to wearing gold chains, half-shaded sunglasses, and silk shirts. As a boy, Gallardo learned shoe making from his older brothers. Then the *fayuca* came, and Gallardo left it all to become a vendor. "We just wanted to make money, to be someone," he says. "Here in Tepito, you know, it's hard to buy a car doing this kind of work [shoe making]. You have to be a professional, an engineer, a doctor, working in an office. But in *fayuca* you could make more than any damn professional."

Gallardo brought it all in—blouses, perfume, calculators. His brothers brought in silk shirts before they were common. Gallardo had five booths and eight workers. "I was selling so much that every third day I'd go to L.A. I wasn't even sleeping. At times I wasn't even eating." A few years into the *fayuca*, Gallardo finally bought himself that car. A Chrysler Le Baron. He made sure it was used. "I didn't know how to drive and I didn't want to wreck a new one.

"I became a womanizer. We'd get back from a trip and we'd go to the Hilton, the Del Prado, really expensive hotels. I just used up my money doing stuff like that. We'd get back from a trip, go to Cancún, rent a boat with some girls, and get drunk. That's how the life was, and that's how many Tepiteños lived it. If I hadn't been a womanizer, I'd have been one of the top *fayuqueros*. But you lose your way. That's what happened to me."

Tepito's children began hanging around with "Juniors"—upper-class kids from upscale neighborhoods of Polanco and Coyoacán. Fathers, flush with cash, gave their sons cars and motorcycles before the kids learned to drive. The Tepiteño accident rate skyrocketed, and some of the young people were killed.

Fayuca provided fertile ground for Tepito's microcapitalist ingenuity. For a while the government sent customs agents to Tepito, stationing them every forty yards around the barrio's perimeter. Tepito got cleaner than ever in its history. Merchants rented barrels and uniforms from street sweepers and used

them to move the merchandise into the barrio. Another fellow put a coffin filled with watches in a hearse, drove into the barrio, and, with men posing as pallbearers, carried the goods past inspectors.

The Castillo family was the example of just how big the *fayuca* trade became. At the height of its empire, the Castillos were displaying the merchandise and signing up buyers, who'd pay in advance for their order. The customers would then camp all night outside the store on Aztecas Street, waiting for the trucks to arrive from Laredo the next morning. The family accepted only 100-peso bills, counted the money with counting machines, and was reputed to deal directly with the federal judicial police commandant in charge of northeastern Mexico. Their empire ended in a bloody shootout with the neighboring Cólin family, clothes sellers, in a dispute that began over the Castillos' trucks disrupting the Cólin family business every morning.

Mexico's entry into GATT, then NAFTA brought the *fayuca* boom to an end. The Mexican government began to lower the tariffs on consumer goods. Customers began finding what Tepiteños were selling in legitimate stores that offered service, guarantees, and receipts and didn't have thugs around the corner waiting to rob the clientele. When the peso was devalued in 1994, sales plummeted further. People still go to Tepito, since merchandise is a little cheaper and carries no sales tax. But the *fayuca* gold rush is a memory.

If anything, the current crisis has added to Tepito's congestion as more people, unemployed or underemployed, have turned to street vending to survive. Today 80 percent of all merchants selling in Tepito are from outside the barrio. Commerce, instead of giving the barrio life, now suffocates it. In some parts of Tepito services like garbage, gas, and telephone repair are impossible to get during the day for all the vendor stalls clogging the streets. Tepito is no longer miserably poor. But neither is it independent and self-sufficient. It is overrun, part of the world, but weaker for it. Tepito gave up the crafts it invented and that sustained it for so long. Now Tepito just sells for a living. And in this day and age only one thing you can sell will turn a profit like *fayuca* once did.

"Now that fayuca *sales have fallen, people say, 'What am I going to do, cut linoleum? Hell, no.' These are people who've developed some bad habits, spending*

big because they used to earn big. The fayuca *ended. No sales. But the costs remained high. People had loans, some had credit cards. Some had dollar loans. The same thing happened. 'Look at that guy. He should be like us because we work the same hours. But look, he's still got his car.' Well, of course, he's selling cocaine. Cocaine just took the place of* fayuca.*"*

—FRANCISCO MORENO

* * *

In an office in the heart of Tepito, Alfonso Hernández lectures visiting college students on the latest threat to the neighborhood's integrity. "They speak pidgin Spanish. Getting along with them is difficult, even harder with the women. We've heard that they fight a lot with their women in the street. But the women always win," says Hernández.

On the cover of the latest edition of the community newspaper is a tarantula—representing cocaine—attacking Tepito. "We don't think it's by chance that drug trafficking arrived at about the same time as these people," Hernández tells the students. It's a remarkably frank expression of hostility. Hernández is an articulate and intelligent man. Still, there's no evidence to show that what he's saying is true: that the forty or so Korean merchants now selling women's clothes in Tepito have anything to do with the wide-open cocaine sales in front of a dozen of the barrio's largest apartment complexes. Still, cocaine and Koreans are the new trends for this historic neighborhood facing the global economy. Both have ignited Tepiteños' old suspicions regarding the motives of the outside world.

"This is a barrio that has resisted, that's been around for more than five centuries, and it's falling apart. Tepiteños haven't found a way to stop the disintegration," says José Alberto López Sustaita, a journalist who covered Tepito for several years. "They're feeling defeated. If you say this to a Tepiteño, he'll tell you to go to hell. They don't admit it. But that's where I think they are."

In Tepito both Koreans and cocaine have their roots in the demise of *fayuca.*

Koreans came first. Koreans, it seems, are something of an economic indicator; their presence says good things about a country's investment climate and business potential. Korean immigrants, both in Mexico and the United States, are middle-class, college-educated folks who are looking for a

small-business opportunity rather than a minimum-wage job. Only the language prevents them from finding work as engineers, architects, and accountants. In Korea, Mexico got good press during the last years of the Carlos Salinas presidency. "Everyone said, 'Mexico: Growing Country,'" says Seung Hoon Han, president of the Korean Merchants Association, with offices a few blocks from Tepito. "We heard that with the Salinas government the Mexican economy was growing and the future looked good." Daewoo, Hyundai, Samsung, and other Korean corporations have been here for years, primarily in the *maquiladora* sector. Tepito's aggressive commerce attracted small businessmen and businesswomen bent on opening their own shops.

Relatively few Koreans ever made the trip. For reasons having to do with immigration law, Mexico's Korean population is much lower than that of other Latin American countries. Argentina, Peru, and Ecuador are each home to several times more Koreans. But a few is a few too many for Tepito. Those Tepiteños who sell or rent to Koreans are viewed as traitors. "Whose side are you on? Those who would screw Tepito or those who are trying once again to save the neighborhood?" wrote Hernández in an article titled "Asians Against Tepiteños."

Tepiteños, by and large, see Koreans as another attempt by the outside world to remake their neighborhood. "Tepito has always defended itself from people who aren't from here but want to come in and change it," said Leopoldo Reyes, a vendor of used tools and a leader of one of Tepito's sixty vendor associations. "They [the Koreans] are leaving now. There aren't as many as there were. They're not surviving the [economic] crisis or all the thieves."

"But the Tepiteño does," added Enrique Gallardo. "They [Koreans] want stratospheric sales. They're not finding them. The Tepiteño survives, bears up."

But that's just talk. In reality, Tepito's business owners, suffering from a letdown as the *fayuca* tailed off and unwilling to return to their funky trades of years gone by, took one look at the Koreans' money and welcomed them warmly. The Koreans struck lease deals with established Tepito vendors—paying well above market rents, according to some—and set up shop.

Meanwhile cocaine arrived. To many Tepiteños cocaine was in no way different from *fayuca*. It was simply another product to sell the rest of the world. After all, no one was going back to eating *migas* and *escamocha*. It's said that as many as a hundred families now sell coke in Tepito, all with police help. The newspapers are beginning to refer to the Tepito Cartel—a group of young men that supposedly controls drug dealing in the area. What is clearly true is that Tepito at night now resembles many U.S. urban cores. Cocaine sales to drive-up customers are made in plain sight, perhaps the only place in Mexico City where this happens. A major selling spot is in front of a *vecindad* where Narcotics Anonymous also has a meeting place; a dealer there made five sales in a half hour one weekday night.

That cocaine—and not the paint thinner or glue that afflict dirt-poor neighborhoods—is Tepito's problem is an indication of how the barrio has risen and at what cost. Tepito teenagers are now snorting coke at alarming rates. Residents complain that this, in turn, has led not just to an increase in crime but an increase in random crime—by which they usually mean that they're now the victims as often as shoppers from outside Tepito.

* * *

"We went to a psychologist. What we didn't know was that our son had been doing coke for more than a year. You're not prepared for this kind of thing. It's a real psychological blow. We went to a clinic and they convinced us to leave him there for at least three months. But then I wanted him home for Christmas. It was the biggest mistake. He lasted another month and a half. Then he'd leave home for days, wouldn't go to work. Yesterday he got home at 3:00 a.m. You begin to realize, 'Where's my watch? Where's my rings? My money?' The other day he stole a gun and sold it.

"I'd give him money to buy diapers for his son, food for his family. But finally you realize it's harmful to give the kid money. There are times when you have to give him tough love. But then there are times when I can't take it and I just give him the money."

—FRANCISCO MORENO

* * *

As Tepito enters yet another century, the likelihood that it will endure is strong. What might not stick around are Tepiteños. All neighborhood schools report a decline in enrollment in the last few years, and Lucio Tapia Elementary School even suspended afternoon sessions this year for lack of students.

The smart *fayuqueros* used their profits to invest in houses and businesses elsewhere. As commerce has taken over, land prices have skyrocketed. Many Tepiteños rent their postearthquake apartments—too small for a Mexican family and now without the added living space the *vecindad* patios provided—as storage for merchandise and have moved to other barrios. The Koreans, too, are leaving. Last year their sales died along with everyone else's. Several have returned to Korea or to greener pastures in Latin America. Even most of the boxers in Tepito's gyms aren't from the neighborhood; more kids are enrolled in pro wrestling classes than are training to be boxers, a nifty metaphor for the substitution of the phony for the real that the neighborhood has made in its economic life.

Some remaining Tepiteños have taken up an ingenious new racket. They've become leaders of the vendors who sell in their streets. There are now sixty-two vendors associations in Tepito. Yet these organizations merely relinquish more Tepiteño independence. The associations are supposed to strike deals with authorities and keep the police from harassing the vendors, whose activity—selling on the street—is not permitted but can be tolerated at the right price. In exchange, they agree to support the PRI/government, something that older generations of Tepiteños would have scorned. "Whenever the party wants us to show up at a rally or a meeting or to vote, we have to do it," says Florentino Solís, a Tepiteño native who leads an organization of 160 *chachareros*—junk sellers. Thus the PRI sells what's not the party's to sell—the public streets—in exchange for keeping the government, which the party also controls, off the vendors' backs.

At the moment, the question of the barrio's future is unanswered. "There's an ambivalence regarding the fact that Tepito is becoming other people's territory," says Ivette Cardenia. "There's one part of Tepito that wants to modernize. As they say, 'We have to change to continue being the same.' There's another wing that's very tied to the traditional. There's great nostalgia for the past."

Alfonso Hernández is one of those who believes Tepito must change to endure. He also thinks he knows what's needed: Las Puertas de Tepito—the Doors of Tepito—a large shopping mall of the kind associated more with Coyoacán and Polanco than a scruffy derelict like Tepito. As planned, the five-story building would have one hundred stalls, banks, and restaurants anchoring the project and eight hundred parking spaces underground. Hernández sees it helping Tepito evolve into a kind of horizontal mall, with customers taking a shopping tour that fans out through the neighborhood's streets but starts in Las Puertas.

The massive development is only in the model stage now, and it's anyone's guess whether it'll be built. But in Tepito's circle-the-wagons view of life, it's already caused quite a stir. People view Hernández as a sellout and too big for his britches, both for proposing the project and for accepting a position in the government. "[Las Puertas de Tepito] is for people who have money and can pay that kind of money to have a spot in the building," says Enrique Gallardo, who is among those who has made the transition from *fayuquero* to vendor leader.

Still, Las Puertas de Tepito offers a vision of Tepito in the twenty-first century preferable to the cocaine-induced urban nightmare, which is the competing alternative at the moment. Las Puertas would be Tepito's bid to recapture the middle-class buyers who left when GATT and NAFTA deprived the barrio of its comparative advantage in *fayuca*. To Hernández and other modernists, Tepiteños, once intrepid voyagers in the global economy, once ingenious microcapitalists, have lost their edge, their creativity, and their imagination and are, of all things, unprepared to compete. This is the legacy of Tepito's entry into the world, a trip that has ended awash in cocaine.

In the *fayuca* era, "we learned something too late," Hernández says. "We learned we hadn't acquired a commercial culture. Most of us were nothing more than distributors. Very few really became merchants. A real merchant knows how to please clients, to reinvest. We didn't learn how to manage capital. In retail, specialization is everything. If Tepito doesn't specialize, it'll die. Specialization brings with it the challenge of providing services to customers. The metal-tubed stand was, in its day, an incredible innovation, as primitive as they look today. Before that, the merchandise was laid on the ground. It was an innovation, but now we need something else. Why? Because customers now want and expect something else."

—1996

THE LAST VALIENTE

The *valientes* have all gone from the valley of Jaripo. Only their legends remain. Most of them have died, and others have faded away and forgotten, eagerly, how it was before. Some have moved north to the United States to live out their days in California Central Valley suburbia, with big American cars and lawns and concrete driveways.

The village of Jaripo is in the northern part of the state of Michoacán. It is surrounded by rugged hills under a big clean sky. Jaripo is a quiet village; the valley, too, is tranquil and fresh. All this is nice, but is also deceptive. Tranquillity is really a sign of abandonment. The valley is quiet because there is no industry and no work, and thus most of its people left long ago. They live instead in Stockton, California; in Chicago, Illinois; and only return every December and January. People here have been emigrating to the United States since World War II. This is why the valley has advanced. Houses that were once of adobe are now two-story homes with marble floors. The cars have license plates from the United States, and the kids return wearing Oakland Raiders and Dallas Cowboys jackets.

A lot has changed in the valley of Jaripo. Yet the stories of how things were still reside beneath the surface, waiting to be told when old men get together in the plaza. That is when they talk about Aristeo Prado.

Aristeo Prado was the last *valiente*.

Dead more than twenty years now, he was like a gunman out of a Western. The way the people of Jaripo tell it, he was a man who for years killed and robbed, who twice escaped from prison and once saved the life of a prison commandant. Some of these stories have some truth to them. But his legend cast a terrifying shadow over the valley. His mere presence would bring Jaripo to a halt. Shop owners would lock their doors. Parents would yank their children inside. "If there was a party in the plaza and he walked into the plaza, the party would stop," says Leonardo Ortega, who grew up in Jaripo. Aristeo went

to the United States and came back changed, trying to live in peace with the world. Then he was ambushed on a city street and passed into legend.

But if his image grew to menacing proportions, others say he never was a mean man.

"I liked the way he wore his hat," says Luisa Moreno, the town pharmacist. "For me he was a fine man. A real man, like few men. Very sincere, very straight. He wasn't afraid. Sometimes people aren't bad. They are made bad. That's what happened to Aristeo."

Aristeo Prado wasn't especially tall or physically imposing. He wasn't what you'd imagine after hearing people talk about him, nothing like how a Hollywood film might portray him. One picture of him, taken later in life, is appropriately blurry. He's white, shirtless, his waist encircled in flab. He is cradling a newborn and looking like a trucker on a day off.

But Aristeo Prado was from Tarimoro, and that contributed to his renown. Tarimoro is a small community about four miles up a bumpy dirt road in the hills above Jaripo. No hamlet in the entire valley had a more fearsome reputation for savage violence than Tarimoro. For years it bathed in the blood of endless family feuds that erupted over minor insults or drunken arguments, over cigarettes and two-peso debts. If today the American-born children of Jaripo's emigrants know one thing about Tarimoro, it's that, in the words of one teenager, "they kill people up there." Tarimoro's children, as young as eight or nine, were said to walk about with loaded pistols. "None of them married a woman because she was their girlfriend," says Luisa Moreno. "They would just steal her. They killed for nothing. There weren't many Saturdays or Sundays that they didn't kill each other."

"There are entire families who've had to leave Tarimoro, giving up all hope of ever returning, because of this," says Luis Magaña, who grew up in Jaripo and now organizes farmworkers in Stockton, California. What happened to Tarimoro was an example of a secondary yet common reason many Mexicans have for emigrating to the United States: the escape from lawlessness and vengeance. Many people from Tarimoro have moved to Merced, California. Others went to Tijuana or Mexico City. Rancho Benito Juárez, another Jaripo Valley community, was formed by Tarimoro families trying to escape the bloodshed.

Tarimoro sits on a promontory above Jaripo, a collection of adobe homes and parched corn patches. A wide, unpaved road leading to it is lined with walls of dark brown rock. In the fields beyond the walls, golden-dried cornstalks peer over these walls in bright counterpoint. Coming out of Jaripo, the road meanders for a couple of miles through the rugged brush and mesquite trees, climbs a small hill, dips, then ascends once again into the hamlet. The music from a lone radio echoes across the fields. The road continues on through Tarimoro, but there's a sense, as in many Mexican ranchos, that this is the end of the line.

The story of how Tarimoro was founded is lost to the ages. There is no mention of it in the many oral histories of emigrants and hacienda workers compiled by a nearby museum. And no one alive remembers why the rancho came to sit on the one part of the Jaripo Valley with no water. Tarimoro depends entirely on the rain that falls. Most of the year it has a barren moonscape look about it, with a limited range of colors that runs from brown to fading olive green to yellow. Wind sweeps hard over the half-bald hill. The folks of Tarimoro, too, have the hard look of desert plants—coarse and unfrivolous, dedicating every fiber to extracting from the land what the land doesn't want to give. Mules and donkeys plod the road to Tarimoro's only watering hole—a small, murky pit at the bottom of a steep hill. "If it weren't for the mules, none of us would take a bath," says one man. Government engineers have tried twice in recent years to drill drinking wells, both times without success. Now it seems the government has given up and left Tarimoro to its dry isolation.

Defined by its isolation, Tarimoro is the classic Mexican rancho.

Ranchos. They are tiny and insignificant. Small hamlets of at most a few hundred people often connected by blood and marriage. Yet they have played a monumental role in Mexico's development.

Ranchos were the vehicle through which large parts of the country were settled. They were formed around, and because of, the hacienda. As haciendas expanded, they would pressure nearby small landowners to sell. These now landless folks, in turn, would leave to look for land in territory farther out on the frontier. On the other hand, when a hacienda ran into financial problems, as many did, it sold piecemeal its far-flung and marginal landholdings, again to small farmers and ranchers. In both cases, the result was these isolated settlements—ranchos—that proliferated through central and northern Mexico.

The people who would take these lands were Mexico's pioneers. They were neither rich nor poor. They had enough to risk on a future and wanted away from the city, the hacienda and its lawyers and hired guns. They settled unforgiving land, then moved on when civilization caught up with them a couple of generations later.

The dry, rocky frontier held for them not a threat but a promise. On the edge of the world, people could escape the suffocating classism of Mexico's towns. A pure meritocracy reigned: your work measured your worth. "You have to face a lot, alone. People who live on the frontier have to take care of problems on their own," says Esteban Barragán, one of Mexico's leading rural historians. "There's no police to resolve conflicts, no judges to resolve problems with others, no ambulances. It's him alone against everything else. And an attitude develops around this. People who grow up in this don't feel tamed."

Ranchero culture came to abhor the government and its representatives. Instead it valued daring and individual initiative. Rancheros were the first Mexicans to emigrate to the United States. The three states with the largest numbers of ranchos—Jalisco, Michoacán, and Guanajuato, in that order—are the states that, also in that order, have sent the greatest numbers of people to the United States. This isn't a coincidence. The United States is simply the latest step into inhospitable territory in the search of a future that the Mexican ranchero has been making for two centuries now.

The rancho formed an exuberant antidote to the paternalism, classism, and fatalism that so often seem the dominant themes of Mexican society. It was a place, however forbidding, where a simple man could reinvent himself, where he was his own master, where life was basic and thus easy to understand, where he handled his own problems and didn't have to go hat in hand to any mayor or lawyer.

This kind of self-sufficiency and aggressive independence was anathema to the PRI regime, which rigorously neglected the rancho. *Ejidos*—communal farms in which land was technically owned by the state and with a bureaucracy and organization that the regime imposed—became the favorite son. Loans for seed, irrigation, and fertilizer, school and health clinic construction—all this was channeled to the *ejido*. The rancho remained free of the regime and thus got nothing. Even academic studies focused far more on the *ejido* than the rancho. Mexico has been paying for these mistakes for years since most *ejidos* proved notoriously unproductive, drained of any dynamism by the bureaucracy the regime imposed.

Yet the world knows Mexico for what the rancho, not the *ejido,* created: tequila, mariachi music, and a good dollop of its classic cuisine. But within Mexico itself few of the rancho's creations resonate like the *valiente.* He populates countless movies and ballads. Virtually every Mexican pueblo has at least one *valiente* about whom people tell stories. Lotería, a children's game similar to Bingo using famous characters instead of numbers, has a spot on its cards for the *valiente.*

The *valiente* emerged because the rancho was a violent, brutal, and lawless place where a man needed to handle a gun, face down threats, and force people to respect him. Some *valiente* reputations grew from small incidents: a man who refused to stand by while a more powerful neighbor tried to take his land by moving a fence. Others became known as *valientes* after taking to highway robbery, or avenging the rape of a sister, or by shooting a man who had insulted him at a party. Out on the rancho, there were a million ways to earn a reputation. Life's choices were stark. The popular imagination distilled life down to two figures: the *valiente* or *el cobarde*—the coward, the one who submits to power and avoids confrontation. There wasn't too much in between. *"El valiente vive hasta el cobarde quiera"* ("The *valiente* lives up to where the coward lets him") is still a common expression in Mexico's ranchos.

In town, property owners, businessmen, and politicians generally saw the *valiente* as a bandit. In the villages and ranchos his feats, as they were retold again and again, inflated into tall tales. People quaked in fear of him or they feasted on his legends to stay sane in the face of life's penetrating unfairness. *Corridos* extolled the *valiente* as a romantic, if doomed, example of human courage. But in reality he showed the wide extremes of human nature: generosity, sadism, nobility, indifference, and mostly the simple human instinct of self-preservation.

For *valientes* were often just poor, common men who when pushed were best characterized by the phrase *"no se dejaba."* The phrase means "he didn't let himself." Within it is packed meanings that have to do with not submitting to power or enemies in superior numbers or the tricks of lawyers and mayors. *No*

se dejaba. He didn't let himself be pushed around.

The *valiente* is disappearing as Mexico's ranchos have connected to the world through roads, schools, electricity, and emigration north. The United States played an important role in his demise. It was the first place the ranchero went that really fulfilled that promise of a future, where his gamble actually paid off. As men from the ranchos went north, they came back different. Dollars paved streets, built those houses with marble floors, and physically transformed the small settlements. The slightest insult was no longer reason for a shooting. Feuds died out, and parties could end without gunfights or corpses.

Nonetheless, while Mexico looks urban, this veneer covers a rancho soul. At birthday parties, weddings, or *quinceñeras,* people in Mexico City or Guadalajara may listen to rap or rock 'n' roll, but before the night is too far gone, the music will switch to *rancheras* or *huapangos* accompanied by plaintive falsetto yelps. "The rancho is depopulating, but there are still a lot of these places," says Barragán. "Today there are still 108,000 ranchos, each with less than one hundred people. Plus many Mexicans retain these [rancho] attitudes. Many people have left for the city, but the rancho is still present. It remains, at least, in our subconsciousness."

Like the rancho, the *valiente,* too, remains at the core of Mexico's soul. He is the man who stands up to the government, the boss, the police, the landowner—the man every Mexican would like to be if he only had the gumption, which is one reason people like to tell his stories. Mexicans have another saying: "The *valiente's* place is the jail or the cemetery." It's a reflection of Mexico's view of justice that the one person who goes alone against power is destined to meet a bad end. Even so, as the *valiente* vanishes from Mexico's horizon to emerge fat and employed in California behind the wheel of a Chevrolet, most people would still like a little bit of his spunk.

Tarimoro was once full of *valientes.* It was also, not coincidentally, the last rancho in the Jaripo Valley to emigrate to the United States. It's as if Tarimoro's own poverty kept its people from leaving. Mexican social scientists say that those who emigrate to the United States aren't the abject poor but the ones who can peer above the daily beating life metes out to see a little hope. Those with every reason to be the first to leave are often the last to go. This was the case with Tarimoro.

Tarimoro is only now going through the slow renovation that neighboring emigrant communities went through twenty years ago. There are cars in Tarimoro now, right next to the mules and donkeys. One family has a house of concrete blocks with real sliding glass windows. Electricity came six years ago and brought refrigeration, radios, televisions. A telephone for long-distance calls was recently installed.

Social life revolves around Luis García's hole-in-the-wall store selling soda, beer, candy, and other odds and ends. García is a thin, crippled, and outgoing man. He can barely walk. Rather he lurches his way about the dark dungeon of his store, then hunches into the window to deliver the goods. But none of this seems to affect his good mood. In front of the store is a bench, where men gather in the afternoon to talk and drink. The bench provides a spectacular view of the mountains rising behind Tarimoro. In these mountains some of the Cristero war—the government's war against the Catholic Church in the 1920s—was played out. Priests hid in the mountain caves and there performed mass for their ranchero flock.

It's here, in front of Luis García's store—as the sunny days of winter pass and the mules and pigs saunter by—that the legend of Aristeo Prado, Tarimoro's last *valiente,* is collected and framed from the shards of memory of people who were around here twenty and thirty years ago.

* * *

He was the fifth of the eight children born to small landowners, Antonio Prado and Abigail Ceja. He had thick, wavy brown hair and, like most kids in Tarimoro, he grew up with barely an elementary school education. At various times in his life Aristeo worked as a field hand, a butcher, a gardener. He spent a good part of his adult life in prison or on the run.

The Prados are remembered as a wild and untamed clan. Antonio, the father, could be brutal. He hit his children and wife with conviction. It's said that Antonio Prado would make his sons fight each other, then smack the one who lost. People remember a long feud the Prados had with some cousins over some land. There are also a lot of stories that the Prados liked to steal women and make them their wives. These stories are used to support the belief among

people from Jaripo that folks from the ranchos were only semicivilized.

One thing that could always be said for the Prados was that if they lived wild, they died that way, too. Carmen Prado, an uncle, was gunned down by soldiers during a rodeo at a nearby rancho. His son, Jorge, had taken a liking to one of the local girls. So he and his father tried to steal her away in front of her family, her neighbors, her friends, and the soldiers who were at the party to keep the peace. As father and son made off with the girl, the soldiers ran up and trained their rifles on them. No Prado shrank from a fight. Carmen went for his gun, but the soldiers had theirs out. They buried Carmen and Jorge together in Jaripo's cemetery.

At eighteen, Aristeo stole himself a wife. His girlfriend, Guadalupe Rodríguez, then fifteen, broke up with him after her family objected to their relationship. Two weeks later he and two friends showed up at her aunt's home in Jaripo, where she was staying. When she left the house on an errand, he grabbed her by the arm and dragged her off down the road to Tarimoro. Seeing this, her brother ran from the house with a gun and began shooting. Aristeo's friends returned fire. Only when Guadalupe decided that she would go freely with Aristeo was the issue settled. "I decided to go with them so they'd stop shooting at each other," says Guadalupe Rodríguez today. "They could have hit me. I could hear the bullets nearby." They were married two days after that but had to go to the town of Villamar since no one in Jaripo would perform the ceremony.

Aristeo's first misstep was killing a young man named Delfino Reyes. He'd been hearing around Tarimoro that Delfino had knocked on his wife's door late at night. In the rancho, this kind of thing was tantamount to adultery. Those who remember say it wasn't true, that it was probably a lie made up by a cousin. Nonetheless, Aristeo had words with Delfino and killed him in a gunfight.

Aristeo fled to Mexicali with his brother Simón, who was wanted for the murder of another man. In Jaripo word spread that they were up north. The brothers were arrested and returned to Michoacán.

They spent the next year in jail in the nearby town of Jiquilpan. As they did their time, however, their brother Mariano was murdered by a friend, Baltazar Castañeda. They were drinking heavily outside a store owned by Castañeda's sister. Townspeople say Mariano tried to force the woman to sell him the store. Guadalupe Rodríguez says they were arguing because the woman wouldn't sell Mariano any beer. Whatever the case, Baltazar pulled a gun and shot Mariano dead. Things worked that way in Tarimoro.

Aristeo and Simón were denied permission to attend the funeral, and between themselves they began to talk about escape. A few months later they paid a guard, scaled a wall, and fled into the hills, leading a jailbreak of several other prisoners.

Not long thereafter Aristeo, gun in hand, appeared at the house of relatives of Baltazar Castañeda. Seeing the fearsome Aristeo at her door frightened the woman of the house so that she took sick. Her family never could cure her after that, and she died two years later. Baltazar Castañeda wasn't seen in the area again.

A year passed. Aristeo spent it living in hiding. Then one night during Easter week he went to Jaripo's plaza for some tacos, and there he was spotted by police officers. Here began the legend of Aristeo Prado.

Fernando Ceja, Aristeo's cousin, remembers how he heard it. "He walked in front of the police. The mayor said, 'Why do I have you? Why don't you grab him and throw him in jail?' How were they going to grab him? They weren't going to get him. They got together, about twelve of them against him, alone without a gun. He didn't have anything. But the way I knew him, if he'd had a gun, twelve would have been too few.

"They followed him. They began shooting at him, but they didn't hit him. He was very clever. I don't know if he saw the bullets. I don't know. But about three cars went after him, shooting. They tracked him all over Jaripo. The priest went through town with a bullhorn, saying, 'What are you doing?' Then one person was sent to tell the priest to be quiet, that he shouldn't be going through town talking.

"Aristeo passed along one of the last streets. One woman saw him and said, 'Come in here, young man.' He went in, and no one felt at all like following him into that house. They knew he was in there behind the door. But they left, and he went running to the hills."

The truth is that Aristeo had a gun and shot it out on Jaripo's streets with relatives of Mayor Nacho Figueroa. Their bullets hit him in the hand and the mouth. The blood gummed up his pistol and it jammed. Now unarmed, and

with an exploded cheek and teeth spewing from his mouth, he ran, zigzagging to avoid their gunfire through the streets of Jaripo. That night Jaripo, which had turned out for the Easter week celebration, locked itself indoors as the hunt for Aristeo Prado shifted from one side of town to the other. He lost the officers in the night when their truck broke down. He jumped over a wall and entered a house, washed his gun and, with half his face torn apart, made it back to Guadalupe's family's house. She told him, "I'm taking you to a hospital. They'll arrest you, but that's better than dying." A cab drove them to the city of Zamora, where police were waiting. They transferred him to a hospital in Morelia, the state capital, where he spent the next few months recuperating.

In Jaripo the stories about him began to evolve and grow more fantastic. He had killed a man and escaped from jail. The police could only catch him when he turned himself in. His presence made a joke of local authorities. The more people talked, the more frightened they became.

"In a small town you know how people imagine things," says Antonio Zaragoza, a restaurant owner who remembers him. "He was a pretty calm guy. My mom had a store, and he would come in from time to time and have a beer."

"From what he told me, he killed eight men. But he was sorry later," says Federico Prado, Aristeo's cousin. Federico Prado is a foreman at a farm near Merced, where he oversees many of the farmworkers from Tarimoro. Short and pudgy with a thick mustache, Prado left Tarimoro with his family in the mid-1960s for Tijuana because Aristeo and his brothers were gunning for them. Cousin against cousin. That was the nature of Tarimoro then. Years later, in California, he and Aristeo reconciled.

An impish grin spreads across Federico Prado's face, and behind glasses his eyes squint with delight and he shakes his head at the memories of his cousin. "He was a good person. If someone was looking for you, he would defend you. He did things that later hurt him. He would regret them later. He had the thinking of a child. When he was doing these things, he was never afraid. But later he would cry."

Aristeo convalesced in the Morelia hospital. He began to notice when the guard would leave his room. One day he also noticed that workers on a floor above had left a rope hanging in front of his window. Aristeo climbed down it and hid in a water tank for several hours as police searched the grounds around the hospital. After they'd moved on, he jumped out of the tank and ran to hide out in a nearby cornfield. That night he made his way to the bus station, where he caught a bus to Jiquilpan.

Word of his escape spread quickly across the valley of Jaripo. He seemed everywhere. At least one child is known to have broken into tears after seeing a vision of Aristeo Prado appear on a rock wall.

Guadalupe Rodríguez remembers: "One night he met a woman and her daughter on the road. They got very scared. He said, 'Why are you afraid of me?' She said, 'Why wouldn't I be afraid, if everyone is talking and saying you steal women and I've got my daughter here?' He walked them home. She said, 'Oh, thank you so much, young man.' People talk and get afraid. It was the same way in Jaripo. The women would go up to this hill to wash and dry clothes. They'd be talking about him, saying Aristeo's going to come by here. They wouldn't go up there alone because they were afraid he'd do something to them."

Jesús Ceja remembers the time. Ceja, at seventy-six, is a lean man and tough as the brush covering the Tarimoro landscape. Known as El Becerro—The Calf—Ceja has thick and calloused hands and only a few teeth. Like many people from Tarimoro, he has light skin that is constantly burned red. He walks slowly about Tarimoro in sandals and a straw cowboy hat, smoking filterless cigarettes that cause him to hack from time to time. Ceja has an iron rod in his arm from Manuel Prado, Aristeo's oldest brother, who shot him during a gunfight years ago.

The 1960s and early 1970s were when the valley, isolated from the rest of the state, was overrun by robber gangs. Ceja became the area's first policeman, under Nacho Figueroa, mostly because he didn't have a weapon to protect himself from the Prados. "They'd go around with pistols and tried to be tough. There wasn't any government at the time," Ceja says. "Not like now. Now there's a lot of government. You do something, and pretty soon they're coming after you. But at the time, there wasn't.

"The Prados formed a gang. They'd rob houses. They'd steal whatever they found. When the road was built and trucks started coming to Jaripo, they'd rob the trucks."

Guadalupe Rodríguez says this wasn't true; otherwise her husband would have had money. "He was always poor. We always lived with his father and ate

at his father's table. And why, then, when they captured him, didn't a lot of people line up to accuse him?"

Whatever the case, Mayor Nacho Figueroa soon asked the state police to hunt the Prados down. One night a squad of officers came over the hills to Jaripo to attack Tarimoro the next day. But in the darkness two of the officers were separated from the squad. By coincidence, they knocked at the home of Simón Prado, not knowing anyone and asking directions to Jaripo. Simón pointed them down a path, and they stumbled off into the darkness. They were surprised moments later when Simón and another man snuck up on them. There the officers were relieved of their rifles and pistols and told to get moving. As they walked away, they pleaded for their guns. They couldn't return to their superiors without their weapons. Simón told them he'd give the guns back to them when he saw fit. The officers returned to Jaripo the next morning, looking, as one man said, "like little lost sheep."

Enraged, the *judiciales* called in the army. The next day "there were soldiers all over the place, something we'd never seen before," says Nacho Figueroa. "The commanders said, 'Bring [the gang] in dead or alive.' And they wanted the guns that had been taken from them, too. They went back to Tarimoro in the middle of the day. There was a gun battle."

The army and police arrested anyone they found in Tarimoro that day.

"I remember one guy from the gang was bleeding from the ear and mouth," says Nacho Figueroa. "They took them over to the main road leading into Jaripo, and there they applied the *"Ley Fuga"* ("Law of Escape") to him and one other. They said, 'Get going,' and they shot them to pieces as they ran."

Simón and Aristeo fled into the hills with the officers' guns and a month later, as promised, sent the weapons back to the officers in the city of Zamora.

For Aristeo, however, this was his end run as a fugitive. He went to Mexicali, where he worked for a time as a gardener and lived with a woman. When Guadalupe joined him, the scorned woman called the police and turned him in.

This time authorities sent Aristeo Prado to Islas Marías Federal Penal Colony. Las Islas Marías form an archipelago off the Pacific coast state of Nayarit. In 1908, the dictator Porfirio Diaz built a penal colony on the island and for many years it was the country's notorious maximum security prison. Today, though, it's a place for prisoners who have demonstrated good behavior in other institutions. Various Mexican universities sponsor programs studying the islands' flora and fauna. Still, the colony retains its infamous reputation. In late 1971 Aristeo Prado arrived on the island.

His time there is remembered only as peaceful. The prison site is really a dusty village with a life and economy of its own. Prisoners live free to travel the island, to work, and to grow what they need to live. Aristeo worked as a butcher and in construction. He bought a house. His wife and young son, Jaime, lived with him for several months. He was released for good behavior in 1975 and headed back to Jaripo.

Yet one episode on the island added to his legend. Aristeo one day spotted an enormous snake slithering through the grass. He grabbed it barehanded. It was long and thick and weighed about thirty pounds. Somewhere there's a photograph of him holding the creature.

For people in Jaripo, this event came to explain why he returned home in 1975, after less than four years in prison for, according to the stories people told, jailbreaks and supposed robberies and killings that surely should have resulted in a life imprisonment. They say that while working in the fields, Aristeo saw the snake slithering toward the commandant overseeing the prisoners. He leapt at it and killed it, saving the commandant's life. There's disagreement about whether he wrung its neck with his bare hands or hacked it to death with a machete. The commandant, they say, was so grateful to this prisoner for saving his life that he arranged for Aristeo's early release. Around Jaripo, the photograph is considered proof of the feat.

For the next three years Aristeo, Guadalupe, and their young children followed farmwork to Nogales, Florida, Mexicali, Merced. In October 1978, as the harvest season wound down in Merced, they returned to Jaripo for good. "We were picking olives when he left," says Federico Prado. "He said, 'You know, I'm leaving. You won't see me anymore because I'm not coming back.' I told him not to go. 'Why are you leaving?' He wanted to start a butcher shop."

So Aristeo Prado returned to Jaripo with some dollars in his pocket and hopes for a future more stable than his past. He wanted to move to Mexico City. Many people from Jaripo had started butcher shops in the capital.

He returned a different man. He was older now, and he had seen another way of life. "He was calmer," said Eberardo Ceja, a former mayor. "He controlled himself. If they didn't provoke him, he didn't provoke them." He had completed his sentence that began with his killing of Delfino Reyes ten years earlier. He was now thirty-one. "He said, 'I don't want any more trouble,'" says Guadalupe Rodríguez. "I've got my children. I just want to live."

But his presence was unnerving, a constant reminder of his legend. It was probably too much to ask of the valley of Jaripo to forget the past. So on November 24, 1978, death came for Aristeo Prado when he was least looking for it.

Like many of the stories surrounding his life, there are versions of what happened. Generally they begin with him stopping in a cantina in Jiquilpan for a beer. Most people say he was going for a gun in his truck. That the men who killed him had been following him all day. Luisa Moreno, the pharmacist, says Nacho Figueroa hired men to kill him and finally do away with his longtime nemesis. So say people in Tarimoro as well. Nacho says Aristeo argued with a man in a cantina. Others say his killers were men he'd beaten in poker. There's disagreement over whether it took two, three, or four men to bring Aristeo Prado down.

The stories aren't that far off. That day Aristeo was driving in Jiquilpan when he passed a small corner store. The owner hailed him. Come have a beer. "I think he knew the owner, or he never would have gotten out of his truck unarmed," says Guadalupe Rodríguez. Aristeo parked and was walking to the store when three men emerged from it. He retreated. There, in broad daylight, they gunned him down. He was going for his pistol that he'd left in his truck. No one was ever arrested for his murder. He left behind three children and a pregnant wife. They laid him in the cemetery in Jaripo. His grave says nothing about his life or legend.

* * *

Aristeo Prado's death would mark the beginning of the end of Tarimoro's savagery.

Two years later the government built the road that exists today out of the *camino real* where the *judiciales* once lost their way. Finally the world was coming to the rancho.

Soon Manuel Prado was dead as well. He was on a bus one day, heading from Jaripo to Tarimoro, when Jesús Ceja—El Becerro—boarded. The men hadn't seen much of each other since the shooting that left Ceja with a metal rod in his shoulder. But in Tarimoro these kinds of things lay like vipers in the grass, waiting to be reawoken. As the bus bounced its way over the rocky road to Tarimoro, each man pretended not to recognize the other. Yet beneath his jacket each man readied his pistol.

Arriving at the rancho, El Becerro rose to leave. It was one of those buses with only one way in or out. Manuel, sitting at the front of the bus, apparently figured he would make his move after El Becerro passed, but El Becerro was wise. As he walked by Manuel, he swiveled quickly. Manuel rose. The two men, two feet from each other, fired off eight rounds. Passengers shrieked and ducked to avoid the bullets in the thunder that enveloped the bus. When it was over, both men were wounded. Manuel was bleeding and lying on the floor. El Becerro was hit in the left hand and chest, but he was still standing. He had recently been made a police officer again, and one bullet hit his plastic police badge, which he had tucked in the shirt pocket over his heart. The bullet deflected and lodged only a few inches under his skin. He'd been able to push Manuel's pistol aside with his hand. When the barrage was over, El Becerro stood bleeding in the passageway. Manuel lay at his feet. El Becerro picked up his rival's pistol, put it to Manuel Prado's head and said, *"Pa' que entiendas"* ("So you understand"), and pulled the trigger.

Two years passed. El Becerro hid out in the hills and returned home at night. Finally, tired of running, he turned himself in and went to jail in Jiquilpan.

About this time, Nicanor Nava was looking for a good cop. Don Nica was from Tarimoro but had moved to Jaripo years before. He was now the town butcher and had been elected mayor. He's remembered as a man who stood against the bloodshed for which his rancho was so well known. Don Nica was also godfather to Antonio Prado, the youngest of the Prado brothers. But in Tarimoro things like that never seemed to count for much. Don Nica's bad luck was that first, he tried to get El Becerro out of jail, so as to be his police chief. His second piece of bad luck about this time was that one day, coming from seeing a cow, he met up with Antonio. Antonio was furious that Don Nica was trying to free El Becerro, his brother's killer. They argued. Under a mesquite tree about fifty yards south of town, Antonio gunned his godfather

down. A cross marks the spot where Don Nica fell. Antonio spent several years in prison. He lives now in Merced.

With that the Prado era in Tarimoro came to an end. It was as if a collective sigh of relief—a burden relinquished—issued from the sunburnt rancho.

By 1987 much of Tarimoro had obtained legal papers through the Amnesty Act. Others simply began emigrating illegally. By the late 1980s most of Tarimoro's young men could be found in Merced. Townspeople in Jaripo believe this had a lot to do with why Tarimoro calmed down. "They were like fighting cocks. Kill for killing. When they saw life elsewhere, they said, 'No, it's better to live,'" says Hervasio Castañeda, a Jaripo shoemaker. "Emigration helped because if I don't see this person who I don't like, after he leaves for two or three years, I've forgotten a little bit. The distance helped."

Eberardo Ceja thinks the people of Tarimoro grew together in the United States. "Before 1980 very few people went up there," he says. "From 1980 on, many young men, thirteen and fourteen years old, would go to work there. There was no more of this family against family. [Up there] it was one family."

Some people in Tarimoro have another, simpler theory explaining the change. It's that those who were causing all the trouble aren't around anymore.

Aristeo Prado's widow has remarried and lives in Merced. She's a grandmother now and works occasionally in the city's canneries. The four children she had with him rarely return to Tarimoro. They aren't rancheros. A son named for him works in a bank and attends junior college. He wanted to be a highway patrol officer, but his mother talked him out of it. Two other sons work in construction. Aristeo's daughter, Patricia, works in a shop in Merced. "I don't tell them about their father," says Guadalupe Rodríguez. "Everyone tells me, 'Your kids are good. They're not like him at all. They don't drink, they don't go around raising hell. They work.'"

Nor does Guadalupe Rodríguez have much to do with Aristeo's brother Antonio. The man Antonio killed, Nicanor Nava, was her uncle, so there's not much to talk about. Simón Prado is a farmworker in the Central Valley and doesn't want to revisit the past.

People in the Jaripo Valley still don't mess with those from Tarimoro. At parties in the plaza, they quietly edge away from folks from Tarimoro who are drunk. But the old days are gone. Emigration has changed Tarimoro forever, bringing new hope and new rules to a once wild place.

One March afternoon, men drink beer outside Luis García's hole-in-the-wall. Mules are tied to one of the posts. The conversation wanders on about agriculture and the United States, when people will start heading north. A breeze occasionally blows dust along and into the eyes of the men at the store. A fine, sharp sunshine clarifies the details—the trees, the gullies, the cleared land—on the hills rising in the distance. The lonely music from a radio wafts across the rancho, telling the story of some drug smuggler.

Up the road walk two teenagers with towels around their necks, heading to the water hole. One is the grandson of El Becerro. His name is Fernando. The other is the son of Manuel Prado. His name is also Fernando. They stop at the store. Fernando Prado walks a dog. He speaks some English and speaks it to a visitor. He lives in a farm labor camp in Merced. It's a desultory, short conversation. The two youths—Prado and Ceja, whose families have fought for years and whose elders shot each other on a bus one day years ago—walk off down the path together.

The past hovers over Tarimoro, but it's fading with time. As in many Mexican ranchos, immigration, contact with the outside world, a few modern conveniences, and a little bit of law enforcement have relegated Tarimoro's violence to the stories of old men. Most people, given a chance, prefer to live in peace.

That's why the *valientes* have all gone from the valley of Jaripo. Only their legends remain.

—1994–2000

THE POPSICLE KINGS
OF TOCUMBO

The winding road between the towns of Cotija and Los Reyes, in the state of Michoacán, runs mostly through fenced green fields of grazing livestock.

Passing the village of Santa Inés, a corridor of trees lines the road, interrupted only to give way to farmhouses and unpaved driveways. Following this road begins to feel like just another drive in the country until you clear a hill, round a turn, and suddenly, on your right, appears an enormous statue of . . . a Popsicle, as big as a three-story house and painted a creamy apricot.

With a confidence and panache rare for a Mexican village, the town of Tocumbo thus greets the world.

Tocumbo is like no other Mexican village. Lavish houses spread across half city blocks. Satellite dishes are everywhere. One man has built himself a private, lighted rapid-soccer court. Some people have tiled the sidewalks in front of their homes with the same tile that covers their house to make sure everything matches. Most remarkable, though, is the widespread level of Tocumbo's development. Even the humblest houses are solid structures of concrete, with gates and glass windows. The village has services that most others in Mexico can only dream of. Tocumbo may be the only town in Mexico with all its streets paved. Its center dividers are landscaped. City hall has two computers. A few blocks away is a gorgeous park, with a swimming pool, dance floor, and picnic grounds. At the center of town is Tocumbo's crown jewel, the Church of the Sacred Heart, designed by Pedro Ramírez Vásquez, the same architect who designed the Basílica to the Virgin of Guadalupe in Mexico City and Estadio Azteca, the country's largest soccer stadium.

Tiny, isolated Tocumbo is "the wealthiest village in Mexico," says Luis González González, dean of the country's rural historians.

The story of how it got that way is one of the great epics of modern Mexican business.

Mexico, generally, has offered only two routes to real economic progress to

its poor and uneducated rural folk. One is emigration to the United States. The other, more recent is growing and smuggling drugs. Michoacán is a major producer of marijuana and second in the country in the number of emigrants it sends north.

But Tocumbo took neither path. Rather, it discovered the Popsicle—*la paleta*. Tocumbans founded, then expanded the "La Michoacana" ice-cream shops, known as *paleterías*. La Michoacana became a business model—a cross between a franchise and a family business while being, technically, neither one. Built on two great Mexican comparative advantages—cheap, luscious fruit and hard work—the Michoacana model proved adaptable enough to allow illiterate rancheros to compete with multinational ice-cream companies and get rich in the process. It's also one of the few Mexican businesses that consistently expanded during the recurring economic crises of the last twenty-five years.

To most Mexicans, the Michoacana name is now almost a brand, connoting fruity, natural, affordable ice cream—though only recently has the name been copyrighted. Tocumbans, the Popsicle kings of Mexico, turned the lowly *paleta* into one of the great Mexican products of the last half century and La Michoacana into one of the most prevalent businesses in the country.

Like sprinkles on a cone, Michoacanas cover Mexico. They have become part of the country's municipal scenery. Simple, bright shops, painted in pinks and yellows and powder blues, they can be set up easily in almost any retail space. Their signs vary widely in style and size; occasionally they are named La Flor de Michoacán or La Flor de Tocumbo. Their storefronts are usually open wide to the public and fronted by refrigerated display cases in which are kept stacks of Popsicles and vats of ice cream and fruit drinks—the three classic Michoacana products. Older *paleterías* are usually painted with balloons and cartoon characters like Mickey Mouse. The newer ones have bright, neon-lighted photographs of the luscious cones, sundaes, and Popsicles to be had within.

No one knows how many Michoacana *paleterías* exist nationwide. Some put the figure at ten thousand. One study estimated between eight and fifteen thousand. Almost every plaza of every town in Mexico has at least one Michoacana. "I don't think there's a town of more than a thousand inhabitants that doesn't have one. In Mexico City alone there are more than a thousand," says José Sánchez Fabián, owner of a Tocumbo *paletería*. (There are four within a five-block radius of my house.) Perhaps only Pemex, the state oil monopoly, and Comex, the paint distributor, have penetrated the country as completely as La Michoacana.

In northern Michoacán, where the economy is dollar dependent, emigration is a tradition, and people from hundreds of villages spend time more time in the United States than in Mexico, Tocumbo is that rare thing. It's a village where virtually no one works in the United States. When Tocumbans visit the United States, they go as tourists. Like emigrant villages for hundreds of miles around, Tocumbo is deserted most of the year. But unlike those villages, its people are scattered across Mexico—in Mérida, Monclova, Mazatlán—running *paleterías*.

Walking around Tocumbo is like taking a quick tour of Mexico: this guy lives in Iguala, Guerrero; this family in Cuauhtitlán, Izcalli; that lady in Ciudad Juárez. Every December these people return to Tocumbo and the village holds the Feria de la Paleta—the Popsicle Fair.

Says Mexico City *paletero* Gerardo Abarca: "You sit around eating tacos in the plaza. You hear the younger kids. One comes up, *"Oye, chico, me hace unos tacos"* with an accent from Mérida. Then a guy walks up, *"Oye, chico, me hace unos tacos,"* with a Sonoran accent. Then a guy from Mexico City comes up, *"Oye, chico . . ."* sounding like people speak here. You hear the entire gamut of Mexico's regional accents. And they're all cousins or they know each other."

Conservatively estimating an average of three employees per *paletería*, La Michoacana employs somewhere around thirty thousand Mexicans—not counting the owners of each shop—making the business as important an employer as many multinational corporations.

And all that is due to a group of men with no education or business experience, rancheros who would have preferred to be back home tending their livestock but became ice-cream men instead.

* * *

Their story begins in the 1940s, when there was every reason to believe Tocumbo would be another village of emigrants. The *bracero* treaty with the United States, which lasted from 1942 to 1964, allowed hundreds of thousands of young men from northern Michoacán to work legally in the north; at

least a hundred men from Tocumbo were working part of the year in the fields of the United States by the mid-1940s.

But Agustín Andrade and Ignacio Alcázar, two cousins, had left Tocumbo a few years before that as boys to find work in Mexico City. And that changed everything.

In Tocumbo, controversy surrounds the origins of La Michoacana. Andrade and Alcázar each claims he was the first to start a Michoacana ice-cream shop in the capital. And each man has his strong supporters among Tocumbans. The first Tocumban to ever start an ice-cream shop was a man named Rafael Malfavón, who opened one near the village plaza. But it was either Agustín Andrade or Ignacio Alcázar, depending on who you believe, who started the businesses in Mexico City, where they flourished.

A 1988 article in the magazine *Contenido* gave the credit to Andrade and in so doing created a scandal among many people in town, since the majority view is that Alcázar set up the first *paletería*. The truth is now lost to history.

The way Agustín Andrade tells it, he was orphaned at age six. By age thirteen, he says he had left Tocumbo and was living in León, Guanajuato, where he worked in an ice-cream shop and learned to make Popsicles. By 1939, at age nineteen, he was living in Mexico City, where work was more plentiful. In 1941, with 600 pesos he'd saved, he started his first *paletería,* in a market on Calle Herreros, near the Lecumberri Penitenciary—now the National Archives.

Alcázar's trek out of Tocumbo began in 1938, at the age of twelve. Alcázar says he was thrown out of school for playing marbles, an incident he still finds unjust. He was fighting frequently with his father. So he left home and walked all the way to Guadalajara. There he sold ice cream, cigarettes, and newspapers in the street. In 1941 he went to Mexico City. He says he arrived with 11 pesos tucked in his overalls. He slept that night in the *zócalo* and awoke to find he'd been robbed. He sold auto parts—mirrors, windshield wipers, and rugs—at intersections. He sold slices of fruit in the parks. For a time he says he also sold old magazines outside a movie theater.

During these years Alcázar went north to work in the United States three times, but he never liked it. He remembered his father, who had emigrated and returned mean. He had learned a little of the ice-cream business from working at Rafael Malfavón's shop in Tocumbo and with another man in

Guadalajara. So in 1943, with some small savings, he says he started the first Michoacana *paletería,* at Balderas and Arcos de Belén avenues. Next to it he put in a car-parts store. For a while he couldn't afford both an apartment and a business, so he slept on the shop floor.

Regardless of who started the first shop, by the late 1940s both men were energetically involved in the business. Their shops were small and humble. They offered only a few flavors, as well as soda and candy. But both men were making a living, and they could stay in Mexico to make it. Soon Andrade and Alcázar were setting up *paleterías* around Mexico City. Andrade himself would go on to start 177 *paleterías,* mostly in the capital. Some he'd sell to a trusted employee. Being something of a ladies' man, he would also give them to his various wives, mistresses, and eighteen children as they came along. Alcázar put in his second *paletería* in the Portales neighborhood and would continue to set up shops around the city as well.

What is not in doubt in the story of La Michoacana is that Alcázar's older brother, Luis, joined him in 1953 and that the Alcázar brothers became the great promoters of the ice-cream shops. Andrade would sell his *paleterías* to employees. But the Alcázar brothers saw a greater opportunity in financing them among the poor folks of Tocumbo. That, more than simply running *paleterías,* became their great business and provided the first impulse to La Michoacana's expansion. Soon the Alcázars were returning to Tocumbo and telling anyone who would listen that they would loan money to anyone who wanted to enter the ice-cream trade; they charged 2 percent interest a month. A *paletero* could pay off the debt in a couple of years using the shop's profits and end up with his own business. The Michoacana pioneers had all grown up together. Often they were related. So bonds of trust held them together.

By the mid-1950s Tocumban men were deciding that owning an ice-cream shop in Mexico City sounded a lot better than a trip to the United States. A long chain of people was pulled out of Tocumbo to Mexico City. Sometimes they'd borrow money from the Alcázars. But usually they'd work in a *paletería,* then buy it from the owner, who was usually a friend or relative. From there they'd use the profits to start a second *paletería.*

These informal financing methods resolved for Tocumbans the problem small entrepreneurs everywhere have of obtaining money for their start-ups.

In Mexico the problem is especially acute. Mexico's banks have long avoided loaning to working-class folks, preferring to court the large and powerful business groups. Mexicans wanting to start a small business usually have to rely on personal savings. But Tocumbans in essence created their own private banking system; in so doing, they made Tocumbo one of Mexico's great finance centers, if measured by the numbers of businesses that grew from the little village.

Every afternoon the new *paleteros* would gather at a *paletería* Ignacio Alcázar owned in northern Mexico City and talk shop. These men began the great dynasties of *paleteros* that exist today.

Marcial Magaña was one of them. He had spent thirteen years working in the United States. He'd heard of Tocumbans making ice cream in Mexico City. So in 1957 he went to Mexico City and started his own *paletería* with money he'd made in the United States. He eventually founded seven more. As time went on, friends and relatives from Tocumbo would arrive and Magaña would finance their *paleterías*.

Back in Tocumbo, his brother-in-law, Miguel Villanueva, remembers sitting in the plaza and hearing people talk about the fabulous business of selling ice cream in Mexico City. "I thought, 'How is it possible that people in Mexico City eat nothing but Popsicles?'" he says. Villanueva decided to see for himself. On the day he married, he and his bride came to Mexico City. Once in the capital, with 45 pesos Magaña loaned him, Villanueva started his first *paletería*. His wife worked the shop while Villanueva worked in a cantina. "Once I'd paid off my debt, I began putting in more *paleterías*. I put one in Colonia Anahuac, then I had two. I didn't need more financing because I had a way to pay for it now."

Magaña is now eighty and left the business twenty years ago to buy an avocado orchard in Tocumbo, which he now tends. Yet all seven of his children have at least one *paletería* apiece—in Mexico City, Guadalajara, Zacatecas, and Mexicali. "I first watched my father make *paletas* when I was six," says his daughter, Ana, who owns a *paletería* in Mexico City. By age eight, part of her daily routine after school was tending the *paletería* attached to the family house. "My nephews are young and in school, but they have to spend an hour a day watching the *paletería*," she says.

Miguel Villanueva, meanwhile, would go on to start another eighteen *paleterías* in Mexico City and Puebla and finance twenty more for newly arriving Tocumbans. Today his eight children own *paleterías*.

And so it went. Friends helping friends, relatives helping relatives. The Alcázar financing model allowed one to make a profit and the other to gain a business.

As it developed, La Michoacana became the ice-cream version of a Mexican handicraft. The back room of each store was where Michoacana ice cream was made. Workers poured ice-cream base into Popsicle molds and churned ice cream with small mixers. *Paleteros* groped their way along, figuring out what worked and sticking with it. It was seat-of-the-pants business administration. Someone found that painting pictures of balloons and Mickey Mouse on the walls attracted children; soon that was standard decor at every Michoacana. Yet being intensely independent rancheros, each owner managed his business his own way. Thus La Michoacana didn't grow into a great corporation. It had no central accounting, no marketing, advertising, or strategic five-year plans. Nor did it develop great factories.

All that proved to be La Michoacana's greatest strength. Its production method kept costs the lowest in the industry. Making ice cream and *paletas* on-site, when needed, also ensured freshness. And La Michoacana needed no large, expensive fleets of refrigerated trucks delivering from a factory to far-flung outlets. So the *paletero* could sell his product at a fraction of the price charged by larger corporations, thus acquiring the loyalty of the vast working-class ice-cream market that valued price above all else.

The Michoacana concept proved endlessly flexible. Corporate ice-cream franchises were bound to sell only what headquarters ordered. But the Michoacana *paletero,* being his own boss, could respond to local tastes. Thus many Michoacanas also sell pie, popcorn, custard, even nachos and pizza.

La Michoacana's great initial weakness was quality. In the early years the *paleterías* could be ratty places, often unclean and uninviting. That began to change in 1959, when an unschooled rancher from Rodeo, a community in the hills above Tocumbo, arrived in Mexico City.

Rafael Abarca had already been to the United States three times to work when he came to Mexico City to apply for papers for another trip north. However, a relative told him about a *paletería* in the Colonia Nueva Santa

María for sale for less than the embassy was charging for legal papers. So he became a *paletero*.

With Rafael Abarca, the Michoacana concept entered its second phase. Abarca, a taciturn man now seventy-four, instilled a higher level of quality in La Michoacana that was copied by many *paleteros*. "I don't remember him ever asking how much something cost," says Juan Valdovinos, who as a teenager worked in an Abarca *paletería*. "He always said, 'I want it done right.'"

Abarca was the first *paletero* to use stainless steel Popsicle molds. *Paleteros* before him had used sheet metal, which rusted easily and often left the Popsicle crooked. He brought in the first refrigerated display cases so that people could see and choose what they were going to eat. Before, ice cream and *paletas* were stored in a large refrigerator at the back of the shop.

The fruit drinks for which La Michoacana is nationally famous were another Abarca innovation. Before that, La Michoacana sold brand-name soft drinks. But the profit margin on sodas was low, distributors were unreliable, and the empty bottles had to be stored. So Abarca began making his own fruit-based *aguas*. He could control quality and availability, and profits were higher than Pepsi or Coke allowed for.

He began using more fruit in his ice cream. He also introduced new flavors. In its early years, La Michoacana sold only chocolate, vanilla, and lime ice cream. Abarca began to experiment with the wide range of Mexican tropical fruit: guanabana, mango, papaya, maguey.

After Abarca, each *paletero* began to adapt his product to local consumer tastes, using the fruit that was cheapest and most popular in his region. Soon daring *paleteros* began to experiment with flavors. Over the years flavors like *chongos zamoranos,* tequila, or cactus apples began to show up in Michoacana display cases.

Meanwhile Abarca's quality, together with the financing and business models the Alcázars had established, allowed La Michoacana to expand beyond Mexico City. Abarca was one of the first to leave the capital. Using the profits from his Mexico City businesses, he put *paleterías* in Tulancingo, Hidalgo, and Tenancingo, State of Mexico. Through the late 1960s and 1970s Abarca set up dozens more—so many, he can't come up with an exact figure. Often, selling the *paleterías* was a matter of necessity as well as profit, since he didn't always have the business administration know-how to manage his far-flung enterprises. There are former Abarca *paleterías* in Hermosillo, Tampico, Morelia, Reynosa, Mexicali, Oaxaca, and Veracruz. He set up at least ten in Tijuana alone, all of which he sold. More recently, he's invested in a *paletería* in malls in Cancún.

During the 1970s, as *paleteros'* standard of living improved, they began to invest in their village. The plaza was renovated in those years. The first streets were paved. Like the financing of their *paleterías,* Tocumbans kept their municipal improvement projects among themselves. Each project was funded by *paleteros'* donations, rarely with much coming from the government. The Popsicle Fair began in 1987 as a way to raise money for the church, which was completed in 1991. Tocumbans also got serious about building new houses. Barrio La Charanda became Tocumbo's Beverly Hills as families there competed to build the most luxurious home—though most of them are vacant most of the year while their owners are off in some part of Mexico tending to their *paleterías.*

Through the 1980s La Michoacana seemed to expand geometrically. Groups of Tocumbans would form partnerships, then scour the countryside looking for towns with an attractive street corner or plaza. As thousands of other retail food outlets floundered and died during the crises of the 1980s, the number of Michoacanas grew.

In part this was due to Tocumbans' habit of keeping financing among themselves. During these crises, banks foreclosed on delinquent businesses. Many thousands of small businesses, started with life savings, simply closed. But since La Michoacana's financing was based on friendship and family ties, loans were forgiven or postponed. Loans rarely went unpaid for long, since the ties that bound Tocumbans remained strong.

Juan Valdovinos came to Mexico City as a fourteen-year-old to work in one of Rafael Abarca's shops. After a while Abarca offered Valdovinos the shop for sale. They haggled a bit; Valdovinos bargained the interest rate down from the normal 2 percent to 1.5 percent a month. They set a price of 120,000 pesos, and over the next eighteen months Valdovinos dutifully paid off his first store. "You'd pay it back because you didn't want to be on bad terms with those who loaned you the money and because you wanted to keep the door

open in case you needed another loan," says Valdovinos, who went on to become mayor of Tocumbo and now owns twelve *paleterías* in the states of Hidalgo and Querétaro.

Yet in part La Michoacana's expansion was also a response to Mexico's recurring economic crises. Instead of consolidating their *paleterías* during these crises, Tocumbans opened more and more shops. They were no longer rancheros; they had learned to be entrepreneurs. They had access to capital through their informal village networks. As sales and profits dropped at one shop, an owner would put in another to earn with two shops what he had been making with one. After the next recession, he'd have five making what two once did.

Tocumbans insisted their children get an education, but the spasmodic crises meant that these young people often couldn't find good-paying work in their profession. "I have a son who's a biologist. He's better off as a *paletero*," says Mario Andrade, a *paletero* for thirty-five years, who owns a shop in Tepic, Nayarit. "Putting him through school back then cost me 50,000 pesos. When he got out, he received a salary of 600 pesos every two weeks. He said, 'How am I going to survive on that?' He asked me for help in putting in a *paletería*. Now he has three."

Thus an entire generation of young Tocumbans, who grew up knowing only economic crisis, didn't become professionals, despite their education. Instead they became *paleteros* like their parents. Many Tocumbans are doctors, engineers, accountants, or lawyers, yet own *paleterías* and work their professions almost as a sideline. This meant there were even more Michoacanas to be founded.

As La Michoacana moved across the country, Tocumbans developed an almost insatiable thirst for labor. Before too long, men from nearby communities—Santa Inés and La Caldera—were working in *paleterías,* then buying out their owners. Some owners come from the nearby city of Los Reyes.

Los Limones, a community near Tocumbo, is the hometown of the Oseguera family. In the 1940s Luis Alcázar had been a sugarcane worker and had stayed at the home of Ignacio Oseguera. Through the 1950s the Oseguera family lost track of Alcázar. Then one day he returned a wealthy man, with stories of money to be made selling ice cream, and offered work to Ignacio's oldest son, Clemente, as a way of thanking the family for its help years before.

In 1959, at age thirteen, Clemente Oseguera went to Mexico City to work in an Alcázar *paletería,* and thus another great Michoacana family dynasty was born. Clemente had seventeen brothers and sisters and eventually pulled them all into the ice-cream business in Mexico City.

His brother, Eleuterio, came in 1962, at age thirteen. By age sixteen he bought his first *paletería* with financing from Luis Alcázar. In the early 1970s, already with five *paleterías* in Mexico City, Eleuterio went south to Oaxaca, then to Chiapas, looking for places to put shops. "I didn't like Mexico City," he says. "It was an adventure. I went looking for the provinces." He settled on Tapachula, on the border with Guatemala, because it was hot all year round. He eventually started eight *paleterías* in Tapachula, then brought his cousins, the Álvarezes, in to work the shops while he expanded north to Laredo and Monterrey.

Today the extended Oseguera family numbers close to a hundred, and those who are old enough run *paleterías*—an estimated four hundred shops at last count, covering most of northern Mexico. Eleuterio alone owns two hundred. The Oseguera clan has branched out into livestock and agriculture. Brother Roberto started his own milk operation. In the 1990s Eleuterio began to diversify into video arcades and gasoline stations—again with financing from Luis Alcázar.

As the years went by, Tocumbans began drawing workers from farther afield. A *paletero* would hire someone. He'd have a cousin back in his hometown who needed work. Pretty soon dozens of men in his hometown would be making *paletas* in far-flung parts of Mexico. El Rodeo, in Michoacán near the border with Guanajuato, is one such village. Another is Tamazunchale, San Luis Potosí. Years ago someone hired a worker from Tamazunchale. Today dozens of people from Tamazunchale now work in or own a Michoacana.

And since anyone could put in a *paletería* and call it La Michoacana, after a while that started happening. By the 1990s Mexico was pretty much jam-packed with *paleterías.* They were sometimes two or three to a plaza.

Paleteros complain that they now face too much competition. This comes not from large corporations like Bing's or Baskin-Robbins, which have notably failed to beat back La Michoacana despite greater resources. Rather, competition comes from other Michoacana *paleteros.* Some *paleteros* no longer use

the name La Michoacana, feeling it's overdone. They've taken names like Las Delicias de Tocumbo, El Lindo Michoacán, or Tocumbo Sí. Eleuterio Oseguera copyrighted the Michoacana name in the early 1990s precisely so he could fight off competitors who weren't from Tocumbo.

All of this worries Tocumbo's younger generation, among them Alejandro Andrade. Andrade is a young capitalist with a mustache and goatee who works daily under a picture of Che Guevara. "He was a fighter," says Andrade of Guevara. "And I have a social conscience." Now thirty-one, Andrade isn't a *paletero,* but he depends on the business nonetheless. He owns a marketing firm, Publicidad Visual Andrade, in an office just off Tocumbo's plaza. There he sells display photos and other Michoacana promotional devices to *paleteros* all over Mexico.

Andrade was a marketing student in Guadalajara in the early 1990s when ice-cream corporations—Bing's, Hollanda, Baskin-Robbins, and Häagen-Dazs—began moving into the Mexican market. He realized La Michoacana lacked a corporate image. So he and an artist friend devised a logo for La Michoacana: an Indian girl holding an ice-cream cone. He also came up with a slogan: *La Michoacana . . . Es Natural.* "It's a children's image. A girl with two eyes but no physical attributes—no nose or mouth, so people can project their own feelings onto it," Andrade says.

Andrade's logo was the first anyone had ever invented for the business that was now almost fifty years old, an indication of how La Michoacana was improvised more than planned. His firm now prints the logo on ice-cream cups and containers, on napkin holders, and on bright neon signs and sells them to hundreds of Michoacana *paleteros.*

His logo is seen across Mexico these days, but initially it flopped. Andrade tried to sell it only to Tocumbo *paleteros,* wanting to keep the image in town, as it were. But a corporate image was anathema to men who'd worked independently all their lives, been successful, and saw no need to change. Some *paleteros* laughed at it. Others promptly returned to their shops and painted the logo on their display cases themselves without paying Andrade a royalty.

So Andrade decided to sell signs and ice-cream containers that bore the logo to anyone. Pretty soon it caught on. "It spread the same way the *paleterías* did, anarchically," Andrade says.

Andrade believes La Michoacana must change to continue to thrive. "[The business model] has worked up to now, but not to its full potential," he says. "Sales, production, administration would be optimized if there were a general agreement among *paleteros* to maintain a certain quality, a corporate image— and not everyone independent and disunified."

To that end, he is trying to form an association of Tocumbo *paleteros*. Two similar attempts have failed because, he believes, they tried to control men who entered the business in part so they wouldn't have to take orders. Rather, Andrade envisions an association acting as a clearinghouse for information on new production and marketing techniques. "There are *paleteros* who don't even know how ice-cream base is made or what kinds there are," he says. "The older *paleteros* who own thirty or forty *paleterías* won't listen to me, but some of the young people will."

The questions about La Michoacana's future preoccupy the younger generation of *paleteros* as well. The great business their fathers did financing others is disappearing, since most Tocumban families now have money and don't need to ask for loans. What started as a business by Tocumbans, solidified by village ties, is now fracturing into large family groups, with each applying its own philosophy.

Among the vanguard of the younger generation is Gerardo Abarca, the oldest son of Rafael Abarca. Gerardo, now thirty-six, was born in Mexico City; on his office wall is his business-administration diploma. The small *paletería* Rafael Abarca bought in the Colonia Nueva Santa María in 1959 has expanded into one of the nicest in Mexico City and, like the Popsicle in Tocumbo, a monument to La Michoacana. It is painted pink and lined with tile; its display cases explode in a hallucinogenic riot of flavors and colors. Upstairs are the Abarca family business offices.

Gerardo has installed Alejandro Andrade's new neon signs with lighted pictures of ice cream and fruit drinks. He's rechristened the family shops La Nueva Michoacana. Two years ago he went to Italy and brought back flavors like champagne strawberry and almond amaretto. Under Gerardo, the Abarcas have been one of the leaders in moving La Michoacana into shopping malls— going after middle-class ice-cream buyers. They now have five mall outlets.

"That's my job: modernizing the business," Gerardo says.

The question facing young *paleteros* like Gerardo Abarca today is how to modernize without losing what customers value most about La Michoacana: its feeling of the pueblo, its low price. The Michoacana model was based on a sensible approach to business that reflected the country folk who founded it: good yet affordable quality, owner independence, hands-on management, nothing too fancy.

La Michoacana was successful because it captured the working classes, who often came to the city from the countryside. Indeed, the business's growth reflected Mexico's transformation from a rural to an urban society over the last four decades. Today Mexico looks modern, but it has distinctly rural roots that remain alive even at the dawning of a new century. Many *paleteros* now find that they, like their businesses and like Mexico itself, straddle that line between rural and urban, traditional and modern.

So it's unlikely that Michoacana *paletas* will be factory made anytime soon. Small, it turns out, is beautiful. "After NAFTA, everyone said Baskin-Robbins and Häagen-Dazs were coming and were going to dominate the market," says Gerardo Abarca. "Americans eat half of all the ice cream eaten in the world. They're wizards with ice cream. But they came here and nothing. Why? Because we kept at doing what we've always done. We haven't followed fads or fashions. It remains what people from the rancho like, and it always will be."

Still, the strengths that allowed La Michoacana to spread across Mexico—each owner's independence and the ease with which people enter the business—now hinder it. The business model invented and improved on by illiterate rancheros was, it turned out, too perfect. The Popsicle kings of Tocumbo are facing perhaps their greatest challenge, created, ironically, by their own success.

In the 1995–96 recession, for the first time in an economic downturn hundreds of Michoacanas closed. This was partly because some *paleteros* simply didn't pay their debts. But it was also because Mexico was so saturated with *paleterías* that not all of them could survive. The old trick of expanding during a recession to maintain profits couldn't work this time.

As people have made lives far from the village, the close ties among Tocumbans that helped build the Michoacana empire aren't always there anymore. Today each family is going its own way. A few *paleteros,* like Eleuterio Oseguera, are diversifying into new businesses, the way major corporations do. Others, like the Abarcas, have followed the sprawl of suburbia and see the shopping mall as the next frontier.

"The older generation knew each other," says Gerardo Abarca. "They lived together until they were twenty or twenty-five. They were all buddies. Then they left to face the future, and that turned out to be leaving the village and getting into *paletas*. It worked. They helped each other enormously, and that's how they got ahead. There was unity [among Tocumbans], like one big family, all used to dealing based on word of honor. That doesn't work among the younger generations. We don't know each other that well. Now if there's no contract, there's no business. And there's competition among the Tocumban families that there wasn't before. Now the new generation will put a *paletería* right in front of you."

—1999

NUEVO CHUPÍCUARO

In 1965 virtually all of Nuevo Chupícuaro at one time or another ambled by the corner of San Pedro and Tarasco streets where Bonifacio Caballero was building his two-story home. With the rebar rising like antennae high above the house and the spaces left for windows, "people said it looked like a large pigeon coop," says Caballero.

But most people in town were awestruck. They'd never seen anything like it owned by a man who, like them, was a poor campesino.

Caballero's home was the first two-story house in Nuevo Chupícuaro (pronounced Choo-PEE-kwa-roh). It cost eleven thousand dollars, money Caballero had made as a farmworker in California. It now includes seven bedrooms, a dining room, a living room, a double kitchen, and two bathrooms—all belonging to a man who worked the fields.

"I was always very poor. I wanted to have a big house. I wanted to leave something for my children," says Caballero, now fifty-seven, with thick graying hair and a bushy mustache, who is still a farmworker in the town of Wasco, near Bakersfield, California.

His children have grown into remarkable American success stories. His oldest daughter works for a NASA contractor, analyzing rocket design. His son is getting his teaching credentials, manages a restaurant, and is conversant in Jack Kerouac and Chicano theater. Another daughter is a preschool teacher, while his youngest daughter is a straight-A student and a cheerleader at Wasco Union High School. "None of this would have been possible in Mexico," he says. "I owe everything to the United States. My children do, too."

Still, Bonifacio Caballero has never considered himself anything but Mexican. And that, more than anything, is why he rents a cramped house in a Wasco labor camp while his magnificent two-story home in Nuevo Chupícuaro sits vacant eleven months a year. It waits for him and his wife, their retirement, and their promised return home. "Chupícuaro is precious," he says.

"When I go to Chupícuaro, life stands still. I'm happy, content."

For him, Mexico will always be home. Bonifacio Caballero is an essay on home. In this global era of fading borders, his story is more relevant than ever. He and his fellow emigrants have spent a lifetime working in a foreign land, all the while planning to come home. With that in mind, they have spent their lives creating the American dream not in the United States but in their Mexican village.

The house that Bonifacio Caballero built set off a construction boom that transformed once humble Nuevo Chupícuaro, in the central state of Guanajuato. Other emigrants to the United States, returning with dollars, followed his example. They rented in the United States and built in Mexico. Long ago dozens of houses in town surpassed the Caballero home in luxury and expense; these now include pillars, fancy patios, sliding glass windows. Some houses look like lost pieces of suburban California, with very un-Mexican lawns, driveways, and walkways to the door.

The town is now an appendage of the California economy. Almost every family has a telephone, and Chupícuaro's listings in the phone book cover a full page, remarkable for a Mexican village its size—and possible only because of dollars.

The town has settled into a yearly routine that is based on emigration north. Beginning in December, the emigrants return, and Chupícuaro swells to three times its normal population of one thousand people. The official fiesta for the town's patron saint, St. Peter, is June 29, but Chupícuaro holds another, bigger party for him on December 29 so returnees can take part. Then in late January the emigrants leave. Business falls off for a couple of months until they've had a chance to recuperate financially and again start sending money back. Things muddle along again until December. Markets run accounts for women whose husbands will drop by in December to settle, paying grocery bills of five thousand dollars and more at a time.

The town has a kindergarten, its own cemetery, its own water district, a drainage system, a health clinic, and its own garbage truck, most of its streets are paved, and it has its own museum. All of that was funded by the dollars of emigrants who, like Bonifacio Caballero, long to someday return to Chupícuaro for good. "Partly [we've built these projects] because we're used to life the way it is up there [in the United States]," says Francisco Aguilar, who worked fields in Modesto, California, and with his savings started a prosperous construction-materials business in Chupícuaro.

I visited Chupícuaro because I was trying to understand Mexican emigration to the United States. As part of that search, I eventually met Bonifacio Caballero and had dinner outside his rented house in that Wasco labor camp. And as the sun went down one summer evening we spoke about immigration, Mexico, Wasco politics, the United States, the history of Chupícuaro, and his empty two-story house.

But the trail that led me to his dinner table, and the questions with which I came, began more than four years before, when I came to live in Mexico. The first thing I did when I arrived in Mexico was visit Jaripo, a village in the neighboring state of Michoacán that seemed supported only by agriculture of the horse-drawn-plow variety. There was no industry, nothing that could maintain an economy. Yet Jaripo had beautiful houses with marble tile, gravel driveways, and wrought-iron gates. A friend told me that the houses all belonged to emigrants in the United States. He pointed out nearby homes of adobe with hard-packed dirt floors and latrines out back. This, he said, was how everyone lived before they'd gone north. This is how people with no connection to the United States and dollars still live in rural Mexico. He then pointed out more houses under construction. These structures wouldn't be finished for years, since their owners worked on them only when they returned in December and January. Walking through Jaripo, I realized that the architecture alone revealed many ways emigration to the United States has changed Mexico.

A few days later I spoke with Gustavo López Castro, a professor of emigration studies at the Colegio de Michoacán, a university in the city of Zamora, Michoacán. "It's the most common thing we see in these villages," he told me. "The first investment is in the house in the village. They have to demonstrate that they've had success [in the United States]."

As the years went by, I traveled to small villages where emigration north was now a tradition. Each one had a network of native sons concentrated in some unlikely town in the United States. Half the village of Totolán, Michoacán, lives in Glendale, California. A good part of Jaripo lives in Stockton, California. Ocampo, Guanajuato, is a virtual extension of Dallas, Texas.

Several hundred people from Tzintzuntzan, Michoacán, work in Tacoma, Washington, or on fishing boats in Alaska.

In the case of Chupícuaro, hundreds of townspeople live in the California Central Valley town of Greenfield. This is due almost entirely to the late José López. López was a field hand with legal papers who found work with a rancher named Mike Reed in 1959. Reed was impressed with his work ethic and asked López if he knew other men who worked as hard. Reed could get legal papers for sixty more. López returned to Chupícuaro, promising work. People thought he was crazy until a Mexican immigration official showed up with papers. López and his sons eventually became labor contractors, funneling a continuous supply of Chupícuaran field hands to the Greenfield economy.

As I traveled to these villages, I paid special attention to the houses. I discovered, as López Castro says, that the houses indeed are everywhere. Villages throughout the central states of Jalisco, Michoacán, Guanajuato, and others are studded with the ongoing efforts of their wandering native children. I have seen water fountains and billiard rooms, two-car garages, onion-domed roofs, winding staircases, emerald lawns, miles of ornate wrought iron, and the sun setting behind a phalanx of satellite dishes. All of it belongs to people who left Mexico as peasants.

The money emigrants invest in their pueblos probably constitutes the largest privately financed urban renewal project on the North American continent today. The Mexican government estimates that emigrants send home roughly five billion dollars a year. Some large though unmeasurable part of that goes into these houses.

Yet what amazed me most of all is that these houses are occupied only in December or January. Most of the year literally hundreds of thousands of handsome homes stand vacant across Mexico as their owners landscape yards in Orange County, run valet parking in Chicago, and pick tobacco in North Carolina.

And this is another reason the houses intrigue me, for I think they tell us something not only about Mexican emigration to the United States but about immigration in general.

We in America like to believe that immigrants dream of coming to the United States, making new lives for themselves, and becoming American. But

I think the houses of Mexican emigrants tell us that's not quite right. They are standing proof that—for those immigrants seeking economic advancement—the real American dream is to earn money and return to show friends and family that they, too, made it in the USA. Naturally. Who doesn't want to go to his high school reunion a success?

If turn-of-the-century European immigrants never went back in large numbers, I don't believe it was from a lack of wanting. It had to do with other factors—war and the difficulty and expense of transportation at the time. My father tells me that my Spanish-immigrant grandfather left his village in Galicia to work in a coal mine and a brewery in Allentown, Pennsylvania, but always dreamed of walking back into his village with money in his pocket. He never could. Geography, the trip's cost, the Depression, the Spanish Civil War, and World War II got in the way.

I think that for many immigrants the idea of actually becoming a U.S. citizen is secondary, if it exists at all. Only the fear of a nationwide version of California's Proposition 187—the voter-approved measure, eventually struck down by a judge, that would have denied illegal immigrants services such as education and medical attention—made Mexicans naturalize in large numbers.

Mexicans are simply one of the few groups who have been able to realize the immigrant's American dream: they can return home in style. Unlike China, Vietnam, Italy, Russia, and other sending countries, Mexico has combined political peace and consistent poverty with geographic proximity to the United States. For Mexicans with dollars, going home has always been quick, safe, and relatively cheap. Unlike immigrants from other countries, Mexicans have never had to perform the excruciating emotional surgery of severing ties to their native land. I don't think this is necessarily a good thing. Many Mexican families can't afford two homes. In the United States they often rent cramped houses in crime and drug-plagued neighborhoods with the worst schools so they can save money to build those beautiful homes, that stand empty and unused, in Mexico.

Nonetheless, this investment keeps Mexico afloat. Thousands of villages would have disappeared years ago had the emigrant decided to cut these ties. Instead villages across the Mexican countryside live a paradox: they are abandoned yet prosperous. The houses stand like giant archaeological artifacts. They

are silent evidence that families have been there. They are proof, oddly, that these families were forced to leave their village to survive and intend to return.

And every winter hundreds of thousands of Mexican emigrants do return, however briefly—the state of Guanajuato alone receives two hundred thousand returnees annually. They have great parties, see old friends, marry, baptize their children . . . and work on their houses. Often they are the most important employers in their villages; emigrants, too, know how to take advantage of cheap Mexican labor.

Chupícuaro is one of these, and if it has a special and rare history, it's still essentially no different from the thousands of other abandoned and prosperous pueblos across Mexico.

I first heard about Chupícuaro from José Hernández, who directs the state office Attention to Guanajuatan Communities Abroad. We were talking about the houses of emigrant Mexico when he brought up the town. He told me of Chupícuaro's history. Years ago the government moved the town to make way for a reservoir. As engineers dug the lake, they found remnants of an ancient Indian culture under the town. That stopped construction. Archaeologists eventually discovered pottery and almost four hundred skeletons. People had been living in Chupícuaro since at least 400 b.c. It was a spectacular find; the most important of Chupícuaro's remains lie in museums in Israel, Los Angeles, Chicago, and Mexico City.

Progress couldn't wait, however, and in 1949 the town was covered in water, dissolving villagers' adobe lodgings and probably burying many other ancient artifacts. Villagers were moved a few miles away into rugged government-built brick houses. The town was renamed: Nuevo Chupícuaro. Yet the new land proved arid and infertile, Hernández said, and Chupícuarans, furious with their government, eventually had to emigrate north, to Wasco and to Greenfield, in California's Central Valley. As they earned dollars, they returned to build in Chupícuaro. "Now you see these spectacular houses, California style, worth maybe two hundred thousand dollars, I'd guess," Hernández told me. "You know how often they use them? Two days, three days a year."

Actually many Chupícuarans use them a few weeks a year, though not much more. Still I was curious. Chupícuaro had antecedents predating Christ. It was rebuilt through U.S. emigration to emerge as a shiny modern pueblo whose residents cross national borders like they cross the street. It seemed worth visiting.

Nuevo Chupícuaro sits quietly on a promontory above a valley carpeted with emerald fields of sorghum, three miles outside the city of Acámbaro in the southern part of Guanajuato, about four hours north of Mexico City. Fittingly, the first thing you notice upon entering the town is something influenced by the Unites States. From atop the town church bursts a strange, gorgeous amalgam of steeples, known as the Torres de la Discordia—the Towers of Discord. Money for the church was donated by returning emigrants in the 1960s. The project organizer hired a foreman, who built the first two towers. But then the foreman and the organizer's son-in-law began to argue about design. Finally the organizer fired the foreman. The son-in-law built the third tower, which is thin and piercing and built to look—this being the late 1960s— like an Apollo moon rocket. (The altar inside the church was built later with a donation from a man living in Modesto who won the California lottery.)

In front of the church, the plaza, refurbished a few years ago using emigrant dollars, is anchored with two bandstands, benches, a fountain, and rows of lush trees. The town museum, a block away, houses lesser artifacts from Chupícuaro's history, recent and ancient.

Besides supporting Chupícuaro's economy, the emigrants' annual return has also fostered a social competition that has further spurred the town's development. The church, the roads, the museum, the houses, the plaza—all are due to emigrants' desire to lose all vestige of their former poverty and outdo each other in showing the success they've had up north.

The cemetery, too, has undergone its own building boom. Townspeople say the cemetery was once a collection of humble iron crosses, similar to many across rural Mexico. But with emigration came money. Now the cemetery looks like a miniature city. It's crowded with large marble tombs, some of which have windows, some of which are enclosed. The tombs are adorned with open Bibles and statues of Jesus and the Virgin Mary and topped with tall steeples and crosses. They are done in marble, contracted from artisans who live in the neighboring state of Michoacán. An ornate marble crypt "is a way of showing how well you've done economically," says Martín Camacho, a pharmacist in Chupícuaro.

"There's a kind of innate democracy in people from Chupícuaro—that one person is worth as much as another," says Father Salvador Rangel, the priest who organized many of the public-works projects and went to California to raise money for them among Chupícuaro's emigrants. "Why should I bow to another? My opinion can be as important as that of another or better. One person builds a house and someone else wants a better one. I think finally that it's healthy when it's channeled toward an idea of progress."

One thing about Chupícuaro that emigration has not measurably helped, but has greatly influenced, is the school. While townspeople will give money for a religious project or a party, they won't donate to improve the school. "They believe that's the government's job," says Juan Francisco Soto, a sixth-grade teacher at José María Morelos Elementary School, where forty of the 240 children leave midyear for the United States. "The impact of emigration has been serious. Many children lose interest in continuing their studies. They think that when they finish junior high school, they're going to leave. Parents don't pressure them to study. They don't see the point. We've got doctors and engineers in town. But the campesinos who go to the United States have better cars."

Still, education aside, emigration has bequeathed campesinos a set of new attitudes. They are now modern members of the global economy. "Talking to them, they say 'I'm going to the United States next week,' like it's so easy, as if they're going to the store," says Diego Mondragón, the museum director, who's never been north. "It's so natural for them." Moreover, emigration and their forced relocation fifty years ago has given people here a distinctly American bias against big government. When, for example, talk turns to Chupícuaro's relationship with Acámbaro, the county seat, people here make heated arguments that resemble "no taxation without representation." "The taxes we pay to Acámbaro we don't get anything for," says José López, son of the Greenfield pioneer and owner of a produce-exporting firm in Chupícuaro. Recently Chupícuaro, urged on primarily by those living in the United States, filed papers with the state to secede and form its own county.

These changes are what I came to Chupícuaro to see, and they fascinate me still. But something even more remarkable gradually dawned on me through the conversations I had with Chupícuarans on both sides of the border.

It came up first in a conversation with the Jaime brothers, Miguel and Javier, who are fountains of information on Chupícuaro's economic history. The brothers are Chupícuaro's construction workers. Now in their late fifties, one or the other has built almost every house in the village, including Bonifacio Caballero's. The housing boom, the Jaimes say, really happened in the 1960s and 1970s, when the town filled out. Since then work has slacked somewhat, and many emigrants have tapered their visits to a few weeks a year. "When [the U.S. Congress] passed the Immigrant-Amnesty Act [in 1986], work really began to drop off. The next year you could see it," says Javier Jaime. "People didn't come back as often. When the peso went from three to a dollar to seven to a dollar [in 1995 and 1996], there was a surge in work, because people could get more for their dollars. There wasn't as much as years before, but there was some."

As we talked, what occurred to me was this: Despite the years of sweat and investment in these gorgeous houses, many emigrants who left in the 1960s aren't retiring to Chupícuaro after all. The final irony of their lives is that they are staying in the United States, while Chupícuaro has become their winter tourist resort—a spruced-up version of the Mexico they left thirty years ago. "This is happening in villages all across Mexico," says López Castro, the emigration scholar, when I spoke with him four years after our first conversation. "Older people are deciding not to come home to live."

Mexican emigrants hoped for a piece of the American dream in Mexico. But despite the modern travel that allows them to return home easier than ever, that dream has proved elusive. Through their U.S. years, these emigrants' dream imperceptibly changed on them. Or more likely, they have changed.

"Most of their lives are spent [in the United States] and their children are there, so they stay," says Javier Olvera, the town's representative to the county government. "I've had friends who've gone north with the same idea. But it's not the same once you have children who are born there. You're not going to make a fifteen- or twenty-year-old come back here, except for maybe a month or two. Home calls you back. It's just that their home is no longer Mexico."

Amazingly, some emigrants have even sold the houses they worked so hard to build to people arriving from the impoverished hamlets that surround Chupícuaro. To these new arrivals, Chupícuaro, with its dollar-erected

economy, is the land of opportunity.

Other Chupícuarans fittingly imagine binational lives for themselves. Francisco Aguilar, now running his construction-materials business, wants to sell some land near Chupícuaro to buy a place in Modesto, California. He may naturalize as an American. Now that Mexico allows double nationality, he can be Mexican and American. "You spend so much time in the United States that you feel part of it," he says. "When I see the fields of the United States, it's like I'm living. To remember is to live. I'd like to live part here, part there, like we've always done."

But Bonifacio Caballero says he will remain Mexican and return to his beloved Chupícuaro after his youngest daughter leaves high school. For his son, also named Bonifacio Caballero, the prospect of his parents' return grows more troubling as it grows closer. "It's always been there, always in the back of my mind, but I don't want to think about it," he says. "I don't think it's the same Mexico that he thought it was going to be when he left thirty years ago. My parents go back for thirty days [every year] and they don't know how life is the rest of the time. They see the town at its peak, the fiestas. The other nine or ten months, it's a ghost town. If they do move back, it'll be a town of old immigrants. I hope it's not a big disappointment."

"I think it's a nice idea, but he doesn't seem to be making any real effort to go back," says Maria Caballero, the oldest child in the Caballero family, who works as a rocket scientist in Maryland. "He keeps making additions to the house so we can all join him there. But I don't think I can live there. I'm used to the conveniences here, big stores, supermarkets. And I don't think they'll go back by themselves. I don't see them living there alone."

Yet thirty-three years after building the house that changed Chupícuaro, Bonifacio Caballero insists he will one day make that two-story house at San Pedro and Tarasco streets his home. His American dream remains intact.

"We are going to return, my wife and I, to enjoy what we have left of life," he says. "It may be an illusion, but we do want to return. I want to be buried in Mexico. I want them to take me to the graveyard with a mariachi band. That's not too much to ask. I want to be buried in my land."

—1998

AFTERWORD

July 2: Another Mexico Emerges

The day after July 2 in Mexico City was a gorgeous, bright, sun-shiny day, with a big blue sky and little trace of the smog that usually carpets the valley of the capital. Rightly so. The PRI had been toppled the day before. A new Mexican Revolution had come, this one without blood or bullets. The first peaceful change of regime in the country's history. Even Mother Nature seemed to agree: it was a new day for Mexico.

The presidential election on Sunday, July 2, 2000 marked a defeat of Mexican history. On that day, the country turned away from the top-down, hierarchical tradition left the country by the Aztecs, the Spanish, the Catholic Church and the dictator, Porfirio Díaz. It was a defeat for the officialist and parasitic tendency in the country's culture that is best represented by the *licenciados* at PRI headquarters. Vicente Fox's election as president was a victory for the future. It reaffirmed the other side of Mexico that this book has tried to describe—the dynamic, energetic, and daring Mexico. This Mexico had grown to be part of the world, was not afraid of it. It had been trying to emerge from under the PRI's sloth for some time. Indeed, in the last few years, it had been finding self-confidence. Business groups, churches, the media, non-profits, and neighborhood groups had moved into civic spaces that once the PRI alone had occupied. What had not changed was Mexico's government and ruling party.

Fox perfectly symbolized the side of Mexico struggling to break free. Rarely had Mexico seen a politician so informal and frank, so willing to create new paradigms and dispense with the bull and pomp of political life. Rarely had Mexico had a politician whose contrasts were on such public display.

Fox is a divorced Catholic and the father of four adopted children. A rancher and former president of Coca-Cola de Mexico who hates business suits, he came from both the rural and cosmopolitan sides of the country. He usually sported an open-collar blue shirt, cowboy boots and a large FOX beltbuckle.

293

He could speak Spanish like a farmer, and English like a New York banker. On a campaign stop with touring motorcyclists, he donned a helmet and leather jacket and rode a Harley. It was such a jarring sight for Mexicans that the stunt earned him the cover of the newsweekly *Proceso*, under the headline, "The Fox Style."

About a couple times a month during the campaign Fox uttered something that shocked the Mexican body politic. He once bent back the index finger of his victory V, leaving the middle finger erect. This was the sign of his rival, Francisco Labastida, the PRI's candidate, he told his crowd. He called Labastida a *mariqueta*—a sissy—and an "electoral pirate." He used the words *los jodidos*—the screwed—to describe those for whom he would fight. To Protestant ministers, he drew parallels between the Catholic Church and the PRI, scandalizing much of the country to make the point that both institutions had held a monopoly on power in Mexico. Toward the end of the campaign, on stage he kicked cardboard coffins emblazoned with the PRI name.

It was all so different. In a country used to slick, silver-tongued politicians, it thrilled some people and turned others off. Temporarily at least, Fox turned the PAN—a party of aristocrats, businessmen, and devout Catholics—into a party of the masses and of the center.

I spent nine days on different tours with the Fox campaign and it was clear he was taking the PAN places it had never gone before. One day he lunched with business people at a posh hotel garden in Zamora, Michoacán. Two hours later we were in the Purepecha Indian village of Tarecuato, where no *Panista* had ever held a rally and many people emigrated to Pomona, California. On another day in Mexico City he breakfasted with finance executives and by noon was speaking before a poor neighborhood on the outskirts of town. One of the reasons Fox won was that he could make these transitions easily and genuinely. He could talk to elites, but he didn't seem to be of them. This attracted many Mexicans to him.

Still, few people expected his victory, and fewer still the suddenness of it. As election day approached, virtually everyone—political observers, most of my colleagues and I, and officials of the Federal Electoral Institute (IFE), the election oversight agency—was prepared for a close contest. The IFE had announced they'd have counts and updates through the early morning hours, continuing if necessary until Wednesday, when official results would be announced. The PRI had 1,300 lawyers lined up to fight what they expected would be numerous suits alleging irregularities at polling places.

But it wasn't necessary. Instead, Mexico left behind the old tawdry machine-style election-day manipulation. Across the nation, most polling places reported orderly, quiet, and serious voting, with high turnout. Then, at 8:00 p.m., Televisa announced its polls showed Fox leading by a sizable margin. By 8:30 p.m.—two and a half hours after polls closed—Joaquín Vargas, president of the Radio and Television Chamber of Commerce, went on radio stations to say that exit polls showed Fox with a 10 percentage-point lead—enough, said Vargas, to declare Fox the next president of Mexico. From then on, the night would be filled with historic moments.

At about 10:30 p.m., Cuauhtémoc Cárdenas, candidate for the center-left PRD, conceded defeat.

Twelve years before Cárdenas stunned the country when he bolted from the PRI and ran a renegade campaign without an organization or media coverage. He unified the fractious left, and drew to him the poor and working classes, peasants, people frustrated with Mexico's corruption and lack of democracy. He traveled the country, speaking in his trademark severe and somber style. In the campaign's closing days, he electrified people, his crowds mushroomed. Many Mexicans still believe he won that election, but had it stolen from him by voter fraud engineered by the PRI/government and a suspicious election-night crash of the vote-counting system. His break with the PRI and his campaign changed Mexican politics and paved the way for other opposition-party victories in state elections and Fox's victory on July 2.

But during the 2000 campaign it was clear that Cárdenas, now sixty-six, was finished. In a strange way, Cárdenas was a reverse barometer of how Mexico had changed. Neither his campaign style nor his rhetoric had changed much since 1988. "(In 1988) he could ignite emotions because he was serious and severe. People looked at him like an Aztec idol, that behind him was hiding all the power of race and identity," said Adolfo Aguilar Zinser, a former aide who broke bitterly with Cárdenas after writing a book critical of his 1994 campaign, and by the time I spoke with him was an advisor to Vicente Fox's campaign. But where once the Cárdenas style seemed new and electrified crowds, now it seemed old and worn. Mexico no longer responded to him the way it once did.

That apparently didn't bother Cárdenas. Polls showed him in distant third place, but he changed little about his campaign approach. It didn't take long to see he wasn't trying to win. His rallies had an empty feel. The sound system was louder than the crowd's applause at most of the rallies I attended. He seemed to expect people to know it was in their interest to vote for him, thus he didn't have to get down in the trenches and work for their vote. It was as if he thought showing up and speaking in small villages was enough. Like a doctor, he was giving Mexico its medicine and they ought to know it was good for them, since he was telling them it was so. Cárdenas was incapable of adapting to the new times he'd helped unleash.

I came to see him as Mexico's Moses. He led the people to the promised land of democracy, but could not enter it himself. Moses, on the other hand, is not recorded as having whined the whole time about his fate. Cuauhtémoc Cárdenas set off on a temper tantrum that lasted the final two months of the campaign. He began to campaign against Fox instead of against Labastida. Following his lead were the whole of PRD leadership and La Jornada, which now lost all journalistic objectivity and, like Cárdenas, attacked Fox daily. Cárdenas reduced himself to playing the same role that the PAN's Diego Fernandez de Cevallos played in 1994: wittingly or not, he became the PRI regime's ally. That was clear even before his last speech in Mexico City's main plaza, when he attacked Fox ten times and Labastida only once.

Cárdenas didn't understand the new Mexico. He tried to make the election a choice between right and left—reduce it to terms he could understand. In a country trying to break from seventy-one years of one-party rule, this was a preposterous idea. Ideologies, policy questions—these didn't matter. They could be argued later, after the PRI was out of the way. That was the job at hand. Moreover, in interviews with both Fox and Cárdenas it was clear to me that there was no substantial difference between them on the most important issues. Cuauhtémoc Cárdenas could have gone down in history as the father of Mexican democracy. Now any such description, to be fair, will also have to include an account of his sad and dubious 2000 campaign.

Certainly the Mexican people saw through him and made him pay the price. He garnered a meager 16.6 percent of the vote, about 3 percent more than polls showed he'd get when he entered the campaign nine months before.

In the following weeks, the PRD folded deep into self-criticism. Yet little of it involved Cárdenas. He remained the party's sacred cow. This was remarkable to watch. Party members who had spent years taking courageous and defiant stands against the PRI system at great personal risk now timidly bowed their heads before Cárdenas's authority and said nothing. No one would say publicly that the reason the party lost so terribly was its candidate. All kinds of other excuses were found. *La Jornada's* pages were filled with members blaming internal divisions, unnamed party leaders, and the PRD's loss of contact with its bases. Cárdenas seemed willing to let the bonfires of the PRD witchhunt consume party president Amalia García. Anyone but himself. Nor on election night was it clear Cárdenas understood the message Mexico was sending him. He told reporters he would not be congratulating Fox. "What's happening to this country is a disgrace," he told *La Jornada*.

At 11:00 p.m., José Woldenberg, president of the Federal Electoral Institute, went on national television and announced that the agency's numbers showed a clear and irreversible trend toward Fox. Woldenberg called the quality of the election "exemplary." "We've had a great day," he said. "We've passed the test. We've showed that we're a country in which a change in government can be made peacefully."

Meanwhile, delirium reined at PAN headquarters in the Del Valle neighborhood of Mexico City, as staffers and volunteers cried and hugged each other. Reporters wandered about, dazed at history in the making. Outside the building a crowd gathered and chanted Fox's name. "The oldest authoritarian system in the world has just fallen," said Carlos Medina Placencia, the PAN's congressional leader, to a crowd of reporters. "What's happened in Mexico tonight has an importance similar to the fall of the Berlin Wall," said Luis Álvarez, eighty, a PAN senator. Álvarez had been president of the PAN, and had twice been its presidential candidate. He was, in turn, jailed twice by the PRI regime. "I'm very, very happy. It's a dream, a dream that's become reality. I always knew the Mexican people would know how to act if given the opportunity."

At 11:05 p.m., President Ernesto Zedillo went on television to do what no president had ever done: announce that a candidate from a party other than the PRI would succeed him. Standing before a painting of Benito Juarez—the

great liberal president of the mid-1800s—Zedillo said he had spoken with Fox and would work with the president-elect to ease the latter's transition into office.

Then it was Labastida's turn. He and his staff had predicted a six-point victory. Many polls showed him leading throughout the campaign. Now before a somber crowd of career party politicians at PRI headquarters on Insurgentes Avenue, Labastida did something that no PRI presidential candidate had ever had to do: he conceded defeat. Flanked by his wife, María Teresa de Uriarte, Labastida said: "The citizens made a decision that we must respect. I'll be the first to do that." He added: "Our party is alive and will continue and will show that it can again gain the trust of a majority of Mexicans."

About an hour later, from the balcony at PAN headquarters, Fox spoke to the throngs of cheering supporters below. *"Me siento a toda maquina, la verdad,* (This feels really good)" he told them, substituting *maquina* for the more base *madre.* "We've all won. Mexico has won. Each family has won. Each Mexican has won. Tonight I'm more in love than ever with my country. This century is the Mexican century." Midway through his speech they sang him "Las Mañanitas"—Mexico's birthday song. He had turned fifty-eight on election day. Finally, he said, "Let's go to the Angel."

People had been at the majestic Angel of Independence monument on Paseo de la Reforma for several hours by that time. They were running through the streets with noisemakers, chanting, blowing horns. Dozens of people skipped through the streets wearing large Fox masks. Masks of ex-President Carlos Salinas are still sold in markets, and used to ridicule the now-exiled former leader. Zedillo once ordered closed a factory that made rubber masks of his likeness, rightly believing they were being used to make fun of him as well. But the Fox masks are used as a symbol of endearment for the man, and as such became another sign of how different the Fox campaign was to Mexican politics.

Amid the bedlam beneath the Angel stood Juan Manuel Hernández, a twenty-four-year-old law student, chanting "Mexico! Mexico!" and waving a Mexican flag. Young people like Hernández were a key to Fox's victory. Polls throughout the campaign showed him with almost half the youth vote. "This is a big change for Mexico," Hernández said above the din around him. "We'll no longer have to be submissive. The people will have a voice. We'll have a government that will take into account non-*Priistas* as well as *Priistas*. We'll have a government concerned for those who've been forgotten, the unprotected."

At about 1:00 a.m. Fox stood before the crowd at the Angel. It began to chant: "Don't fail us! Don't fail us!" "We can't fail Mexico," Fox told them. "Let's go home now and go to sleep. Tomorrow our work begins."

* * *

In the days following July 2, the spectacle the PRI made of itself was especially bizarre for those of us used to the pomp and self-assuredness of the ruling party. Suddenly naked, without a president to protect them and tell them what to do, *Priistas* were now rattled. Improbably, some became versed in the Rights of Man. Politicians who'd spent their lives wallowing in the muck of presidentially protected corruption, suddenly were sounding like Thomas Jefferson, having in the span of three days discovered the beauty and necessity of counterbalances on presidential power.

Perhaps most ironic was Manuel Bartlett. Bartlett had been a candidate for the PRI's presidential nomination and was now a senator-elect. He had been in charge of the election system in 1988 the night the vote-counting computer system "crashed." He had been Interior Minister when DEA Agent Enrique Camarena was killed and American diplomatic officials say he will have to answer questions about the case before a grand jury the next time he goes to the United States. Now Bartlett was sounding like a great democrat. He insisted that the new Congress would be strong and independent, a concept anathema to *Priistas* when they held power. He said that Fox would be checked by Congress. "Very checked," he emphasized, for anyone who missed the point.

Priistas spent the first few days blaming each other for their defeat. President Zedillo, especially, was attacked for recognizing Fox's victory so quickly. Meanwhile, Cuauhtémoc Cárdenas suggested that Zedillo had paved the way for Fox, though earlier Cárdenas had criticized the president for an unprecedented campaign of public-works inaugurations favoring Labastida in the months before the election. *Proceso* went one step further. It blamed Zedillo, Salinas, and Miguel De La Madrid.

Mexicans like to blame their presidents, but all that missed the point. The PRI lost because its structure was made obsolete and irrelevant by the global economy. During the Cold War, the country could get away with a protected economy and a mammoth, unaccountable, and inefficient one-party state. The system had rewarded herd-thinking and submission, and made an untouchable king of the sitting president. What naturally grew from this was corruption, appalling waste, a government that could not respond to its people, and a country unable to compete in the world. Carlos Salinas didn't doom the PRI. It was the nature of the PRI itself, the design of the Mexican one-party state that was failing. Now the country needed an agile and competent government.

The PRI system was simply a load Mexico could no longer carry. Like an old snakeskin, the PRI was crumbling, crusty, unnecessary and in the way. In the end Mexicans shrugged it from their backs with surprising ease. Within the week, there were proposals to rename the party, reform it, separate it from its junkie-like dependence on the president, and have it come up with some ideas of its own for once. All radical proposals for the PRI. Until July 2 it appeared invincible. Suddenly it was charging into the distance and out of sight.

I spent time at PRI headquarters after the election. What became clear, as I walked through its halls, was the way the party had deluded itself. Years of winning rigged elections convinced it that it could win a fair race, too. What led the party to this self-deception was the same PRI structure that wholly submitted to authority for so many years. Now this submission clouded the truth. "What we created was a pyramid of lies," said one *Priista* I spoke with. "If I'm, say, state president of the PRI and they ask me how the campaign's going, I have to say, 'Fine.' I can't go against the structure. They ask me about the opposition, I say, 'No, they're very few. There's almost no opposition presence.' So there's a lie that comes up from below. The local PRI president, the state PRI president, they all lie to the one above. We all try not to see reality. I have to lie although I know it's not reality in order not to lose my job. We all try to please the one above." The best example of this was in the border state of Tamaulipas, where during the campaign Gov. Tomas Yarrington publicly told Francisco Labastida that he didn't need to campaign in his state because his victory was already guaranteed. Labastida lost Tamaulipas by 76,000 votes.

The day I visited PRI headquarters, people were taking down Labastida signs, emptying offices. In the press office, a secretary was talking on the phone: "We're a little sad, but we're OK. We're still here. We don't know until when, but we're still here. There's still hope." In the lobby, I bought a PRI domino set and some PRI playing cards, hoping they'd be collectors' items sometime soon. I was the clerk's first customer in a few days.

As I walked through PRI-land, the theme of the party's self-deception stayed with me. I remembered my visit to Mérida, Yucatán ten days before the election. My time there coincided with major rallies by Fox and Labastida. The Fox rally was on a Thursday and attended by fifteen thousand screaming and enthusiastic people who'd come to see no one but Vicente Fox.

Mérida is one of the few cities in Mexico without a police force in its employ. Control of the police was taken from the city by a PRI governor in 1969 after the PAN won Mérida City Hall for the first time. Yucatán's governor, Víctor Cervera, one of most hardline of *Priistas*, uses the officers at his discretion. So despite fifteen thousand people marching through downtown, creating the expected traffic havoc, no police were in evidence anywhere. It didn't seem to matter. Rally organizers improvised some traffic control and Fox arrived to deafening frenzy in the city's plaza. It was the kind of excitement his presence increasingly created as the election approached.

Yet it all seemed dwarfed the next day when Francisco Labastida held a rally at the city's soccer stadium. This time police were out in force directing traffic, which included hundreds of buses from across the state, many of which were government owned. The size of the crowd was impressive. More than fifty thousand people showed up. However, it didn't have half the enthusiasm of the Fox crowd the day before. Rather, the feeling was empty and blasé. Rock groups and pop singer Juan Gabriel were scheduled to perform, as if Labastida himself wasn't enough to bring people out. In fact he wasn't.

I was standing on the soccer field, about fifty yards from an exit when Labastida began to speak. As his speech progressed, I noticed people beginning to leave. At first it was only a trickle. I could dodge them easily enough. But soon, many hundreds of folks were pouring out of the stadium. I had intended to stay, but before long the flow was so thick that resisting it was impossible. I left with it. Labastida, meanwhile, continued his speech. As we

neared the exit, the crush of exiting people was intense. Little children were getting caught underfoot. Frantic mothers, holding crying infants, looked up at me with fear in their eyes. It was scary. We needed several minutes to move twenty yards. But finally, we squeezed through to the parking lot and breathed a sigh of relief. Back on the stage, Labastida continued his speech, oblivious to the folks piling out on him.

The scene was just a great big metaphor for the PRI and its campaign. But, in fact, the party used the size of the rally, and others like it, as proof that it had Yucatán and the country locked up.

I had actually gone to the Yucatán not to see Labastida, but to watch Víctor Cervera in action. In all Mexico, there likely is no governor who better symbolizes the old style of PRI politics—and how the ruling party kept power for seventy-one years—than Cervera. Like the PRI nationally, Cervera had used government programs to solidify loyalty to him and his machine. He had achieved a remarkable omnipresence. Poor rural folks tended to view him as a great benefactor; the urban middle class saw him as a populist thug. But when people on all sides of Yucatán politics discussed Cervera they used terms like "invincible" and "omnipotence."

"Cervera doesn't miss one opportunity to show that only with his participation can problems be solved," said one man who had spent many years as a PRI political operative in rural areas, but who by that time was a Cervera enemy.

Cervera was like the PRI in that way. His best-known program is one in which he holds large events in small towns and distributes merchandise. This includes bicycles, sewing machines, water tanks, rolls of barbed wire, washing machines, and blenders.

The way the story was reported, it appeared that this merchandise was being given away to convince rural folks to vote PRI. That turned out not to be true. The government provided the stuff at half price and on credit. Early in the campaign at many of these rallies, people were being urged to vote PRI as they received their bicycles and sewing machines. However, that stopped as election coverage intensified and foreign and national reporters came to the state. Cervera, meanwhile, said the merchandise was designed to help the poor, and not for political ends. Yet his critics contended that the merchandise could just as easily be delivered without the governor's presence and that he only did this to cultivate his image as benefactor and to keep people beholden to the party.

The point of it all, it seemed to me, was not so ham-handed as one bicycle, one vote. It was, rather, part of a more subtle and constant process of creating an image of the government as magnanimous, the fountain of beneficence— the same rigorous way that Coca-Cola has created an image as refreshing and thirst-quenching.

One day, the governor visited Homun, a town of about seven thousand people about an hour from Mérida. There he oversaw the distribution of three hundred Hoover Milenia washing machines, inaugurated the opening of a senior center, and a street-paving project—all state funded.

I returned to Homun a couple days later and met a man named Nestor Ix. Mr. Ix was a sixty-three-year-old Mayan Indian campesino, a jovial and gregarious man, and we got to talking about the election and the governor. Mr. Ix, it turned out, was to be director of a polling place on July 2, and was intent on making sure, he said, that "there's no funny business." I asked Mr. Ix if he could enumerate for me all the *apoyos*—or aid—he received from the state. It took a while. But finally, we calculated that Mr. Ix receives 370 pesos a month because he is nearing retirement, and looking forward to getting double that when he turns sixty-five. He gets crop subsidies twice a year. The state government also gives him fertilizer for his bean field and half the equipment he needs every year for his bee business. He has a bicycle and his wife has a sewing machine, both thanks to the state. Six programs for one man. Not surprisingly, Mr. Ix told me, "I'm a *Priista* in my heart."

I later spoke with the town mayor, Evelio Echevarría, who enumerated even more *apoyos* that Homun receives from the state. This included building virtually the entire Homun school infrastructure, paving most of its streets, a food program for old people, a food program for school children, scholarships for school-age children, and a summer-camp program. All this in addition to the farm and retirement programs that Mr. Ix received. Homun performed almost none of the functions normally associated with a town government. The town, like Mr. Ix, depended on the state.

Among *Priistas*, Cervera was considered the master politician. Across the country it was the Cervera model of politics the PRI put in practice—believing that people would be indebted to them for the *apoyos* the PRI handed out.

But July 2 would show that these kinds of programs—the classic PRI buy-offs—were reaching diminishing returns. People were happy to accept half-priced merchandise, but many of them weren't fooled. Most importantly, after being bought off for years, they'd lost all enthusiasm for the party, even if they were going to vote for it. In the end, a lot of them just didn't bother to go to the polls.

In the weeks before the election, I also went to Chimalhuacan, a shantytown suburb of 1.2 million people in the state of Mexico, just east of Mexico City, to attend a massive party for mothers. Among Mexico's working classes, PRI politics, like church-going, has largely been the woman's job. While her husband worked, the woman faced daily the lack of municipal services: paved streets, drinking water, storm drainage, garbage pickup. She fought for these scarce services and thus came into contact with the local PRI, which required her support before attending to her needs. The more support she showed, the more likely her problems would be addressed. One thing was certain: those who didn't join up got nothing. Thus the PRI turned the horrible scarcity in poor neighborhoods from a political liability into a tool to maintain party loyalty. The party's genius was always in using its people's poverty and vulnerability for its own political benefit.

Legions of stout working-class housewives have been the cornerstone of PRI power, found at rallies in aprons or T-shirts, aggressively leading cheers for some slick politician. During the 2000 campaign, one place the PRI was counting on was Chimalhuacán, where Guadalupe Buendía is the political boss.

Mrs. Buendía is a stout woman who is also known as La Loba (The Wolf). She has long been one of the great political operators in the Mexico City area. If it's helpful to think of the PRI as a political machine—a nationwide Tammany Hall—then La Loba is a particularly powerful ward boss, whose base of support are working-class women.

Chimalhuacán formed on land that was once the bed of the now-dried Lake Texcoco. Beginning in the 1970s, the newly vacant land was invaded and squatted by poor people looking for a cheap place to build a home. Vast neighborhoods—one of which is named for Mrs. Buendía—have no paved streets.

Mrs. Buendía's family had been small landowners when all this happened, and lost chunks of it to organized and violent squads of squatters. Finally she subdivided her family's last parcel and became a fighter for municipal services in her subdivision. She was effective, if also brutal and coarse. Before too long other neighborhoods joined her. She formed the Organización de Pueblos y Colonias (OPC).

Today, the OPC is made up of bakers, garbage collectors, bus drivers, bicycle taxi drivers, and above all thousands of housewives. The OPC has its own full-time gynecologist on staff who gives free exams, and enough members to field a league of 40 soccer teams. OPC is almost a government in itself, helping members get electricity installed, legal land title, and more. Moreover, through political participation, its members have a readymade social life, no small thing in a city where there are virtually no opportunities for recreation or entertainment. At the top is Guadalupe Buendía, who brokers OPC support to the PRI. Her walls are covered with photographs of her with governors, presidents, senators.

Long ago, La Loba had figured out how the PRI system was set up. When I met her, she was directing the water district and was reported to occasionally cut service to those neighborhoods where opposition parties dominated. The press portrayed her as a little dictator. She has a foul mouth and a fierce temper. But many Chimalhuacán women love her. Key to her power is making sure that women know that she gives away food at low cost, legalizes land titles, and pressures state bureaucrats for money for street pavings. They know that belonging to the Organización de Pueblos y Colonias is the best way to get services their families need. "On one hand, she likes helping people," said one man in the OPC. "On the other, you know, it gives her power."

Another important component of her very visible largesse is an annual party for Chimalhuacán's mothers. I was spending time in Chimalhuacán doing a story on La Loba and was invited to the party.

This year's party was going to be crucial, since it was an election year and the PRI stood a chance of losing. Also, La Loba's son, Salomon, was running for state legislature, and her cousin, Carlos Cornejo, was running for Congress. They were the future of Mrs. Buendía's power base.

The party was held under a yellow tent in a vacant lot almost the size of a football field. Under the tent were fifteen thousand chairs. Soon they were filled by women of all ages and sizes, joined only by their poverty. As the event

got underway, the announcer kept booming through the massive speakers, "This party is for you, the mothers." But the true motive was other. Signs for the PRI and its candidates were everywhere. "Who are you going to vote for?" first the announcer, then La Loba, asked incessantly through the day. "The Priii!" the crowd would respond. The announcer would lead the women in cheers: "The PRI! The PRI! Rah! Rah! Rah!" Similar cheers went up for Salomon, for Carlos, for the mothers, and, of course, for Mrs. Buendía.

In working-class Mexico, anything free is worth grabbing; Mexico is, after all, a country where people read their junk mail. Knowing this, the PRI never dreamed of holding a rally without giving away lots of stuff. Each woman was given a plastic bucket emblazoned with the PRI logo and the faces of Salomon and Carlos, and containing comic books that detailed the exemplary life led by Francisco Labastida. Next came PRI T-shirts and caps. All of it was avidly snapped up. "We're celebrating those who gave us life: you, the mothers," said Salomon, above the T-shirt chaos. "Those who don't get a T-shirt will get a cap. There'll be more gifts. So just remain in your seats."

Indeed, that day Mrs. Buendía would raffle off six refrigerators, two televisions, two dozen irons, four stoves and a clothes washer. In the past, she had raffled off parcels of land and farm animals.

The real show began about 1:00 p.m., when Paquita la del Barrio arrived. Paquita is a mountain of a woman and Mexico's best female singer, a cross between Tammy Wynette and Katie Webster. Her songs are invariably about unfaithful men, and women who make them suffer for their transgressions. Frequently in mid-song she'll start in with *"Me estas oyendo, inútil?"* (Are you listening to me, you useless bum?), and go off on a rant against an offending male. Adding her to the bill was a deft touch. The crowd roared as she took the stage. To these women, for whom part of life's struggle is bearing abusive and faithless husbands, Paquita was sweet, vicarious revenge. They twisted and swayed on her phrasing, singing every lyric. Paquita left more than an hour later, and was followed by more political promotion, more cheers for the PRI, more exhortations to vote PRI on July 2.

At this point, over the cheers, commenced a pulsing disco music as the announcer proclaimed the arrival of "the best Chippendales in the Mexican Republic." Over the next hour out they came: A cop, then a soldier, a college student, a Ricky Martin look-alike, Batman, a pirate. The crowd, already wound up over Paquita, just went berserk. Close to the stage, I was in a mosh pit of thirty-five- and forty-year-old women clamoring at the jiggling buttocks and pelvic thrusts. Some women giggled uncontrollably. Others would reach up and stroke the men's thighs as if they were fine vases. Still others lost all restraint, lunging to grab great hunks of beefcake. The screams were deafening. The temperature rose fifteen degrees at least. After it appeared the women could take no more, the men ran back on stage together in their g-strings— one now wearing underwear with the PRI logo on the butt. Once again the crowd went wild, clamoring and grasping.

Finally, five of the men formed a line, four donning underwear that each showed one letter of the word, "V-O-T-A" (Vote). Last in line was the fellow with the PRI logo. Together, they wiggled again, then left the stage. Quickly Mrs. Buendía went to the microphone. And as a sea of women before her poured sweat and roared like a tidal wave, she yelled above the din: "So, *compañeras*, who are you going to vote for?" To this, fifteen thousand women let out a thunderous orgiastic groan—"The Prriiiiiii!"—then seemed to collapse in exhaustion and it was over. No hotshot Internet executive could have branded his dotcom any better than La Loba branded the PRI that afternoon.

Yet it was an indication of how far the PRI was divorced from its people that it squandered this advantage. Over the next two weeks Mrs. Buendía was hotly criticized by PRI higher-ups for hiring the strippers. The newsweekly *Proceso* published photographs of the event. The Fox campaign made a national television spot featuring pictures of the strippers and ridiculing the PRI. Then the PRI governor of the state of Mexico called Mrs. Buendía to reprimand her for staging the show. So did the state PRI chairman.

My ears were ringing as I left the tent that day; I wouldn't be able to hear well for the next two days. I shuffled out amid thousands of stout working-class women who sustained the world's oldest one-party regime. They were returning to bleak existences, in homes of concrete blocks on trash-strewn streets of rocks and dust. I'd always wondered what these women saw in this party that had done so little for them. But that day they looked dazed and happy, and they clutched their PRI T-shirts, their PRI caps and their plastic PRI buckets. It was a remarkable event, and I didn't see anything wrong with

it. Mrs. Buendía, it seemed to me, like any good politician, knew her people. Bringing in male strippers seemed a creative way of doing politics. A rousing performance like that was healthier than fostering dependence on government largesse, the way Víctor Cervera did in the Yucatán. After all, Chimalhuacán is poor and life is hard. Said one middle-aged woman: "When are we ever going to have the money to see a show with such handsome men?"

"I didn't want to hurt anyone," Mrs. Buendía said later, stung by the public criticism. "It was a healthy thing. They say that in my country men and women have the same rights. Then, why can men watch this kind of thing, and women can't? Why can men see what they want, cheat on us, mistreat us, and we can't do anything?" But she had the last laugh. On July 2, Carlos and Salomon both won their districts, while the PRI lost heavily elsewhere in the state of Mexico and in the Yucatán. Víctor Cervera later gave a speech in which he scolded the state's young people for believing in the "mirage of change" that Fox represented. But with a governor's election in the Yucatán a year away, it seemed a matter of time before Cervera was, like his party, history.

It turned out that Mrs. Buendía herself was soon to be history, as well. A couple of months after the election, she was in jail on murder charges. Her people had battled with followers of the new mayor, Jesús Tolentino Román, who was also from the PRI. Fifteen people died. Mrs. Buendía was upset that Román, who was not from Chimalhuacán, had been made candidate by the state PRI over her objections, and then, when elected, would not share power with her. Their sides clashed the day Román was supposed to be sworn in. Following the bloody incident, she went into hiding for a week before being arrested. As of this writing, she was awaiting trial in Almoloya de Juárez, Mexico's maximum security prison.

* * *

After spending time at PRI headquarters, I decided to drop by the pillars of PRI support not far away. At Calle Vallarta 8, near the Monument to the Revolution, stands a beige seven-story concrete block of a building that houses the Congress of Mexican Workers (CTM)—the coalition of unions that had been a PRI bulwark since the party's inception in 1929.

Power had not been good for the CTM. Over the years, it built a solid reputation for outright disregard for the rights and working conditions of its members. The CTM became, in many ways, like a pro wrestler: aping what it would like the world to believe it is, though everyone knew it wasn't.

Farmworkers like Luis Guerrero in Baja California have never had a CTM representative defending them when they lose an eye, or when growers dust them, along with the crops, with pesticides. Likewise, female *maquiladora*—assembly plant—workers, like those in Ciudad Juarez, report never having a CTM representative come to their aid when plant managers ask them for bloody tampons as proof they're not pregnant. Both the farmworkers and *maquiladora* workers have CTM dues deducted directly from their paychecks.

In the CTM lobby I met Alfonso Godinez, who explained to me that "the CTM lives from its workers' dues." He said this without a trace of irony. He mentioned this to draw the distinction between the CTM and the PRI, whose bureaucrats were largely on the government payroll, directly or indirectly. Yet Godinez himself lives from those workers' dues. He is a CTM political analyst, part of its vast bureaucracy, and has never himself been a union member.

In front of the building stands a statue of Fidel Velázquez. For most of his life, Velázquez was one of Mexico's most powerful men. He died in 1997, at the age of ninety-seven. He was CTM leader under eleven presidents, and, behind his trademark dark glasses, was known throughout Mexico as one of the country's kingmakers. His approval was needed for all presidential nominations. In his day, Velázquez was one of Mexico's more quotable political figures. Among his more famous quotes was: "He who moves doesn't come out in the photo"—a motto for those wanting to be nominated for president and how they should comport themselves with the utmost of discretion leading up to the anointing. Another famous quote was: "We came into power by the bullet and by the bullet they'll have to remove us."

With Velázquez dead, Mexicans chose the ballot. Velázquez's quotableness, and to some extent his power, diminished as he reached his nineties. Every day he looked more like an iguana lizard. He expressed himself in a senile mumble and a billow of cigar smoke, and held a weekly Monday press conference in which he was almost impossible to understand. In those press conferences he came to stand for the PRI regime. It didn't matter that no one could understand what he said. Fidel Velázquez, like the regime, didn't really need

to explain himself to anyone. Though he controlled millions of workers, he was unaccountable.

Velázquez was replaced by Leonardo Rodríguez Alcaine, also known as "Whitey" (La Guera), for his light skin, freckles, and sandy hair. "Whitey" Rodríguez Alcaine himself has a particularly sharp tongue; he once threatened to have sex with a nosy reporter's sister, though those weren't the words he used. One of the things "Whitey" Rodríguez Alcaine said before the election was that he would call a general strike of all workers if Fox won. But in a meeting with Zedillo and other PRI leaders following the party's defeat, "Whitey" Rodríguez Alcaine apparently had his agenda reset. On July 4, the CTM ran an ad in Mexico City newspapers, signed by Rodríguez Alcaine and other union leaders, tamely announcing that the organization would abide by the results of the election. In other words, the general strike was off. It said something about the PRI and the CTM that two of the ad's signees—Juan José Osorio, of the musicians union, and Salvador Angulo, of the paperworkers union—had actually died a few years before the ad appeared.

The mood around the CTM's offices following the election was not improved by "Whitey" Rodríguez Alcaine's public about-face. "People are really upset," Godínez said. "But the problem we've had here in the CTM has been our submission. Whatever the party said, we went along with." On tables in CTM offices was the PRI magazine *Examen*—"Examination." Since this was something the PRI had never performed on itself, the theme of the party's self-delusion returned. I remembered a high-level PRI political operator who met with reporters before the election and claimed that the party would win by six percentage points. He eagerly explained that Fox was so weak that the PRI would likely even win the governorship of his home state of Guanajuato. Instead, the PRI lost the presidency by six percentage points and the Guanajuato governor's race by more than twenty-two. The articles in *Examen* were, themselves, testament to this kind of officially imposed delirium. "Preserving our national sovereignty: upholding a regime of rights and liberties" read one article. Reading that, and knowing the PRI's history, I didn't know whether to laugh or cry.

A similar response was provoked by the CTM motto: "For the Emancipation of Mexican Workers." "Workers saw their leaders weren't defending their rights, so they voted for the opposition," Godínez said under his breath and looking around stealthily as he stood in the vast marbled lobby of the CTM building. "Often the leaders fooled themselves into believing that people were going to vote for the PRI. They'd ask them and workers would say, 'I'm voting PRI'—only because they were afraid. But since the vote is now free and secret, when they were alone in the ballot box they voted for the opposition." Ironically, the CTM may now become the vigorous defender of workers' rights that it never was as part of the state, Godínez believed. "Sometimes fighting for workers' interests was against the interests of the PRI and the government," he said. "Now you'll see the CTM is going to fight for all the rights of workers because the opposition is in the presidency. Now the CTM will have to earn its bread."

Two blocks away from the CTM, at Calle Lafragua 3, the Confederación Nacional de Organizaciónes Populares (CNOP) had not changed much since I'd first visited it five years before. The same names graced the roster in the lobby. The CNOP was the PRI's attempt to control that part of Mexican society that lived outside the government. The CTM needed the government's help in negotiations with the business class. The Confederación Nacional Campesina (CNC) depended on the government for things like fertilizer subsidies. After a while, the interests of these two umbrella groups were transformed into the political interests of their leaders, and the groups themselves were coopted.

However, the PRI/government had no easy way to do that with the rest of Mexican society. Hence, the need for the CNOP, which was its connection to grassroots and small-business groups, like florists and bicycle-taxi unions and economists.

On the fifth floor I found Benito Barco, a *licenciado*, sitting at a desk in a cubicle that comprised the offices of a group with the hefty name of the National Front for Citizen Participation. Lic. Barco was its secretary general. The Front had formed in 1992 to absorb PRI members from working-class neighborhoods who were upset with the party and not fully incorporated into the party structure, he told me.

The Front's job is what's known in Mexican politics as *gestión social*—a kind of negotiating to push the government (usually the city or state) to invest in public works and services in poor neighborhoods where members of groups

like the National Front live. It's what La Loba does, or did. Usually *gestión social* involves more than dialogue. It implies at least the threat of sit-ins, highway takeovers, and the like as a way pressuring government officials. *Gestión social* was necessary because the PRI/government usually wouldn't act on its own. It became part of Mexican political culture under the PRI—a lobbying method for the powerless.

Barco was a dapper man, with a thin mustache and glasses, a pressed white shirt and red tie. He was a lifelong *Priista/licenciado*, who came to the National Front in 1995 from a post in the Mexico City government. Right now, the Front's main job, apart from doing *gestión social* on behalf of its members, he said, was to gain recognition as a "political group" in the eyes of the IFE, which oversees public funding of national political organizations as well as elections. That designation would bequeath the Front an annual budget of somewhere between 1.2 and 1.6 million pesos a year. Barco conceded it'd be hard to achieve since the National Front, despite its name, isn't very national, with only 2,500 members in three states.

I asked Barco why he thought the PRI had lost. He enumerated the reasons. The distance between leaders and the rank-and-file, the bureaucratization of the PRI—too many *licenciados*, in other words. The party was too accustomed to receiving *linea*—orders—from the president and the elite, and had stopped acting on its own, he said. "You also have to understand that this is the modern era," he told me. "People thought they held the option to choose in their hands. It's part of modern Mexico and the opening to democracy. This is one of the reasons the party's had problems."

The Front itself has problems, and likely not much future. It was able to do *gestión social* on behalf of its members because it was a PRI affiliate and the PRI controlled the government and would usually only help its affiliates. There doesn't seem much reason to belong to the Front with the PRI out of power. So before too long Lic. Barco may find himself looking for work. Still, he said, shortly before I left, "we shouldn't view this (political change) as a tragedy. As an activist in the party, it's been interesting living through this experience." I thanked him and left the cubicle of the National Front for Citizen Participation.

From there I proceeded to the tenth floor where, more than five years later,

I found myself again at the door of Severo Arellano and the National Association of Private Schools (ANEP). Time had been good to Mr. Arellano. His office had moved and remodeled. It was now lighter. The stained windows were no more. The office had three phones, which, like loud parrots, rang each with a different blare. Mr. Arellano himself looked better, sharper. He wore a black suit, with a white shirt and red tie.

He didn't show any sign of remembering who I was and I didn't remind him. But this time we had more time to talk. Mr. Arellano turned out to be sixty-four, a teacher of engineering, a former military officer, and a lifelong member of the PRI. He'd joined back when the party was at the vanguard of the country's industrial development and, like many older Mexicans, he'd never lost that feeling for it. On his walls were the same photos of Mr. Arellano with President Zedillo. Midway through the interview, another shoeshine guy came in and was getting down to work when Mr. Arellano shooed him away, telling him to return after the interview. The ANEP had started in 1947, he told me, and for most of its life had been an unaffiliated non-profit. Mr. Arellano had been a member for twenty-five years and was its president for the last six.

The organization affiliated with the PRI in 1992. Its directors felt it had a better chance of resolving the problems of private schools from inside the PRI than from outside it, he said. That logic may no longer hold. After all, what's the point of belonging to the PRI if the party isn't in power?

That's how José Juan Rosales saw it. I'd met Rosales on the tenth floor of the CNOP just before entering Mr. Arellano's office. He and his wife, Elizabeth, an elementary school teacher, had come to the ANEP to see about a refund for a teacher-education class Elizabeth took. She felt she was being overcharged. "This is all going to come falling down," Rosales said, looking around the tenth floor of the CNOP. What does the ANEP do, I asked them. They looked at each other. "Not much but charge membership fees, right?" Rosales said, looking at his wife. She nodded.

Actually, the ANEP gives continuing education classes for teachers and represents schools in problems they have with the Ministry of Education—an advocate for private schools, in other words. Mr. Arellano and I sat chatting for a few minutes about the association—625 member schools in Mexico City and another 800 in outlying states—the election results and the future of the CNOP.

"Interesting times, no?" I asked.

"Uffff," he said, shaking his head and raising his eyebrows.

Finally, I came around to what had brought me to his office five years before. I asked again for some names and numbers of private schools. "They're not willing to talk," Mr. Arellano said, clearly reluctant and all these years later still not sounding like an advocate. "They're not willing to dialogue with you."

That hadn't been my experience with social organizations in general, I told him.

"No," he went on. "They close their doors and they give their classes. They don't receive people, nor do they give reports or anything. I could give you names, but it won't help you."

"Well, I'm used to being told no," I said.

Mr. Arellano chuckled and paused, then said, "What is it you want?"

It was like pulling teeth, but finally, it happened. Mr. Arellano donned his spectacles and went looking over the list of private schools that was right there on his desk. So it was that five years after I'd first asked, I got a few names and numbers of private schools—for free, the old data-base problem that we'd once faced apparently having been resolved. Severo Arellano had changed, however slowly. He was like Mexico in that way, I suppose. As I write this, I still haven't called the private-school contacts that took so long to come by. They're like parking spaces in New York—so rare you don't want to touch them, you just want to look at them in awe. I'll get around to it at some point. I'm waiting for a special moment.

* * *

Not long after the election, I had a drink with my favorite Mexican philosopher, Dr. Arturo Nájera, the former *Bronxista* from Veracruz. Dr. Nájera had actively sought work with the Labastida campaign. He was a veteran of several campaigns, including Labastida's primary campaign the November before. Still, his offer was refused. It was an indication of the arrogance with which the PRI's political operators viewed the race that they felt they could turn down experienced help. Instead, the doctor had found work in the Health Ministry, where he'd been for several months.

We spent the evening talking about Vicente Fox, power and politics, about

Carlos Salinas, corruption and drug smuggling, and above all about the meaning of the election, the PRI's defeat, and the nature of human freedom. The party was now going to be without a president to tell it what to do, what to think, how to act. So I wondered about the future of the famous party discipline that had created the Bronx in the Congress. "I think it's going to break apart," he said. "There won't be anyone who can control [legislators]. Before the control was, 'If you don't get in line, we'll replace you. We'll take your job.' Now, without any way of pressuring people, this discipline and iron control will relax. The conditions are right to break these chains controlling internal freedom. In losing, people win their liberty."

Though his party had lost, he was not at all sad. "I think this awakening among our people is what was lacking. I didn't want my party to lose. But people woke up and voted. I don't agree with those who say that people voted more with their stomachs than with their heads. I think people thought. They believed they needed a change. Not all of them went to university. But we have to respect these people who voted against us."

He spoke of Catholicism. He was a Catholic but almost never went to church. There was a lot about it he didn't like. His youngest daughter, however, had on her own become an avid Catholic. He was proud that she was doing it on her own, instead of having either religion or agnosticism imposed on her by him. He noted that Vicente Fox was openly going to mass, something that was taboo for every PRI president, given the party's and the Revolution's anti-clerical slant. He saw parallels in Fox breaking these taboos, his daughter's independence, and the independence his fellow Mexicans had shown at the ballot box. The results of July 2 represented a resurgence of the human being, Nájera believed.

"I think the most important liberty isn't the external, but rather the internal. Breaking internal chains, even though we might not have been aware they existed. Sometimes they're so deeply ingrained in us that we don't allow ourselves to dissent. They're symbolically, psychologically very important. They represent the dependence on the mother or father figure, the dependence on the clan. We can't dissent against he who rules. That's why we give him all this support," he said, as he made a half-bow.

"The fundamental value in the human being is liberty. Within the voting

booth, their ten, twenty thirty seconds of free reflection, this liberty was there. I'm very proud of being Mexican because we all had this opportunity to be free for those twenty seconds. We'll continue being free. I don't feel sad. I feel very satisfied. Personally, it may go badly for me, but I'm not worried."

With the PRI no longer in power, he had decided to leave the public sector and start up a private clinic again and see how things went. A buoyant economy would help him along, he felt. Many private doctors had had to close offices precisely because people had been hit so hard by the recurring economic crises. He hoped that era was now over.

"I think this will be very positive for Mexico," he said. "These groups in power had become insolent and arrogant. Hopefully those who come in will come in humble and realize that people are tired of so much arrogance and decisions from above and discipline. If the Roman Empire ended, if the English Empire ended, if the Spanish Empire ended, why wouldn't this *Priista* empire also end?"

* * *

The day after he was elected president, Vicente Fox met with President Ernesto Zedillo. When he left that meeting, Fox came out to meet with reporters for the first time as president-elect. He spoke about many things that afternoon. But one that struck me was a simple, astonishing announcement. Fox announced he would be choosing his cabinet ministers according to their expertise in the area they would administer. He also said they would be chosen before September so that they could get to know their agencies before the December 1 swearing-in.

It was a good way to begin. Under the PRI, cabinet ministers usually were political allies of the president, with little knowledge of the fields they administered. For example, José Antonio González Fernández, an attorney, was Zedillo's last Secretary of Health. He had also been PRI president and Labor Secretary, and admitted to having no expertise in health issues. Cabinet ministers were usually announced only a day before the new president took office. The logic of the PRI system was never accountability, efficiency, or responsiveness to constituents. It was self-preservation and satisfying the different groupings within its political elite that vied for power. So a lot of what would seem obvious and basic in well-run public administration was never put in place—like choosing cabinet ministers with expertise.

At a press conference with foreign reporters the following day, Fox announced another obvious change. He would also be proposing a number of measures to strengthen municipal government. I think this is one of the most important tasks he faces. In the global economy, regional and local governments, not the nation-state, are the key forces in attracting investment, job creation, and in promoting synergies that lead to technological advance. Capable local government makes democracy function, since it is closest to the people.

But this is precisely where Mexico is weakest. Most Mexican cities, towns and villages are crippled, dependent, and poor—like Homun in the Yucatán. Under the PRI, tax proceeds have been turned over to the central government, which then doles fifteen percent of it back to states, five percent to cities, and keeps eighty percent for itself. Because re-election is prohibited, every three years the mayor and his entire staff leaves. A new mayor enters and must learn from scratch.

Thus, municipalities have no money for the most basic services, such as paving streets or providing drinking water. Nor often do they have the administrative know-how to, say, let a public-works contract out for bid. Municipal weakness is the reason for Mexico's contaminated water supply and Moctezuma's Revenge. It is why Mexican police departments have to ration bullets and don't have enough cars or guns for their officers. It is one reason why so many cities, like Tijuana, are ringed with shantytowns.

In Mexico, economic growth has largely come without true development precisely because municipalities are so incapable. Indeed, I believe many Mexicans' impoverishment has almost as much do to with this as with low wages. When jobs come to a city, so do people wanting those jobs. But local government cannot hope to keep up with the infrastructure demands this economic boom has created. So a Mexican with a job still has to walk to work in knee-deep water when it rains, or risk having his house taken out in a flood because the city hasn't provided storm drainage.

Municipalities often cannot design policies to attract the jobs that will keep their people from heading to the U.S. or turning to drug smuggling. And they are simply too hamstrung to provide a local bulwark against the

effects of drug smuggling. In the United States, cities and towns do this by providing capable police, libraries, recreation departments and more. Most Mexican municipalities can do none of that.

Changing all this implies reorganizing—a redistribution of power and responsibility—each level of Mexican government. The PRI never was going to do this. Its system was predicated upon weak municipalities and states dominated by a powerful central government, headed by the president. With Fox, that thorough reorganization can now begin. Fox promised to increase states and cities share of total tax revenues from twenty percent to forty-five percent during his six years in office. A longer-term reform, he said, will be making states and cities fully autonomous—with a civil service and responsibilities for setting local taxes and planning priorities.

I was thinking about the many governmental changes Mexico had to make when, not long after these press conferences, I went to the state of Chiapas. I went to cover the campaign for governor. But I also went because I was searching for white elephants and what they said about Mexico's past, and its potential for the future.

Elefantes blancos dot Mexico like acne—useless, unwanted or unnecessary projects that served only as magnificent wastes of money and fountains of corruption. Every state and most cities have some white elephant project—some pointless bridge or unused convention center—its residents point to and shake their heads.

These projects are offensive or ridiculous, and are grotesque misappropriations of money in a country so poor. I think white elephants will be one of the PRI's lasting contributions to the country it ruled for so long. These projects are artifacts of a political culture and regime that is now slowly passing. I can imagine at some point they might be studied by political scientists and sociologists, like the Roman Coliseum and Egypt's pyramids, for clues to a political system. Certainly, nothing illustrates quite as well or as permanently the system's arrogance and wastefulness.

They exist because governors and mayors—who usually promote these local projects—have had virtually unquestioned power in their fiefdoms. Since by law they couldn't be re-elected, they had little fear of their constituents' wrath. Added to that is Mexicans' feeling that mayors and governors have not done their jobs unless they produce *obras*—works. Thus, something inconspicuous but necessary—say, computerizing government bureaucracy—was less politically appealing than building some highway or convention center that could be inaugurated and pointed to for years to come.

Moreover, under the PRI local planning decisions were often made in Mexico City. A planner from León, Guanajuato once told me of a highway extension Mexico City bureaucrats had designed for his city. After much work and expense designing the extension, they came to León. There they discovered they'd been using long outdated maps and the highway they'd planned was going to run through an entire neighborhood. The project was quietly canceled.

Chiapas leads the country in malnutrition and illiteracy. Eight out of ten of its residents live in what the census bureau calls "extreme poverty." It should be a wealthy state, since it is rich in natural resources. One reason it is not is the wasteful and unproductive way its public money is used. No place in Mexico is richer in white elephants. This is largely due to a peculiarity of the state: In 176 years of independence, the state has had 166 governors. Replacing Chiapas governors is a game virtually every Mexican president has engaged in. And every governor, in turn, comes in wanting to place his mark on the state.

"This is the tragedy of Chiapas," Carlos Gutiérrez, manager of the Ciudad Real Hotel in San Cristóbal de las Casas, told me. "The state's backwardness—at least most of it—is due to the lack of political continuity. Mexico traditionally has been a country of six-year administrations. We Mexicans complain that every six years there's a total change in the federal government, plans, ideas, ways of doing things. But in Chiapas, we wish we could have a change every six years. Instead, it's every one, two years. You can't do much with that."

On display in Chiapas are the worst habits of *Priismo*, and, not coincidentally, the best examples of white elephants. The state capital, Tuxtla Gutiérrez, for example, possesses what residents claim is the largest kitchen in Latin America. It is part of the enormous Póliforo, one of the most lavish convention centers in Mexico. Yet anyone who's been to Tuxtla will understand why few people would want to hold a convention there. It is a frankly unattractive city, far from the rest of Mexico, and must compete with places like Cancún, Cuernavaca, and Acapulco.

This is why the elegant multi-million-dollar Póliforo and its enormous kitchen are mostly used for local weddings and birthday parties.

Another problem in attracting conventions is another famous Tuxtla white elephant: the Llano San Juan Airport. The land the airport was built on—owned by a former governor—gets so much fog that the airport is unusable four months a year. "The airport was born dead," said one Tuxtla resident. The state has refurbished an old military airport for use when Llano San Juan is fogged in. Meanwhile, state officials are discussing building yet another airport—this time, presumably, on land that doesn't suffer from fog banks.

In the mountains above Tuxtla, the tourist town of San Cristóbal itself has been endowed with its share of white elephants. San Cristóbal still doesn't have enough garbage trucks to serve all its far-flung and unpaved shantytown neighborhoods. But it has two theaters, neither one of which is used more than a few times a year. In the late 1980s, Gov. Patrocinio González ordered the renovation of the town's landmark 400-seat theater, Teatro Daniel Zebadúa. The next governor, Elmer Setzer, did him one better. He ordered the construction of a 1,100-seat theater—the gorgeous and entirely unnecessary Teatro de la Ciudad Hermanos Domínguez—coincidentally on land that was owned by his wife. ("Curiously, all these projects seem to be built on land owned by governors," said Carlos David Alfonzo, a state legislator from San Cristóbal.) The Zapatista Army of National Liberation (EZLN), the peasant Indian army that rebelled on Jan. 1, 1994, was said to be so upset that the Teatro de la Ciudad and not a hospital had been built that during their uprising they planted dynamite in the theater and were ready to blow it up.

San Cristóbal also spent $120,000 on a fountain at a park lagoon that is little more than a tube spraying water in the air. "It looks like a broken water pipe," said one man. The town's mayor at the time I visited had been public works director in the previous administration. As public works director, he was ordered to build speed bumps around town. As mayor, he took out all the speed bumps. In none of these projects did San Cristóbal residents have much say. But as I was researching them, I came upon Jorge Alberto Ruiz Cacho, a local architect, and the controversy surrounding the cathedral plaza in San Cristóbal. By the time I met him, Ruiz Cacho had for six years been fighting the city's plans for the plaza.

San Cristóbal's cathedral, indeed its entire downtown, is listed as an historic monument. Visitors will attest to the inviting nature of its colonial architecture—one reason the town is a major tourist attraction. However, the cathedral plaza has a history of public-works shenanigans. For many years, the space was home to a neoclassical building used as a priests' residence. But in 1964, the director of a junior high school got approval from a bureaucrat in the Education Ministry in Mexico City to knock it down and put up an addition to his school. This apparently came without the knowledge of anyone in San Cristóbal. Perhaps fearing public reaction, the school director hired workers to come in after midnight one night and destroy the building. In its place, he put up a boxy, universally despised junior high annex.

That in turn was torn down in 1982 and for many years the area was a vacant lot used for parking. Later, an underground parking lot was built, while the plaza above remained barren. By the mid-1990s, the city had money to do something with the space. Ruiz Cacho told me that since 1994 city officials had drawn up and actually installed two different designs for the plaza. In neither case had they consulted with the public, local architects, engineers or civic groups.

The first design—to which only Ruiz Cacho, then a city councilman, complained—consisted of large concrete cylinders surrounded by benches. They were so ugly that city officials themselves tore them out. The second renovation took ridiculous turns. It wasn't just that again no one outside city government was asked about the very centerpiece to their downtown; nor that the scale of the project was too large for the city's quaint colonial architecture; nor that there weren't enough trees. It was also that instead of wrought-iron benches, long slabs of modernistic concrete (at $1,200 apiece, enormously heavy and looking very out of place) were laid out. These benches had no way for rainwater to drain from them, so city workers had to go back and drill holes in them. The lamps were large space-age things that looked, as one man said, like "flying saucers." Instead of wrought-iron guardrails and handrails, black tubes were installed, looking like something out of the Mexico City subway. Heavy concrete planters were placed in areas where they appear now to jeopardize the integrity of the parking structure below. Who knew what was going to happen during the next earthquake, Ruiz Cacho told me. What's more, the project

capped above-ground filters installed to absorb carbon monoxide from the parking lot; the toxic emissions now accumulate below.

One renowned architect visited and called the design "ignominious." That appeared to be townspeople's verdict as well, for as the project was being completed, a strange thing happened. People in town began to protest publicly. Suddenly Ruiz Cacho wasn't the only one who hated how the plaza was turning out. The Chamber of Commerce wrote a letter to the mayor. Local architects went on a radio station to complain.

Then an even stranger thing happened. City officials actually halted the project; the lamps and benches were removed, and when I visited a few days later, the plaza was mostly bare and the project was "under review." The cathedral project in San Cristóbal is thought to be the first public-works project in Chiapas ever stopped by citizen protest. "The first renovation was ugly, the second was worse," said Ruiz Cacho. "City officials think that if they consult with the public, they'll lose prestige as the authority. On the contrary, asking the public's opinion they earn its trust."

Ruiz Cacho estimated the city had spent $1.5 million on the two plaza projects and had nothing to show for it. Still, the reaction to the cathedral plaza marked a small, but important change of political culture. It's hard to imagine another project going through San Cristóbal again without some citizen input.

The political renovation currently going on in the country promises to largely do away with the white elephants that flourished under the PRI's closed system of government—projects like the cathedral plaza in San Cristóbal or the Poliforo or the Llano San Juan airport. "This is all part of the change that's happening in a society that now participates and is demanding," Carlos David Alfonzo, the state legislator, told me. "Before it would accept anything."

To see more of these changes, while in Chiapas I also visited the offices of Vision Chiapas 2020 in Tuxtla Gutierrez. Vision Chiapas 2020 is an effort to set development priorities for the state's most important industries—tourism, coffee, ranching and others—for the next two decades. Some two thousand people participated—people from the business sector, political and environmental groups, the state and federal government. The idea was to have a development plan that outlasts governors and that can direct state spending on public works—thus hopefully avoiding any more white elephants and getting better use out of tax monies. (The new governor, Pablo Salazar, signed on to the plan during his campaign. He also committed himself to staying for the full six years in office.)

The many dozens of proposals they came up with got down to the detail of building rest areas near important tourist spots and establishing a system of micro-credits for small coffee growers. Chiapas 2020 is the kind of thing that happens so often in the United States as to be of only passing news interest. But in Mexico setting long-term planning goals is earth-shakingly new. Even more so if it involves the private sector and non-profit groups and not just the government.

Those involved in the project wax romantically about the change in political culture they're trying to achieve. They go on about how it's no longer just the government who decides what should be built and where with public money. They talk about the responsibility the public now has to participate in these decisions. I don't know what the concrete results of Vision Chiapas 2020 will be over the next twenty years. But right now the project says a lot about how a more open and efficient way of governance is emerging in Mexico. For that I found it worthwhile. The most backward state in Mexico has realized that the old culture of closed government and white elephants is simply too costly a burden to bear.

"In the final analysis, what this 2020 project has achieved has been to get people to participate," said Carlos Gutiérrez, the owner of the Ciudad Real in San Cristóbal, who is in charge of pushing tourism infrastructure projects for Vision Chiapas 2020. "Mexicans are very apathetic. We complain, criticize a lot, but when it comes time to take part, we step back. What we' re saying is, 'Don't just criticize. Propose something, but then also work with us to see that what you've proposed becomes reality.'"

* * *

I believe this is the Mexico of the future. It is a Mexico that gradually leaves behind the timid submission to authority and begins to act for itself, like the folks in San Cristóbal. It is the Mexico of Chalino Sánchez, of Zeus García, of Luis Guerrero and the Popsicle Kings of Tocumbo. It is a Mexico

that refuses to carry the weight of the Aztec king, of the Spanish noble, of the PRI *licenciado*.

Long-term regional planning; consulting with the citizenry on plaza renovations; creating a local government that can pave roads and build storm drains; selecting cabinet ministers based on their expertise. Again, these are simple and obvious changes. But to Mexico they are new and refreshing, and will go a long way to making government more accountable and effective. They are changes the PRI was never going to make. They won't immediately turn Mexico into a wealthy and just society. But they will release the country to pursue policies that better provide for people's real needs. They should help shed government waste and self-imposed binds on development. As they do that, they should help prepare Mexico for more equal participation in the global economy.

July 2, finally, was due to Mexicans' realization of how the world had changed around them and how far behind they'd fallen in the global economy after years under the PRI government's twisted logic. By defeating that logic, the stage is set to unleash the dynamism of another side of Mexico, dynamism that has been chained like a dog up to now. The *Priista/licenciado* will now have to work for a living. He will become another elite victim of the global economy, just like the party bureaucrats of the Soviet Union and the flabby managers of General Motors.

To fully participate in the global economy, Mexico faces huge and long-term challenges. Among them is a complete transformation of its education system to produce citizens who can think analytically and creatively—something public schools don't often do now. Mexico also needs a real and vital union movement. Workers need to participate in economic growth; unions help that happen. Mexico needs to wean itself from dependence on its own cheap labor and move toward investments in technology that only higher worker wages provoke.

But the first step is a fair, open, and efficient government. That, I believe, is all Mexico has ever needed to truly develop. Proof of that are the millions of Mexicans who go to the United States, thrive through hard work, buy homes, send their children to college and retire with dignity. None of that could they have achieved in a PRI-controlled Mexico.

Now, I think, as these changes are implemented, the flow of Mexicans to the United States will begin to staunch considerably. Mexican wages won't have to equal those in the U.S. for this to happen. As the gap between them closes, the hazardous trip north will seem increasingly less worthwhile. Moreover, the simple hunch that things are getting better, and the government is at least theirs, will keep more Mexicans at home.

In my opinion, the great Mexico story of the next decade will be watching a country, backward for so long, begin to develop and not just lurch haphazardly between uncontrolled growth and savage recession. It will be watching a country evolve from a dusty political/economic joke to one that is robust and part of the world.

Another Mexico is ascendant, and it's a good thing.

APPENDIX: STORY UPDATES

The Ballad of Chalino Sánchez

The murder of Chalino Sánchez remains unsolved; so, too, that of Saúl Viera. Yet Chalino's legacy lives on. His recordings still sell well at record shops and swap meets. Radio station La K-Buena (105.5 FM) in Los Angeles now airs *narcocorridos* sung by young men who sound like Chalino, and the Chalinazo is still a popular style of dress.

Marisela lives with her children in Paramount. A few Hollywood producers and directors took an interest in making a movie of her husband's life. She said she decided against participating, however, when Musart, which still claims to own the rights to Chalino's music, threatened to tear up the recording contract of her son, Adan, if she pursued the offers.

Lynching in Huejutla

Two years after the lynching, the case of the six people arrested and charged with murder and sedition remains under review by a judge.

Huejutla quickly repaired the damage done by the mob that night. But the memory of what happened there has not faded. Huejutla now has riot police. Some Huejutlans are wary of venturing too far into Veracruz for fear of retribution.

José Luis Fayad left office when his term expired in 1999. The lynching brought to an end his political career, which once seemed bright, and Fayad himself has suffered health problems. Omar Fayad left the attorney general's office in 1999 to become chief of a special national police force. He is now running for Congress. Jesús Murillo Karam left his job as governor in 1999 to become a subsecretary of the Interior Ministry. In 2000 he left that job to work on the presidential campaign of PRI candidate Francisco Labastida.

José Santes's widow, Verónica Hernández, has not remarried. She receives 1,000 pesos a month, interest from a trust fund established by the state government of

Hidalgo. However, no one in the family knows where the trust fund is deposited or under whose name. They fear that with time, future governments will stop the payments, leaving her and her four children to fend for themselves. The family of Salvador Valdez received nothing.

The girls' families still live in López Mateos but don't often come downtown. Meanwhile every March 24 priests hold a mass at the bandstand where the two men died.

Telenovela

The telenovela continues to reflect Mexico's social transformation.

Azteca's *El Candidato* was a telenovela about a campaign in a country that is trying to transform its political system from a one-party state to a democracy. *El Candidato* was also the first interactive telenovela, in which viewers could use the Internet and e-mail to give their opinions of the show and its plot twists.

Women's roles continue to expand beyond that of the pitiful María. Several novelas have aired steamy sex scenes, showing lovers in bed, and two novelas have included homosexual characters written with seriousness and involved in love relationships.

One novela that proved too far ahead of its time was *Tentaciones (Temptations)*. The plot revolved around a priest who is torn between his vows to God and his love for a woman, who turns out to be his half sister. Protests from citizen and church groups led to its early cancellation.

International sales of Mexican telenovelas continue strong. Verónica Castro remains out of television work but has continued her recording career. Fausto Zerón-Medina continues to publish *Saber Ver.* Angélica Aragón has been active in other telenovelas, has directed a play, and has worked in a Hollywood movie.

The *Jotos* of La Fogata

The *joto* colony near Mazatlán's Zona de Tolerancia remains constant and in flux.

Violeta did not return from Guadalajara. La Bella and La Mónica went back to their hometown of Tepic, Nayarit. La Daniela returned to her family in Culiacán. New queens have arrived to take their places.

Abenamar, La Calabasa, La Estrella, La Cindi, and Martina remain at the colony, working every night in El Famoso and banned all but one night a year from La Fogata by Marta Caramelo, who continues to scold them about their lifestyle.

The thirtieth annual pageant at La Fogata, held during Carnival 2000 in Mazatlán, was a big success and won by La Cindi, who received her crown from Abenamar.

Things have not gone well, however, for José García Medina, La Prieto. María de Jesús apparently discovered his homosexual trysts. She has taken the kids, left home, and is filing for divorce. Friends say that García has been desperately sad and, always thin, has lost even more weight. He is planning to move to Tijuana.

San Quintín

Luis Guerrero works as a night watchman guarding a farm. Vicente Guerrero is still an assistant preacher at the Apostolic Assembly of the Faith in Christ Jesus. In 1999 he married Libni López, whom he met through the church. He now works as an administrator in the new social security hospital, the same one that Indians took over a highway to have relocated.

Zeus and the Oaxaca Hoops

Los Angeles remains one of the great centers of Zapoteco basketball. Raza Unida continues as dominant as ever. In 2000 the team traveled to Madera, in California's Central Valley—the farthest it's gone in search of hoops—to play in, and eventually win, the Copa Benito Juárez organized by the Oaxacan community there.

Zeus García still works as a busboy, is raising Ervin, and now writes a regular basketball column for *El Oaxaqueño*.

The Dead Women of Juárez

The case of the Juárez women grew increasingly political as the list that Esther Chávez kept grew from eighty-six murdered women to nearly 200 over the next few years. Congresswomen visited Juárez and demanded better protection for women, more investment in law enforcement. Feminist groups pressured authorities for action. Journalists covered the case incessantly.

Partly due to the sensitive political nature of the case, a special prosecutor's office, set up in February 1998, went through four directors in eight months. By 1999, though, the office achieved some stability.

The case's big break came in March 1999. A fourteen-year-old *maquiladora* worker said she'd been raped, her panties removed, dumped, and left for dead by a bus driver on one of the *maquiladora* routes. She identified the bus driver as Jesús Guardado.

Guardado in turn implicated three other bus drivers: Bernardo Hernández, José Gaspar, and Agustín Toribio.

Under interrogation by police, the bus drivers said Sharif had hired them to rape and kill young women to make it look as if the real killer were still at large. The bus drivers said Sharif paid them $1,200 for every two pairs of panties they turned in. The women they chose, they said, had to fit a certain physical description.

Sharif allegedly used as a go-between Víctor Moreno, an American citizen and alleged drug smuggler who came regularly to the prison where the Egyptian was being held to visit his brother-in-law. Police allege that Moreno found the drivers and arranged for the delivery of the panties and the money.

Sharif denied these accusations, saying the police had tried the same tactic with Los Rebeldes. However, the bus drivers' confessions convinced a judge, who sentenced Sharif to thirty years in prison. The trial of Moreno and the bus drivers—who have since recanted their confessions, saying they were made under torture—was still going on as of this writing.

So far, though, investigators believe they can attribute only sixty-four murder cases to Sharif and the two gangs he allegedly hired. That leaves more than 130 cases of murdered women that have nothing to do with Sharif, Los Rebeldes, or the bus drivers.

Many of them have been solved, but they add credence to Jorge Ostos's rhetorical question: "Do we have a serial killer or simply a whole bunch of psychopaths roaming the streets?"

One of these cases is Sandra Juárez's. The investigation into her death has been caught in a jurisdictional no-man's-land. El Paso County Sheriff's detectives first handled the case because her body was found on the U.S. side of the Rio Grande. Soon, though, it became apparent that she had never been to the United States but rather floated or was placed there. Sheriff's detectives say

they transferred the case to Ciudad Juárez detectives. Ciudad Juárez investigators say their records show it's an El Paso County case. Not surprisingly, no one has been arrested.

Meanwhile, the case's high profile has forced investment in Juárez's criminal-justice infrastructure. Detectives have gone through training in sex-crime and homicide investigation. There are now gloves with which to handle evidence and bags to put that evidence in. One more social worker has been added to the office that handles sex-crime and domestic-violence reports.

Juárez now has 250,000 *maquiladora* jobs, a fifth of all *maquila* jobs nationwide.

West Side Kansas Street

The Zamora version of West Side Kansas Street began to drift apart within a year after I wrote about it. José Cervantes, for one, decided he'd had enough. The last time I saw him he had grown out his hair, was lifting weights, and had the bright and cheerful look of the boy in the photo album dancing with his mother.

Memo Cervantes finally went to the United States, where he worked as a field hand in California's Central Valley. Simio moved away from Avenida Juárez to the state of Sonora. Juan Briseño moved back to Watsonville. Others—Chin, Camarena, Miguel Núñez—remain on La Juárez, picking tomatoes and frying their brains with cheap alcohol and the fumes of shoe glue.

Meanwhile, in Maywood, the original West Side Kansas Street remains strong and involved in drug dealing and car theft. Police there say WKST recruits newly arrived Mexican youths who return to Mexico and start their own cliques back home.

Leaving Nueva Jerusalén

Amid the publicity surrounding the expulsion of the seventy-five families, police were finally forced to arrest Agapito Gómez and sent him to jail in Morelia, where he was charged with the rape of six young girls at Nueva Jerusalén, including that of María Remedios Cruz Vigueres.

But the case grew more complicated. One day the prosecutor in Turicato sent María Remedios's mother, Georgina Vigueres, without protection, to Nueva

Jerusalén to serve a summons on a man who was to be a witness in the case against Gómez—something by law the prosecutor should have done himself. The prosecutor told Señora Vigueres that he didn't have anyone to serve the summons and if she wanted the case to proceed, she'd have to serve it herself.

So Señora Vigueres returned to Nueva Jerusalén with her fourteen-year-old son, Juan. While she was there, guards at the village grabbed her, procured a rope, and were about to hang her. One of them shot Juan in the shoulder, who pulled a gun from his mother's purse and shot and killed one of the guards, Jesús Cruz López.

For this Señora Vigueres was arrested. A judge found her guilty of being an "accomplice to homicide" and sentenced her to fifteen years in prison.

A few months later, with the PRI now in power in both Turicato and the state legislature, Agapito, who had the tumor removed from his neck, was released from jail, a judge citing lack of evidence that he had raped the six young girls—though no DNA tests had been performed on María Remedios's child. He has returned to Nueva Jerusalén.

Señora Vigueres's sentence has since been overturned and she is now being retried under a new judge.

The victory of Vicente Fox has if anything strengthened the ties between Nueva Jerusalen and the PRI. The PRI still controls the state government, but it is reeling and wounded and will likely have to rely more than ever on the sect for votes in future elections.

Meanwhile Ausencio Velázquez Huerta, the sect's *encargado del orden*—the unofficial police chief—was shot to death on the road to Puruarán by an unknown assailant. His case remains unsolved. Pedro Reyes, the former mayor of Turicato, was also murdered as he returned to his home in Puruarán one night in early January 2000—shot four times in the back. His killing, too, has not been resolved.

Tepito

Tepito's cocaine nightmare has intensified, and the "Tepito Cartel" has grown.

Police say the organization is more of a drug-dealing gang and doesn't fit the definition of a cartel since it doesn't control production. Nonetheless, Tepito remains one of the few places in Mexico where drug sales take place in public.

Gangland-style murders occur with some frequency in the *barrio bravo*.

Police enter Tepito en masse, if they enter at all.

Las Puertas de Tepito has not been built, and the streets of the barrio are as clogged as ever with the world's crapola. Still, Tepito retains some of its cynical sense of humor regarding the outside world. Within weeks after the potency pill Viagra went on the market, Tepito had a pirate version on sale.

Nuevo Chupícuaro

Bonifacio Caballero recently bought twenty acres of land outside Wasco, which he leases to some friends who grow roses. His plans are to dig a well, build a house, and raise crops and a few animals. Though his children say his health is failing, he still speaks of returning to Chupícuaro.

His youngest daughter is attending California State University, Bakersfield, in a program for gifted students.

His son, Bonifacio Caballero, has offers to teach elementary school in Los Angeles and Kern County. "In Chupícuaro," writes Bonifacio Caballero the younger, "every time I've gone back, I spend less time there. I notice new families, many from other states, some from the capital. The 'Fiesta de San Pedro,' which was mostly a local party, has turned into a lavish, eight-day *pachanga* that gets out of hand every year more and more.. . . The buildings, well, yes, there are some new homes. But not like that 'boom' in the early eighties and nineties—no, not to that scale. Even the local economy there is not the same. Some friends of ours who were very prominent have had to come to the United States for work for the first time. I myself am lost in a duality, a multicultural nightmare coming undone, imploding and exploding at the same time. I don't believe I'll ever live there for more than a few weeks. I am planning on going to Cuba this summer. Life is good."

ACKNOWLEDGMENTS

This book is the product of my attempt to journalistically explore a country and to tell some of its stories, particularly those of people whose voices don't make headlines or show up on television. These people always tell the most fascinating stories, and Mexico is full of them.

The remarkable changes Mexico experienced in the last several years inevitably wound their way into much of my reporting. So finally I came to be interested in each story not simply for its own merit in what it could provoke in human interest, but also for what it could say about Mexico.

Several interviews helped shape my thinking about Mexico. Richard Rodriguez, one of America's best essayists, granted me interviews on two occasions. The first especially, a discussion about the concept of the border in the global age, stays with me still, informing much of what I write about. Early on in my time in Mexico an interview with Gustavo López Castro, professor at the Colegio de Michoacán, started me thinking about the great themes involved in immigration. An interview with Esteban Barragán, a scholar of ranchero culture at the Colegio, gave me hope for Mexico when, at a low moment, I despaired that the *"Priista/licenciado"* culture was all there was to the country.

The person who introduced me to Mexico is farmworker-organizer Luis Magaña, a man I admire from Jaripo, Michoacán, who now lives near Stockton and is one of today's great Californians. Through the years his help and generosity, as well as that of Luisa Moreno and Guadalupe Ramos, were deeply appreciated. Nor could any of this have been accomplished without the support and love of Guadalupe Chavira.

I think journalism is the most fascinating and fulfilling endeavor imaginable. That I now exercise it as a profession is due in large measure to the editors I've had. Reporters need solid, creative editors. I've had several.

Frances Fernandez, then at the *Orange County Register,* was probably the

best first editor a reporter could have asked for: tough, caring, motherly, and demanding.

My second job was covering crime at *The Record* in Stockton, one of the best news towns in California. This was also the most exciting job I've ever had, and it shaped me as a reporter in many ways. I remember fondly most everyone at *The Record.* Bruce Spence, the editor who hired me, is still the best newspaperman I've ever worked for. I consider it my great fortune as a young reporter to have spent time under his tutelage. Richard Hanner, my city editor at *The Record,* worked closest with me. For his daily effort to form and strengthen my reporting, I will always be grateful. I also thank Mike Fitzgerald, Dana Nichols, the copy desk folks who kept me honest, Mike Klocke and Jeff Hood and the rest of the sports desk, and especially Dianne Barth and Paul Feist, two great reporters, for the friendship and encouragement they extended to a guy from out of town.

I'm grateful for the enormous help given me by gang investigator Dale Wagner, a tough detective of German descent who is fluent in both Spanish and gang life and is one of the great people of the Stockton police department.

I'd like also like to thank Lyn Watts at the *Tacoma News-Tribune,* though my experience in the drizzling rain of the Pacific Northwest didn't work out as we'd hoped.

Sandy Close, with whom I worked at the Pacific News Service, is probably the most exciting editor in American journalism. A conversation with her generates enough great ideas and new perspectives to last months.

As a freelancer, I was greatly aided, both financially and professionally, by an Alicia Patterson Fellowship that I received in 1998. Much of what is in this book could never have been completed without the help of that fellowship and the Alicia Patterson Foundation itself. My thanks in particular to Margaret Engel, the foundation's director, and to Joel Millman of *The Wall Street Journal.*

I am also indebted to the editors at newspapers and magazines, many of whom I've never met, who ran my stuff and paid me for it. Freelancers, especially those living abroad, put a premium on editors who are open, enthusiastic, and trustworthy.

Mike Zamba and Lonnie Iliff hired me at the short-lived but nonetheless inspired *Mexico Insight Magazine* and thus allowed me to move to Mexico.

Mexico Business Magazine—now MB—has kept me in business since I became a freelancer. For that I'm particularly grateful to Martha Liebrum, Angelo Young, Claire Poole, and Alger González Parra.

I thank Gail Bensinger, at the *San Francisco Examiner,* for her spirited encouragement through the years. Chris Shively, Darlene Stinson, and the great man of Mexico correspondents, Dudley Althaus, at the *Houston Chronicle* have been a joy to work with, as have Lynne Walker and David Gaddis Smith at the *San Diego Union-Tribune.* I thank all the editors I've worked with at the *Riverside Press-Enterprise,* my first newspaper client. So, too, I thank Robert Ruby and Hal Piper, two gentlemen of journalism, at the *Baltimore Sun,* Chris Lehman at *Newsday,* and Gary Spiecker at the *L.A. Times* Sunday opinion page.

My thanks also to Tom Christie, John Payne, and Sue Horton at the *L.A. Weekly;* Randy Johnson at United Airline's *Hemispheres* magazine; Kate Rounds at *Ms.* magazine; Ignacio Rodríguez, editor of *Milenio,* Mexico's best news magazine; and Mike Zellner at *Latin Trade* magazine.

I'm also greatly indebted to Professor Linda Hall and to David Holtby, both at the University of New Mexico, for taking an interest in this project from far away.

Freelancers need to stick together. For their support and help along the way I thank Joel Simon and Ruben Martínez—together we made up the Pacific News Service Mexico City bureau—as well as Franc Contreras and my sister in freelancing, Leslie Moore. I also thank Leon Lazaroff for his help when I was getting started.

Mexico is blessed with an excellent foreign correspondent corps. Space limits my ability to recognize them all. However, I'd like in particular to say thanks to Keith Dannemiller and Sergio Dorantes, two great photographers; Elizabeth Malkin and Eduardo Garcia, two great business reporters; friends and journalists Rick Sandoval, Susan Ferriss and Mary Beth Sheridan, Jim Smith and Maxine Hart, Paul and Georgia de la Garza, Ricardo and Lauren Chacon, Lucy Conger, Tim and Jan McGirk, Sam Dillon and Julia Preston, Tracey Eaton, Molly Moore and John Anderson, Susana Hayward, Dolly Mascarenas and Eloy Aguilar, Danny Mora and Sarahi Vilchis, and to all the folks who still get together Fridays at the Nuevo Leon Cantina to talk about Mexico and whatever else comes to mind.

I'd like also to say thanks to the friends I've made and keep still from Claremont High School and from Barrington Hall at U.C. Berkeley—as well as the spouses and children they've added through the years. Through our shared history, my Claremont friends have helped keep me centered and directed and laughing. Barrington Hall remains for me one of the great liberating experiences, a place that encouraged me to create a life of my own design. I also tip my hat to the great singer, currently in semiretirement, Larry "The Loveman" Pope, himself a product of that philosophy.

My wonderful brothers, Benjamin and Joshua, have always been sources of love and support for their itinerant sibling. I remember, too, our brother Nathaniel here.

Finally I'd like to thank the many people, too numerous to name—those who appear in this book and some who don't—who gave their time and their perspectives, recounted their experiences, and tolerated my questions, helping me as they went to understand their side of Mexico.

—SAM QUINONES